CAMBRIDGE STUDIES IN
MEDIEVAL LIFE AND THOUGHT

Edited by M. D. Knowles, Litt.D., F.B.A.
*Emeritus Regius Professor of Modern History in the
University of Cambridge*

NEW SERIES VOL. X

MONASTIC TITHES

FROM THEIR ORIGINS TO THE TWELFTH CENTURY

MONASTIC TITHES

FROM THEIR ORIGINS TO THE
TWELFTH CENTURY

BY

GILES CONSTABLE

Associate Professor of History
Harvard University

CAMBRIDGE
AT THE UNIVERSITY PRESS
1964

PUBLISHED BY
THE SYNDICS OF THE CAMBRIDGE UNIVERSITY PRESS

Bentley House, 200 Euston Road, London, N.W. 1
American Branch: 32 East 57th Street, New York 22, N.Y.
West African Office: P.O. Box 33, Ibadan, Nigeria

Printed in Great Britain at the University Printing House, Cambridge
(Brooke Crutchley, University Printer)

CONTENTS

AUTHOR'S NOTE

The preparation and publication of this book
were made possible by grants from the
American Council of Learned Societies, the
publication grant as a result of a contribution
from the United States Steel Foundation.

LIST OF ABBREVIATIONS

This list includes the principal primary sources, collections, periodicals, and works of reference used in the preparation of this work. To save space in the notes, all papal documents cited by the JE or JL number alone were consulted in the editions cited there, usually the *PL*, and all chartularies, which are listed separately here, have been cited by the name alone. Place-names are always a problem. To avoid confusion, I have in general used the native form of place-names, except where there is a well-established English form (such as Rome, Milan, Florence, Naples, Venice, Munich, Brussels, etc.), and the English form of personal names, in order to avoid mentioning the same person by a variety of names. Thus, in the names of monasteries, I have followed almost exclusively the locations listed in L. H. Cottineau, *Répertoire topo-bibliographique des abbayes et prieurés* (Mâcon, 1939), but I have as a rule given the name of the patron saint in the English form, unless the Latin or modern foreign form is better known, as with the titular churches of the cardinals in Rome. The secondary material which has been used is so varied that a list could merely be entitled 'Works Consulted' and would not really be a bibliography of monastic tithes. But an index of authors cited has been provided in order to facilitate finding the full titles of works cited in an abbreviated form.

AASS *Acta sanctorum* (Antwerp, 1643 ff.).
A. f. kath. KR *Archiv für katholisches Kirchenrecht.*
A. f. Urk. *Archiv für Urkundenforschung.*
APRI *Acta pontificum Romanorum inedita*, ed. J. von Pflugk-Harttung (Tübingen–Stuttgart, 1880–8).
Bibl. Clun. *Bibliotheca Cluniacensis*, ed. M. Marrier and A. Duchesne (Paris, 1614).
Bull. Clun. *Bullarium sacri ordinis Cluniacensis*, ed. Pierre Symon (Lyons, 1680).

CC   *Corpus christianorum (Series latina).*

CDRHF   Chartes et diplômes relatifs à l'histoire de France publiés par les soins de l'Académie des Inscriptions et Belles-lettres.

Comp. 1   Bernard of Pavia, *Compilatio prima,* ed. Emil Friedberg, *Quinque compilationes antiquae* (Leipzig, 1882).

De Clercq, *Législation,* 1   C. de Clercq, *La législation religieuse franque de Clovis à Charlemagne,* Université de Louvain: Recueil de travaux publiés par les membres des Conférences d'Histoire et de Philologie, II, 38 (Louvain–Paris, 1936).

De Clercq, *Législation,* II   C. de Clercq, *La législation religieuse franque,* II: *De Louis le Pieux à la fin du IXe siècle* (Antwerp, 1958).

Decretals   Gregory IX, *Decretals,* ed. Emil Friedberg, *Corpus iuris canonici* (Leipzig, 1879), II.

Decretum   Gratian, *Decretum,* ed. Emil Friedberg, *Corpus iuris canonici* (Leipzig, 1879), I.

Dict. d'arch.   *Dictionnaire d'archéologie chrétienne et de liturgie* (Paris, 1907–53).

Dict. de droit   *Dictionnaire de droit canonique* (Paris, 1924 ff.).

Dict. d'hist.   *Dictionnaire d'histoire et de géographie ecclésiastiques* (Paris, 1912 ff.).

EPRI   *Epistolae pontificum Romanorum ineditae,* ed. S. Löwenfeld (Leipzig, 1885).

Gams, *Series*   P. B. Gams, *Series episcoporum ecclesiae catholicae* (Regensburg, 1873–86).

GC   *Gallia christiana* (Paris, 1715 ff.).

GP   *Regesta pontificum Romanorum: Germania pontificia,* ed. A. Brackmann (Berlin, 1910 ff.).

Hefele–Leclercq, *Conciles*   C. J. von Hefele, *Histoire des Conciles,* ed. and tr. H. Leclercq (Paris, 1907 ff.).

IP   *Regesta pontificum Romanorum: Italia pontificia,* ed. P. Kehr (Berlin, 1906 ff.).

JE, JK, JL   Philip Jaffé, *Regesta pontificum Romanorum,* 2nd ed. by F. Kaltenbrunner (JK: to 590), P. Ewald (JE: 590–882), and S. Löwenfeld (JL: 882–1198) (Leipzig, 1885–8).

M² Johann F. Böhmer, *Regesta imperii*, 1: *Die Regesten des Kaiserreichs unter den Karolingern, 751–918*, ed. E. Mühlbacher, 2nd ed. J. Lechner (Innsbruck, 1908).

Mansi, *Collectio* *Sacrorum conciliorum nova et amplissima collectio*, ed. J. D. Mansi (Florence–Venice, 1759 ff.).

MGH, *Capit.* Monumenta Germaniae historica, *Leges*, II: *Capitularia regum francorum*, ed. A. Boretius and V. Krause (Hanover, 1883–97).[1]

—— *Conc.* *Leges*, III: *Concilia*, ed. F. Maassen and A. Werminghoff (Hanover, 1893–1924).

—— *Const.* *Leges*, IV: *Constitutiones et acta publica imperatorum et regum*, ed. L. Weiland, J. Schwalm, etc. (Hanover, 1893–1926).

—— *Dipl. Karol.* *Diplomata Karolinorum: Die Urkunden der Karolinger*, ed. A. Dopsch, J. Lechner, M. Tangl, and E. Mühlbacher (Hanover, 1906).

—— *Dipl.* *Diplomata regum Germaniae ex stirpe Karolinorum: Die Urkunden der deutschen Karolinger*, ed. P. Kehr and T. Schieffer (Berlin, 1932–60) and *Diplomata regum et imperatorum Germaniae: Die Urkunden der deutschen Könige und Kaiser*, ed. T. Sickel, H. Bresslau, etc. (Hanover–Berlin, 1879–1959).

—— *Epp.* *Epistolae*, ed. P. Ewald, L. M. Hartmann, etc. (Berlin, 1887–1939).

—— *Formulae* *Leges*, V: *Formulae Merowingici et Karolini aevi*, ed. K. Zeumer (Hanover, 1886).

—— *Leges* in fol. *Leges* in folio, ed. G. H. Pertz, J. Merkel, etc. (Hanover, 1835–89).

—— *Libelli* *Libelli de lite imperatorum et pontificum saec. XI. et XII. conscripti* (Hanover, 1891–7).

—— *SS* *Scriptores* in folio (Hanover, 1826–1934).

—— *SS Merov.* *Scriptores rerum Merovingicarum*, ed. W. Arndt, B. Krusch, etc. (Hanover, 1884–1920).

MIÖG, MÖIG *Mitteilungen des Instituts für österreichische Geschichtsforschung* (from 1923–42: *Mitteilungen des österreichischen Instituts für Geschichtsforschung*).

---

[1] On the reliability of this edition, which was severely criticized by Simon Stein, see F. L. Ganshof, *Recherches sur les capitulaires* (Paris, 1958), pp. 37 ff., and other references given in my article in *Speculum*, XXXV, 226 n. 12.

Monasticon   William Dugdale, *Monasticon anglicanum*, ed. J. Caley, H. Ellis, and B. Bandinel (London, 1817–30).

NA   Neues Archiv der Gesellschaft für ältere deutsche Geschichtskunde.

ODCC   The Oxford Dictionary of the Christian Church, ed. F. L. Cross (Oxford, 1957).

PL   Patrologia latina.

PU   Papsturkunden volumes in the *Nachrichten der Gesellschaft der Wissenschaften zu Göttingen.*

Rev. bén.   Revue bénédictine.

Rev. d'hist. ecc.   Revue d'histoire ecclésiastique.

RHGF   Recueil des historiens des Gaules et de la France (Paris, 1738–1904).

Santifaller, *Elenco*   L. Santifaller, 'Saggio di un Elenco dei funzionari, impiegati e scrittori della Cancelleria Pontificia dall'inizio all'anno 1099', *Bullettino dell'Istituto storico italiano per il Medio Evo*, LVI (1940).

Sav. Zs.   Zeitschrift der Savigny-Stiftung für Rechtsgeschichte.

Schiaparelli, *Diplomi*, I   *I diplomi di Guido e di Lamberto*, ed. L. Schiaparelli, Fonti per la storia d'Italia, XXXVI (Rome, 1906).

—— *Diplomi*, II   *I diplomi di Berengario I*, ed. L. Schiaparelli, Fonti per la storia d'Italia, XXXV (Rome, 1903).

—— *Diplomi*, III   *I diplomi di Ugo e di Lotario, di Berengario II e di Adalberto*, ed. L. Schiaparelli, Fonti per la storia d'Italia, XXXVIII (Rome, 1924).

SMGBOZ   Studien und Mitteilungen zur Geschichte des Benediktiner-Ordens und seiner Zweige.

Spicilegium   Luc d'Achery, *Spicilegium*, 2nd ed. (Paris, 1723).

Stumpf   Karl F. Stumpf-Brentano, *Die Reichskanzler vornehmlich des X., XI., und XII. Jahrhunderts*, II: *Die Kaiserurkunden des X., XI., und XII. Jahrhunderts chronologisch verzeichnet* (Innsbruck, 1865–1883).

Thesaurus   Thesaurus novus anecdotorum, ed. E. Martène and U. Durand (Paris, 1717).

Ughelli, *Italia sacra*   F. Ughelli, *Italia sacra*, 2nd ed. (Venice, 1717–22).

Wattenbach, *Geschichtsquellen* W. Wattenbach, *Deutschlands Geschichtsquellen im Mittelalter*, 6th ed. (Berlin, 1893–4).

Wattenbach–Holtzmann, *Geschichtsquellen* W. Wattenbach, *Deutschlands Geschichtsquellen im Mittelalter: Deutsche Kaiserzeit*, ed. R. Holtzmann, 3rd ed. (Tübingen, 1948).

Wattenbach–Levison, *Geschichtsquellen* W. Wattenbach, *Deutschlands Geschichtsquellen im Mittelalter: Vorzeit und Karolinger*, ed. W. Levison and H. Löwe (Weimar, 1952 ff.).

CHARTULARIES

Abingdon   *Chronicon monasterii de Abingdon*, ed. Joseph Stevenson, Rolls Series, 2 (London, 1858).

Acy   A. Vattier, 'Cartulaire du prieuré de Saint-Nicholas d'Acy', *Comité archéologique de Senlis: Comptes-rendus et Mémoires*, 3rd ser. 1 (1886), 50–80.

Afflighem   *Cartulaire d'Afflighem*, ed. E. de Marneffe, fasc. 1, Analectes pour servir à l'histoire ecclésiastique de la Belgique, II, 1 (Louvain, 1894).

Altenberg   *Urkundenbuch der Abtei Altenberg*, ed. Hans Mosler, I, Urkundenbücher der geistlichen Stiftungen des Niederrheins, III, 1 (Bonn, 1912).

Altluxemburg   *Urkunden- und Quellenbuch zur Geschichte der altluxemburgischen Territorien bis zur burgundischen Zeit*, ed. C. Wampach, 1 (Luxemburg, 1935).

Aniane   *Cartulaire d'Aniane*, ed. l'abbé Casson and E. Meynial, Société archéologique de Montpellier (Montpellier, 1900).

Arezzo   *Documenti per la storia della città di Arezzo nel medio evo*, ed. Ubaldo Pasqui, 1, Documenti di storia italiana pubblicati a cura della regia deputazione toscana, XI (Florence, 1899).

Aureil   G. de Senneville, ed., 'Cartulaires des prieurés d'Aureil et d'Artige en Limousin', *Bulletin de la Société archéologique et historique du Limousin*, XLVIII (1900).

Autun   *Cartulaire de l'église d'Autun*, ed. A. de Charmasse (Paris–Autun, 1865–1900).

Bâle   J. Trouillat, *Monuments de l'histoire de l'ancien évêché de Bâle*, 1 (Porrentruy, 1852).

Basse-Fontaine   Cartulaire de l'abbaye de Basse-Fontaine, ed. C. Lalore, Collection de principaux cartulaires du diocèse de Troyes, III (Paris–Troyes, 1878).

Bobbio   Codice diplomatico del monastero di S. Colombano di Bobbio fino all'anno .MCCVIII., ed. C. Cipolla, Fonti per la storia d'Italia, 52–4 (Rome, 1918).

Bonnevaux   Cartulaire de l'abbaye de N.-D. de Bonnevaux, ed. Ulysse Chevalier, Documents historiques inédits sur le Dauphiné, VII (Grenoble, 1889).

Bourbourg   Un cartulaire de l'abbaye de N.-D. de Bourbourg, ed. I. de Coussemaker (Lille, 1882–91).

Breme   Cartario della Abazia di Breme, ed. L. C. Bollea, Biblioteca della Società storica subalpina, 127 (Turin, 1933).

Cambron   Cartulaire de l'abbaye de Cambron, ed. J.-J. de Smet, Monuments pour servir à l'histoire des provinces de Namur, de Hainaut et de Luxembourg, II, 1 (Brussels, 1869).

Cavour   Cartario della Abazia di Cavour, ed. B. Baudi di Vesme, E. Durando and F. Gabotto, Biblioteca della Società storica subalpina, 3 = Corpus chartarum Italiae, 3 (Pinerolo, 1900).

Chalais   Les Chartes de l'ordre de Chalais, ed. J.-Ch. Roman, Archives de la France monastique, XXIII–XXV (Ligugé–Paris, 1923).

Chartreuse   Recueil des plus anciens actes de la Grande-Chartreuse (1086–1196), ed. B. Bligny (Grenoble, 1958).

Clairvaux   Recueil des chartes de l'abbaye de Clairvaux, ed. J. Waquet, fasc. 1 (Troyes, 1950).

Cluny   Recueil des chartes de l'abbaye de Cluny, ed. A. Bernard and A. Bruel, Collection de documents inédits sur l'histoire de France (Paris, 1876–1903).

Conques   Cartulaire de l'abbaye de Conques en Rouergue, ed. G. Desjardins, Documents historiques publiés par la Société de l'École des Chartes (Paris, 1879).

Durbon   Chartes de Durbon, ed. Paul Guillaume (Montreuil-sur-Mer, 1893).

Erfurt   Urkundenbuch der Erfurter Stifter und Klöster, I, ed. A. Overmann, Geschichtsquellen der Provinz Sachsen und des Freistaates Anhalt, N.R. 5 (Magdeburg, 1926).

Farfa Il regesto di Farfa, ed. I. Giorgi and U. Balzani, Biblioteca della R. Società romana di storia patria (Rome, 1879 ff.).

Fontmorigny Albert Huchet, Le chartrier ancien de Fontmorigny (Bourges, 1936).

Fulda Urkundenbuch des Klosters Fulda, ed. E. E. Stengel, I, Veröffentlichungen der historischen Kommission für Hessen und Waldeck, x (Marburg, 1913).

Gellone Cartulaire de Gellone, ed. P. Alaus, l'abbé Cassan and E. Meynial, Société archéologique de Montpellier (Montpellier, 1898).

Gimont Cartulaire de l'abbaye de Gimont, ed. A. Clergeac, Archives historiques de la Gascogne, 2nd ser. 9 (Paris–Auch, 1905).

Gladbach Urkunden und Regesten zur Geschichte der Stadt und Abtei Gladbach, ed. E. Brasse, I (M. Gladbach, 1914).

Glastonbury The Great Chartulary of Glastonbury, ed. Aelred Watkin, Somerset Record Society, 59, 63, 64 (Frome, 1947–56).

Göttweig Das Saal-Buch des Benedictiner-Stiftes Göttweig, ed. W. Karlin, Fontes rerum Austriacarum, II, 8 (Vienna, 1855).

Grenoble Cartulaires de l'église de Grenoble, ed. J. Marion, Collection de documents inédits sur l'histoire de France (Paris, 1869).

Halberstadt Urkundenbuch des Hochstifts Halberstadt und seiner Bischöfe, ed. G. Schmidt, I, Publicationen aus den k. Preussischen Staatsarchiven, 17 (Leipzig, 1883).

Heiligenkreuz Urkunden des Cistercienser-Stiftes Heiligenkreuz im Wiener Walde, ed. J. N. Weis, I, Fontes rerum Austriacarum, II, II (Vienna, 1856).

Heisterbach Urkundenbuch der Abtei Heisterbach, ed. F. Schmitz, Urkundenbücher der geistlichen Stiftungen des Niederrheins, II (Bonn, 1908).

Héronval Cartulaire de Héronval [ed. E. Tassus] (Noyon, 1883).

Hospitaliers Cartulaire général de l'Ordre des Hospitaliers de S. Jean de Jérusalem, ed. J. Delaville Le Roulx, I (Paris, 1894).

Ilsenburg Urkundenbuch des...Klosters Ilsenburg, ed. E. Jacobs, I, Geschichtsquellen der Provinz Sachsen, 6 (Halle, 1875).

Josaphat   Chartes de Terre Sainte provenant de l'abbaye de N.-D. de Josaphat, ed. H.-F. Delaborde, Bibliothèque des Écoles françaises d'Athènes et de Rome, XIX (Paris, 1880).

Jumièges   Chartes de l'abbaye de Jumièges (v. 825 à 1204), ed. J.-J. Vernier, Société de l'histoire de Normandie (Rouen–Paris, 1916).

Kaufungen   Urkundenbuch des Klosters Kaufungen in Hessen, ed. H. von Roques, I (Cassel, 1900).

Köln   Quellen zur Geschichte der Stadt Köln, ed. L. Ennen and G. Eckertz, I (Cologne, 1860).

La Charité-sur-Loire   Cartulaire du prieuré de la Charité-sur-Loire, ed. R. de Lespinasse (Nevers–Paris, 1887).

La Ferté   Georges Duby, Recueil des pancartes de l'abbaye de la Ferté-sur-Grosne 1113–1178 ([Aix-en-Provence] 1953).

Land ob der Enns   Urkunden-Buch des Landes ob der Enns (Vienna, 1852 ff.).

La Trinité de Vendôme   Cartulaire de l'abbaye cardinale de la Trinité de Vendôme, ed. C. Métais, Société archéologique du Vendômois (Paris–Vendôme, 1893–7).

Leno   Francesco Zaccaria, Dell'antichissima Badia di Leno libri tre (Venice, 1767).

Lérins   Cartulaire de l'abbaye de Lérins, ed. H. Moris and E. Blanc, Société des Lettres, Sciences et Arts des Alpes Maritimes (Saint-Honorat de Lérins–Paris, 1883–1905).

Longpont   Le cartulaire du prieuré de Notre-Dame de Longpont (Lyons, 1879).

Lyon   M.-C. Guigue, Cartulaire lyonnais (Lyons, 1885–93).

Mâcon   Cartulaire de Saint-Vincent de Mâcon, ed. M.-C. Ragut (Mâcon, 1864).

Mainz   Mainzer Urkundenbuch, I, ed. M. Stimmung, Arbeiten der historischen Kommission für den Volksstaat Hessen (Darmstadt, 1932).

Marmoutier (Anjou)   Paul Marchegay, Archives d'Anjou (Angers, 1843–54), II: *Cartae de rebus abbatiae Majoris Monasterii in Andegavia.*

Marmoutier (Blésois)   Marmoutier: Cartulaire Blésois, ed. C. Métais (Blois, 1889–91).

Marmoutier (Dunois) Cartulaire de Marmoutier pour le Dunois, ed. Ém. Mabille (Châteaudun, 1874).

Marmoutier (Vendômois) Cartulaire de Marmoutier pour le Vendômois, ed. C. A. de Trémault, Société archéologique du Vendômois (Paris–Vendôme, 1893).

Melsa Chronica monasterii de Melsa, ed. E. A. Bond, Rolls Series, 43 (London, 1866–8).

Merseburg Urkundenbuch des Hochstifts Merseburg, ed. P. Kehr, 1, Geschichtsquellen der Provinz Sachsen, 36 (Halle, 1899).

Messina I diplomi della cattedrale di Messina, ed. Raffaele Starrabba, Documenti per servire alla storia di Sicilia, Prima Serie: Diplomatica, 1 (Palermo, 1876–90).

Mittelrhein Urkundenbuch zur Geschichte der mittelrheinischen Territorien, ed. Heinrich Beyer (Coblenz, 1860 ff.).

Molesme Cartulaires de l'abbaye de Molesme, ed. J. Laurent, Collection de documents publiés avec le concours de la commission des antiquités de la Côte-d'Or, 1 (Paris, 1907–11).

Montiéramey Cartulaire de l'abbaye de Montiéramey, ed. C. Lalore, Collection des principaux cartulaires du diocèse de Troyes, 7 (Paris–Troyes, 1890).

Muri Die ältesten Urkunden von Allerheiligen in Schaffhausen, Rheinau und Muri, Quellen zur Schweizer Geschichte, 3 (Basel, 1883).

Namur Actes des comtes de Namur de la première race, 946–1196, ed. F. Rousseau (Brussels, 1936).

Nogent-le-Rotrou Saint-Denis de Nogent-le-Rotrou 1031–1789: Histoire et Cartulaire, ed. H. de Souancé and C. Métais, Archives du diocèse de Chartres, 1, 2nd ed. (Vannes, 1899).

Nonenque Cartulaire et documents de l'abbaye de Nonenque, ed. C. Couderc and J. L. Rigal, Archives historiques du Rouergue, 18 (Rodez, n.d. [1954]).

Old Wardon The Cartulary of the Cistercian Abbey of Old Wardon, Bedfordshire, ed. G. H. Fowler (Manchester, 1931).

Oña Colección diplomática de San Salvador de Oña, ed. Juan del Alamo, Consejo superior de investigaciones científicas: Escuela de estudios medievales, XII, XVII (Madrid, 1950).

Ordre du Temple   *Cartulaire général de l'Ordre du Temple*, ed. G. A. M. J. d'Albon (Paris, 1913).

Orval   *Cartulaire de l'abbaye d'Orval*, ed. Hippolyte Goffinet (Brussels, 1879).

Ourscamp   *Cartulaire de l'abbaye de Notre-Dame d'Ourscamp*, ed. M. Peigné-Delacourt, Mémoires de la Société des Antiquaires de Picardie: Documents inédits concernant la province, 6 (Amiens, 1865).

Padova   Andrea Gloria, *Codice diplomatico padovano dal secolo sesto a tutto l'undecimo* and *Codice diplomatico padovano dall'anno 1101 alla pace di Costanza*, I, Monumenti storici pubblicati dalla deputazione Veneta di storia patria, 1, 2 and 4 (Venice, 1877–9).

Paulinzelle   *Urkundenbuch des Klosters Paulinzelle*, ed. E. Anemüller, Thüringische Geschichtsquellen, 7 (Jena, 1889–1905).

Pforte   *Urkundenbuch des Klosters Pforte*, ed. P. Boehme, Geschichtsquellen der Provinz Sachsen, 33 (Halle, 1893–1904).

Pontefract   *The Chartulary of St John of Pontefract*, ed. R. Holmes, Yorkshire Archaeological Society, 25 and 30 (York, 1899–1902).

Preuilly   *Chartes et documents de l'abbaye cistercienne de Preuilly*, ed. A. Catel and M. Lecomte, Société d'archéologie, sciences, lettres et arts du département de Seine-et-Marne (Montereau, 1927).

Quimperlé   *Cartulaire de l'abbaye de Sainte-Croix de Quimperlé*, ed. L. Maître and P. de Berthou, Bibliothèque bretonne armoricaine, 4, 2nd ed. (Rennes–Paris, 1904).

Raitenhaslach   *Die Urkunden des Klosters Raitenhaslach, 1034–1350*, ed. E. Krausen, Quellen und Erörterungen zur bayerischen Geschichte, N.F. XVII, 1 (Munich, 1959).

Ramsey   *Cartularium monasterii de Rameseia*, ed. W. H. Hart and P. A. Lyons, Rolls Series, 79 (London, 1884–93).

Redon   *Cartulaire de l'abbaye de Redon en Bretagne*, ed. A. de Courson, Collection de documents inédits sur l'histoire de France (Paris, 1863).

Reims   Pierre Varin, *Archives administratives de la ville de Reims*,

I. 1, Collection de documents inédits sur l'histoire de France (Paris, 1839).

Rievaulx *Cartularium abbathiae de Rievalle*, ed. J. C. Atkinson, Surtees Society, 83 (Durham–London–Edinburgh, 1889).

Ronceray Paul Marchegay, *Archives d'Anjou* (Angers, 1843–54), III: *Cartularium monasterii beatae Mariae Caritatis Andegavensis*.

St Benoît-sur-Loire *Recueil des chartes de l'abbaye de Saint-Benoît-sur-Loire*, ed. M. Prou and A. Vidier, 1, Documents publiés par la Société historique et archéologique du Gatinais (Paris–Orléans, 1900–7).

St Bertin *Les Chartes de Saint-Bertin*, ed. Daniel Haigneré, 1, Société des antiquaires de la Morinie (St Omer, 1886).

St Bertin (alt.) *Cartulaire de l'abbaye de Saint-Bertin*, ed. B. Guérard, Collection de documents inédits sur l'histoire de France (Paris, 1840).

St Corneille de Compiègne *Cartulaire de l'abbaye de Saint-Corneille de Compiègne*, ed. E. Morel, 1, Société historique de Compiègne (Montdidier, 1904).

Ste Croix de Bordeaux *Cartulaire de l'abbaye de Sainte-Croix de Bordeaux*, ed. A. Ducaunnès-Duval, Archives historiques du département de la Gironde, 27 (Bordeaux, 1892).

Ste Croix d'Orléans *Cartulaire de Sainte-Croix d'Orléans*, ed. J. Thillier and E. Jarry (Orléans, 1906).

St Cybard *Cartulaire de l'abbaye de Saint-Cybard*, ed. P. Lefrancq, Société archéologique et historique de la Charente (Angoulême, 1930).

St Cyprien *Cartulaire de l'abbaye de Saint-Cyprien de Poitiers*, ed. L. Rédet, Archives historiques du Poitou, 3 (Poitiers, 1874).

St Étienne de Dijon *Chartes de l'abbaye de Saint-Étienne de Dijon [des origines à 1100]*, ed. J. Courtois, Collection de textes relatifs au droit et aux institutions de la Bourgogne (Dijon–Paris, 1908).

St Gallen *Urkundenbuch der Abtei Sanct Gallen*, ed. H. Wartmann (Zürich, 1863 ff.).

St Gregory, Canterbury *Cartulary of the Priory of St Gregory, Canterbury*, ed. A. M. Woodcock, Camden Third Series, 88 (London, 1956).

St Hubert   Chartes de l'abbaye de Saint-Hubert en Ardenne, ed.
   G. Kurth, I, Collection de chroniques belges (Brussels,
   1903).

St Jean d'Angély   Cartulaire de Saint-Jean-d'Angély, ed. G. Musset,
   Archives historiques de la Saintonge et de l'Aunis, 30 and 33
   (Paris, 1901–3).

St Loup de Troyes   Cartulaire de l'abbaye de Saint-Loup de Troyes,
   ed. C. Lalore, Collection des principaux cartulaires du
   diocèse de Troyes, I (Paris, 1875).

*St Maixent   Chartes et documents pour servir à l'histoire de l'abbaye
   de Saint-Maixent*, ed. A. Richard, Archives historiques du
   Poitou, 16–18 (Poitiers, 1886).

*St Martin des Champs   Recueil de chartes et documents de Saint-
   Martin-des-Champs*, ed. J. Depoin, Archives de la France
   monastique (Ligugé–Paris, 1912–21).

St Martin de Tulle   J.-B. Champeval, 'Cartulaire de l'abbaye
   bénédictine Saint-Martin de Tulle', (suite) *Bulletin de la
   Société scientifique, historique et archéologique de la Corrèze*,
   XIX (1897), 621–43.

*St Pierre à Gand   Chartes et documents de l'abbaye de Saint Pierre au
   mont Blandin à Gand*, ed. A. van Lokeren (Ghent, 1868).

St Rufus   Codex diplomaticus ordinis sancti Rufi Valentiae, ed.
   U. Chevalier, Collection de cartulaires dauphinois, IX, I
   (Valence, 1891).

*San Solutore di Torino   Cartario della Abazia di San Solutore di
   Torino*, ed. F. Cognasso, Biblioteca della Società storica
   subalpina, 44 = Corpus chartarum Italiae, 23 (Pinerolo,
   1908).

*St Sernin   Cartulaire de l'abbaye de Saint-Sernin de Toulouse
   (844–1200)*, ed. C. Douais (Paris–Toulouse, 1887).

*St Stephan in Würzburg   Urkundenbuch der Benediktiner-Abtei
   St. Stephan in Würzburg*, I, ed. F. J. Bendel, Veröffentlichungen
   der Gesellschaft für fränkische Geschichte, III, I (Leipzig,
   1912).

*St Symphorien d'Autun   Recueil des actes du prieuré de Saint-
   Symphorien d'Autun de 696 à 1300*, ed. A. Déléage (Autun,
   1936).

St Vaast d'Arras Cartulaire de l'abbaye de Saint-Vaast d'Arras, ed.
E. van Drival, Documents inédits concernant l'Artois, 6
(Arras, 1875).

San Venerio del Tino Le carte del monastero di San Venerio del Tino,
ed. G. Falco, 1, Biblioteca della Società storica subalpina,
90.1 = Corpus chartarum Italiae, 63.1 (Pinerolo, 1917).

St Victeur au Mans Cartulaire de Saint-Victeur au Mans, ed. P. de
Farcy and B. de Broussillon, Société d'agriculture, sciences
et arts de la Sarthe (Paris, 1895).

St Victor de Marseille Cartulaire de l'abbaye de Saint-Victor de
Marseille, ed. B. Guérard, Collection de documents inédits
sur l'histoire de France (Paris, 1857).

St Vincent du Mans Cartulaire de l'abbaye de Saint-Vincent du Mans,
ed. R. Charles and S. M. d'Elbenne, Société historique et
archéologique du Maine (Mamers-Le Mans, 1886–1913).

St Wandrille Ferdinand Lot, Études critiques sur l'abbaye de Saint-
Wandrille, Bibliothèque de l'École des Hautes Études, 204
(Paris, 1913).

Saintes Cartulaire de l'abbaye royale de Notre-Dame de Saintes, ed. T.
Grasilier, Cartulaires inédits de la Saintonge, 2 (Niort, 1871).

Salem Codex diplomaticus Salemitanus: Urkundenbuch der Cister-
zienserabtei Salem, ed. F. von Weech, 1 (Karlsruhe, 1883).

Salzburg Salzburger Urkundenbuch, ed. W. Hauthaler and F.
Martin (Salzburg, 1910 ff.).

Sauxillanges Cartulaire de Sauxillanges, ed. H. Doniol, Académie
des sciences, belles-lettres et arts de Clermont-Ferrand (Clermont-Ferrand–Paris, 1864).

Savigny Cartulaire de l'abbaye de Savigny, ed. A. Bernard,
Collection de documents inédits sur l'histoire de France
(Paris, 1853).

Scarnafigi Documenti di Scarnafigi, ed. G. Colombo, Biblioteca
della Società storica subalpina, 12 = Corpus chartarum
Italiae, 8 (Pinerolo, 1902).

Schleswig-Holstein Schleswig-Holstein-Lauenburgische Regesten und
Urkunden, ed. P. Hasse, 1 (Hamburg–Leipzig, 1886).

Speyer Urkunden zur Geschichte der Stadt Speyer, ed. Alfred
Hilgard (Strasbourg, 1885).

Staffarda   *Cartario della Abazia di Staffarda*, ed. F. Gabotto, G. Roberti and D. Chiattone, Biblioteca della Società storica subalpina, 11–12 = Corpus chartarum Italiae, 7–8 (Pinerolo, 1901–2).

Stavelot-Malmédy *Recueil des chartes de l'abbaye de Stavelot-Malmédy*, ed. J. Halkin and C.-G. Roland, I (Brussels, 1909).

Steiermark *Urkundenbuch des Herzogthums Steiermark*, ed. J. Zahn, I (Graz, 1875).

Stoneleigh *The Stoneleigh Leger Book*, ed. R. H. Hilton, The Dugdale Society, 24 (Oxford, 1960).

Strassburg *Urkundenbuch der Stadt Strassburg*, ed. Wilhelm Wiegand, I (Strasbourg, 1879).

Subiaco *Il regesto Sublacense*, ed. L. Allodi and G. Levi, Biblioteca della R. Società romana di storia patria (Rome, 1885).

Tiglieto *Cartari minori*, III: *Carte inedite e sparse del monastero di Tiglieto*, ed. F. Guasco di Bisio, F. Gabotto and A. Pesce, Biblioteca della Società storica subalpina, 69 (Turin, 1912–23).

Tiron *Cartulaire de l'abbaye de la Sainte-Trinité de Tiron*, ed. L. Merlet, Société archéologique d'Eure-et-Loir (Chartres, 1883).

Toussaints de Châlons *Chartes de Toussaints de Châlons*, ed. C. Lalore, Collection des principaux cartulaires du diocèse de Troyes, 4 (Paris–Troyes, 1878).

Unser Lieben Frauen zu Magdeburg *Urkundenbuch des Klosters Unser Lieben Frauen zu Magdeburg*, ed. G. Hertel, Geschichtsquellen der Provinz Sachsen, 10 (Halle, 1878).

Uzerche *Cartulaire de l'abbaye d'Uzerche*, ed. J.-B. Champeval (Paris–Tulle, 1901).

Vaux de Cernay *Cartulaire de l'abbaye de Notre-Dame des Vaux de Cernay*, ed. L. Merlet and A. Moutié, Société archéologique de Rambouillet: Documents pour servir à l'histoire du département de Seine-et-Oise (Paris, 1857–8).

Vigeois *Cartulaire de l'abbaye de Vigeois en Limousin (954–1167)*, ed. M. de Montégut (Limoges, 1907).

Vignory *Cartulaire du prieuré de Saint-Étienne de Vignory*, ed. J. d'Arbaumont, Société historique et archéologique de Langres (Langres, 1882).

Walkenried   *Die Urkunden des Stiftes Walkenried*, 1, Urkundenbuch des historischen Vereins für Niedersachsen, 2 (Hanover,
1852).

Wirtemberg   *Wirtembergisches Urkundenbuch* (Stuttgart, 1849 ff.).

Xanten   *Urkundenbuch des Stiftes Xanten*, ed. P. Weiler, 1, Veröffentlichungen des Vereins zur Erhaltung des Xantener Domes
e. V., II (Bonn, 1935).

Yonne   *Cartulaire général de l'Yonne*, ed. Maximilien Quantin
(Auxerre, 1854–60).

Zwetl   *Das 'Stiftungen-Buch' des Cistercienser-Klosters Zwetl*, ed.
J. von Frast, Fontes rerum Austriacarum, II, 3 (Vienna, 1851).

INTRODUCTION

THE PROBLEM
OF MONASTIC TITHES

THE purpose of this work is to study the tithes paid to and by monks in the Middle Ages and in particular to explain why by the twelfth century, in spite of earlier theory and practice, most monks received tithes and many were freed from payment. This subject, like other aspects of monastic economy, has not received much attention from historians.[1] In most works monks are included with the clergy as receivers rather than payers of tithes, although in the early Middle Ages the monastic and clerical orders were distinct and monks were as a rule forbidden to receive and required to pay tithes.

---

[1] All students of monastic privileges and economy are agreed that the existing works are inadequate. The most notable exceptions in the field of tithes are the works of Georg Schreiber, especially *Kurie und Kloster im 12. Jahrhundert*, Kirchenrechtliche Abhandlungen, LXV–LXVIII, 2 vols. (Stuttgart, 1910), and his collected essays in *Gemeinschaften des Mittelalters* (Münster in Westf., 1948). There are also valuable sections on monastic tithes in the works of G. G. Coulton, though he was principally concerned with the late Middle Ages; in the posthumous work by Jean-Berthold Mahn, *L'Ordre cistercien et son gouvernement des origines au milieu du XIIIe siècle*, Bibliothèque des Écoles françaises d'Athènes et de Rome, CLXI (Paris, 1945, reprinted 1951); and in Catherine Boyd, *Tithes and Parishes in Medieval Italy: The Historical Roots of a Modern Problem* (Ithaca, 1952). The best general books on tithes are by Paul Viard, *Histoire de la dîme ecclésiastique principalement en France jusqu'au Décret de Gratien* (Dijon, 1909) and *Histoire de la dîme ecclésiastique dans le royaume de France aux XIIe et XIIIe siècles* (Paris, 1912), which will be cited hereafter as Viard, *Dîme*, I and II. Viard paid little attention to monastic tithes, however, and his works, though based on the sources and full of common sense, tend to be legalistic and to generalize on the basis of insufficient evidence. The important work of Émile Lesne, *Histoire de la propriété ecclésiastique en France*, Mémoires et travaux...des Facultés catholiques de Lille, VI, XIX, XXX, XXXIV, XLIV, XLVI, L, and LIII, 6 vols. in 8 (Lille, 1910–43) deals principally with the revenues of the secular clergy. Tithing was known in several religious systems, but the comparative history of tithes has not yet been seriously studied: see W. H. D. Rouse, *Greek Votive Offerings* (Cambridge, 1902), pp. 39–94, and the few references given by H. F. Schmid, 'Byzantinisches Zehntwesen', *Jahrbuch der österreichischen byzantinischen Gesellschaft*, VI (1957), 68.

Tithes in general have long been used in religious and political polemics.[1] Liberal and Protestant historians in particular have tended to regard tithes as an onerous and iniquitous tax, a sign of the oppressive rule of the Church in the Middle Ages, and an inevitable cause of friction between the clergy and the laity.[2] This view is largely based on a preconceived dislike for any compulsory ecclesiastical tax, not on contemporary evidence. Resistance to tithes and evasion of payment certainly existed in the Middle Ages, especially in the fourteenth and fifteenth centuries, but not on the scale suggested by some writers. The vast majority of tithes were faithfully paid, and most of the countless references to tithes in medieval sources are concerned with their possession rather than their payment or enforcement. Over-emphasis on the oppressive nature of tithes and the difficulties of collection tends therefore to obscure their economic importance. Tithes were, according to Pöschl, 'the most important tax in the economic development of western Europe';[3] and although at first sight this opinion may appear to be the pardonable exaggeration of a specialist, further consideration confirms that no tax in the history of Europe can compare with tithes in length of duration, extent of application, and weight of economic burden. Who paid and who received these tithes is an important question for historians.

The history of monastic tithes will be studied here under three headings, covering roughly from the seventh to the twelfth century. The first heading deals with the theological and canonical doctrine of tithing and its application through the Carolingian period, when most monasteries still paid tithes and very few possessed them. The second heading covers the possession of tithes by monasteries in the three following centuries; and the third, the fact that many monks in the twelfth century were

---

[1] Most early works on tithes are tendentious. Tithes are still a lively political, religious, and economic issue in some countries, such as Italy (cf. Boyd, *Tithes*, pp. 1–25); and many recent books on tithes are without scholarly value.

[2] See my article on 'Resistance to Tithes in the Middle Ages', *Journal of Ecclesiastical History*, XIII (1962), 172–85.

[3] Arnold Pöschl, 'Das karolingische Zehentgebot in wirtschaftsgeschichtlicher Beleuchtung', *Die feierliche Inauguration des Rektors der Grazer Universität ...1927/8* (Graz, 1927), p. 19.

freed from paying tithes of goods produced by themselves or for their own use. Taken together, these developments amounted to a minor revolution in economic practice, monastic theory, and canon law. In the twelfth century controversies raged all over Europe between the former owners of tithes and the newly freed monks, who often refused to pay tithes which had for centuries belonged to other institutions or families. Theory was meanwhile made to fit practice, and the canonists produced out of the conflicting sources a reasonably consistent doctrine of monastic tithes. On this basis Popes Hadrian IV and Alexander III worked out in the second half of the century a practical compromise taking into account the interests of both the payers and the owners of the tithes. This finally was accepted by the Fourth Lateran Council as the universal law of the Church. A fourth heading could be added on the legal disputes in the later Middle Ages. But these were mostly settled in terms of the solution established in the twelfth century; and the history of monastic tithes will be considered here down to the time of Alexander III, whose long pontificate marked in many respects a turning-point in the history of the Church and ushered in the 'legal' period of consolidating and defining the reforms and changes of the previous century.[1]

After the twelfth century tithes tended to lose their character as a distinctively ecclesiastical revenue and to become a form of property held by both laymen and ecclesiastics.[2] Pöschl remarked on this 'transformation of the obligatory tithe from a charge on persons to a charge on land' at the turn of the thirteenth century. 'At the same time and in connection with this', he pointed out, 'the right to own tithes came to be based less on official position than on private feudal and landed relationships.'[3] Plöchl called this a change from a *Steuerbegriff* to a *Vermögensbegriff*, that is,

---

[1] Ulrich Stutz, *Geschichte des kirchlichen Benefizialwesens* (Berlin, 1895) was planned to go to the time of Alexander III, but only the first part of vol. I was published.

[2] Cf. Ernst Klebel, 'Zehente und Zehentprobleme im bayrisch-österreichischen Rechtsgebiet', *Sav. Zs.* LVIII, Kan. Abt. XXVII (1938), 241–2 and 259–61.

[3] Arnold Pöschl, 'Der Neubruchzehent', *A. f. kath. KR*, XCVIII (1918), 20.

tithes became a matter of property rather than of taxation.[1] At the same time, in an effort to solve the complexities of rival claims to tithes, the lawyers established a clear concept of exemption or immunity from tithes and defined more closely the distinctions between 'predial', 'personal', and 'mixed' tithes and between 'old field' and 'noval' tithes. From this time on, therefore, monasteries were simply one of many claimants for possession of tithes, and the earlier controversies over whether they should receive or pay tithes were all but forgotten.

In the early Middle Ages, however, monastic tithes were a matter not only of economics but also of doctrine, canon law, and monastic theory. Their history lies in the borderland between theory and practice and must be studied against a background of changes in property relationships, in the theory of tithing, and in the nature of the monastic order. Laws were unwritten at this time. Practice made theory, and custom consecrated abuse. In the foundation charter of Cluny, for instance, it was strictly forbidden 'to grant [the property of the abbey] as a benefice to any person'; but fifty years later Abbot Maiolus declared in a charter that 'Custom is law, although unwritten, and it is now established as law by common usage that any ecclesiastical property may be granted for a rent to anyone, even to laymen, by the authority of a charter'.[2] So it was with tithes. The theologians and legislators were agreed that tithes should be paid only to churches where the sacraments were administered, but both monks and laymen were able to establish by mere usage their right to hold tithes. Monks were increasingly ranked as legitimate receivers of tithes, moreover, both because they tended to merge with the clergy as more monks were ordained and even exercised pastoral functions, and were no longer treated as laymen or as a separate order of society, and because in the eleventh and twelfth centuries monks were commonly considered the *pauperes Christi*, who had impoverished themselves for Christ and were entitled

[1] Willibald Plöchl, *Das kirchliche Zehentwesen in Niederösterreich*, Forschungen zur Landeskunde von Niederösterreich, v (Vienna, 1935), pp. 99–109.
[2] *Cluny*, I, 126, no. 112, and II, 181, no. 1088 (repeated III, 360, no. 2217, in a charter of 993/1048).

to receive rather than pay tithes. These developments were not universally accepted, however, and monastic tithes thus became an issue in a great dispute over the nature of monasticism and the ideal form of monastic life.

The following study is necessarily based on a wide variety of sources, including theological and legal as well as strictly historical records, and above all on charters. 'On the law of monastic exemptions...,' wrote Kuttner, 'which had such an incisive effect on the ecclesiastical structure of mediaeval Europe, the written law of the early Middle Ages was almost silent; the charters remain our chief evidence until deep into the twelfth century, when lawsuits on exemption cases begin to occupy in abundance the judicial practice of the Roman pontiffs.'[1] The same is true of monastic tithes, and the historian often has to use charters of uncertain authenticity. In view of the unreliability of many existing editions, the manuscript tradition of every charter should in theory be examined independently. Not only must faulty copies be corrected, interpolations excised, and rank forgeries rejected, but spurious claims authenticated by genuine charters and genuine claims in forged charters must also be discovered and assessed at their real worth.[2] To compensate for these hazards, the student of monastic tithes at least has an abundance of documents. Nearly every monastic chartulary contains charters dealing with tithes. And in presenting the evidence he can therefore hope to make up by quantity for occasional failings in quality.[3]

[1] Stephan Kuttner, 'Methodological Problems Concerning the History of Canon Law', *Speculum*, xxx (1955), 544.

[2] See Albert Brackmann's review of Schreiber, *Kurie*, in *Göttingische gelehrte Anzeigen*, CLXXV (1913), 276 and 287–8, and Harry Bresslau, *Handbuch der Urkundenlehre*, 2nd ed. (Leipzig–Berlin, 1912–31), I, 96, who stressed the danger of faulty copies of early medieval documents. Some examples of false claims in genuine charters will be found in case 1 in the Appendix. The tendency of recent scholarship, however, seems to be to rehabilitate documents previously condemned as forgeries: cf. Georges Despy, *Les chartes de l'abbaye de Waulsort: Étude diplomatique et édition critique*, I (Brussels, 1957), who has shown that several charters condemned by Léon Lahaye and Ernst Sackur are authentic (see the review by Bryce Lyon, in *American Historical Review*, LXIV, 689–90).

[3] Even the most reliable scholars in this field have occasionally made use of forgeries: Léon Levillain, *Examen critique des chartes...de l'abbaye de Corbie*,

Even in authentic documents the terms may be obscure and ambiguous (sometimes, it seems, also to contemporaries), and a great deal was often left unsaid. The word *decima* was used in many senses, ranging from a literal tenth, quite distinct from the ecclesiastical tithe, to various kinds of secular rents and taxes.[1] *Fratres* and *monasterium* may refer not to a real monastery but to secular clerics leading a communal life, who performed pastoral work and were entitled to receive tithes.[2] Tithes were usually not mentioned in routine documents concerning possession of land, and arrangements that were mutually understood and accepted might become explicit only if disputes arose.

A more subtle difficulty is to estimate the effectiveness of the charters, the relation between the written rights and the economic realities. In theory the monastic privilege was intensely individual. It was 'a totality of subjective rights' and 'a confirmation and grant of individual rights with permanent validity'.[3] German historians in particular have warned that the position of each

Mémoires et documents publiés par la Société de l'École des Chartes, v (Paris, 1902), p. 179 n. 1, used a document proved false by A. Werminghoff, in *NA*, XXVIII (1903), 49–59; E. E. Stengel, *Die Immunität in Deutschland bis zum Ende des 11. Jahrhunderts*, 1: *Diplomatik der deutschen Immunitäts-Privilegien vom 9. bis zum Ende des 11. Jahrhunderts* (Innsbruck, 1911), p. 553, cited two forged tithe-privileges (M² 1768 and 1801); and Émile Lesne, 'La dîme des biens ecclésiastiques aux IXe et Xe siècles', *Rev. d'hist. ecc.* XIV (1913), 502, cited several suspicious papal charters (see pp. 210, 213, 217 below).

[1] On the varied use of the word *decima*, see William M. Newman, *Le domaine royal sous les premiers Capétiens (987–1180)* (Paris, 1937), pp. 19–20; Boyd, *Tithes*, pp. 1–4; Schmid, in *Jb. d. öst. byz. Ges.* VI, 45–110, on the secular tithes in the East generally and esp. 102–10 on tithes in the West; and my article on 'Nona et Decima', *Speculum*, XXXV (1960), 224–50.

[2] On the ambiguity of these terms and the confusion of secular with regular canons, see John Dickinson, *The Origins of the Austin Canons and Their Introduction into England* (London, 1950), p. 37, and Gerhart Ladner, *The Idea of Reform* (Cambridge, Mass., 1959), p. 388, who said that 'Members of these basilican communities were also designated as *custodes, clerici, fratres, pauperes*, and even as *monachi*; but they were obviously not monks in the sense of the theoretical distinction between the monastic and the clerical lives'.

[3] The first definition is that of Gerd Tellenbach, *Church, State and Christian Society at the Time of the Investiture Contest*, tr. R. F. Bennett, Studies in Mediaeval History, III (Oxford, 1940), p. 17; and the second that of Leo Santifaller, 'Die Verwendung des Liber Diurnus in den Privilegien der Päpste von dem Anfängen bis zum Ende des 11. Jahrhunderts', *MÖIG*, XLIX (1935), 239.

monastery must be studied in terms not of its relation to the papacy and the general privileges of its order but of its individual relations with the local secular and ecclesiastical authorities and its special legal position.[1] Papal privileges for German monasteries, according to Brackmann, often only confirmed the grants of local authorities. Even within a specific congregation or order, such as the Cistercians, there was no strict uniformity of rights and privileges.[2] From the day it was granted, a charter might be ineffective or at least subject to negotiation, and it cannot be used as conclusive evidence of the real economic and legal position of the monastery.

These difficulties must be kept in mind as a warning against relying too heavily on individual documents or generalizing exclusively on the basis of papal privileges. The emphasis on local conditions may itself be carried too far, however, and be based too narrowly on conditions in the Holy Roman Empire, where in the twelfth century the influence of Rome was weaker and the monasteries were more dependent on regional powers than in other parts of Europe. Even in the Empire the position of a monastery often depended on a balance of local and central powers, among which the papacy might be decisive.[3] In spite

[1] This has been called 'das territorialgeschichtliche Forschungsprinzip' by Schreiber, 'Kirchliches Abgabenwesen an französischen Eigenkirchen aus Anlass von Ordalien' (1915), in Gemeinschaften, p. 152. Both Albert Brackmann and Hans Hirsch, however, severely criticized Schreiber's own Kurie for concentrating too narrowly on papal policy: see Gött. gelehrte Anzeigen, CLXXV, 278, and Hirsch, Die Klosterimmunität seit dem Investiturstreit (Weimar, 1913), partly tr. by Geoffrey Barraclough, Mediaeval Germany, 911–1250: Essays by German Historians (Oxford, 1938), II, 139. Cf. also Schreiber's reply, 'Studien zur Exemtionsgeschichte der Zisterzienser' (1914), in Gemeinschaften, pp. 393–4, and pp. 255 ff. below.

[2] Brackmann, in Gött. gelehrte Anzeigen, CLXXV, 286: 'Diese völlig verschiedene Behandlung der einzelnen Zisterzienserklöster zeigt, dass für den Rechtsinhalt und die Formulierung des Privilegs nichts die Ordenszugehörigkeit sondern die Rechtsverhältnisse des einzelnen Klosters massgebend waren'; see also his Die Kurie und die Salzburger Kirchenprovinz, Studien und Vorarbeiten zur Germania Pontificia, I (Berlin, 1912), p. 78.

[3] Cf. J.-F. Lemarignier, 'L'Exemption monastique et les origines de la réforme grégorienne', À Cluny (Dijon, 1950), pp. 300–1: 'On a même été jusqu'à dire que les bulles [for Fulda and Hersfeld] n'avaient d'autre objet que de colorer d'une teinte canonique un privilège essentiellement royal et que

of the difficulties of authenticity, interpretation, and evaluation, it still seems possible to discover from the charters and other sources certain broad tendencies in the position of monks and the nature of monastic economy.

l'exemption apparaissait comme quelque peu masquée par une manifestation de l'"Eigenkloster". En réalité, les deux choses se juxtaposent, de même que diplômes et bulles coexistent: il y a exemption vis-à-vis des évêques et sujétion vis-à-vis du prince.'

CHAPTER I

TITHES IN
THE EARLY MIDDLE AGES

I. THE CHRISTIAN THEORY OF TITHES

THE history of tithes in the Middle Ages starts with the Bible and the works of the theologians and exegetes. Both the Old and New Testaments contain many references to tithes; and their payment, unlike any other specific and regular charge in the Middle Ages, was based directly upon divine precept.[1] In the book of Leviticus, for instance, the Lord instructed the children of Israel through Moses that 'All tithes of the land, whether of corn, or of the fruits of trees, are the Lord's, and are sanctified to Him.... Of all the tithes of oxen, and sheep, and goats, that pass under the shepherd's rod, every tenth that cometh shall be sanctified to the Lord' (xxvii. 30, 32). In the New Testament Jesus referred somewhat slightingly to tithes: 'Woe to you, scribes and Pharisees, hypocrites because you tithe mint and anise and cummin; and have left the weightier things of the law; judgment and mercy and faith. These things you ought to have done and not to leave those undone' (Matt. xxiii. 23, cf. Luke xi. 42 and xviii. 12). Even here tithes were considered a matter of the law and a thing to be done. The Epistle to the Hebrews, which throughout the Middle Ages was commonly attributed to St Paul[2] and in which

---

[1] The following remarks are not intended to explain the systems of tithing mentioned in the Bible, which would require a book to themselves, but to describe briefly biblical tithing as it was understood in the Middle Ages. The Bible is cited in the Douay version, as being closer to the Vulgate than is the King James version.

[2] Cf. Alfred Wikenhauser, *New Testament Introduction*, tr. Joseph Cunningham (New York, 1958), pp. 58 and 465–6, who pointed out that the Epistle to the Hebrews was the only New Testament book of which the authorship was 'seriously disputed in the Middle Ages' but was generally accepted as the work of St Paul in the West after the fourth century.

Abraham gave a tenth of his spoils to the priest-king Melchizedek, the prototype of Christ, was used to show not only that the new priesthood was superior to the old but also, although the reference to tithes was incidental, that all Christians must tithe their entire income.

The Bible does not clearly indicate, however, to whom the tithes must be paid and how they should be used. Most references in the Old Testament treated tithes as the special property of God and as the perquisite of his ministers. In Num. xviii. 20–8 they were called the inheritance of the sons of Levi. In Neh. x. 37–8 and xiii. 5 the servants at the altars of the Lord, including even the singers and the porters, were expected to live off tithes. In both these sources the Levites themselves had to set aside 'the tenth part of the tenth' for the Aaronites who officiated at the central sanctuary. In the book of Deuteronomy, however, another system of tithing was found in addition to the annual tithe for the feast at the Temple. 'The third year thou shalt separate another tithe of all things that grow to thee at that time, and shalt lay it up within thy gates. And the Levite that hath no other part nor possession with thee, and the stranger and the fatherless and the widow, that are within thy gates, shall come and shall eat and be filled' (Deut. xiv. 28–9, cf. xxvi. 12). This 'other' tithe was thus to be used for a triennial feast at the home of the donor, who was to invite the Levite and other needy persons. In the deuteronomist book of I Kings, furthermore, Samuel even referred to tithes which might be exacted by the king: 'Moreover he [the king] will take the tenth of your corn, and of the revenues of your vineyards, to give his eunuchs and servants.... Your flocks also he will tithe, and you shall be his servants' (I Kings viii. 15 and 17).

Modern scholars have explained in several ways these different references to tithing in the Old Testament. Deuteronomy may refer to an earlier system which was superseded by the purely Levitical tithe, or possibly to the custom of tithing in northern Israel as contrasted with Judah.[1] Any inconsistency in the Bible, however, was abhorrent to the medieval commentators, who

[1] Cf. *The Interpreter's Bible*, ed. G. A. Buttrick, etc. (New York–Nashville, 1953), II, 424–6.

attacked these passages in Deuteronomy with a full battery of exegetical weapons. Some of them tried a literal interpretation. The Venerable Bede, for instance, maintained that the 'other tithe' was for the priests.[1] Rabanus Maurus admitted that he was puzzled by the two tithes and emphasized that the Levites were placed first among those to whom the 'other tithe' was to be given and suggested, following Bede, that this and the tithe in Deuteronomy xxvi. 12 was the Levitical or sacerdotal tithe as distinct from the tithe mentioned in xiv. 22–7.[2] The author of the *Glossa ordinaria* in the twelfth century adopted almost verbatim Rabanus's interpretation of xiv. 28–9,[3] but he saw the tithe in xiv. 22–7 in a moral sense as the good works which men should perform every year, applying Rabanus's exegesis of Num. xviii. 20–8, that tithes in general signify spiritually the observance of the law, the integrity of the catholic faith, and the perfection of good works.[4] The *Glossa ordinaria* on Deut. xxvi. 12, however, suggested a parallel with Tobias 1. 6–7, that 'those who were far from the Temple gave in the third year the tithes of three years to the poor and to the Levites who were with them'.[5] In the thirteenth century Thomas Aquinas gave a fully literal explanation of these

[1] Bede, *In Pentateuchum commentarii: Deuteronomium* to xiv. 28, in *PL*, xci, 386: '*Separabis mihi aliam decimam,* id est sacerdotibus, ac si per hoc sacerdotibus diceret.'
[2] Rabanus Maurus, *Enarratio super Deuteronomium,* ii, 7, in *PL*, cviii, 888–90.
[3] *Glossa ordinaria* to Deut. xiv. 29, in *PL*, cxiii, 466. The *Glossa ordinaria* were long attributed to Walafrid Strabo in the ninth century but are now known to have been composed in the circle of Anselm of Laon in the twelfth century, and the section on the Pentateuch is thought to be by Gilbert the Universal, before 1128: see Joseph de Ghellinck, *Le mouvement théologique du XIIe siècle,* 2nd ed., Museum Lessianum: Section historique, x (Brussels–Paris, 1948), pp. 104–12, and Beryl Smalley, *The Study of the Bible in the Middle Ages,* 2nd ed. (Oxford, 1952), pp. 52–66.
[4] Rabanus Maurus, *Enarrationes in librum Numerum,* ii, 23, in *PL*, cviii, 701; repeated with the same abbreviations in the *Glossa ordinaria,* in *PL*, cxiii, 409 and 465–6. Cf. the interpretations of Gregory the Great, cited p. 12 n. 2 below, and in the *Quaestiones super Exodum* (attributed to Bede or to Wigbod in the eighth century), xxxvii, in *PL*, xciii, 376–7, where first-fruits were compared to the beginning and tithes to the consummation of good works. On these see Friedrich Stegmüller, *Repertorium biblicum medii aevi* (Madrid, 1950 ff.), ii, 189 and v, 440, nos. 1654–62 and 8376.
[5] *PL*, cxiii, 482.

passages and wrote in the *Summa theologica* that 'In the Old Law
men were bound to pay three kinds of tithe': one for the Levites,
as in Num. xviii; a second, 'which was reserved for the offering
of sacrifices', as in Deut. xiv. 22–3; and a third tithe given for
charity every third year, as in Deut. xiv. 28–9.[1]

These literal and moral interpretations, however, failed to
explain satisfactorily why the tithe in Deuteronomy was paid
only every third year and to strangers, orphans, and widows as
well as to the Levites. These difficulties were best met by an ana-
gogical exegesis.[2] Bruno of Segni, who died in 1123, interpreted
the third year as the age of grace, following the two ages before
and under the law.

For by this ['other tithe' in xiv. 28], I think that a spiritual understanding of the law is meant; for there are ten words of the law, and
previously certain Jews by their literal understanding and observance
gave one tithe. But when the third year came, that is, the third age of
time, another tithe was given, by which the same ten words were
spiritually understood.... From this tithe live the Levites and the
clerical order; from this whoever delights in spiritual things may eat
and be filled. The pilgrims, who are the Gentiles coming to the faith,
and the orphans and the widows, who have left the most evil father and
husband, the Devil, receive this [tithe].[3]

---

[1] Thomas Aquinas, *Summa theologica*, II. 2, q. LXXXVII, a. 1, tr. by the
Fathers of the English Dominican Province (London, 1911–22), IX, 91–6.

[2] Gregory the Great in his commentary on I Kings xv and xvii, where
Samuel referred to a royal tithe, also avoided a literal interpretation. Under the
rule of evil kings, he explained, the righteous will lose some of their virtue and
property. The example of the wicked will reduce, or tithe, the flocks of the
elect, which he interpreted as 'the hosts of spiritual virtues'. Elsewhere Gregory
again compared the crops of grain and grapes to the good works which set an
example to the faithful, but this time he said that the eunuchs and servants
were those striving to be good, for whose benefit the good examples (the
tithes) were collected: Gregory the Great, *Opera omnia* (Paris, 1705), III. 2,
184–6 and 196–7.

[3] Bruno of Segni, *Expositio in Deuteronomium* to xiv. 28–9, in *PL*, CLXV, 508.
On Bruno, see Max Manitius, *Geschichte der lateinischen Literatur des Mittelalters*, Handbuch der Altertumswissenschaft, IX, 2 (Munich, 1911–31), III, 49–50,
and Joseph de Ghellinck, *L'Essor de la littérature latine au XIIe siècle*, Museum
Lessianum: Section historique, IV–V (Brussels–Paris, 1946), I, 157, who called
him 'conseiller influent sous quatre pontificats'.

The great twelfth-century mystical theologian Rupert of Deutz also interpreted this passage allegorically. He began his commentary on Deut. xxvi. 12 with the remark that 'Literally, this is a precept of piety; mystically, however, it is a demonstration or prophecy of the apostolic work'.[1] For him the essential meaning was that in the era of grace (the third year) tithes might be given to the Gentiles (the strangers, orphans, and widows) as well as to the Jews (the Levites). The differences in the Bible were thus reconciled in various ways, and the ambiguity was not allowed to compromise in any respect the absolute nature of the law of tithing.

The theologians and commentators emphasized above all the universality of the obligation to pay tithes. Even if Christians cannot, as they should, sell all and give to the poor, said St Jerome in his commentary on Mal. iii. 10, they should at least imitate the Jews by giving tithes and first-fruits.[2] Some theologians went further and maintained that since the justice of Christians must exceed that of the scribes and Pharisees, they should give more than a single tithe.[3] For tithes are paid, according to St Caesar of Arles in a sermon universally attributed to St Augustine in the Middle Ages, for the sake not of God who receives them but of those who pay them, whose eternal salvation depends upon faithful payment.[4] And a follower of Caesar said that both

[1] Rupert of Deutz, *In Deuteronomium*, II, 3, in *PL*, CLXVII, 959. On Rupert, see pp. 173–5 below and, on his Trinitarian concept of history, Morton W. Bloomfield, 'Joachim of Flora', *Traditio*, XIII (1957), 278 n. 126, with bibliographical references.

[2] *PL*, XXV, 1571. Cf. Louis Thomassin, *Ancienne et nouvelle discipline de l'église*, III, 1, 2.5, ed. M. André (Bar-le-Duc, 1864–7), VI, 10, who cited St Jerome as evidence that even monks must pay tithes, but the reference is not explicit.

[3] Cf. Paul the Deacon, *In sanctam regulam commentarium* (Monte Cassino, 1880), pp. 418–19 (see p. 206 and n. 3 below); Walafrid Strabo, *Libellus de exordiis et incrementis rerum ecclesiasticarum*, XXVIII, in MGH, *Capit.* II, 512–13 (cited p. 34 below); 909 council of Trosly, can. 6, citing Matt. v. 20, in Mansi, *Collectio*, XVIII, 282 (see p. 35 below); and Odo of Cluny, *Vita S. Geraldi*, I, 14 and 28, in *Bibl. Clun.* pp. 75 and 80. Thomas Aquinas, *loc. cit.* p. 12 n. 1 above, also cited Matt. v. 20 in reference to tithes, but he did not draw the conclusion that Christians should pay more than a tenth.

[4] Caesar of Arles, serm. XXXIII, ed. Germain Morin, in *CC*, CIII, 142–7, also published as serm. CCLXXVII *de reddendis decimis* among the works of St Augustine

worldly success and bodily health depended on the payment of tithes.[1]

The same points were made by the Carolingian theologians. 'Abraham taught by his deeds', wrote Walafrid Strabo, 'and Jacob by his promises, then the law established and all the holy fathers recount that tithes must be given to God and to the priests of God.'[2] Rabanus Maurus, in a passage describing the structure of the Church, used two verses from Leviticus to stress the universal character of tithes. The Church, he said, is divided into three professions: the clergy, who govern and serve in churches; the monks, 'who live far from the activities of this life and free from worldly cares, either in a monastery under the discipline of a rule or in solitary places as best they can'; and the laity, 'that is, those who are married and all others devoted to worldly activities'.

The Lord figuratively described these three professions,...as three types of animals when in Leviticus [xxvii. 30 and 32] he spoke through Moses: 'Of all the tithes of oxen, and sheep, and goats, that pass under the shepherd's rod, every tenth that cometh shall be sanctified to the Lord. All tithes of the land, whether of corn, or of the fruits of trees, are the Lord's, and are sanctified to him.'...By cattle, of course, are meant the clergy....By sheep, however, the simplicity of monks is

(Paris, 1836–9), v, 3089–92, and tr. M. M. Mueller, The Fathers of the Church, xxxi (New York, 1956), i, 162–7: 'See, we have shown you how the tithes benefit us rather than God' (p. 163). This sermon was frequently cited by medieval theologians, including Thomas Aquinas, who believed, however, that tithes were intended to support the clergy and said that 'the payment of tithes is due not for its own sake, but for the sake of the ministers' (Summa theologica, II. 2, q. LXXXVII, a. 2, ed. cit. IX, 98). This sermon was printed without identification from an eighth-century manuscript at Einsiedeln by Paul Piper, 'Superstitiones et paganiae Einsidlenses', Mélanges...Émile Chatelain (Paris, 1910), pp. 302–4, and was cited from this by Schmid, in Jb. d. öst. byz. Ges. VI, 99 n. 328 as evidence of the theory of tithing in the eighth century.

[1] PL, LVII, 901. This sermon clearly derived from Caesar of Arles, but it was published as sermon XXVI in the appendix to the works of Maximus of Turin. 'Il reste beaucoup à faire pour éliminer les pièces apocryphes du bagage littéraire dont la déconcertante légèreté de Bruni a chargé saint Maxime de Turin', said B. Capelle, 'Les Tractatus de baptismo attribués à saint Maxime de Turin', Rev. bén. XLV (1933), 108.

[2] Walafrid Strabo, De exordiis, XXVIII, in MGH, Capit. II, 512.

implied; and by goats, the life of secular men, that is, of the laity, is expressed.[1]

All men, therefore, whatever their position in the Church, had to pay tithes. Like prayer, charity, and the Ten Commandments, it was a personal religious obligation from which there could be no exemptions.[2] 'Tithe is a due', wrote Watson, 'which must, at the risk of his soul, be paid by every believer.'[3] And the act of rendering tithes, as Schreiber said, took on 'a certain liturgical character' and was treated as 'an act of worshipping God'.[4]

In theory even the clergy were required to pay tithes. The passages in Gen. xiv. 20 and Heb. vii. 2 where Abraham gave a tenth of all his spoils to Melchizedek were interpreted to mean not only that tithes must be paid to the Christian clergy, represented by Melchizedek, which had superseded the old Levitical priest-

---

[1] *Thesaurus*, V, 521. In his *Expositiones in Leviticum*, VII, 17, Rabanus interpreted these passages in such a way as to stress the absolute obligation of tithes, in *PL*, CVIII, 583–5; but in the epitome of Rabanus attributed to Walafrid Strabo the words 'of all the tithes' in Lev. xxvii. 32 were glossed 'of all the orders which are under the discipline of Christ', in *PL*, CXIV, 850. Ralph of Flavigny in the twelfth century, however, interpreted this passage to mean that all types of people (the cattle, sheep, and goats) must render to the Lord what is his (the tithes): *In Leviticum libri XX*, I, 1–2 and XX, 6–7, in *Maxima bibliotheca veterum patrum* (Lyons, 1677), XVII, 51–4 and 246–7.

[2] A follower of Abelard in the twelfth century stressed that divine grace rather than human virtue was necessary to fulfil the law of tithing, like the Ten Commandments: *Commentarius Cantabrigiensis in epistolas Pauli e schola Petri Abaelardi*, IV: *In epistolam ad Hebraeos*, ed. Artur Landgraf, Publications in Mediaeval Studies, II, 4 (Notre Dame, Ind., 1945), p. 749. Thomas Aquinas maintained 'that man's obligation to pay the tithe arises partly from natural law [the duty to support the clergy], partly from the institution of the Church [the proportion of a tenth]': *Summa theologica*, II. 2, q. LXXXVII, a. 1, *ed. cit.* IX, 95. And St Charles Borromeo, whose Milan Penitential derived largely from the eleventh-century penitential of Burchard's Corrector, considered failure to pay tithes a theft from God and a breach of the Seventh Commandment: H. J. Schmitz, *Die Bussbücher und die Bussdisciplin der Kirche* (Mainz, 1883), p. 824, and J. T. McNeill and H. M. Gamer, *Medieval Handbooks of Penance*, Columbia Records of Civilization, XXIX (New York, 1938), p. 363.

[3] E. W. Watson, in *The Cambridge Medieval History* (Cambridge, 1911–36), VI, 533.

[4] Georg Schreiber, *Untersuchungen zum Sprachgebrauch des mittelalterlichen Oblationenwesens* (Wörishofen, 1913), p. 17 n. 2.

hood,[1] but also that all men must pay tithes, since in the person of Abraham the Levites themselves paid tithes, just as Abraham's other descendants paid tithes to their brethren the Levites.[2] Also in Num. xviii. 26 the Levites were forced to pay tithes to the Aaronites, which according to Bruno of Segni meant that the Christian clergy must pay tithes.[3] Peter the Venerable in the twelfth century wrote to the Cistercians that 'In the days of the Fathers not only laymen paid tithes but also churches to churches and monasteries to monasteries both from the work of peasants and from their own produce'.[4] In practice, however, since they were the receivers of the tithe, the clergy either kept the tithes paid by themselves or absorbed this duty into the general obligations of their office.[5] The theory that everyone without exception must pay tithes was not forgotten, however, and was involved in the religious disputes of the eleventh and twelfth centuries.

Every type of revenue, furthermore, was subject to tithes. The view that tithes were a purely agricultural tax was unknown in the

---

[1] Atto of Vercelli, for instance, repeatedly based the superiority of the Christian to the Levitical priesthood on the example of Melchizedek, the prefiguration of Christ: *Argumentum in epistolam ad Hebraeos*, in Atto of Vercelli, *Opera*, ed. C. Burontius (Vercelli, 1768), II, 212–13. Cf. the arenga to a charter of 1125/9 in *St Maixent*, I, 313, no. 287 (cited p. 109 below).

[2] Cf. Alcuin, *Expositio in epistolam Pauli apostoli ad Hebraeos* to vii. 4–5, in *PL*, C, 1063–4, and *Glossa ordinaria* on the same passage, in *PL*, CXIV, 654–5, probably by Anselm of Laon (Smalley, *Bible*, p. 60). Both commentators cited Chrysostom on this point. Hugh of Amiens in the twelfth century used the payment of tithes by Abraham to Melchizedek as evidence that all men, including the Levites, must pay tithes: *Contra haereticos*, I, 8, in *PL*, CXCII, 1262–3. Maimonides also held that 'All are bound to give tithe of cattle: priests, Levites, and (lay) Israelites': *The Code of Maimonides, Book Nine: The Book of Offerings*, tr. Herbert Danby, Yale Judaica Series, IV (New Haven, 1950), p. 83.

[3] Bruno of Segni, *Expositio in Numeros* to xviii. 20–8, in *PL*, CLXIV, 487.

[4] Peter the Venerable, ep. I, 35, in *Bibl. Clun.* p. 705.

[5] Cf. Thomas Aquinas, *Summa theologica*, II. 2, q. LXXXVII, a. 4, *ed. cit.* IX, 102–3: 'Now tithes are due to the clergy as being ministers of the altar and sowers of spiritual things among the people. Wherefore those members of the clergy as such, i.e. as having ecclesiastical property, are not bound to pay tithes.' But clerics 'who do not dispense spiritual things to the people' must pay tithes unless exempted by the papacy, and even the pastoral clergy had to pay tithes from their personal property.

early Middle Ages.[1] Abraham's tithing of his spoils, Jacob's promise to give God tithes of all things given to him (Gen. xxviii. 22), and Jesus's reference to 'the tithe of mint and anise and cummin' were used to show that tithes must be paid even from the smallest things.[2] St Ambrose stressed that tithes are due from every substance given to man by God, including profits from trade and hunting.[3] Caesar of Arles in his pseudo-Augustinian sermon on tithes said that 'If you do not possess the tithes of earthly fruits, as does the farmer, whatever your talents procure for you belongs to God. He asks for tithes from the source of our livelihood. Pay tithes of military service, business, or a trade.'[4] The author of a sermon attributed to Eligius of Nim-

[1] Many historians have maintained the contrary: P. Imbart de la Tour, 'Les paroisses rurales dans l'ancienne France, II: L'organisation de la paroisse à l'époque carolingienne', Revue historique, LXIII (1897), 28, who said that the tithe 'affectait la terre, non la personne'; Viard, Dîme, I, 105–6, who wrote that 'La dîme ne porte donc pas sur tous les revenus des fidèles mais sur les seuls produits de l'industrie agricole' (though in Dîme, I, 150 and II, 8, he stressed that tithes were owed from all types of revenue); Watson, in Camb. Med. Hist. VI, 534–5; and more recently Schmid, in Jb. d. öst. byz. Ges. VI, 93 ff., who held that tithing in the West grew out of late Roman agricultural taxes taken over by the barbarian invaders and that tithes were not levied from non-agricultural revenues. This view depends, however, on legal distinctions introduced into the theory of tithing in the twelfth and thirteenth centuries (see pp. 267–8 and 287 ff. below) and upon modern canon law, according to which the tithe is 'une charge réelle du bien-fonds et non pas un impôt personnel' (G. Lepointe, in the Dictionnaire de droit canonique, IV, 1233). In the early Middle Ages, however, tithes were a personal obligation owed from all types of income and never only from agricultural revenues. In Wales, indeed, tithes seem to have been levied not from land but only from personal property and income: T. P. Ellis, Welsh Tribal Law and Custom in the Middle Ages (Oxford, 1926), I, 37, 197, and 208.
[2] On Matt. xxiii. 23, see Hilary of Poitiers, cap. XXIV, in PL, IX, 1050; Walafrid Strabo, De exordiis, XXVIII, in MGH, Capit. II, 513; Paschasius Radbertus, X, 23, in PL, CXX, 777–9; and Thomas Aquinas, Summa theologica, II. 2, q. LXXXVII, a. 2, ed. cit. IX, 99. On Heb. vii. 2, see the Commentarius Cantabrigiensis, ed. Landgraf, p. 744: 'id est de omnibus illis, que habebat in preda, dedit illi decimam'. These spoils, the commentator later stressed (p. 749) were not unlawful plunder but God's gift to Abraham.
[3] Ambrose, serm. XXV, 2, in PL, XVII, 677; cf. serm. XXIV, 3, ibid. 674.
[4] Caesar of Arles, serm. XXXIII, 1, in CC, CIII, 144, and tr. Mueller, I, 164. This passage was cited by Pope Nicholas II in his privilege for St Peter at Perugia in 1059 (cited p. 95 below) and by Thomas Aquinas, Summa theologica, II. 2, q. LXXXVII, a. 2, ed. cit. IX, 98–9, who said that 'tithe must be paid before

wegen, who died in 630, likewise said that 'Everyone should give a tithe from whatever skill or trade he exercises to God in [the form of] the poor or the churches'.[1] Cassian in his *Collationes* went even further: 'We who are ordered to give tithes of our property and all our profits should even more also give tithes of our conduct, occupation, and achievements, wherefore they are clearly discharged in the reckoning of Lent. For the number of all the days [of a year]...is tithed by the number of thirty-six and a half days.'[2] Gregory the Great also compared the fast days of Lent, which Christians devote to God, to a tithe of their time. 'Just as you are ordered in the law to give tithes of your things,' he wrote, 'strive to give Him also tithes of your days.'[3]

These tithes were the property of God, not a voluntary offering by man, and the obligations of charity were in no way fulfilled by paying tithes. 'First of all,' said Caesar of Arles, 'give tithes of all your profits to the Church for the clergy and the poor; and give alms from the nine-tenths which remain in your possession.'[4]

everything else on one's entire produce'; cf. also pseudo-Maximus, serm. XXVI, in *PL*, LVII, 902. Caesar again stressed that tithes belong to God in serm. XXXIII, 2 and in serm. XXXIV, 3 (*CC*, CIII, 144–5 and 148–9) and that tithes must be paid 'ex omnibus fructibus et ex omnibus lucris' in serm. I, 12 (*CC*, CIII, 9–10).

[1] MGH, *SS. Merov.* IV, 755.

[2] Cassian, *Conlationes*, XXI, 25, ed. Michael Petschenig, Corpus scriptorum ecclesiasticorum latinorum, XIII, 2 (Vienna, 1886), p. 600. On the term *conversatio*, which I have here translated as 'conduct', see the introduction on 'La langue de Saint Benoît' by Christine Mohrmann in the edition of St Benedict's *Regula monachorum* by Philibert Schmitz (Maredsous, 1955), pp. 34–9. St Dorotheus, *Doctrina* XV, in *Patrologia graeca*, LXXXVIII, 1787, also compared Lent to the tithes of the year.

[3] Gregory the Great, *Homilia*, I, 16, to Matt. iv. 1–11, *ed. cit.* I, 1494–5 (with editorial notes in III, 315 C–D). This passage was cited by the council of Trosly in 909, can. 6, in Mansi, *Collectio*, XVIII, 283 (cited p. 35 below); and both the Penitential of Theodore of Canterbury and the Confessional of Egbert (cited p. 25 n. 1 below) referred to Lent as the period 'when we pay the tithes of the year'.

[4] Caesar of Arles, serm. XIV, 3, in *CC*, CIII, 71, and tr. Mueller, I, 81; cf. serm. XIII, 3: 'Decimas de fructiculis vestris ad ecclesiam reddite...qui solebat furtum facere vel res alienas invadere, etiam de propria substantia incipiat pauperibus erogare' (*CC*, CIII, 66); serm. XIX, 3: 'Decimas ante omnia de fructiculis vestris ecclesiis reddite...' (*CC*, CIII, 89); and serm. LX, 1: '...de omnibus fructibus decimas reddat, et de novem partibus quicquid suis necessitatibus superfuerit, minuta peccata quae cotidie subripiunt redimat...' (*CC*, CIII, 263). Cf. pseudo-Maximus, serm. XXVI, in *PL*, LVII, 903, and Ambrose, serm.

Man was thus a sort of share-cropper with God, who had, as it were, a proprietary interest in the works of man and was entitled to a tenth part of his proceeds.

2. THE EARLY PRACTICE OF TITHING

Very little is known about the actual payment of tithes in the first centuries of Christianity. Their early history is a subject, said Hartridge, 'on the details of which learned authorities will probably for ever disagree'.[1] 'The faithful may have paid the tithe voluntarily and spontaneously,' according to Leclercq, 'but we are not in a position to cite any canonical or conciliar text before the fourth century which requires the payment [of tithes].'[2] Almost nothing is known, furthermore, about the possible survival of ancient secular tithes in the early Middle Ages and about the disappearance of tithing in the East.[3] It is

xxiv, 3, in *PL*, xvii, 674, who cited Deut. xii. 6 to prove that payments to the Church should be given before alms.

[1] R. A. R. Hartridge, *A History of Vicarages in the Middle Ages* (Cambridge, 1930), p. 1.

[2] *Dict. d'arch.* iv. 1, 995, where there is a useful survey of the early history of tithes; see also Thomassin, *Discipline*, iii, 1, 2–11, *ed. cit.* vi, 8–70, which in spite of its age is still of value; the first volume of Viard, *Dîme*; and Boyd, *Tithes*, pp. 26–46.

[3] The best account of this subject that I have found, though old, is in Thomassin, *Discipline*, iii, 1, 3–9, *ed. cit.* vi, 21–3, 26, 30, and 45. Chrysostom and other early fathers of the Greek church mentioned the ecclesiastical tithe, but later it apparently died out, although various secular payments of a tenth were known in the Byzantine Empire: cf. George Ostrogorsky, in *Camb. Econ. Hist.* i, 200, and Schmid, in *Jb. d. öst. byz. Ges.* vi, 45–110. The ecclesiastical tithe is not discussed by Emil Herman, 'Die kirchlichen Einkünfte des byzantinischen Niederclerus', *Orientalia christiana periodica*, viii (1942), 378–442, who treated tithes in the West as a Carolingian innovation (p. 404), or by Kenneth Setton, 'On the Importance of Land Tenure and Agrarian Taxation in the Byzantine Empire, from the Fourth Century to the Fourth Crusade', *Amer. J. Philology*, lxxiv (1953), 225–59. The introduction of tithes into the East after the Latin conquest in 1204 was a constant source of trouble: see Leo Santifaller, *Beiträge zur Geschichte des lateinischen Patriarchats von Konstantinopel (1204–1261), und der venezianischen Urkunde* (Weimar, 1938), pp. 65–6. In 1219 the non-Latins living in the Latin Empire of Constantinople were allowed to pay one-thirtieth in place of one-tenth for ten years: see R. L. Wolff, 'Politics in the Latin Patriarchate of Constantinople, 1204–1261', *Dumbarton Oaks Papers*, viii (1954), 271, who on pp. 257–60 discusses the tithes paid by the Latin conquerors. In Sicily it appears that only the Latin population were

probable, however, that the normal ecclesiastical tithe in the Middle Ages originated in the precepts of the Bible and remained a purely religious obligation, enforced by ecclesiastical sanctions only, until it was made a part of secular law by the Carolingian rulers in the eighth century.[1]

By the fifth and sixth centuries tithes were well established in the old areas of Christianity in the West. Viard and Beck found extensive evidence of tithing at this time in the Frankish kingdoms and in south-eastern Gaul;[2] and San Martín established, largely on the basis of liturgical sources, that tithes were known in Visigothic Spain before the Moslem conquest.[3] In Italy, the compulsory *collata* or *collatio*, which was used for pilgrims and the poor and from which Gregory the Great specifically exempted the blind, may have been the same as the ecclesiastical tithe.[4] Cassian referred to tithes as being given for the uses both of the poor and of the Levites.[5] Eugippius recorded in his life of the missionary St Severinus, who died in about 482, that many people in Noricum

forced to pay tithes, since an alleged diploma of King William I (forged probably in the mid-thirteenth century) granted the abbey of St Mary at Josaphat a church 'cum decima unius molendini aliisque decimis bonorum hominum latinorum': C. A. Garufi, *I documenti inediti dell'epoca normanna in Sicilia*, I, Documenti per servire alla storia di Sicilia, I, 18 (Palermo, 1899), p. 72, no. 29; cf. Karl Kehr, *Die Urkunden der normannisch-sicilischen Könige* (Innsbruck, 1902), p. 353, and Lynn White, *Latin Monasticism in Norman Sicily*, The Mediaeval Academy of America, Pub. XXXI (Cambridge, Mass., 1938), pp. 205–9.

[1] Schmid (see p. 17 n. 1 above) is almost alone among serious modern scholars in asserting the secular origins of medieval tithes. His view that 'the strongest root of the western ecclesiastical law of tithing' was the transfer to the Church of state lands from which secular agricultural tithes were owed is not supported by any contemporary evidence, which shows, on the contrary, that tithes were not purely agricultural and were certainly not restricted to state lands given to the Church. Jesús San Martín, *El diezmo eclesiástico en España hasta el siglo XII* (Palencia, 1940), pp. 117–27, stressed that in Spain there was no connection between the ecclesiastical tithe and the secular dues of a tenth.

[2] Viard, *Dîme*, I, 41–55, and Henry G. J. Beck, *The Pastoral Care of Souls in South-East France during the Sixth Century*, Analecta Gregoriana, LI (Rome, 1950), p. 329.

[3] San Martín, *Diezmo*, pp. 37–76 and 157–62. Cf. Gonzalo Martínez Diez, 'El patrimonio eclesiástico en la España Visigoda', *Miscelanea Comillas*, XXXII (1959), 24–9, who concluded on the basis of an independent examination of the literary and liturgical evidence that tithes existed in Visigothic Spain but were rare and not enforced by the Church.   [4] Boyd, *Tithes*, pp. 28–35.

[5] Cassian, *Conlationes*, XXI, 2–3, ed. cit. pp. 574–5.

paid tithes on account of the charitable example of Severinus, who 'in his letters exhorted the people of Noricum to give tithes...with which the poor may be fed'. When their crops failed, Severinus told the people that 'If you had offered tithes for the poor, not only would you enjoy an eternal reward but you would also be able to abound in worldly comforts'.[1] Caesar of Arles frequently mentioned tithes in his sermons. 'Before the tribunal of the eternal Judge', he warned, 'a man will appear guilty of as many murders as the number of poor souls who have died of hunger where he lived because he refused to pay tithes, for he reserves for his own use the possessions assigned by our Lord to the poor.'[2] This suggests that tithes might be given directly to the poor, but as a rule Caesar stressed that tithes were not the same as charity and belonged neither to the giver nor to the ultimate receiver, the poor, but to God, and that they should properly be given to the Church for distribution to those in need.[3]

This view of tithing is found in various sources of the sixth and seventh centuries. The earliest conciliar texts referring to tithes come from Merovingian Gaul. In 567 the bishops of the province of Tours urged in a pastoral letter that tithes should be paid for the use of the poor and the redemption of captives.[4] The second council of Mâcon in 585 decreed that:

[1] Eugippius, *Vita s. Severini*, XVII–XVIII, ed. H. Sauppe, in MGH, *Auctores antiquissimi*, I. 2 (Berlin, 1877), 17, and tr. G. W. Robinson, *The Life of Saint Severinus by Eugippius*, Harvard Translations (Cambridge, Mass., 1914), pp. 64–5 and 66–7; cf. Viard, *Dîme*, I, 44–5 and, on the *Vita*, Wattenbach-Levison, *Geschichtsquellen*, pp. 44–8.

[2] Caesar of Arles, serm. XXXIII, 3, in *CC*, CIII, 146, and tr. Mueller, I, 166; cf. pseudo-Maximus, serm. XXVI, in *PL*, LVII, 902–3.

[3] Caesar stressed in several sermons that tithes must be paid to the churches or priests: serm. I, 12; XIX, 3; XXX, 2; and XXXIII, 2; in *CC*, CIII, 9–10, 89, 130, and 145. He was less clear in serm. X, 3, and XVI, 2 (*CC*, CIII, 53 and 77) but implied in both that tithes should be given *for* rather than *to* the poor. Viard, *Dîme*, I, 49, and Leclercq, in *Dict. d'arch.* IV. 1, 999, said that opinion at this time was divided on whether tithes should be given to the clergy or directly to the poor.

[4] MGH, *Conc.* I, 136–8. According to De Clercq, *Législation*, I, 45, this decree was 'le premier texte mérovingien qui parle de la dîme'. On ecclesiastical aid to captives generally, see Alfons Dopsch, *Wirtschaftliche und soziale Grundlagen der europäischen Kulturentwicklung aus der Zeit von Caesar bis auf Karl den Grossen*, 2nd ed. (Vienna, 1923–4), II, 223–4.

The faithful should restore the ancient custom and should each give to the clergy who administer the ceremonies to the people their tithes, which the priests may use either for the poor or for the redemption of captives, while by their prayers they seek peace and deliverance for the people. Let anyone who scorns these most beneficial statutes be severed for ever from the limbs of the Church.[1]

According to Gregory of Tours, the hermit Hospitius, who lived near Nice in the late sixth century, attributed the Lombard invasions to the wickedness of the people and their failure to pay tithes. 'Tithes are not given,' he said, 'the poor are not nourished, the naked are not clothed, the pilgrims are not received in the guest-house and adequately fed. For this reason this scourge is coming.'[2] In the sermon attributed to Eligius of Nimwegen, the listeners were told to bring their offerings and tithes to the churches and to give their tithes to God 'in [the form of] the poor or the churches'.[3] King Sigebert II in about 653 granted the tithes from certain royal estates to the church of Speyer 'for the profit of the churches or the support of the clergy or the sustenance of the poor'.[4] St Philibert, abbot of Jumièges and Noirmoutier in the second half of the seventh century, was said to have tithed the income of his monastery 'for the redemption of captives and the sustenance of the poor'.[5] And the Venerable Bede reported

[1] MGH, Conc. I, 167; cf. the text with many variants in Mâcon, p. ccxliv. On this council, see Viard, Dîme, I, 55–9, who pointed out that its decrees applied only to Burgundy; Hefele–Leclercq, Conciles, III. 1, 209; and De Clercq, Législation, I, 98. Dopsch, Kulturentwicklung, II, 324, suggested that the State gave these tithes to the Church as compensation for confiscated lands; but this is reading conditions in the eighth century back into the sixth, and Dopsch's citation of Stutz to support his view was called 'unverständlich' by Karl Voigt, Staat und Kirche von Konstantin dem Grossen bis zum Ende der Karolingerzeit (Stuttgart, 1936), p. 285.

[2] Gregory of Tours, Historia Francorum, VI, 6, ed. Henri Omont and Gaston Collon, revised by René Poupardin, Collection de textes pour servir à l'étude et à l'enseignement de l'histoire, XLVII (Paris, 1913), p. 213.

[3] MGH, SS. Merov. IV, 753 and 755.

[4] MGH, Diplomata imperii in fol., 1 (Hanover, 1872), p. 24, no. 24, and Speyer, p. 1, no. 1, in the arenga. The authenticity of this charter, although parts of it may not be original, was accepted by both the editors, by Louis Duchesne, Fastes épiscopaux de l'ancienne Gaule, 2nd ed. (Paris, 1907–15), III, 164, and by Brackmann, in GP, III. 3, 90.

[5] MGH, SS. Merov. V, 596. Philibert actually sent his monks overseas

that Eadberct, who succeeded Cuthbert as bishop of Lindisfarne in 687, 'in accordance with the law gave a tenth part to the poor every year not only of animals but also of all crops and fruits, and also of clothes'.[1]

The sermons of Caesar of Arles, circulating under the name of St Augustine, spread the doctrine that tithes were no substitute for charity and must be paid to the clergy. Their influence on Carolingian legislation can be traced through an anonymous *Homilia sacra* and the *Scarapsus* of St Pirmin. The homily was at one time attributed to Caesar himself but is now thought to be a 'product of the South Gallic-Visigothic cultural area' in the first half of the seventh century. The section on tithes is not complete, but the author clearly knew the works of Caesar of Arles. 'Bring to the churches every year', he said, 'the tithes from all your [*gap in text*]...and from your herds. Give alms from the nine parts, and let him who has more give more in alms.'[2] This passage was used and enriched with biblical citations by St Pirmin in his *Scarapsus de singulis libris canonicis*.

Give to the churches every year the tithes from all your fruits and animals. Give alms from the nine parts remaining to you, and from

with the tithes in order to ransom captives. On the *Vita*, see both the editor's remarks on pp. 568–73 and Wattenbach–Levison, *Geschichtsquellen*, p. 138.

[1] Bede, *Historia ecclesiastica gentis Anglorum*, IV, 27 [29], ed. Charles Plummer (Oxford, 1896), I, 276.

[2] The only edition of this homily is with two other works in *Gennadii Massiliensis presbyteri liber de ecclesiasticis dogmatibus, veteris cuiusdam theologi Homilia sacra, Marcialis episcopi Lemovicensis epistolae*, ed. G. Elmenhorst (Hamburg, 1614), pp. 47–55, esp. p. 51 on tithes. The attribution to Caesar of Arles was authoritatively rejected by G. Morin in his edition of Caesar's sermons (reprinted in *CC*, CIV, 966). Gall Jecker, *Die Heimat des hl. Pirmin, des Apostels der Alamanen*, Beiträge zur Geschichte des alten Mönchtums und des Benediktinerordens, XIII (Münster in Westf., 1927), pp. 103, 125 n. 8, and 158, discussed the date and sources and concluded that it was 'Produkt des südgallisch-westgotischen Kulturgebietes'; cf. Martin of Braga, *Opera omnia*, ed. Claude Barlow, Papers and Monographs of the American Academy in Rome, XII (New Haven, 1950), p. 165. The sermons of Caesar of Arles may also have influenced the passages on tithes in the so-called Letter from Heaven, probably composed in the late sixth century in north-east Spain or southern Gaul: see Robert Priebsch, *Letter from Heaven on the Observance of the Lord's Day* (Oxford, 1936), p. 23.

these redeem your sins, as it is written, 'For alms delivereth from death: and the same is which purgeth away sins'. He who is rich and has much should give much.... And he who is poorer should give little, in accordance with his means.... And he who has nothing from which to give alms, let him have the good will to do so, and this will count for the deed.[1]

St Pirmin was the founder of Reichenau and the apostle to the Alemanni in Baden and Alsace. But he was probably a Visigoth in origin, and the *Scarapsus*, which was apparently written at Meaux in 718/24, seems to reflect Spanish usage.[2] It clearly shows the spread of the doctrine of tithing all over Christian Europe.

How seriously these injunctions were taken by the masses is hard to say. Many historians have maintained that before they became a part of secular law in the eighth century tithes were rarely paid because they were a purely moral obligation.[3] The distinction between secular and religious obligations, however, was certainly narrower in the Middle Ages than it is today, and many Christians may have felt that the duty to pay tithes was no less compulsory because it was not enforced by civil law. This view is supported by the so-called Penitential of Theodore of Canterbury, which, since its purpose was strictly practical, is a better guide to actual usage than theological and legal sources. Though the text is occasionally obscure, this penitential suggests that the payment of tithes was a matter of course in the seventh century. Only priests were specifically excused from payment, and the very poor from undue pressure to pay. Laymen were apparently expected to pay tithes from all types of revenue to

---

[1] Pirmin, *Scarapsus*, XXIX, ed. Jecker, *Pirmin*, pp. 68–9. The biblical citation is from Tobias xii. 9. In cap. XXIV, pp. 57–8, Pirmin cited other biblical texts supporting the payment of tithes.

[2] See Jecker, *Pirmin*, p. 183; Germain Morin, 'Saint Pirmin en Brabant, thèse invraisemblable?', *Rev. d'hist. ecc.* XXXVI (1940), 8–18, who accepted that Pirmin came from Spain or Septimania; and San Martín, *Diezmo*, pp. 81–3.

[3] Cf. René Aigrain, in *Histoire de l'Église*, ed. A. Fliche and V. Martin (Paris, 1934 ff.), v, 558, who wrote that 'la dîme resta...une marque de générosité dont les chrétiens zélés furent seuls à s'acquitter'. Tithes were certainly not voluntary in the sense that men were considered free to pay them or not as they saw fit.

the Church, and they were to be used for the poor and for pilgrims.[1]

The origin and influence of Theodore's penitential, and especially of the canons concerning tithes, are a subject of dispute among scholars. Some have suggested that it was based on oral opinions given by Theodore and written down in the late seventh or early eighth century; others, that it had nothing to do

---

[1] Paul W. Finsterwalder, *Untersuchungen zu den Bussbüchern des 7., 8. und 9. Jahrhunderts*, I: *Die Canones Theodori Cantuariensis und ihre Überlieferungsformen* (Weimar, 1929) has the best text of this penitential, although severely criticized by, among others, Wilhelm Levison, 'Zu den Canones Theodori Cantuariensis' (1930) in his *Aus rheinischer und fränkischer Frühzeit* (Düsseldorf, 1948), pp. 295–303 and McNeill–Gamer, *Handbooks*, pp. 54–5 and 58–60, who gave a translation of this penitential on pp. 179–215. The most complete collection of Theodore's canons is called U, and includes four canons relating to tithes. (1) U II, 2, 8 (p. 314): 'Presbiter decimas dare non cogitur'; cf. D 45, G 156, and Co 21 (pp. 243, 268, and 272). (2) U II, 14, 1 (p. 332): 'Ieiunia legitima tria sunt in anno per populum XL ante pascha, ubi decimas anni solvimus et XL ante natale domini et post pentecosten XL dies et noctes'; cf. D 155 (p. 251: 'Ieiunia legitima sunt in XL mis. In primo decimae reddendae sunt.'), G 61 (p. 259), and Co 189 (p. 283). McNeill and Gamer translated the *ubi* as 'when', but it probably means 'by which' or 'with which' and refers to the doctrine that Lent is the tithe of the year (see p. 18 above). The same phrase occurs in the so-called Confessional of Egbert (*c.* 950–1000), XXXVII, in McNeill–Gamer, *Handbooks*, p. 248. (3) U II, 14, 10 (p. 333): 'Tributum ecclesiae sit, sicut consuetudo provinciae, id est ne tantum pauperes in decimis aut in aliquibus rebus vim patientur'; cf. D 53, G 158, Co 59 (pp. 244, 268, 274). McNeill and Gamer translated the second phrase as: 'that is, so that the poor may not so greatly (?) suffer violence on this account in tithes or in any matters'. A comparison with the other versions, however, suggests that it means: 'so long as the poor suffer no violence in [paying] tithes or anything'. (4) U II, 14, 11 (p. 333): 'Decimas non est legitimum dare nisi pauperibus et peregrinis sive laici suas ad ecclesiam'; cf. G 157 (p. 268: 'Decimae non sunt legitimae dare nisi pauperibus et peregrinis sive laicis ad ecclesiam.'). This is the most important and difficult to interpret of the four canons. McNeill and Gamer translated it: 'It is not lawful to give tithes except to the poor and to pilgrims or for laymen [to give] to their own churches.' F. M. Stenton, *Anglo-Saxon England*, 2nd ed., Oxford History of England, II (Oxford, 1947), p. 154, using the edition in Haddan and Stubbs, *Councils*, wrote that 'Theodore...ruled that tithe could lawfully be given only to the poor, to pilgrims, and by laymen to their churches'. Cf. Boyd, *Tithes*, p. 32. These interpretations all treat *suas* as agreeing with *ecclesiam*, whereas in fact it seems to be a substantive for 'their tithes', and the canon means that 'It is not legitimate to give tithes except to the poor or to pilgrims or for laymen [to give] theirs [except] to the church'.

with Theodore himself.[1] All are agreed, however, that it drew on varied sources and includes Greek, Roman, and Celtic as well as strictly Anglo-Saxon elements;[2] and most are of the opinion that the canons concerning tithes (which are the earliest known reference to tithing in England)[3] derived from Ireland and that the Irish penitentials were responsible for the spread of tithing on the Continent.[4] There is little evidence about tithes in Ireland at this time, however, and the only references in contemporary Irish penitentials show no correspondence with the canons of Theodore.[5] On the other hand, the marked resemblance of Theodore's canons to the continental sources on tithes strongly suggests that they derived from the Continent, and the reference to

[1] Wilhelm Levison, *England and the Continent in the Eighth Century*, Ford Lectures, 1943 (Oxford, 1946), p. 99; Wattenbach–Levison, *Geschichtsquellen*, Beiheft: Rudolph Buchner, *Die Rechtsquellen*, p. 68, who said that the canons 'in Wirklichkeit nicht von dem Erzbischof von Canterbury selbst stammen'.

[2] In addition to the works cited in the preceding note, see Finsterwalder, *Canones*, pp. 199–205; Paul Fournier, 'De quelques infiltrations byzantines dans le droit canonique de l'époque carolingienne', *Mélanges...Gustave Schlumberger* (Paris, 1924), I, 69–70; and Paul Fournier and Gabriel Le Bras, *Histoire des collections canoniques en Occident depuis les fausses décrétales jusqu'au Décret de Gratien*, Bibliothèque d'histoire du droit (Paris, 1931–2), I, 56, who said that 'les recueils théodoriens ne sont pas de simples pénitentiels anglo-saxons: la pénitence n'y tient qu'une demi-place et les sources en sont extrêmement variées, n'excluant même pas l'élément celtique'.

[3] R. H. Hodgkin, *A History of the Anglo-Saxons* (Oxford, 1935), II, 433; Stenton, *Anglo-Saxon England*, p. 154.

[4] Cf. Dopsch, *Kulturentwicklung*, II, 325 and n. 169; James F. Kenney, *The Sources for the Early History of Ireland*, I: *Ecclesiastical*, Columbia Records of Civilization, XI (New York, 1929), 228–9; Boyd, *Tithes*, p. 33, who said that '...by general agreement it was those Irish collections that spread the idea of the tithe in that period'. Watson, in *Camb. Med. Hist.* VI, 534, and Hodgkin, *Anglo-Saxons*, II, 433, even maintained that tithing originated in England and spread from there to the Continent.

[5] The section on tithes in the so-called Irish Canons (*c.* 675), in McNeill–Gamer, *Handbooks*, pp. 128–30, is based largely on Exodus and Leviticus. The *Senchus Mor*, in *Ancient Laws of Ireland*, ed. W. N. Hancock (Dublin–London, 1865–1901), II, 345 and III, 13–15, 33–5, and 41, probably reflects usage in the ninth and tenth centuries: cf. Charles Gross, *The Sources and Literature of English History from the Earliest Times to about 1485*, 2nd ed. (London, etc., 1915), p. 261, and Kenney, *Sources*, p. 325 n. 103. According to Levison, *England*, p. 106, the payment of tithes 'was insisted on...in Irish sources', but he gave no examples. Usage in Wales (see p. 17 n. 1 above) suggests that there were considerable differences between the Celtic and continental systems of tithing.

Lent as the tithe of the year may even point to eastern influence. 'The Franks had no need', as Viard remarked, 'of foreign preachers to know the legal necessity of the tithe.'[1] But Theodore's penitential, whatever its origins, certainly spread the idea and practice of tithing on account of its wide distribution and immense popularity among the Anglo-Saxon missionaries.[2]

These missionaries also played an important role in the history of tithes in other ways. They apparently consulted Pope Zachary on the proper use of tithes, and his reply, written in 748, is preserved among the correspondence of Boniface and Lull.

The distribution of the tithes of the faithful offered in church is not to be under the control of the giver, for the ordinances of the holy fathers provide that the bishop is to divide them into four parts....It is established that the disposition of church funds will be in the hands of the bishop together with his attendant clergy. It is written that 'They that serve the altar partake with the altar.' Out of these revenues provision shall be made for alms to the poor, the building of churches, the equipment of altars, and the decoration of every church, according to the income.[3]

[1] Viard, Dîme, I, 67–8. The council of Mâcon in 585, a century before the compilation of Theodore's Penitential, already referred to tithing as 'the ancient custom'.

[2] On the influence of Theodore's Penitential, see Finsterwalder, Canones, introd. (list of manuscripts); Kenney, Sources, p. 244; Fournier–Le Bras, Collections, I, 84–9; McNeill–Gamer, Handbooks, pp. 58–60; and Stenton, Anglo-Saxon England, p. 140, who said that Theodore's decisions 'came to influence the whole penitential system of the West'. The influence of the canons concerning tithes can be seen in the Confessional of Egbert, XXXVII, in McNeill–Gamer, Handbooks, p. 248; the Merseburg Penitential, CXXVI; and the First Vallicellian Penitential, CXXXIII, which conflated Theodore's U II, 2, 8 and II, 14, 11 into: 'Decimas non sunt legitimas dare nisi pauperibus et peregrinis nec non cogitur presbyteris decimas dare', in H. J. Schmitz, Die Bussbücher und die Bussdisciplin der Kirche, II: Die Bussbücher und das kanonische Bussverfahren (Düsseldorf, 1898), p. 367, and McNeill–Gamer, Handbooks, pp. 439–40. Misunderstandings such as this may partly explain the hostility of the Frankish bishops to the insular penitentials: see Fournier–Le Bras, Collections, I, 98–100; McNeill–Gamer, Handbooks, p. 27; and Levison, England, p. 100.

[3] MGH, Epp. III, 365, and tr. Ephraim Emerton, The Letters of Saint Boniface, Columbia Records of Civilization, XXXI (New York, 1940), p. 154; JE 2288; Santifaller, Elenco, p. 244. Cf. Boniface's letter to the archbishop of Canterbury in 747, in MGH, Epp. III, 354.

The full importance of this letter will be discussed later, but Zachary here for the first time applied to tithes the general rules of the Church governing the distribution of its revenues. He reasserted the Old Testament theory that the priests themselves were entitled to use tithes and added the upkeep of churches to the exclusively charitable uses found in the earlier sources.

A few years later, probably in 765, Lull received an important order from Pepin the Short. 'You shall so provide and ordain on our authority', wrote the king, 'that everyone, willy-nilly, must pay his tithe.'[1] The exact purpose and legal force of this letter are not known. It may have been a general measure for all of Pepin's realm, as some scholars have claimed; or its application may have been limited to a particular region or period of time.[2] It is proof of Pepin's interest in tithes, however, and strongly supports the argument of Perels that 'It was really King Pepin...who by virtue of his secular authority imposed the ecclesiastical tithe on all the Franks as a compulsory offering'.[3]

The civil enforcement of tithes by Charlemagne, which began with the famous capitulary of Heristal in 779,[4] must therefore be seen as a confirmation of existing practice and a con-

[1] MGH, Capit. I, 42, no. 17.
[2] Ulrich Stutz, 'Das karolingische Zehntgebot', Sav. Zs. XLII, Germ. Abt. XXIX (1908), 187 considered it a circular letter to the Frankish episcopate in 765; Leclercq, in Dict. d'arch. IV. 1, 1002, called it 'une formule d'ordre général'; Viard, Dîme, I, 70–4, said it was a general order applying only to the year 765; Pöschl, Inauguration, p. 18, on the other hand, regarded it as a purely local measure; and De Clercq, Législation, I, 145, stressed that it contained nothing extraordinarily new. Pepin's grant of tithes to the bishopric of Utrecht in 753 (MGH, Dipl. Karol. no. 4, confirmed by Charlemagne in 769, ibid. no. 56) was called 'die älteste Nachricht über die Schenkung von Zehnten in einer fränkischen Königsurkunde' by Dopsch, Kulturentwicklung, II, 325; but cf. the grant of Sigebert II to Speyer in 653, cited p. 22 n. 4 above.
[3] Ernst Perels, 'Die Ursprünge des karolingischen Zehntrechtes', A. f. Urk. III (1911), 250; cf. Boyd, Tithes, p. 37 n. 40, on the roles of Pepin and Charlemagne in the civil enforcement of tithes. Dopsch, Kulturentwicklung, II, 323–6, attributed the introduction of compulsory tithes to Charles Martel (cf. his view cited p. 22 n. 1 above).
[4] MGH, Capit. I, 48, no. 20. 7 (cf. p. 44 n. 1 below). On the general effect of this legislation, see De Clercq, Législation, I, 303–4.

tinuation of his father's policy rather than as a radical innovation or new departure.[1] His measures did not transform the tithe overnight from a voluntary into a compulsory due, as is sometimes said. They meant that from now on the secular authorities would assist the clergy in enforcing payment of tithes. This interpretation in no way reduces the practical importance of the step. 'It is one of the best known facts of history', said Stutz, 'that the first kings of the Arnulfian or Carolingian house ordered the payment of tithes by all subjects in their realm.'[2] Many historians have speculated over the motives of the move. Some have suggested that the tithe was a recompense given to the Church in return for the royal grants of ecclesiastical lands to lay vassals.[3] But this view is based on a confusion of the ecclesiastical tithe with the secular *nona et decima* paid as a rent to the Church by holders of *precaria verbo regis*.[4] The payment of normal tithes, as Perels pointed out, was not restricted to those who held church lands.[5] Pöschl, on the other hand, associated the civil enforcement of tithes with the growing administrative and military role of the clergy in the Carolingian empire. 'The ecclesiastical tithe was the necessary compensation', he said, 'for the extensive requisition by the State of the Church and its lands.'[6] This view seems to attribute, however, an astonishing foresight and economic realism to Pepin and Charlemagne in their dealings with the Church. In view of the well-established precedent for tithing, it seems unnecessary to seek any more specific or elaborate reason for the civil enforcement of tithes than the general concern of the

---

[1] This point was emphasized by Georg Waitz, *Deutsche Verfassungsgeschichte*, IV, 2nd ed. (Berlin, 1885), pp. 120–1.

[2] Stutz, in *Sav. Zs.* Germ. Abt. XXIX, 180.

[3] Alfons Dopsch, *Die Wirtschaftsentwicklung der Karolingerzeit*, 2nd ed. (Weimar, 1921–2), II, 23, and *Kulturentwicklung*, II, 324–5; Watson, in *Camb. Med. Hist.* VI, 534; Levison, *England*, p. 106; F. L. Ganshof, *Feudalism*, tr. Philip Grierson (London, etc., 1952), p. 18: 'In order to give the Frankish Church some sort of compensation for its losses, Pepin III made obligatory the payment of tithes by all the inhabitants of the kingdom.'

[4] See my article in *Speculum*, XXXV, 224–50, where I tried to show that the normal ecclesiastical tithe had nothing to do with the technical *nona et decima*.

[5] Perels, in *A. f. Urk.* III, 242.

[6] Pöschl, *Inauguration*, p. 36; cf. also p. 31.

early Carolingian kings for the interests of the Church and for
uniformity of practice throughout their realm.[1]

The possibility of papal influence should also not be overlooked,
since in 786 two papal *missi*, George of Ostia and Theophylact of
Todi, accompanied by an envoy from Charlemagne, Abbot
Wigbod, visited England and held two councils which approved,
among others, a canon concerning tithes. It cited the standard
biblical texts on tithing and decreed 'that all men should strive to
give tithes from everything they possess, because it is the special
property of the Lord, and they should support themselves and
give alms from the nine parts'.[2] There is no evidence that tithes
were yet enforced in England by civil law. King Ethelwulf in
855 made his famous 'Donation' of 'the tenth part of his land
over all his kingdom', but this tithe may have been personal or
even secular, and the grant can hardly be called an official ordinance on tithing.[3] The earliest known civil enforcement of tithes

[1] This is the view, broadly speaking, of Viard, *Dîme*, I, 83–5, who called the
measure 'une manifestation particulière de la politique ordinaire de Charlemagne vis-à-vis de l'Église'; Lesne, *Propriété*, II. 1, 109–11: 'Il [Pepin] rend la
dîme obligatoire, non précisément parce qu'il dépouille les églises, mais parce
qu'il a souci des intérêts de l'Église franque...' (p. 111); Hans von Schubert,
Geschichte der christlichen Kirche im Frühmittelalter (Tübingen, 1917–21), p. 551,
who referred to the ecclesiastical tithe as 'ein Stück der karolingischen Reform';
Voigt, *Staat u. Kirche*, pp. 331–3; and Émile Amann, in *Histoire de l'Église*, ed.
Fliche and Martin, VI, 91, who suggested that Charlemagne was also concerned to help the parish churches.

[2] This canon is known from the report sent to Pope Hadrian by George of
Ostia, in *Councils and Ecclesiastical Documents Relating to Great Britain and Ireland*,
ed. Arthur Haddan and William Stubbs (Oxford, 1869–78), III, 456–7, and in
MGH, *Epp*. IV, 25–6; cf. Watson, in *Camb. Med. Hist.* VI, 534; Stenton, *Anglo-
Saxon England*, pp. 214–16, who distinguished these legatine councils from those
held in 787 (p. 216 n. 5); and Levison, *England*, pp. 16, 106–7, and 127–9.
There is also an unsatisfactory account in Hefele–Leclercq, *Conciles*, III.2, 995–7.

[3] *The Anglo-Saxon Chronicle*, ed. Benjamin Thorpe, Rolls Series, XXIII
(London, 1861), II, 57, and *English Historical Documents*, 1: ca. 500–1042, ed.
Dorothy Whitelock (London–New York, 1955), pp. 174 and 483–5; cf.
Æthelwulf's grant in 854 in *Glastonbury*, I, 143–4, no. 202. On this 'Donation',
see W. H. Stevenson, in his edition of *Asser's Life of King Alfred* (Oxford, 1904),
pp. 186–91, who suggested that the king booked the land to his thegns in order
that they might use it and grant it freely to religious houses, in which case the
'tenth part' had nothing to do with the ecclesiastical tithe. The Premonstratensian
Adam of Dryburgh in the twelfth century wrote that Æthelwulf, 'Eleemosynis

in England dates from the middle of the tenth century.[1] The close coincidence of the English conciliar decree of 786 and the Carolingian ordinances on tithes is interesting, however. The connection of George of Ostia with the Frankish court and the presence of Charlemagne's representative may, as Levison suggested, mean that the English decree reflected the situation in the Carolingian kingdom.[2] But it is possible that both the Frankish kings and the English councils were influenced by a broad policy inspired by the papacy and the Anglo-Saxon missionaries and designed to regularize the payment of tithes all over the Christian world.

3. CAROLINGIAN LEGISLATION ON TITHES

The civil enforcement of tithes in the Carolingian empire led to a series of practical problems which were new in scope if not in principle. Four questions in particular had to be clearly answered in order to establish an effective system of universal tithing. Who had to pay tithes? From what? To whom? And how should the tithes be used? The answers to these questions were laid down in the legislation of the Carolingian period and set the stage for the subsequent history of tithing.[3]

The answers to the first two questions were given in the Bible and clearly stated by the exegetes and theologians. Both kings and bishops sought by a long series of decrees to force every Christian to tithe his entire income. The doctrine that alms must

sane sic operam dabat ut totam terram suam pro Christo decimaret, et partem decimam per ecclesias monasteriaque divideret': *De tripartito tabernaculo*, II, 13, 113, in *PL*, CXCVIII, 716. But this only shows that the Donation was later considered a normal tithe.

[1] See p. 42 below. Levison, *England*, p. 107, was of the opinion that the earlier, purely ecclesiastical command to pay tithes was 'without general effect'; but the civil laws in England, like the Carolingian decrees, probably only ratified existing usage.

[2] Levison, *England*, p. 107.

[3] Thomassin, *Discipline*, III, I, 9, *ed. cit.* VI, 37–45, stressed that the law of tithing, in spite of regional differences, continued unchanged into at least the eleventh century. He also found 'une grande uniformité pour quelques points' in ecclesiastical legislation on tithes from the eleventh to the sixteenth centuries. Among the points he mentioned was that the obligation to pay tithes was considered universal, a matter of divine right, and imprescribable.

be given after tithes had been paid to the Church, which derived from Caesar of Arles through the *Homilia sacra* and the *Scarapsus* of St Pirmin, was reasserted in a diocesan statute of 789/813,[1] in the famous collection of capitularies drawn up by Benedictus Levita in the middle of the ninth century,[2] and in the *Constitutiones* of Archbishop Oda of Canterbury, who died in 958 and had close connections with the abbey of Fleury.[3] Hardship or poverty were in theory no excuse for escaping tithes.[4] Even slaves, according to the council of Mainz in 888, must pay tithes.[5] Neither rank, wealth, nor position gave any basis for freedom from tithes. The king and his vassals were expected to pay like everyone else.[6] Bishop Gerbald of Liège, in his diocesan statute of 787/810, ordered tithes to be paid by everyone in his diocese, 'whether nobles or servants, or whether bishop or abbot or count or royal vassal or one who has his own property'.[7]

In accordance with the Bible, even those who specially served the Lord, the clerics and monks, were supposed to pay tithes. In a letter written in 823/4, Agobard of Lyons discussed the

[1] De Clercq, *Législation*, I, 284–5 and 371.

[2] MGH, *Leges* in fol., II. 2: *Capitularia spuria*, II, 192, p. 83; cf. Emil Seckel, 'Studien zu Benedictus Levita, VII', *NA*, XXXV (1909–10), 146–9, who suggested that this statute derived from a Burgundian synod, after 800, and from Caesar of Arles and Pirmin; and Jecker, *Pirmin*, p. 106. On the dates of the collections of False Decretals, see Schafer Williams, 'The Pseudo-Isidorian Problem Today', *Speculum*, XXIX (1954), 704, who dated them 845/55, and Ganshof, *Capitulaires*, p. 71, who suggested 847/52.

[3] *PL*, CXXXIII, 950; cf. Stenton, *Anglo-Saxon England*, p. 442, and G. Schoebe, 'The Chapters of Archbishop Oda (942/6) and the Canons of the Legatine Councils of 786', *Bulletin of the Institute of Historical Research*, XXXV (1962), 75–83, esp. 82–3 on tithes.

[4] Viard, *Dîme*, I, 106 and 226–8 and II, 4–5, 32, and 38–9. There is no definite evidence that the *collata* or *collatio* from which Gregory the Great exempted the blind (see p. 20 above) was really the same as tithes.

[5] Mainz 888, can. 22, in Mansi, *Collectio*, XVIII, 70; cf. Hefele–Leclercq, *Conciles*, IV. 2, 692, and De Clercq, *Législation*, II, 322.

[6] See Smaragdus of St Mihiel, *Via regia*, XII, in *PL*, CII, 953, which was written for Louis the Pious between 812 and 815: cf. M. L. W. Laistner, *Thought and Letters in Western Europe, A.D. 500 to 900*, 2nd ed. (London, 1957), p. 315. On this point cf. also Waitz, *Verfassungsgeschichte*, IV, 121–2, and Louis Halphen, *Charlemagne et l'Empire carolingien*, L'Evolution de l'Humanité, XXXIII (Paris, 1947), p. 178.

[7] De Clercq, *Législation*, I, 359–60; cf. 280.

biblical origins of tithes and stressed that 'Tithes from all things [were] paid by all the people to the other ministers, who also from these tithes which they had received paid tithes to the priests'.[1] Rabanus Maurus, as seen above, compared the cattle, sheep, and goats in Lev. xxvii. 32 to the three professions of clerics, monks, and laymen.[2] And the *Capitulare monasticum* issued at Aachen in 817 laid down 'That tithes should be given to the poor from everything that is given in alms both to the church and to the brothers'.[3] In point of fact the clergy were probably not forced to pay tithes,[4] but there is evidence that some clerics took seriously the obligation to tithe their income for the benefit of the poor. A charitable bishop like St Anskar, in the first half of the ninth century, gave not only a tithe from all his revenues, including the tithes he received, but also a double tithe every fifth year from his livestock.[5]

Alcuin was almost alone among his contemporaries in urging a more moderate policy, especially in exacting tithes from newly converted Christians, and his letters throw valuable light on the difficulties of enforcing the universal tithe. 'We know that it is highly meritorious to tithe our property,' he wrote to Charlemagne in 796, 'but it is better to lose the tithe than the faith. Even we, who have been born, raised, and trained in the catholic faith, are barely willing to tithe our property fully; how much more unwilling are those of tender faith and childish spirit and grasping disposition.' He wrote in the same year to Archbishop Arn of Salzburg advising him not to collect tithes from the Saxons. 'Be a preacher of piety,' he urged, 'not an exactor of tithes.'[6] It is

---

[1] MGH, *Epp.* v, 169.   [2] See pp. 14–15 above.

[3] MGH, *Capit.* I, 347, no. 170.49; on this council, see De Clercq, *Législation*, II, 17–26.

[4] Cf. the canon in the Penitential of Theodore (cited p. 25 n. 1 above): 'Presbiter decimas dare non cogitur.'

[5] Rimbert, *Vita s. Anskarii*, xxxv, in MGH, *SS*, II, 719; cf. Wattenbach, *Geschichtsquellen*, I, 248–9. See also pp. 201 ff. below on the payment of tithes by monks in the Carolingian period.

[6] MGH, *Epp.* IV, 158 and 154; cf. the letters to Megenfridus in 796 and to Charlemagne in 799, *ibid.* pp. 161 and 289. On Alcuin and tithes, see James W. Thompson, *Feudal Germany* (Chicago, 1928), p. 394 n. 4, although Viard, *Dîme*, 193–4, warned that he should not be seen as 'un adversaire déterminé de la dîme'.

possible that as a result of these arguments some special concessions were made to the recent converts in the East;[1] but Alcuin's position was exceptional, and as a rule the law of tithing was applied without exception to all Christians.

The legislators also followed the biblical commentators in demanding tithes from all types of income. They recognized no legal distinctions between 'real' (or 'predial'), 'personal', and 'mixed' tithes, between 'noval' and 'old field' and between 'great' and 'small' tithes.[2] Theodulph of Orleans in his first diocesan statute, drawn up before 813, wrote:

Those who are engaged in trades and commerce should be warned against seeking worldly gain more than eternal life....Just as tithes and alms must be given by those who seek their food, clothing and other necessities by work in the fields and other labours, the same should be done by those who apply themselves to trades for their necessities. For God gives to every man an art by which he may live, and from his art, from which he derives the necessary support for his body, every man should also administer support to his soul, which is a greater necessity.[3]

Walafrid Strabo in his *Libellus de exordiis et incrementis rerum ecclesiasticarum* emphasized that the Jews gave tithes 'of herds and fruits and of all monies' and that 'Since the Jewish people observed the law of tithes with such diligence that they gave tithes from the smallest herbs, such as rue, mint, and cummin, as the Lord is witness, why should not the evangelical people (among whom the number of priests is greater and the observance of the sacraments more sincere) fulfil the same command with greater zeal?'[4] It is, of course, true that in the ninth century most revenues were from agricultural sources; and the soldiers,

---

[1] See p. 73 and n. 2 below.

[2] These distinctions naturally influenced the practical workings of the system of tithes in this period, but they were not yet defined or established in law. Viard, who relied heavily on the distinction between 'real' and 'personal' tithes, admitted that he found no trace of it in the sources before the middle of the twelfth century: *Dîme*, I, 158; cf. pp. 267–8 and 287 ff. below.

[3] Theodulph's first collection, XXXV, in *PL*, CV, 202. On the date, see De Clercq, *Législation*, I, 259–62.

[4] Walafrid, *De exordiis*, XXVIII, in MGH, *Capit.* II, 512–13.

merchants, and craftsmen often neglected and even forgot their obligation to pay tithes. The synod of Trosly in 909 attacked this negligence with energy.

Many men neglect and scorn the justice of God; they seek to prescribe the injustice of their parsimony; and they steal and take away from God with sacrilegious recklessness the due part of tithes and claim, at the risk of their own disaster, that they owe no tithes from military activity, trade, crafts, the shearing of wool, and other trades given them by God. Such men should listen not to us but to the commands of the Bible and the holy examples of the fathers on these matters. They should know that we are not, as they say, now demanding something new but are repeating what was established by God's law and given by the devotion of the fathers.

The council then cited a battery of biblical and patristic texts showing that Christians must pay more tithes even than the Pharisees and that tithes are owed not only from every kind of produce, revenue, and skill given by God but also from men's time, in the form of fasting in Lent. It concluded that those who failed to pay tithes would certainly be damned unless they gave satisfaction to God and to the Church by reform and penance.[1]

The question to whom the tithes should be given was more difficult. The theologians agreed that tithes must be paid to the Christian sacerdotal order, which was thought to have super-seded the Levites. In practice this seems to have been interpreted as the churches where the sacraments were administered. The council of Mâcon in 585 declared that tithes should be paid 'to the

---

[1] Trosly 909, can. 6, in Mansi, *Collectio*, XVIII, 281–3 (quoted passage on 281). On this council, see Hefele–Leclercq, *Conciles*, IV. 2, 722–5, and Auguste Dumas, in *Histoire de l'Église*, ed. Fliche and Martin, VII, 270–1, who said that its claim to tithes from all types of revenue was a novelty. For evidence that tithes were owed from non-agricultural revenues in the eleventh century, see the charter of the bishop of Arezzo in 1033, cited p. 71 below, and the long list of revenues from which tithes had to be paid in the so-called *Leges Edwardi Confessoris*, VII–VIII, in *Die Gesetze der Angelsachsen*, ed. Felix Liebermann (Halle, 1898–1916), I, 631–2, which were compiled, according to Gross, *Sources*, p. 265, 'by a cleric of French birth, probably between 1130 and 1135'. Liebermann, *Über die Leges Edwardi Confessoris* (Halle, 1896), pp. 53–5, discussed this passage and remarked that 'Zehnt wird von Naturalwirthschaft, aber auch von *negotiationes*, entrichtet'. See also the evidence cited pp. 103–4 below.

clergy who administer the ceremonies to the people'. The Anomalous Laws in Wales, which embodied early Celtic custom, decreed that tithes 'were payable to the individual priest and not to the Church', meaning, presumably, not to bishops or monks.[1] And Pope Zachary in 748 called tithes an altar due, to which 'they which wait upon the altar' had a definite claim.

This doctrine was confirmed and defined by the Carolingian theologians. Walafrid Strabo spoke of tithes as being given 'to God and to the priests of God', and Jonas of Orléans argued strongly 'that tithes must be given to priests, yes indeed to God in his priests', and not be distributed at the pleasure of the donor.[2] Archbishop Hincmar of Rheims maintained that only bishops who performed pastoral functions were entitled to any share of parochial dues. 'Bishops must take care', he said, 'that they [the priests] should reap the *spiritalia* only from those in whom they sow the *carnalia* and should not eat their produce unless they pay the price of preaching and intercession.'[3] Archbishop Amulo of Lyons also referred in a letter to the baptismal church, where the sacraments were administered, as the proper place to pay tithes; and Bishop Ralph of Bourges, whose diocesan statute dates from 854, ordered all Christians in his diocese to pay their tithes to the churches where they heard mass and where their children were baptized.[4] Pope Leo IV in a letter written to the bishops of Brittany in 847/8 said that 'It seems not only to me but also to greater men that tithes should be paid only to churches where holy baptism is given'.[5] Tithes therefore tended to become a

---

[1] Ellis, *Welsh Law*, I, 197.

[2] Walafrid, *De exordiis*, XXVIII, in MGH, *Capit.* II, 512; and Jonas of Orléans, *De institutione laicali*, II, 19, in PL, CVI, 205. De Clercq, *Législation*, II, 74–6, associated the composition of Jonas's work with the council of Paris in 829.

[3] Wilhelm Gundlach, 'Zwei Schriften des Erzbischofs Hinkmar von Reims', *Zs. für Kirchengeschichte*, X (1889), 125. The terms *spiritalia* and *carnalia* here refer respectively to the altar revenues and to the sacraments.

[4] Amulo of Lyons (841–52), ep. I, 7, in PL, CXVI, 82; and Ralph of Bourges, XXI, in PL, CXIX, 714. On the date, see De Clercq, *Législation*, II, 345.

[5] MGH, *Epp.* V, 595; JE 2599; *Decretum*, C. XVI, q. I, c. 45. See, on the date, René Merlet, 'L'Émancipation de l'église de Bretagne et le concile de Tours (848–851)', *Le Moyen Âge*, XI (2nd series, II, 1898), 10 n. 1, and Boyd, *Tithes*, pp. 78–9, who said in error that the letter was addressed to the English episcopate and referred to dividing tithes into four parts.

parochial revenue given almost in return for the sacraments.[1] One priest, about 835, applied this theory so literally that he withheld communion until his parishioners had paid their tithes.[2] But the synod of Trosly in 909, while strongly asserting the parochial nature of tithes, maintained that priests should administer the sacraments even if they received no tithes or oblations.[3]

Civil decrees attempted to enforce this doctrine as a practical measure both to ensure universal payment of tithes and to strengthen parochial organization. The authorities were concerned not only to prevent evasion or private distribution of tithes but also to protect the existing parish churches from the claims to tithes of more recent foundations.[4] Charlemagne decreed in the capitulary of Salz in 803 that tithes must be paid to baptismal churches, 'where worship was made of old', and specified that these churches should keep the tithes even if the land from which they were paid was given to a cathedral or monastery.[5] If anyone built a church on his own land, he continued in the same capitulary, 'the other older churches should on this account lose no right or tithe, which should always be paid to the older churches'.[6] Louis the Pious repeated these decrees. In the so-called capitulary of Worms in 829, which may in fact have been a list of instructions to his *missi*, Louis decreed that 'Anyone who takes the tithe from the church to which it justly belongs and for payment, friendship, or any other cause gives it to another church, will be forced by our count or *missus* to give

---

[1] Cf. Thomas Aquinas, *Summa theologica*, II. 2, q. LXXXVII, a. 1–4 (cited pp. 13 n. 4, 15 n. 2 and 16 n. 5 above).

[2] MGH, *Epp.* V, 521–2 (letter by Rabanus Maurus).

[3] Trosly 909, can. VI, in Mansi, *Collectio*, XVIII, 281.

[4] On this development in Italy, see Boyd, *Tithes*, p. 43 and n. 54 (bibliography).

[5] MGH, *Capit.* I, 119, no. 42. 2; cf. Hefele–Leclercq, *Conciles*, III. 2, 1123–4; De Clercq, *Législation*, I, 206–7; Ganshof, *Capitulaires*, pp. 13–14. Note that Charlemagne required even cathedrals and monasteries to continue paying tithes to the previous owner. This statute was included in Regino of Prüm, *Libri duo de synodalibus causis et disciplinis ecclesiasticis*, I, 52, ed. F. G. Wasserschleben (Leipzig, 1840), p. 48, which was compiled about 906, according to Fournier–Le Bras, *Collections*, I, 245.

[6] MGH, *Capit.* I, 119, no. 42. 3; *Decretum*, C. XVI, q. I, c. 44. Cf. the so-called capitulary of 813, in *Capit.* I, 174, no. 78.19, and De Clercq, *Législation*, I, 248.

back the amount of the tithe with his fine'.[1] Three years later Lothar instituted a similar inquiry in Italy and told his *missi* to force men to pay their tithes to the churches where they had been baptized and received the sacraments.[2] A contemporary diplomatic formula for use in charters also stipulated that a daughter church should usurp from its mother no right, 'neither tithe nor baptism nor burial', except the celebration of divine services.[3]

Ecclesiastical legislation was equally firm. A diocesan statute in 800/813 decreed 'That every church should have a boundary of the estates from which it receives the tithes'.[4] The five reforming councils in 813 took steps both to enforce the payment of tithes and to protect the rights of parish churches.[5] The canon of the council at Chalon-sur-Saône, which was later included in Gratian's *Decretum* and other canonical collections, was directed particularly against the claims of the higher clergy to tithes.

Certain brothers, moreover, complained that some bishops and abbots had refused to give tithes to the churches where their peasants heard mass. Then this holy council decreed that the bishops and abbots might order the tithes from the fields and vineyards which were for the support of themselves or the brothers to be brought to [their] churches. Members of the *familia*, however, must give their tithes [to the churches] where their children were baptized and where they heard masses throughout the whole course of the year.[6]

---

[1] MGH, *Capit.* II, 13, no. 191.6; cf. De Clercq, *Législation*, II, 63–8, who was of the opinion that neither cap. 191 nor 192 was really issued by the council of Worms.

[2] MGH, *Capit.* II, 64, no. 202.9; cf. De Clercq, *Législation*, II, 85–6.

[3] MGH, *Formulae*, p. 264. This formulary, which was compiled in western France after 858, incorporated earlier elements.

[4] MGH, *Capit.* I, 178, no. 81.10; = Ansegisis, *Collectio*, I, 149, *ibid.* 412; cf. De Clercq, *Législation*, I, 291; Buchner, *Rechtsquellen*, p. 80; and Ganshof, *Capitulaires*, p. 12 n. 33, and (on Ansegisis), pp. 69–70.

[5] Arles 813, can. IX and XX; Rheims 813, can. XXXVIII; Mainz 813, can. XXXVIII and XLI (see p. 40 below); Chalon-sur-Saône 813, can. XVIII (see n. 6 below); and Tours 813, can. XVI (see p. 49 below); in MGH, *Conc.* II, 251–2, 257, 270–1, 277 and 288; cf. Hefele–Leclercq, *Conciles*, III. 2, 1135–48.

[6] Chalon-sur-Saône 813, can. XVIII, in MGH, *Conc.* II, 277 and, with several variants, *Decretum*, C. XVI, q. I, c. 46; cf. Lesne, in *Rev. d'hist. ecc.* XIV, 491–2 and, on the *familia*, Ursmer Berlière, *La familia dans les monastères bénédictins du moyen âge*, Académie royale de Belgique: Classe de Lettres..., Mémoires in-8°, XXIX. 2 (Brussels, 1931), p. 3.

The higher clergy were thus allowed to pay the tithes from their own produce to their own churches, but their dependants must pay tithes to the parish churches.

This policy was hard to maintain and unpractical in a period when Christianity was expanding, new churches were needed, and private control over ecclesiastical property was growing. Throughout the ninth century many cathedrals and abbeys in fact received tithes, and many landholders disposed of the tithes from their estates as they pleased. An eighth-century formula from the region of Paris provided for the endowment of a church with 'the entire tithe both from those vineyards and from the other property which we have bought or acquired in that place'.[1] Charlemagne himself decreed in the capitulary *De villis* that 'Our officials should pay tithes fully from our entire income to the churches on our estates, and our tithes should not be given to someone else's church except where it was established in the past'.[2] In about 830 one Lempteus and his wife founded a church at Satolas (Isère), with the approval of the archbishops of Vienne and Lyons, and endowed it among other things with 'a full tithe from all the property which we now possess or shall acquire in the future'. They further specified in the charter that 'We reserve for ourselves, however, while we live, the right to dispose otherwise of these tithes in case of need or desire to restore or build a church somewhere else'.[3] Jonas of Orléans at about the same time bitterly complained of landlords who refused to pay tithes, paid them unwillingly, or kept the tithes of churches *in iuris sui proprio*.[4]

Ecclesiastical policy towards these irregularities tended to vary regionally. In the older areas of Christianity—including Italy, some parts of France, and England—the rights of the existing

[1] René Poupardin, 'Fragments du recueil perdu de formules franques dites "Formulae Pithoei"', *Bibliothèque de l'École des Chartes*, LXIX (1908), 660; cf. Buchner, *Rechtsquellen*, p. 52.

[2] MGH, *Capit.* I, 83, no. 32.6. On this much-discussed capitulary, see Buchner, *Rechtsquellen*, p. 79, and Ganshof, *Capitulaires*, p. 110, who dated it between 770 and 800. On the term *conlaboratus*, which I have translated 'income', see F. L. Ganshof, 'Manorial Organization in the Low Countries in the 7th, 8th and 9th Centuries', *Trans. Roy. Hist. Soc.* 4th series, XXXI (1949), 57.

[3] *Grenoble*, p. 14, no. A7.

[4] Jonas of Orléans, *De institutione laicali*, II, 19, in *PL*, CVI, 204.

churches were on the whole maintained.[1] A synod at Pavia in
845/50 complained that 'certain laymen who have proprietary
churches either on their own lands or on benefices neglect the
bishop's arrangement and give their tithes not to the churches
where they receive baptism, preaching, confirmation, and the
other Christian sacraments, but they assign them as they wish
either to their own churches or to their own clerics'.[2] Bishop
Herard of Tours in his collection of statutes compiled in 858
forbade laymen to transfer tithes from one church to another.[3]
And as late as 922 the synod which met at Coblenz under the
auspices of Charles the Simple and Henry I decreed that 'A layman, cleric, or person of either sex who gives away a place in his
possession or a piece of property has no power to take away the
tithe which was duly assigned to a previous church'.[4]

In more recently converted areas, however, where the parochial
organization was less firmly established, there were signs of
weakening even in the early ninth century. The council of Aachen
in 818/19 allowed the tithes from new estates to be paid to
churches 'newly constructed there'.[5] The councils of Mainz in 847
and 852 both confirmed the decree of the council of Mainz in 813
that 'Tithes and other possessions should not be taken from long-
established churches and given to new oratories';[6] but the 847

[1] Cf. Boyd, Tithes, pp. 81 and 155.
[2] MGH, Capit. II, 82–3, no. 210.11; Decretum, C. XVI, q. I, c. 56; cf. Hefele–
Leclercq, Conciles, IV. 2, 1320–1, and De Clercq, Législation, II, 129–31.
[3] Herard of Tours, CXXXV, in PL, CXXI, 774; on the date, see De Clercq,
Législation, II, 352.
[4] MGH, Const. I, 630, no. 434.8; Decretum, C. XVI, q. I, c. 42; on this council
see Georg Waitz, Jahrbücher des deutschen Reiches unter König Heinrich I, 3rd ed.
(Leipzig, 1885), p. 65.
[5] MGH, Capit. I, 277, no. 138.12; cf. Hefele–Leclercq, Conciles, IV. 1, 27–9
and 31, who dated this statute in 817, and De Clercq, Législation, II, 6–36, who
studied the three councils at Aachen in 816, 817, and 818/19 and associated
cap. 138 with the last, which was primarily concerned with the secular clergy.
On this particular statute, cf. Stutz, Benefizialwesen, pp. 257–9, and Paul
Thomas, Le droit de propriété des laïques sur les églises et le patronage laïque au
moyen âge, Bibliothèque de l'École des Hautes Études: Sciences religieuses,
XIX (Paris, 1906), p. 85.
[6] MGH, Conc. II, 271; cf. Arles 813, can. XX, ibid. 252 (see p. 38 n. 5 above);
Decretum, C. XVI, q. I, c. 43. The re-enactments in 847 and 852 differed slightly
in wording.

council added the proviso 'without the consent and advice of the bishop',[1] and the 852 council decreed before the confirmation that 'Bishops must be received with due honour, in order that they may perform their ecclesiastical office, in the churches of monks or laymen and in chapels on the demesne and held in benefice, where tithes are paid'.[2] Both councils therefore accepted that under special circumstances tithes might be transferred to a proprietary church. These concessions were not universally accepted even in the East. The council of Mainz in 888 repeated without any proviso the prohibition of 813.[3] And a council at Metz in 893 decreed 'That henceforth no lord may receive any part of the tithes from his church, but only the priest who serves in that place where the tithes were consecrated in the past...', though this was directed principally against lay possession of tithes.[4] Both the landlords and the priests of the new churches were opposed to a rigid policy of protecting the old churches, however;[5] and in 895 the famous council of Tribur decreed as a compromise that 'If he [a landlord] cultivates new land in a forest or uninhabited place four or five miles away [from an existing church] and builds a church and has it consecrated, with the consent of the bishop, he may then provide a suitable and learned priest and then finally may give the new tithe to the new church, saving however the authority of the bishop'.[6] A few

[1] MGH, *Capit.* II, 179, no. 248.11; cf. Hefele–Leclercq, *Conciles*, IV. 1, 131–6, and De Clercq, *Législation*, II, 138–42.

[2] MGH, *Capit.* II, 186, no. 249.3; cf. Hefele–Leclercq, *Conciles*, IV. 1, 191, and De Clercq, *Législation*, II, 208.

[3] Mainz 888, can. XIII, in Mansi, *Collectio*, XVIII, 67; cf. Hefele–Leclercq, *Conciles*, IV. 2, 691–2, and De Clercq, *Législation*, II, 208.

[4] Metz 893, can. II, in Mansi, *Collectio*, XVIII, 78; cf. Hefele–Leclercq, *Conciles*, IV. 2, 688–90, who dated this council 888 and considered it a preliminary meeting for the council at Mainz later that year, and De Clercq, *Législation*, II, 337–8, who re-dated the council to 893 (p. 337 n. 5).

[5] Cf., especially on the East, the masterly pages of Stutz, *Benefizialwesen*, pp. 239–47, who stressed the importance of pressure from the lay proprietors rather than from the Church, and Erica Widera, 'Der Kirchenzehnt in Deutschland zur Zeit der sächsischen Herrscher', *A. f. kath. KR*, CX (1930), 33–110, esp. 61–75, who also considered the transfer of tithes to proprietary churches as a result of the wishes of the lay owners.

[6] MGH, *Capit.* II, 221, no. 252.14; cf. the similar statute, of uncertain origin, found in only one manuscript of Regino of Prüm, *De synodalibus causis*,

voices were still raised in favour of the old system, as at Coblenz in 922, but this decree laid the basis for future policy.

Some concessions were made even in Italy and England. An important council at Ravenna in 898, which was attended by both Pope John IX and the Emperor Lambert, listed and enforced by threat of excommunication many secular decrees requiring tithes to be paid to baptismal churches unless, it was specified, the bishop gave his permission, presumably to pay the tithes to other churches.[1] King Edgar of England also established that:

All payment of tithe is to be made to the old minster, to which the parish belongs, and it is to be rendered both from the thegn's demesne land and from the land of his tenants according as it is brought under the plough. If, however, there is a thegn who has on his bookland a church with which there is a graveyard [i.e. with some parochial rights], he is to pay the third part of his own tithes into his church. If anyone has a church with which there is no graveyard, he is then to pay to his priest from the [remaining] nine parts what he chooses.[2]

By the tenth century, therefore, almost any church performing pastoral functions was—with the consent of the local bishop—allowed to receive at least a share of the tithes.

1, 44b, *ed. cit.* p. 45: 'Ut novalia rura, quae iuxta cultos agros fiunt, ecclesiae antiquae decimentur, et si ultra millaria quatuor vel quinque in saltu quaelibet digna persona aliquod novale collaboraverit, ibidemque cum sui consensu episcopi ecclesiam construxerit, post consecrationem ecclesiae provideat presbyterum, eiusque conductu de eodem elaboratu decimas eidem ecclesiae conferat.' Regino described this council in his chronicle as directed '...contra plerosque seculares, qui auctoritatem episcopalem inminuere temptabant...': ed. Friedrich Kurze, MGH, SS in usum schol. (Hanover, 1890), p. 143. Cf., on the council, Hefele–Leclercq, *Conciles*, IV. 2, 697–707, and De Clercq, *Législation*, II, 328–35, and, on this statute, Stutz, *Benefizialwesen*, pp. 262–3; Thomas, *Droit*, pp. 85–6; and Schreiber, *Gemeinschaften*, p. 110.

[1] Ravenna 898, can. I, in Mansi, *Collectio*, XVIII, 230 (dated 904) and MGH, *Capit.* II, 124, no. 230.1; cf. Hefele–Leclercq, *Conciles*, IV. 2, 717–18; Louis Duchesne, *Les premiers temps de l'état pontifical*, 3rd ed. (Paris, 1911), pp. 302–3; and E. Amann, in *Histoire de l'Église*, ed. Fliche and Martin, VII, 27–8.

[2] II and III Edgar (959–963), in *English Hist. Docs.* I, 395; for later laws on tithes see *Gesetze*, ed. Liebermann, I, 146–9 (I Athelstan), 277 (Cnut 1027, no. 16), 384 (law of the Northumbrian priests, no. 60); also Herbert Meritt, 'Old English Entries in a Manuscript at Bern', *Journal of English and Germanic Philo-*

The fourth and most disputed question of tithing in the Carolingian period was the distribution of tithes after they had been
paid to the parochial clergy. In the Bible, as seen above, the tithe
was used for the Levites and Aaronites and, in Deuteronomy, for a
charitable feast. According to the early Christian sources, tithes
belonged not to the clergy or to the poor, like other ecclesiastical
revenues, but to God,[1] and they were to be used exclusively for
those of God's children who were in need, especially pilgrims,
captives, and the poor. The insistence upon payment to the clergy
was to prevent evasion and the confusion of tithes with alms.
As their payment was enforced and regularized, however, tithes
came to be regarded as a normal clerical revenue and as subject
to the canonical rules of episcopal control over ecclesiastical
property[2] and of distribution either by quadripartition between
the bishop, clergy, fabric, and poor (the so-called 'Roman'
division) or by tripartition between the bishop, clergy, and
fabric, omitting the poor (the 'Spanish' system).[3] Pope Zachary

logy, XXXIII (1934), 344 and 347–8, who printed from a tenth-century manuscript an interesting text which may be associated with Edgar's law: 'Æthel-
weard makes known to Ceolbeorht that I will that you render the two portions
of the tithe from Bedwyn and from Lambourn to God's servants for provisions
at Bedwyn and they shall divide it among themselves as seems fit to you'; and
Stenton, *Anglo-Saxon England*, pp. 155–6.

[1] On the concept that the property of the Church belongs to the poor and is
only dispensed by the clergy, see Thomassin, *Discipline*, III, III, 26–33, *ed. cit.*
VII, 344–85.

[2] On the control of the bishop over ecclesiastical property in the early
Middle Ages, see Thomassin, *Discipline*, III, II, 1 ff., *ed. cit.* VI, 509 ff.; Émile
Lesne, *L'Origine des menses dans le temporel des églises et des monastères de France
au IXe siècle*, Mémoires et travaux publiés par des professeurs des Facultés
catholiques de Lille, VII (Lille, 1910), p. 1; Edouard Fournier, *Les origines du
vicaire général* (Paris, 1922), pp. 38–9; Sergio Mochi Onory, *Vescovi e città* (*Sec.
IV–VI*) (Bologna, 1933), pp. 138 ff.; Aigrain, in *Histoire de l'Église*, V, 558, who
said that the bishop was 'l'administrateur-né des biens de son église' at the time
of Gregory the Great; and Boyd, *Tithes*, pp. 77–8. This right was later invaded
by the proprietary claims of monasteries, laymen, and the lower clergy; but it
was maintained in principle throughout the Middle Ages: *Decretum*, C. x,
q. 1; Ulrich Stutz, 'The Proprietary Church as an Element of Mediaeval
Germanic Ecclesiastical Law', tr. in Barraclough, *Mediaeval Germany*, II, 35 ff.;
and Thomas, *Droit*, pp. 58–61.

[3] The origins of these two rules are far from clear: see Stutz, *Benefizialwesen*,
pp. 24–41, and Boyd, *Tithes*, pp. 75–9. Quadripartition was first mentioned in a

seems to have been the first to apply these rules of episcopal control and canonical division to tithes in his letter of 748. But they will be discussed separately here, since there were great differences in theory and practice on the subject of distribution.

The rule of episcopal control was apparently not applied to tithes in the fifth, sixth, and seventh centuries, perhaps on account of their special nature as God's property, but it found unanimous approval among the Carolingian theologians and legislators because it was both practical and in accord with canon law. Charlemagne in the capitulary of Heristal decreed that tithes must be dispensed 'by order of the bishop'.[1] The anonymous diocesan statute of 800/13 also decreed 'That tithes are under the bishop's authority with regard to how they shall be dispensed by the priests'; and this canon was later included in the influential collections of Ansegisis, Benedictus Levita, and Regino of Prüm.[2] Jonas of Orléans and Hincmar of Rheims agreed that the diocesan bishop must supervise the distribution of tithes.[3] And a council at Pavia in 850 decreed that 'He who tries to dispense his tithes in accordance with his own wish and not the order of the bishop is doubly guilty: once, because he impiously steals the property of

---

letter by Pope Simplicius in 475 (*Decretum*, C. XII, q. II, c. 28; JK 570) and was described in greater detail by Pope Gelasius in 494 (*Decretum*, C. XII, q. II, c. 27; JK 636). Tripartition was mentioned by several councils in the sixth and seventh centuries, beginning with I Orléans 511, can. XV, in MGH, *Conc.* I, 6, and *Decretum*, C. X, q. I, c. 7 (cf. Hefele–Leclercq, *Conciles*, II. 2, 1012, and De Clercq, *Législation*, I, 11); see also Tarragona 516, can. VIII, in Mansi, *Collectio*, VIII, 542–3, and *Decretum*, C. X, q. I, c. 10; Carpentras 527, in MGH, *Conc.* I, 40–3, esp. 41; and IX Toledo 655, can. VI, in Mansi, *Collectio*, XI, 28, and *Decretum*, C. XII, q. III, c. 4. On the application of the two rules, see pp. 54–5 n. 4 below.

[1] MGH, *Capit.* I, 48, no. 20.7; cf. the Lombard form (*ibid.*), which reads 'per iussionem et consilium episcopi in cuius parrochia fuerit', and the instructions to the *missi* in Aquitaine in 789, in *Capit.* I, 65, no. 24.11 (cf. De Clercq, *Législation*, I, 178). On the relation of the Lombard to the common form of the capitularies, see De Clercq, *Législation*, I, 162; Boyd, *Tithes*, p. 40; and Ganshof, *Capitulaires*, p. 17.

[2] MGH, *Capit.* I, 178, no. 81.4; = Ansegisis, *Collectio*, I, 143, *ibid.* p. 412; Benedictus, I, 45, in MGH, *Leges* in fol., II. 2, 49 (cf. Seckel, in *NA*, XXXI, 73); Regino, I, 43, *ed. cit.* p. 45.

[3] Jonas of Orléans, *De institutione laicali*, II, 19, in *PL*, CVI, 204–5; Hincmar, in *Zs. f. Kirchengeschichte*, X, 124.

the Lord and secondly, because he presumes to violate sacred property with sacrilegious rashness'.[1]

This doctrine was strongly supported in the collections of False Decretals, of which the principal object, according to Fournier and Le Bras, was to restore 'the independence, authority, and prestige of the episcopate'.[2] Pseudo-Isidore repeatedly asserted, in both genuine and forged decrees, the rule of episcopal control over ecclesiastical property and revenues.[3] Benedictus Levita cited no less than five times the canons of the council of Gangra, in about 345, confirming the authority of the bishop over all oblations given to churches.[4] He included the decrees on tithes from the capitulary of Heristal and from the diocesan statute of 800/13, both of which asserted episcopal control over tithes.[5] Benedictus was especially concerned over grants and sales

[1] MGH, *Capit.* II, 121, no. 228.17; on this council, cf. Hefele–Leclercq, *Conciles*, IV. I, 188, and De Clercq, *Législation*, II, 134. The term *dominica substantia*, which I have translated 'property of the Lord', may simply mean 'ecclesiastical property', as was suggested in another context by Seckel, in *NA*, XXXIX, 413. See also the council of Pavia in 845/50, in MGH, *Capit.* II, 82–3, no. 210.11, and *Decretum*, C. XVI, q. I, c. 56 (cited p. 40 n. 2 above).

[2] Fournier–Le Bras, *Collections*, I, 133; cf. Walter Ullmann, *The Growth of Papal Government in the Middle Ages* (London, 1955), p. 182, who said that 'The primacy of the Roman Church is, next to ecclesiastical freedom from lay jurisdiction, the most vital principle with which Pseudo-Isidore operates'. The primacy of Rome, however, was a weapon with which to exalt episcopal power.

[3] *Decretales Pseudo-Isidorianae*, ed. Paul Hinschius (Leipzig, 1863), pp. 30 (forged *Canones apostolorum* of Clement, can. XLI; *Decretum*, C. XII, q. I, c. 24), 144 (forged letter of Urban I, c. 3; *Decretum*, C. XII, q. I, c. 16), 272–3 (Council of Antioch, can. XXV), and 681 (Council of Gangra, can. VIII, cited in a letter by Pope Symmachus; *Decretum*, C. XVI, q. I, c. 57).

[4] Benedictus Levita, I, 24; II, 370 (g); III, 7–8 and 261 (g), in MGH, *Leges* in fol., II. 2, 47, 92, 105, and 119; cf. Seckel, in *NA*, XXXI, 69; XXXV, 484; XXXIX, 332; and XL, 34, who identified the Dionysio-Hadriana as the source of these canons. Benedictus asserted the control of the bishop over ecclesiastical property more generally in the forged capitulary II, 370; III, 261: 'ut episcopi rerum ecclesiasticarum in omnibus iuxta sanctorum canonum sanctiones plenam semper habeant potestatem' (also probably forged); and Add. IV, 57, in *ed. cit.* pp. 91–2, 118–19 and 150; cf. Seckel, in *NA*, XXXV, 480 (on II, 370) and XL, 31 (on III, 261), who pointed out parallel canons in the Dionysio-Hadriana and Hispana.

[5] Benedictus, I, 45 (statute of 800/13, cited pp. 38 n. 4 and 44 n. 2 above), I, 94; and Add. IV, 127 (capitulary of Heristal, cited pp. 28 n. 4 and 44 n. 1

of tithes without the advice and consent of the bishop. Priests must not sell tithes before they are harvested, he declared in a capitulary of doubtful origin, and tithes must be sold for the repair of churches and the redemption of captives only 'by the advice of the diocesan bishop and other good priests'.[1] Later he again maintained that 'No priest or deacon, or any cleric or layman, should sell, give, mortgage, or borrow against tithes before he has faithfully collected them all and gathered them properly in the barns on the enclosure of the church to which they belong', and that they should then be disposed of in accordance with the orders of the bishop and the decree of Pope Gelasius.[2]

These capitularies and canons deeply influenced contemporary legislation as well as later canonical collections, and thus firmly established the doctrine of episcopal control over tithes.[3] Herard of Tours, many of whose statutes were inspired by the False Decretals, laid down 'That tithes should be both faithfully given by the people and canonically distributed by the priests, and each year they should give an account of their distribution to the bishop or to his ministers, lest they should incur the losses of frauds and appear, which God forbid, the slayers of the poor by taking away their necessities'.[4] The synod of Trosly in 909 cited from the collections both of Ansegisis and of Benedictus Levita in its decree that 'every priest by his ordination and supervisory office holds his parish with its endowment and the tithes of the church, subject, that is, to the advice and supervision of the bishop, in accordance with the ancient and divinely established rules', and that tithes and other parochial revenues must be 'under the authority and supervision of the bishops and the rule and

above), in MGH, *Leges* in fol., II. 2, 49, 55 and 155; cf. Seckel, in *NA*, XXXI, 73 and 92. See also Add. III, 83, *ed. cit.* p. 143 (cited p. 49 n. 1 below).

[1] Benedictus, III, 214, in MGH, *Leges* in fol., II. 2, 115; cf. Seckel, in *NA*, XXXIX, 413, who considered this capitulary probably forged.
[2] Benedictus, Add. IV, 144, in MGH, *Leges* in fol., II.2, 156; cf. Add. IV, 89, *ed. cit.* p. 152.
[3] Cf. Stutz, *Benefizialwesen*, p. 241: 'Zum Zehnt blieb der Bischof immer in näherem Verhältniss als zu den übrigen Einkünften einer solchen Pfarrkirche'; Thomas, *Droit*, pp. 62–5; Pöschl, in *A. f. kath. KR*, XCVIII, 176–80; and Widera, in *A. f. kath. KR*, CX, 37–9.
[4] Herard of Tours, XXXV, in *PL*, CXXI, 766.

dispensation of the priests'. The synod further stressed that in forbidding laymen to control tithes it was defining the government of the bishop and not arrogating for itself the power of God.[1] The synod of Hohenaltheim in 916, which also drew on the False Decretals in order to buttress ecclesiastical authority, likewise decreed that 'Tithes are in the power of the bishop and his priests'.[2] And another German council, held at Augsburg in 952 and attended by King Otto I, again asserted 'That all tithing is in the authority of the bishop, and if it is neglected the emendation must be settled before the bishop or his agent'.[3]

The question of the use of tithes was closely related to that of episcopal control but far more controversial. Under the old theory, although the bishops and clergy controlled the tithes, they were not considered to own them or even to be entitled to a share. Pope Zachary's letter in 748 is typical of the confusion on this subject in the eighth and ninth centuries, for although he cited both the precept that priests should live from the altar and the canonical rule of quadripartition, which divided ecclesiastical revenues between the bishop, clergy, fabric, and poor, he then said that tithes should be used for building, equipping, and decorating churches as well as for helping the poor and thus in

---

[1] Trosly 909, can. VI, in Mansi, *Collectio*, XVIII, 280–1 (cf. pp. 35 and 37 above). The distinction between the episcopal *potestas et dispositio* and the priestly *regimen et dispensatio* (p. 280D) may have been clearer in words than in practice.

[2] MGH, *Const.* I, 623, no. 433.18. On this council, see Ernst Dümmler, *Geschichte des Ostfränkischen Reiches*, 2nd ed., Jahrbücher der deutschen Geschichte (Leipzig, 1887–8), III, 605–10, and Manfred Hellmann, 'Die Synode von Hohenaltheim (916)', *Historisches Jahrbuch*, LXXIII (1953), 127–43, revised and reprinted in *Die Entstehung des deutschen Reiches*, ed. Hellmut Kämpf, Wege der Forschung, I (Darmstadt, 1956), 289–312. Both Dümmler and Hellmann stressed the influence of the False Decretals on the canons of this council (cf. Hellmann, p. 310, on can. XVIII concerning tithes); but this thesis has been questioned by H. Fuhrmann, 'Die pseudoisidorischen Fälschungen und die Synode von Hohenaltheim (916)', *Zeitschrift für bayerische Landesgeschichte*, XX (1957), 136–51 (see *Rev. d'hist. ecc.* LIV, 998–9). The decree on tithes probably derived from the statute of 800/13 (cited p. 44 above) through the collections of either Ansegisis, Benedictus Levita, or Regino.

[3] MGH, *Const.* I, 19, no. 9.10; cf. Rudolf Köpke and Ernst Dümmler, *Kaiser Otto der Grosse*, Jahrbücher der deutschen Geschichte (Leipzig, 1876), p. 206.

fact only added the fabric of the church to the traditional charitable uses of tithes.[1]

A few sources in the Carolingian period still adhered to the view that tithes should be used exclusively for charity. Theodulph of Orléans, for instance, maintained in his second diocesan statute, drawn up about 813, although also citing the rule of quadripartition, that:

Priests should be taught and also warned that the tithes and oblations which they receive from the faithful are for the support of pilgrims, the poor, and travellers, and must be used not as their own property but as entrusted funds, concerning which they will render an account to the Lord and will be damned unless they faithfully distribute them to the poor and those mentioned above.[2]

This statute was included in the canonical collections of both Benedictus Levita and Regino of Prüm.[3] The so-called St Hubert Penitential, compiled in Gaul about 850, also stressed that 'Those who manage the funds of the poor and receive the tithes of the people and who take therefrom anything for themselves or for their worldly gain must make restitution as the wicked invader of the property of the Lord'.[4] Herard of Tours called anyone who misused tithes a 'slayer of the poor' in his diocesan statute cited above. And Benedictus Levita in another capitulary on tithes and oblations, again of doubtful origin, emphasized that priests 'are the dispensers not of their own property but of the property of the Lord'.[5]

A small step further was to allow the use of tithes for the upkeep of churches, like Zachary in his letter of 748. The council of

---

[1] For Zachary's letter, see pp. 27–8 above. There were very few references in secular legislation to the uses of tithes. The *Leges langobardorum*, Charlemagne, no. 94, in MGH, *Leges* in fol., IV, 504, referred to quadripartition, but this may be of later origin.

[2] De Clercq, *Législation*, I, 324; on the date, cf. p. 266.

[3] Benedictus, III, 375, in MGH, *Leges* in fol., II. 2, 125; cf. Seckel, in *NA*, XLI, 171–2; Regino of Prüm, I, 353, *ed. cit.* pp. 164–5.

[4] *Poenitentiale Hubertense*, XLVIII, in Schmitz, *Bussbücher*, II, 337, and McNeill–Gamer, *Handbooks*, p. 293; cf. p. 45 n. 1 above on the term *dominica res*.

[5] Benedictus, III, 214, in MGH, *Leges* in fol., II. 2, 115; cf. Seckel, in *NA*, XXXIX, 413 (cited p. 45 n. 1 above).

Tours in 813 decreed 'That tithes given to individual churches should be dispensed with great care by the priests on the advice of the bishops for the use of the church and of the poor'.[1] And in a fragmentary Italian capitulary of uncertain date Louis the Pious or his son Lothar decreed that tithes, 'concerning which we have heard many controversies between the bishop or other priests and our counts and vassals and other faithful men', should be spent by the priest of the local church for lights or distributed to the poor.[2] In these sources neither the bishop nor the priest was supposed to take any part of the tithe for his own use.

The support of the priest was often added to the poor and the fabric as a suitable use for tithes and so formed a special rule of tripartition for tithes. Zachary's citation of I Cor. ix. 13, 'They that serve the altar partake with the altar', implied that priests might use tithes, but he had not included their support in his list of the proper uses for tithes. Other sources were more specific. The expanded version of the *Regula canonicorum* of Chrodegang of Metz, drawn up probably in the second half of the eighth century, decreed:

Concerning the division of tithes: the priests of the people should receive the tithes and keep the names of those who have given in writing on the altar; and they should divide the tithes before witnesses in accordance with canon law: they should choose the first part for the decoration of the church; they should dispense the second part through the hands of the faithful, mercifully and in all humility, for the use of the poor and pilgrims; the priests should keep the third part, however, for themselves alone.[3]

[1] Tours 813, can. xvi, in MGH, *Conc.* II, 288 (see p. 38 n. 5 above), cited by Benedictus Levita, Add. III, 83, in MGH, *Leges* in fol., II. 2, 143. The *Relatio* of 829 (cited p. 53 below) also urged the use of tithes 'for the uses of the churches and of the poor of Christ'; and a similar doctrine was confirmed by the council at Coblenz in 922 (cited p. 56 below). The terms 'church' and 'churches' here may, of course, refer to more than the upkeep and include the support of the clergy.

[2] MGH, *Capit.* I, 336, no. 168.8.

[3] *Spicilegium*, I, 579. On this expanded version of Chrodegang's rule, see *S. Chrodegangi Metensis episcopi (742–766) Regula canonicorum*, ed. W. Schmitz (Hanover, 1889), introd. p. v; De Clercq, *Législation*, I, 146–7; and Dickinson, *Canons*, p. 17.

A similar division in almost the same words is found in an anony-mous ecclesiastical statute of the early ninth century; and Jonas of Orléans, writing about 829, said that:

It is the duty of the bishop to arrange how much of these oblations from the faithful should be used for the fabric of the church, how much in furnishing lights, how much in tending guests and nourishing the poor, and how much in supplying the needs of the priests and the others who perform with them the service of Christ.[1]

Also in England, according to Ælfric and the laws of Ethelred, the priest was expected to use the tithes for the repair of the church, the poor, and the servants in the churches.[2] This rule of tripartition, however, though it was occasionally supported by references to canon law, had no connection with the 'Spanish' rule of tripartition between the bishop, clergy, and fabric. It derived historically from the addition of the clergy and the fabric, as suitable uses for the property of God, to the traditional chari-table use of tithes.[3]

This addition was justified by several authors on the grounds of the services performed by priests for the entire Christian com-munity. Walafrid Strabo, for instance, said that tithes are given not only to honour God but also

in order that the priests and ministers of the Church may be relieved from the care and worry of bodily needs...and made more free for

---

[1] MGH, *Capit.* I, 106, no. 36.7; and Jonas of Orléans, *De institutione laicali*, II, 19, in *PL*, CVI, 204–5. On the so-called capitulary, see De Clercq, *Législation*, I, 289–90, who considered it to be a diocesan statute of 800/13; P. W. Finster-walder, 'Quellenkritische Untersuchungen zu den Capitularien Karls des Grossen', *Historisches Jahrbuch*, LVIII (1938), 421, who connected it with the council of Tours in 813 and dated it 813/20; and F. L. Ganshof, 'La fin du règne de Charlemagne: Une décomposition', *Zeitschrift für schweizerische Geschichte*, XXVIII (1948), 442 n. 26; cf. Buchner, *Rechtsquellen*, p. 79.

[2] Cited by Felix Makower, *Die Verfassung der Kirche von England* (Berlin, 1894), p. 340 n. 6.

[3] Thomassin, *Discipline*, III, II, 18, *ed. cit.* VI, 573–6, who maintained that the rule of quadripartition was ancient and universal, explained the frequent omission of any reference to the bishop's share as a result of voluntary grants by the bishops to the priests for the sake of the poor. Makower, *Kirche*, p. 340 n. 6, also suggested that the rule of tripartition in England developed out of omitting the episcopal share from quadripartition.

meditation of divine law and the administration of instruction and the willing performance of spiritual service and that the tribute of the people may be offered in a daily oblation to the Lord as well as contribute, in accordance with the canons, to the support of the poor and the repair of churches.[1]

Walafrid apparently knew that canonically tithes should be used for the poor and the fabric of churches but regarded the support of the clergy as an equally worthy use. Bishop Ralph of Bourges in his diocesan statute of 854 maintained that everyone should pay tithes

in order that the priests (who by their holy prayers and oblations invoke the mercy of Almighty God for the sake of peace, the salvation of the entire Christian people, the crops of the earth, the sick, and the dead) may have food, clothing, and other things they need and in order that they may be able to offer assistance to guests and pilgrims, to orphans and widows, and to the weak and ill.[2]

Hincmar also regarded those who performed pastoral functions as entitled to a share of the tithes and oblations and, although he discussed the rule of quadripartition, criticized bishops who failed to use tithes and oblations for the upkeep of churches and the care of guests, dependants, and the poor and who left the priests barely enough to survive.[3]

None of these arrangements gave any part of the tithe to the bishop, who in at least one source was specifically forbidden to take a share. In the first capitulary of Mantua the young King Bernard of Lombardy decreed that 'From the tithes which are offered by the people to the parochial or baptismal churches, no part shall be brought to the cathedral or to the bishop'. This statute was apparently issued in 813, when the five reforming councils met north of the Alps, and according to the prologue it was designed to eradicate 'the evils which have come to light in the holy church of God in our times'. The reference to tithes

[1] Walafrid, *De exordiis*, xxviii, in MGH, *Capit.* II, 513.
[2] Ralph of Bourges, xxi, in *PL*, cxix, 714 (cited p. 36 above).
[3] Hincmar, in *Zs. f. Kirchengeschichte*, x, 134. Stutz, *Benefizialwesen*, pp. 347–50, remarked that in the ninth century episcopal charges often bore heavily on the parish churches.

therefore shows that the bishops were claiming part of the tithes. It was not, as Boyd called it, a 'derogation from the general rule', but was a strict application of the prevailing theory and practice.[1]

The canonical rules of quadripartition and tripartition, both of which awarded a share to the bishop, were first seriously applied to tithes in the East, where the special nature and traditional uses of tithes were less well established. The two councils at Freising and Reisbach in 800 cited the decree of Pope Gelasius and ordered that the tithes should be divided between the bishop, clergy, poor, and fabric.[2] At the council of Salzburg in 807, over which Arch-bishop Arn presided, the bishops complained that tithes were being paid to monasteries and, after the Gelasian decree was read, the abbots agreed to return 'the episcopal portions to the bishops'.[3] An anonymous south German diocesan statute drawn up before 813 instructed the priests to divide the tithes 'in accordance with canon law into four parts', one for themselves, one for the fabric and lighting the church, one for pilgrims, widows, orphans, and the poor, and one for the bishop.[4] Bishop Haito of Basel (806-22) specifically discussed the application to tithes of the rules of quadripartition and tripartition. 'According to the canon of Toledo', he wrote, 'a third part [of the tithe] belongs to the bishops; but we do not want to exercise this right and wish to have only a quarter, in accordance with the usage of the popes and the observance of the holy Roman church.'[5]

This opinion, which combined a good knowledge of canon law with a bad knowledge of history, clearly prevailed in the East in

[1] MGH, Capit. I, 195, no. 92.11 (dated 787?); cf. Charles de Clercq, 'Capitulaires francs en Italie à l'époque de Charlemagne', Hommage à Dom Ursmer Berlière (Brussels, 1931), pp. 251-60 and Législation, I, 229-30, who dated it 813; Boyd, Tithes, pp. 42-4; and Buchner, Rechtsquellen, p. 80.
[2] MGH, Conc. I, 209 (cf. 214), and Capit. I, 228, no. 112.13; cf. Seckel, in NA, xxix, 281 n. 2; Hefele-Leclercq, Conciles, III. 2, 1101-6; De Clercq, Législation, I, 252-7.
[3] MGH, Conc. I, 234; cf. Stutz, Benefizialwesen, pp. 215-16; Hefele-Leclercq, Conciles, III. 2, 1239; De Clercq, Législation, I, 257.
[4] Published by Seckel, in NA, xxix, 292; cf. De Clercq, Législation, I, 288-9.
[5] MGH, Capit. I, 364, no. 177.15; cf. De Clercq, Législation, I, 283. An almost identical canon, attributed to a 'Council of Cologne, can. 6', is found in Burchard of Worms, Decretum, III, 135, in PL, CXI, 700.

the ninth century. The influential Walafrid Strabo, who died in 849, supported the rule of quadripartition of tithes in his book on ecclesiastical property.[1] The two councils at Mainz in 847 and 852 repeated the canon of the council of Tours in 813 that tithes should be divided between the Church and the poor but added to it the decree of Pope Gelasius on quadripartition; and the 852 council further added that one part definitely belonged to the bishop.[2] The synod of Tribur in 895, which in many respects summed up the development of tithing in the East, also clearly asserted that tithes should be divided into four parts.[3]

The bishops in the West were more cautious about claiming a share of the tithe. Pope Zachary, Theodulph, and Hincmar all mentioned the rule of quadripartition in connection with tithes, but they did not really apply it. More conservative doctrines, excluding the bishop, are found in most of the sources. The earliest conciliar reference to quadripartition of tithes in France was in the *Relatio* addressed to Louis the Pious by the bishops in 829.

Although the canons teach that a quarter of the tithes and oblations of the faithful is at the disposition of the bishop, none the less, wherever the bishop has his own property, let him be content with what he has; but when he has no property for his church, let him take for himself and his household as much of the aforesaid quarter as he needs, not, God forbid, as much as he avariciously desires. And if he has no need, let him take nothing from the aforesaid quarter, but let him leave it to be expended in accordance with his orders for the uses of the churches and the poor of Christ.[4]

This passage clearly shows the contrast in the attitudes in the West and in the East, where the bishops were less reluctant to take a quarter of the tithes.

The confusion between the old and new rules and the growing influence of canon law can also be seen in the collections of

---

[1] Walafrid, *De exordiis*, xxviii, in MGH, *Capit.* ii, 512–13.

[2] MGH, *Capit.* ii, 178–9 and 185–6, nos. 248.10 and 249.3; cf. pp. 40–1 above on these councils.

[3] MGH, *Capit.* ii, 220, no. 252.13; cf. p. 41 above on this council.

[4] MGH, *Capit.* ii, 32, no. 196.8, and *Conc.* ii, 633; cf. Hefele–Leclercq, *Conciles*, iv. 1, 65; De Clercq, *Législation*, ii, 71; and Ganshof, *Capitulaires*, p. 29 n. 97.

False Decretals. Benedictus Levita in particular applied almost every possible rule to tithes in one place or another. Seckel, indeed, commented that 'The proportions according to which the ecclesiastical revenues should serve their different ends was a matter of indifference to Benedict: now he renounces any fixed proportion, now he supports tripartition, now he favours the quadripartition adopted in the *Capitula*'.[1] With regard to tithes, Benedict was the victim of the inconsistency of his sources, but on the whole he seems to have regarded tithes as a normal ecclesiastical revenue and to have inclined towards their division into four parts with one for the bishop.[2] Pseudo-Isidore cited the Gelasian decree on the use of oblations and other church revenues, but he did not specifically refer to tithes.[3]

Throughout the Carolingian period, therefore, there was a wide variety of overlapping rules and opinions governing the distribution of tithes, and it is often impossible to say which practice prevailed in any particular region or period.[4] On account

[1] Seckel, in *NA*, xxix, 286, citing among other canons of Benedictus I, 209 (= Ansegisis, *Collectio*, I, 80) and Add. IV, 57, which applied tripartition respectively to voluntary gifts to churches and to altar revenues, but not specifically to tithes. Canon Add. III, 83, derived from the council of Tours in 813 (see pp. 38 n. 5 and 49 above), divided tithes between the church and the poor.

[2] Benedictus was not definite on this point, but canon III, 214 (see p. 46 n. 1 above; probably forged) referred to tithes and oblations 'unde pauperes recreari debent vel ecclesiae restaurari seu clerici vivere, sive episcopi recipi, hospites et peregrini pasci ac venerari', and Add. IV, 144 (cited p. 46 above) specifically said that tithes should be distributed according to the order of the bishop and the Gelasian decree. Canon III, 375, derived from Theodulph's second diocesan statute (see p. 48 above), referred to quadripartition but said that tithes should be used for pilgrims, travellers, and the poor. Cf. Add. IV, 58, in MGH, *Leges* in fol., II. 2, 150-1, which applied quadripartition generally to ecclesiastical revenues and oblations.

[3] *Decretales Pseudo-Isidorianae*, p. 654 (cap. XXIX).

[4] The application of the two rules of quadripartition and tripartition, both in the Carolingian period and later, is a disputed subject among historians. Some of the examples cited below (see index, under 'tithes') suggest that at no time was there any strict uniformity, even on the regional level. Quadripartition certainly tended to prevail in canon law (cf. *Decretum*, C. XII, q. II, cc. 26-31); and Stutz, *Benefizialwesen*, pp. 241-2, was of the opinion that it was more common in the Germanic areas, where papal influence was stronger, and that tripartition prevailed 'in den altchristlichen Gebieten, wo man an das gallo-spanische Kirchenrecht anknüpfte, und wo der Episkopat wegen seiner

of the spread of canon law and episcopal control of conciliar
legislation, the bishops were eventually able in most places to

Vergangenheit immerhin noch eine grössere Machtstellung besass als in den
neuen...'. Schreiber, *Gemeinschaften*, pp. 185–93, 323, and 358, on the other
hand, regarded tripartition as peculiarly Germanic. It is true that the earliest
references to tripartition of tithes were in the East; and later tripartition
seems to have prevailed, though quadripartition was also used, in southern
Germany (modern Austria): see Plöchl, *Zehentwesen*, p. 46; Ferdinand
Tremel, 'Das Zehentwesen in Steiermark und Kärnten von den Anfängen bis ins
15. Jahrhundert,' *Zs. des historischen Vereines für Steiermark*, XXXIII (1939), 11;
and the Muri and Salzburg charters (cited pp. 69 and 101 below), which
refer to fifths as well as to thirds and quarters of tithes. *The Earliest
Norwegian Laws*, ed. Laurence Larson, Columbia Records of Civilization,
XX (New York, 1935), pp. 40–1, however, support Stutz's view that
quadripartition was introduced into newly converted regions, such as Norway,
where the system of tithes was introduced in the time of Sigurd I (1122–30),
according to Knut Gjerset, *History of the Norwegian People* (New York, 1915),
I, 334. Quadripartition prevailed in Sweden and Iceland as well as Norway, in
contrast to Denmark, where the tripartite rule was followed, according to
Ivar Nylander, *Das kirchliche Benefizialwesen Schwedens während des Mittelalters*,
Rättshistoriskt Bibliotek, IV (Lund, 1953), pp. 205–6. The *Acta Murensia* (see
pp. 62–3 and 69 below) repeatedly refer to quadripartition in Switzerland; and
and in the twelfth century Pope Hadrian IV enforced quadripartition in the
diocese of Worms (see p. 283 below). In France, in the tenth century, Abbo of
Fleury referred to both systems (see p. 81 below); and in the diocese of
Toulouse the bishop claimed sometimes a third and sometimes a quarter of the
tithes; cf. the council of Toulouse in 1056 (cited p. 89 below); the St Sernin
charters (cited pp. 95 n. 3, 100 n. 3, 101 n. 1, below); and Elisabeth
Magnou, *L'Introduction de la Réforme grégorienne à Toulouse*, Cahiers de l'Association Marc Bloch de Toulouse: Études d'histoire méridionale, III (Toulouse,
1958), p. 49. In Italy, Popes Alexander II and Hadrian IV enforced quadripartition of tithes (see pp. 89 and 283 below); but the case between the bishopric of Messina and the abbey of Lipari–Patti (cited p. 129 below) and cases III
and VIII in the Appendix show that in the twelfth century tripartition as well as
quadripartition were used in Sicily, Piedmont, and Lombardy. On England,
where tripartition between the clergy, fabric, and poor long prevailed, see
Makower, *Kirche*, p. 340 n. 6, and Hartridge, *Vicarages*, p. 2. Finally, on
Spain, cf. MGH, *Capit.* II, 459–60, no. 303, where the bishop of Barcelona
complained to Charles the Bald at Attigny in 874 that a certain priest had
usurped two (out of three) parts of the tithe of his parish and Charles confirmed
the authority of the bishop over tithes, though whether he took a third for
himself is uncertain; on this decision, see Hefele–Leclercq, *Conciles*, IV. 2, 1348,
and De Clercq, *Législation*, II, 295. San Martín, *Diezmo*, p. 21 n. 2, said that
quadripartition appeared in Spain in the eleventh century; and case VII in the
Appendix shows that the papacy enforced tripartition of tithes in Spain in the
middle of the twelfth century.

establish their right to a quarter or even a third of the tithes. But in some areas, such as England, the special tripartition of tithes between the poor, the fabric, and the priests survived as late as the eleventh century; and according to several sources the bishop was sometimes denied a share. The synod of Metz in 893, for instance, assigned the tithes entirely to the parish priest, 'for his support, for supplying lights, for the fabric of the church, and for obtaining sacerdotal vestments and other suitable needs of his office'.[1] The conservative council at Coblenz in 922, after attacking the use of tithes by laymen to feed their servants and dogs, confirmed the old doctrine that tithes should be used 'for the repair and lighting of the churches and the reception of guests and the poor'.[2] Late in the tenth century Abbo of Fleury in his collection of canons still denied the bishops any share of the oblations, though he did not mention tithes.[3] These conservative opinions gradually gave way, however, to the view that tithes were a part of the normal revenues of the Church and subject to the same rules of control and distribution. Paschasius Radbertus in his commentary on Matthew regarded tithes as given simply 'for the use of the priests'.[4] A century later the synod of Ingelheim in 948, which was the first German synod in thirty years to be attended by a papal legate, decreed that cases concerning refusals to pay tithes must be settled 'in the holy synod by those priests for whose use they are deputed'.[5] Thus the special character of tithes as the property of God, to be used exclusively for charity, was increasingly neglected, and they were treated like any other ecclesiastical revenue.

[1] Metz 893, can. II, in Mansi, *Collectio*, XVIII, 78 (see p. 41 above). The old charitable use of tithes was here entirely omitted.

[2] MGH, *Const.* I, 631, no. 434.18 (see p. 40 above).

[3] Abbo of Fleury, XXXIX, in *PL*, CXXXIX, 491; cf. Fournier–Le Bras, *Collections*, I, 324, who dated this collection about 993, and p. 81 below, where Abbo, in his letter to 'G.', allowed the bishop a third or a quarter of the tithes but still maintained that they should be used for pilgrims, orphans, widows, and the repair of churches.

[4] *PL*, CXX, 779 B.

[5] MGH, *Const.* I, 15, no. 6.9; cf. Köpke and Dümmler, *Otto*, pp. 162–5.

CHAPTER II

MONASTIC POSSESSION OF TITHES

THE possession of tithes by monks falls under two headings. The first, which will be considered in this chapter, concerns the payment to a monastery of tithes by men working on lands not belonging to the monks or cultivated for their use. These are the tithes later referred to as 'from the labour of other men'. The second heading concerns the possession by monks of their own demesne tithes, that is, of tithes from goods produced by themselves or for their own use. A monastery which owned its demesne tithes might keep or distribute itself the tithes it would otherwise have had to pay to someone else, and it was in effect freed from the obligation of paying any tithes at all. This second aspect became a matter of who paid tithes and how they were used, therefore, and belongs in the chapter on monastic payment of tithes. This distinction between *decimas alieni laboris* or *aliorum hominum* and *decimas proprias* or *indominicatas* is fundamental to the study of monastic tithes.

I. FROM THE SEVENTH TO THE ELEVENTH CENTURY

According to the sources cited in the previous chapter, all Christians were required to pay tithes to the church where they received the sacraments. At that time most monks were either laymen or considered a third order of society, distinct from both the clergy and the laity; their churches, if they had them, performed no pastoral functions; and they were not entitled to receive tithes. Doubtless from the earliest times a certain number of tithes were privately given to monks, and Cassian referred in his *Collations* to the payment of tithes to hermits in Egypt in the fourth century.[1]

[1] Cassian, *Conlationes*, XIII, 7, and XXI, 1–2, *ed. cit.* pp. 403 and 574; cf. Thomassin, *Discipline*, III, 1, 4.9–10, *ed. cit.* VI, 19–20, and Viard, *Dîme*, I, 32.

But in the West, where circumstances with regard to monks and tithes were different, there is no evidence of extensive payment of tithes to monks before the eighth century.[1] The example of St Radegundis, who died in 587 and tithed her income before presenting the remainder to monasteries, suggests that monks were not supposed to receive tithes and that laymen who paid tithes at all as a rule gave them to the sacramental clergy.[2]

The earliest known references to monastic possession of the tithes of 'other men' occur in the seventh century. The papal privilege of 643 for Bobbio, if genuine, may apply to the tithes from lands worked either by the monks themselves or by other men;[3] but in a charter of 692 for the abbey of Our Lady at Le Mans, Bishop Aiglibertus of Le Mans instructed the agents or *missi* in charge of ten estates (*villulae*) belonging to the cathedral 'that we have granted to the monastery of the blessed Mary... all the tithes from the said estates...and we order that without any delay you should give [these tithes] to the *missi* of the monastery'.[4] Pardessus was inclined to doubt the authenticity of this charter precisely on the basis of this grant of tithes;[5] but every historical phenomenon has its 'first' example, and the charter was defended as authentic by Julien Havet and has been accepted by more recent scholars.[6] Almost half a century later,

---

[1] Cf. A. Hamilton Thompson, in *Camb. Med. Hist.* v, 676, who said that 'The examples of St Benedict gave no precedent for the possession of appropriated parish churches or tithes...'; and T. P. McLaughlin, *Le très ancien droit monastique de l'Occident*, Archives de la France monastique, XXXVIII (Ligugé–Paris, 1935), who cited no examples of monastic possession of tithes in the period between St Benedict and the ninth century.

[2] MGH, *SS Merov.* II, 366. This Life was written soon after 600.

[3] See p. 212 below.

[4] *Actus pontificum Cenomannis in urbe degentium*, ed. G. Busson and A. Ledru, Archives historiques du Maine, II (Le Mans, 1901), pp. 206–7.

[5] *Diplomata, Chartae, Epistolae, Leges*, ed. J.-M. Pardessus (Paris, 1843–9), II, 226 n. 1: 'Verum, in charta quam nunc exhibemus, fatemur nulla nobis deprehensa fuisse vitia unde hanc supposititiam pronuntiare liceat; etsi aliquam suspicionem injiciant decimae hac aetate monasteriis concessae.'

[6] Julien Havet, 'Les actes des évêques du Mans', *Œuvres de Julien Havet* (*1853–1893*), I: *Questions mérovingiennes* (Paris, 1896), p. 394 (text on p. 429); cf. Duchesne, *Fastes*, II, 339; Leclercq, in *Dict. d'arch.* IV. 1, 1001; and Viard, *Dîme*, I, 63–4.

in 740, Duke Transmundus II of Spoleto gave the abbey of Farfa 'each year the tithes of the wine, grain, and oil, and of the *tertium* which is gathered by the people from the region where Mellitus is *actionarius* and the same tithe fully from Subusualdo'.[1] In 763 Duke Theodicius gave Farfa in addition the tithes of his grain at Amiterno and of his wine at Interocro, 'except for twelve measures of grain from the tithe of Amiterno which are customarily given in the church of St Vittorino there, which that church has the right to hold'.[2] In Alsace in 754 the abbey of Hornbach was given two estates 'with the lands and half of the tithing (*decimatio*) of the church', although *decimatio* here may refer not to the tithe itself but to the land from which the tithes were gathered.[3] These scattered documents show that by the middle of the eighth century monastic possession of tithes, though rare, was not unknown and that monks occasionally owned the tithes from certain lands or types of revenue or the excess over a specified quantity or proportion of the tithe which was allotted to the local church.

During the reigns of Pepin and Charlemagne, and partly as a result of their enforcement of tithes as a civil obligation, tithes played a more important role in monastic economy, and by the beginning of the ninth century many monasteries clearly derived a considerable proportion of their revenues from tithes. An imperial formula of 814, derived from a charter for Stavelot and Malmédy, confirmed the possession of tithes among other

[1] *Farfa*, II, 27, no. 7: '...decimas de vino, et de grano, seu et de oleo, vel de tertia quae a populo colligitur de massa ubi mellitus actionarius est, et de subusualdo omnia in integrum ipsam decimam per singulos annos in ipso monasterio dare debeamus.' The *tertium* was a customary agricultural due.

[2] *Farfa*, II, 57, no. 53: '...exceptis duodecim modiis grani, decimae ipsius curtis amiterninae quae per consuetudinem dare debent ibidem in ecclesia sancti victorini, quam ipsa ecclesia licentiam habeat tollendi.'

[3] J. D. Schöpflin, *Alsatia...diplomatica* (Mannheim, 1772–5), I, 33, no. 26: '...cum terris seu decimacione dimidie ecclesie' (it could mean, 'with the lands or tithing of half the church'); cf. Albert Bruckner, *Regesta Alsatiae aevi merovingici et karolini*, I: *Quellenband* (Strasbourg–Zürich, 1949), pp. 104–5, no. 174, and pp. 116–18, no. 193, where there are references to possession of tithes and the tithing in a suspicious charter of Bishop Eddo of Strasbourg for Ettenheimmünster.

property for a monastery.[1] And the famous *Statuta* of Adalhard of Corbie, which were promulgated in 822, show that at least one great Carolingian abbey forced its more important tenants to pay their tithes to the monastery, in spite of the repeated royal and ecclesiastical decrees requiring the payment of tithes to parochial churches only. 'This is the account', Adalhard wrote, 'of the tithes which our vassals and householders must give. They must both give and bring to the monastery tithes from everything which they produce from the soil for their own use, both great and small, such as grain, wine, garden vegetables, etc.' If the benefice was far from the monastery, the tenant might arrange with the *portarius* to sell the tithe and bring the proceeds to the abbey. These arrangements, however, applied only to tenants holding benefices of at least four *mansi*, 'since those who hold less should pay their tithes fully in the same manner, not to the monastery, however, but to the church or priest where his dependants (*familia*) customarily pay their tithe'.[2] This practice was probably unusual in the early ninth century. The great polyptych of St Germain des Prés, for instance, which was compiled between 790/811 and 823/6, contains no reference to tithes of any sort.[3] But the situation at Corbie rapidly became the rule rather than the exception.

The growth of monastic possession of tithes in the ninth century was not simply a matter of usurpation, as seems to have been the case at Corbie, where a strong abbey gathered the tithes properly

[1] MGH, *Formulae*, p. 317; cf. MGH, *Dipl.* Louis the German, no. 147 (873, for Stavelot): 'Decimas etiam de fiscis nostris, quas anteriores nostri concesserunt, et nos dare cum integritate precipimus.'

[2] Adalhard of Corbie, *Statuta*, xvii, ed. Benjamin Guérard, *Polyptique de l'abbé Irminon* (Paris, 1844), ii, 334, and ed. Léon Levillain, 'Les statuts d'Adalhard', *Le Moyen Âge*, xiii (2nd ser. iv, 1900), 385–6; see also stat. ix, ed. Guérard, ii, 323–6, and ed. Levillain, pp. 370–5, where Adalhard regulated with great care the method of tithing, especially on distant estates. Cf. Émile Lesne, 'L'Économie domestique d'un monastère au IXe siècle d'après les statuts d'Adalhard, abbé de Corbie', *Mélanges...Ferdinand Lot* (Paris, 1925), pp. 409–18, and Luc Dubar, *Recherches sur les offices du monastère de Corbie jusqu'à la fin du XIIIe siècle*, Bibliothèque de la Société d'histoire du droit des pays flamands, picards et wallons, xxii (Paris, 1951), pp. 27–31.

[3] *Polyptyque de l'abbaye de Saint-Germain des Prés*, ed. Auguste Longnon (Paris, 1886–95).

belonging to the parish churches. The developments concerning tithes in general discussed in the first chapter also opened ways for monks to own tithes; and particularly the application to tithes of the normal rules governing the distribution of ecclesiastical revenues made it possible for monks to receive tithes to which they would previously have had no right. Of great importance was the recognition of the right of the bishop to supervise the tithes and, as a rule, to take a share for himself. The share of the parish priests was thus cut down to a quarter or at most a third; and the bishop could assign the sections for the fabric and the poor—with the addition, if he wished, of his own section—to a monastery. Even the priest's share might be divided. A priest named Atto, for instance, complained to Louis the Pious that he had agreed to serve a church in return for half the tithes which belonged to a priest named Frotwin, and that he had still received nothing after a year and a half.[1] Frotwin could have given the remaining half of his share of the tithes to a monastery.

The hard-won permission to pay tithes to a new church was also very important. The claims of existing churches were technically protected, and the bishop had to give his permission; but in practice any proprietary church could assert its claim to tithes. It is impossible to discuss fully here the so-called proprietary church system and the rights of the founder or 'owner' over an appropriated church. Such a relationship between ecclesiastical institutions, by which one church or monastery held another as its property, was later called incorporation; and its principal significance, according to Pöschl, was economic. 'The tithes and entire revenue of all these [dependent] churches were paid to the ruling monastery.'[2] The need for new churches and for regular services in existing churches also promoted the

---

[1] *Monumenta Moguntina*, ed. Philip Jaffé, Bibliotheca rerum germanicarum, III (Berlin, 1866), pp. 324–5; cf. Stutz, *Benefizialwesen*, p. 247 n. 36, and p. 264 n. 9.

[2] Arnold Pöschl, 'Die Inkorporation und ihre geschichtlichen Grundlagen', *A. f. kath. KR*, CVII (1927), 49 (where he defined 'incorporation' as 'Abhängigkeitsverhältnisse kirchlicher Anstalten untereinander') and 159, and CVIII (1928), 59; cf. G. G. Coulton, *Five Centuries of Religion* (Cambridge, 1929–50), III, 171–2.

foundation and acquisition of proprietary churches by monasteries.[1] At first these churches were usually served by a priest or
vicar, who was supported either by a fixed income paid by the
monastery or by an agreed proportion (frequently the canonical
quarter or third) of the church's revenues.[2] Later the monks
themselves often served as priests,[3] and the monastery took the
entire income. Many monasteries thus sought systematically to
acquire churches and to exercise parochial responsibilities and so
derived an increasing part of their income from the tithes and
parochial revenues, or *altaria*, of dependent churches.[4]

Under special circumstances a monastic church might even
itself be elevated into a parish church served by the monks, as was
La Chapelle-Aude in 1075 by the archbishop of Bourges, who
specified that 'The tithe of those who live within the town (*burgum*)
should be paid to the monks who serve the church of La Cha-
pelle'.[5] Or a parish church might become a monastery and retain
its parochial rights. The founders of the abbey of Muri in Switzer-

---

[1] Cf. Thomassin, *Discipline*, III, 1, 10, *ed. cit.* VI, 46–53; Francesco Gosso,
Vita economica delle abbazie Piemontesi (*Sec. X–XIV*), Analecta Gregoriana,
XXII (Rome, 1940), pp. 177–94, who said that 'Sia per costituire la dotazione
delle abbazie fondate, sia per provvedere alle necessità del ministero in tanta
scarsità di clero, i monasteri ricevevano sovente la donazione di capelle e
qualche volta anche di chiese parrocchiali, di pievi' (p. 189); and Philibert
Schmitz, *Histoire de l'ordre de Saint Benoît* (Maredsous, 1942–56), I, 318–22, who
stressed the need for further study of the juridical questions concerning monastic
possession of parishes.

[2] See Imbart de la Tour, in *Rev. hist.* LXVIII, 8; Henri Sée, *Les classes rurales et
le régime domanial en France au moyen âge*, Bibliothèque internationale d'économie politique (Paris, 1901), pp. 462–5 and 469–70; Viard, *Dîme*, II, 105–7;
and Hartridge, *Vicarages*, pp. 10–15.

[3] See pp. 145–7 below.

[4] Important though it was, possession of churches was certainly not the only
and perhaps not even the principal way in which tithes came into the possession
of monks, as some scholars have suggested: cf. Widera, in *A. f. kath. KR*, CX,
61–71, who saw the 'Germanic' law of the proprietary church as 'eine zusam-
menfassende, allgemein gültige Begründung' for the transfer of tithes to monks,
and Coulton, *Five Centuries*, III, 156–62 and ch. 11. On this topic, see the sensible
remarks of Thomassin, *Discipline*, III, II, 21 and 24.3, *ed. cit.* VI, 586–7 and 602.
On the distinction between the *ecclesia* and the *altaria* (parochial revenues), see
Thomas, *Droit*, pp. 76–8, and Hartridge, *Vicarages*, p. 12.

[5] Émile Chénon, *Histoire et coutumes du prieuré de la Chapelle-Aude* (Paris,
1915), p. 96.

land, in 1027, for instance, took over the existing church with its tithes and other revenues and property, according to the *Acta Murensia*, 'on condition that they would have with them a secular priest who would minister to the people'. The lay parishioners soon proved disturbing to the monks, however, and the first provost, Reginald, built another church, dedicated to St Goar, for the congregation, although the abbey church remained the mother church, with full parochial rights. The abbot received the cure of souls from the bishop and appointed and supported a priest in the new church, which received no permanent endowment, and specifically no tithes, except for the tithes of Wallenswil. That the priest in fact received other tithes was 'more for charity and to supply a means of living than for justice or obligation, and the abbot has the power to give to another or to keep for himself'. No part of the parochial tithe was owed to the bishop, but the author admitted that every fourth year the tithe belonged to the bishop, who thus collected the equivalent of an annual quarter.[1] The monks also held many tithes outside the original parish. A charter of 1064, issued when the new monastery church was dedicated, confirmed their possession of 'the tithes of all the churches on this side of the river [Arc], almost as far as Windisch'.[2] Later they acquired tithes and fractions of tithes over a large area where they held no land or proprietary churches,[3] though occasionally the *Acta* mentions that a local church was baptismal and therefore entitled to the tithe.[4]

At the same time many tithes passed into the hands of laymen and were treated by them like secular revenues. Already in the early ninth century ecclesiastical and secular decrees were promulgated forbidding the payment of any rent or performance of any secular service by a priest in return for tithes or other

---

[1] *Muri*, pp. 21–2, 58–9, and 66–7. The *Acta Murensia* was composed in the middle twelfth or thirteenth century, but it incorporated earlier elements: cf. Wattenbach, *Geschichtsquellen*, II, 392, and Hans Hirsch, 'Die Acta Murensia und die ältesten Urkunden des Klosters Muri', *MIÖG*, XXV (1904), 209–74 and 414–54, who supported a date of about 1150 (p. 240).

[2] *Muri*, p. 29.

[3] See p. 69 below.

[4] *Muri*, pp. 77 and 80.

ecclesiastical revenues or property.[1] This spread of lay control
over tithes, like that of monastic possession, was a result both of
usurpations, episcopal grants and sales, and the proprietary church
system.[2] 'From the ninth century', said Imbart de la Tour, 'tithes
were usurped by landlords and given, sold, and enfeoffed both
in their own and in free parishes.'[3] He maintained that in the
tenth century the tithe became in effect a seigneurial due and a
rent on land;[4] and some historians have even suggested that these
secularized and enfeoffed tithes entirely lost their spiritual significance.[5] There was nothing basically incompatible at this period,
however, between secular control over tithes and their religious
nature, which was never altogether forgotten. In broad terms the
'secularization' of tithes was an aspect of 'le triomphe du régime
bénéficial', as it was called by Edouard Fournier: the general
subdivision of absolute property rights, the breakdown of

[1] MGH, Capit. I, 277, no. 138.10 (Louis the Pious in 818/19) = Ansegisis,
Collectio, I, 85, ibid. p. 407; also in the collections of Regino, Burchard, Ivo, and
Gratian (Decretum, C. XXIII, q. VIII, c. 25); and MGH, Capit. I, 333, no. 167.4
= 845 Council of Meaux, can. LXIII (Capit. II, 413, no. 293.63), and in the
collections of Burchard, Ivo, and Gratian (Decretum, C. XXIII, q. VIII, c. 24).
A charter in Cluny, I, 356-7, no. 378 (929), gave the monks a church 'which has
neither tithes nor other [property] for which service is due to a secular lord', and
shows the need for these decrees against requiring service in return for tithes.
[2] The origins of infeudated tithes have long puzzled historians. 'Or dont soit
procedee ceste espece de Disme, c'est perauanture la chose la plus obscure qu'il
y ait en notre Histoire...', said Etienne Pasquier, Les recherches de la France, III,
41 (Paris, 1621), p. 309. Thomassin, Discipline, III, I, 11, ed. cit. VI, 54-70, discussed
several views on the question and concluded that 'Tous ces sentiments n'ont
rien d'incompatible et n'ont rien que de vraisemblable en distinguant diverses
sortes de ces dîmes inféodées...' (p. 65); Waitz, Verfassungsgeschichte, IV, 123,
recognized that tithes never belonged to the king as such and were held by
laymen as grants from prelates; and Albert Hauck, Kirchengeschichte Deutschlands, 8th [unchanged] ed. (Berlin, 1954), IV, 53 n. 4, said that 'Das Eigentum
der Laien an Zehnten erklärt sich zum Teil aus dem Eigenkirchenwesen; sie
konnten aber auch durch Verleihung in den Besitz von Zehnten kommen'.
[3] Imbart de la Tour, in Rev. hist. LXIII, 30.
[4] Ibid. LXVII, 23, and LXVIII, 21-2.
[5] On the secularization of tithes, see Jacques Flach, Les origines de l'ancienne
France (Paris, 1886-1917), I, 336-7; Sée, Classes rurales, pp. 114-16, 460-2, and
472; Thomas, Droit, pp. 69-72; Viard, Dîme, I, 136-9 and 207; Hartridge,
Vicarages, pp. 3-5; P. S. Leicht, Il diritto privato preirneriano, Biblioteca della
Rivista di Storia del diritto italiano, IX (Bologna, 1933), p. 167; and Newman,
Domaine, p. 19.

episcopal control over the temporal property of the diocese, and the formation of ecclesiastical benefices and *mensae*.[1] More narrowly, laymen came to have definite proprietary rights over tithes and felt free to grant or sell them as they wished to other laymen or to ecclesiastical institutions.[2]

A good example of this attitude is found in the chronicle of Ebersheim, which records that the Empress Ricgardis came to the abbey some time between 862 and 893/6 and:

gave to [its patron] St Maurice for divine services thirty acres of fields and vineyards and a farm at Kinzheim together with the tithe of this whole allod; thus she performed great penance, since she had forcibly deprived the church of St Maurice of its tithes at Sigolsheim. For she built on her land in this estate a church dedicated to St Peter and required first her own tithes and then all the tithes of the entire estate [to be paid] to it, except for the farm of St Maurice and his *familia* and the allod of the Holy Mother of God and her *familia*.[3]

The authenticity of this grant is uncertain,[4] but it shows the way in which a great magnate treated tithes and gave them to an abbey with one hand while taking them away with the other.

There are countless references to tithes in monastic charters of the ninth and tenth centuries, and it is not always possible to tell whether the monks originally gained possession by usurpation, by payments from their proprietary churches, by grants of the episcopal or other canonical portions of the tithe, or by gifts, restora-

[1] See Fournier, *Vicaire*, p. 39, and Lesne, *Menses, passim*. Imbart de la Tour, in *Rev. hist.* LXVII, 33, remarked that 'On peut dire qu'au XIe siècle l'unité religieuse du diocèse n'existe plus'.

[2] On the proportion of tithes held by laymen in the late medieval and early modern periods, see *Chartes du Forez*, xv: *Les Dîmes en Forez* (Mâcon, 1957), pp. 188–96 and 208: 'Sur 220 paroisses foréziennes, 64 seulement ont toutes leurs dîmes en main ecclésiastique, à un moment donné au moins; dont 2 seulement prouvées au XIIIe s....En Forez, nous voyons plus de dîmes en mains laïques qu'en mains ecclésiastiques' (pp. 188, 208). In England in 1831 Lord Lansdowne still declared 'his opinion that tithes were property, sacred property': *Three Early Nineteenth Century Diaries*, ed. A. Aspinall (London, 1952), p. 49. It was the property rather than the tithe which he regarded as sacred.

[3] *Chronicon Ebersheimense*, xv, in MGH, *SS*, XXIII, 439.

[4] Bruckner, *Regesta*, pp. 386–7, no. 648, accepted it as authentic, but cf. *GP*, III. 3, 45–6 on the forgeries in this chronicle.

5   C M T

tions, or sales by laymen (who might themselves have acquired the tithes in any of these same ways). In the ninth, tenth, and eleventh centuries the Church kept up an intermittent campaign to recover churches, tithes, and other usurped ecclesiastical property from the hands of laymen; and in an article on the restoration of private churches in France at this time Mollat stressed that when usurped property was restored to the Church little attention was usually paid to the proper recipient and that monks were often given revenues to which they had no canonical right.[1] Dumas also said that 'The majority of such restitutions did not help the parish churches: the repentant proprietors preferred to give their tithes to religious houses, which were favoured by the faithful; monasteries of monks or canons were the principal beneficiaries of these good resolutions'.[2]

In most charters concerning monastic tithes no attention was paid to their spiritual character. Tithes were freely given, bought, sold, and exchanged like any secular revenue, even by the kings and bishops who issued stringent decrees forbidding such transactions. Tithes alone from specific lands and products, as in the early grants to Our Lady at Le Mans and Farfa, and lands or churches with their tithes were given to monasteries simply as a valuable form of property. Louis the German in 873 confirmed a grant to Lamspringe by the bishop of Hildesheim of 'certain tithes in his diocese'.[3] Charles the Bald in 877 gave all the tithes from several estates and two-thirds of the tithes from others to St Cornelius at Compiègne.[4] And among the acts of the Emperor Arnulf are grants of churches with tithes to St Maximin at Trier

---

[1] Guillaume Mollat, 'La restitution des églises privées au patrimoine ecclésiastique en France du IXe au XIe siècle', *Revue historique de droit français et étranger*, 4th ser. XXVII (1949), 399–423; cf. Thomassin, *Discipline*, III, I, 10. 7, ed. cit. VI, 49–51.   [2] Dumas, in *Histoire de l'Église*, VII, 286.

[3] MGH, *Dipl.* Louis the German, no. 150. The charter has been altered and is not above suspicion.

[4] *Recueil des actes de Charles II le Chauve*, ed. A. Giry, M. Prou, F. Lot and G. Tessier, CDRHF (Paris, 1943–55), II, 448–54 (451–2 on tithes), no. 425. Cf. the large grants of tithes to monasteries in Spain by the French kings Lothar and Louis V in the tenth century: *Recueil des actes de Lothaire et de Louis V rois de France (954–987)*, ed. Louis Halphen and Ferdinand Lot, CDRHF (Paris, 1908), pp. 23–5, 111–16 and 120–4, nos. 11, 49 and 51 (for Cuxa, Ripoll, and Vallès).

and St Emmeram at Regensburg and confirmations of episcopal grants of tithes to the nuns of Ridigippi and Möllenbeck, to whom the bishop of Minden gave at their foundation the tithes from a hundred and twenty carucates belonging to the bishopric 'on condition that the monastery pays to the see each year five pounds in silver or gold and receives the bishop once a year as in other places in his diocese'.[1] Rents or payments of this kind were often exacted in return for grants of tithes.[2] Sometimes the grants were also frankly feudal in nature. The bishop of Paderborn 'by the hand of his advocate' gave the episcopal tithes in his diocese to the advocate of the nunnery of Schildesche.[3] And in 993 the bishop of Autun granted some tithes to the abbot of St Symphorien at Autun for his lifetime in return for annual payment of the synodal dues.[4]

Tithes already belonging to a monastery might be granted to another monastery or even, with proprietary churches and abbeys, to bishops and laymen. The tithes of the little abbey of St Martin near Dijon, for instance, were given to the great abbey of St Stephen by Bishop Isaac of Langres (c. 856–80), whose grant was confirmed by Bishop Argrimus in 899, and were restored to St Stephen, after being usurped by a layman, by Bishop Hericus in 934.[5] Louis the Child in 905 gave the abbey of Pfäffers, with its

---

[1] MGH, *Dipl.* Arnulf, nos. 10, 12, 41 and 147. Cf. Louis the Child, no. 36 (904), granting some land with all its appurtenances and tithes to an individual monk, Umcrim of St Mihiel, who had single-handed restored a deserted cell and after whose death the land was to revert to his abbey. The formulas used by the Saxon emperors in granting tithes to monasteries are listed by Widera, in *A. f. kath. KR*, cx, 95–7.

[2] An exchange between a bishop and a layman of the episcopal tithes in the diocese of Worms for nine *mansi* of land was confirmed in MGH, *Dipl.* Otto III, no. 85 (992).

[3] Confirmed in MGH, *Dipl.* Otto II, no. 74 (974); cf. Otto II, no. 302 and Otto III, no. 91 for Reepsholt and Nivelles.

[4] *St Symphorien d'Autun*, p. 41, no. 16. The bishop was probably glad to ensure payment of the synodals, which may have been hard to collect, by granting the tithes.

[5] *St Étienne de Dijon*, pp. 29–30 and 55–7, nos. 16 and 36; cf. Duchesne, *Fastes*, II, 190, on Bishop Isaac of Langres. During the reign of King Lothar (954–86), Bishop Achardus gave part of a church belonging to St Stephen, together with its tithes, to a canon of Langres and his nephew: *ibid.* pp. 66–7, no. 44.

churches, tithes, and other possessions, which had previously been held as a benefice by the Marquis Burchard, as a proprietary grant (*in proprium*) to the bishop of Constance.[1] And in 989 the archbishop of Cologne gave his demesne estate at Winnigen, together with its tithe 'which belonged to the monastery of St Victor [Xanten]', to St Martin the Great at Cologne, 'in order to relieve the very great poverty of the monastery and the need of the monks'.[2]

In many cases the canonical rules for paying and distributing tithes seem to have been entirely disregarded. When the bishop of Gerona in 957 gave various tithes, first-fruits, and oblations to Bañolas 'in order that the abbots and monks serving God in that place may spend and distribute them in accordance with the rule of St Benedict',[3] he had apparently forgotten that tithes and parochial revenues were not mentioned by St Benedict and that canon law placed the distribution of tithes in the hands of the bishop and clergy. Monks themselves freely used tithes for barter. In 896 an elaborate agreement was made between a layman Roger and the monks of St Maximin at Trier. Roger built a new church on his land in a parish belonging to the monks and endowed it with some land and with the tithes from several estates belonging to the monks (who had apparently paid tithes to Roger). The monks in addition endowed the new church with various tithes previously paid to their parish church. The church was to be served by the parish priest and was to belong to the monastery after the death of Roger and his wife.[4] The monks thus eventually recovered, as part of the endowment of the new church, tithes which had either belonged to their parish church or been paid from their own lands.

As time went on fewer grants were made of the entire tithe of an area, either with or without the land or church to which the tithe properly belonged, and fractional and specific grants became

[1] MGH, *Dipl.* Louis the Child, no. 38. Though an old foundation, Pfäffers was called an *abbatiuncula* in this charter and was probably still a very small house.
[2] *Xanten*, p. 5.
[3] *Marca hispanica*, ed. Pierre de Marca (Paris, 1688), p. 874.
[4] *Altluxemburg*, I, 138–41.

more common. Grants of episcopal tithes were by their nature usually restricted to the quarter or third to which the bishop was entitled. Many laymen, also, only held parts of tithes, which might be further subdivided by inheritance or subinfeudation before being given to a monastery. Provision might also be made out of the tithes for the parish priest, as in the grant to Farfa in 763. In 778, according to a later charter, the bishop of Strasbourg gave to the new abbey of Eschau, among other property, the estate of Rufach with its church and 'with four parts of the tithes belonging to that church; but the said bishop gave the fifth part to the parish priest on account of the richness of the estate and the immensity of the tithes'.[1] And the abbey of Muri in the eleventh century owned many fractions of tithes outside the region where it held all the tithe. At Stallikon, in the present canton of Zürich, the monks owned 'at first the third part in the tithe; then two parts in the part of the others who receive the tithe with us; for at first it is divided into four, of which the third is ours; of the fourth part which remains, when it is divided into five, two parts are ours, the other parts belong to the others'. The *Acta Murensia* later says, however, that at Stallikon the monks held a quarter of the tithes and an eighteenth (rather than two-fifths) of another quarter.[2] Be this as it may, one quarter belonged to the abbey, another quarter was divided between the abbey and other owners, and the remaining half may have been devoted to its canonical uses. More simply, the abbey of Prüm in 893 kept two-thirds and gave one-third to the priest out of the tithes 'of grain and hay...and also of burial dues and the royal rent, if tithes are given', at Basnach.[3]

A grant might also be restricted to certain specific types of produce. As early as about 817 the bishop of Liège gave the tithe

---

[1] Bruckner, *Regesta*, pp. 172–3, no. 272; *GP*, III. 3, 29. Cf. *Spicilegium*, III, 372: the bishop of Clermont consecrated a new church and endowed it with the entire tithe from six villas and estates, with half the tithe from eleven villas and estates, and with two parts (out of three?) of the tithe from seven villas and estates.

[2] *Muri*, pp. 77 and 97; cf. pp. 71–2, 75, 82, and 127–8 for other complicated divisions of tithes.

[3] *Altluxemburg*, I, 127–8.

of the cheese from all his estates and of the wine from three estates (to which he later added two more) to the abbey of St Hubert in the Ardennes 'in order that the monks leading a regular life there may have enough and to spare for food and clothing'.[1] Tithes of wine were a favourite form of gift to monasteries. Innocent II mentioned a grant of tithes of wine made to Gengenbach by the Empress Ricgardis some time before 888.[2] And Conrad II confirmed an episcopal grant to St Martin at Minden:

on condition that no injustice or harm is done to the monks in the tithing of the wine and that they should remember when drinking this wine that previously they had not even a cupful of wine from his whole diocese and should therefore intercede more frequently with God on behalf of ourselves, our beloved wife G. and our son king H., at whose request we gave this vineyard to bishop S.[3]

Another common form of dividing tithes was in terms of the control and use of the land. On the little lordship of Solutré in Burgundy, in 888/927, the abbey of St Laurence at Mâcon owned the tithes from the lord's condamines and vineyards and from uncultivated lands; all other tithes were divided between the parish churches of St Julian and St Peter.[4] A few years later, in 932/3, the monks of Cluny built a church at Solutré on some land given them by the king of Burgundy; and it was consecrated by the bishop of Mâcon and endowed with various tithes previously paid to the parish churches, but it remained subject and paid an annual due to the church of St Julian.[5] In the early eleventh century, St Emmeram owned the tithes from many scattered parcels of land, and a rich but recent foundation like Cluny held

---

[1] St Hubert, p. 6, no. 4, and La chronique de Saint-Hubert dite Cantatorium, ed. Karl Hanquet, Commission royale d'histoire: Recueil de textes pour servir à l'étude de l'histoire de Belgique (Brussels, 1906), p. 14.

[2] Wirtemberg, II, 7–9, no. 310; JL 7949; GP, III. 3, 77–8, no. 1.

[3] MGH, Dipl. Conrad II, no. 192; cf. Henry III, no. 68 for a grant (possibly spurious) of the obscure 'royal tithe' to St Mary at Münster.

[4] Mâcon, pp. 130–1, no. 204; cf. André Déléage, La vie rurale en Bourgogne jusqu'au début du onzième siècle (Mâcon, 1941), I, 454.

[5] Cluny, I, 393–5, no. 408.

any number of tithes and fractions of tithes from lands and churches not owned by the abbey.[1]

Lastly, monks might be given the tithes from specific revenues. Tithes of agricultural rents have already been mentioned, but tithes of commercial revenues were also not unknown. St Peter at Ghent received the tithes of the port of Ghent on the River Scheldt from the count of Flanders in 936/41, with the confirmation of Louis IV in 950.[2] Otto I in 961 gave to SS Maurice and Innocent at Magdeburg 'the entire tithe in the above-mentioned regions and towns from the products and all the profits (*utilitates*) from which Christians give and should give tithes, whenever by the grace of God they may become Christians'.[3] And in 1033 the bishop of Arezzo made a yet more specific grant to the hermits at Camaldoli of 'all the tithes of those things that are bought and sold for profit by the citizens of Arezzo, both in the city and the suburbs, and by all the traders and merchants in our diocese'. He went on to remind the merchants, who had apparently asked for a remission of the tithes from their business at Camaldoli, 'how grave a sin it is not to give tithes to God (which the poorest peasants never dare withhold from the just labour of their hands) from the profits of your trade, which you rarely if ever exercise without danger of grave fraud and without the crime of perjury'.[4]

These divisions of tithes, like their secularization, were an aspect of the broad economic development of the tenth and

---

[1] See K. T. von Inama-Sternegg, *Deutsche Wirtschaftsgeschichte* (Leipzig, 1879–1901), II, 476–8, for an analysis of the *Descriptio censuum* of St Emmeram in 1031, and Guy de Valous, 'Le domaine de l'abbaye de Cluny aux Xe et XIe siècles', *Annales de l'Académie de Mâcon*, 3rd ser. XXII (1920–1), 364, and my article on 'Cluniac Tithes and the Controversy Between Gigny and Le Miroir', *Rev. bén.* LXX (1960), 591–624.

[2] *Recueil des actes de Louis IV, roi de France (936–954)*, ed. M. Prou and P. Lauer, CDRHF (Paris, 1914), p. 39, no. 15. The tithe was described in the charter as 'the tenth which those who stop in the port should pay to God for the assistance of their souls', so that it can hardly have been a secular toll or customs due.

[3] MGH, *Dipl.* Otto I, no. 231. This grant clearly envisaged that tithes would be paid in the future by converted pagans.

[4] Jean Mabillon, *Annales ordinis s. Benedicti* (Lucca, 1739–45), IV, 357–8, and (a somewhat different version) *Arezzo*, I, 220–1, no. 153.

eleventh centuries. As Ferdinand Lot remarked in his book on St Wandrille:

When one examines the series of charters of the eleventh and twelfth centuries, it is striking that the fortune of the institution rarely consists of entire domains, as in the eighth and ninth centuries, but consists of tithes, of fractions of tithes, of rents, etc., received from the domains where other lords, lay or ecclesiastical, had rights at least equal to those of the monastery.[1]

It was part of 'the triumph of the benefice' and the economic and religious division of the diocese. Monasteries were no longer given absolute rights over whole estates but conditional rights in and over parts of estates, among which tithes were a valuable and sought-after revenue.

This picture may seem at first sight in complete contrast with the picture of careful control and regulation of tithing which was presented, on the basis of different kinds of evidence, in the first chapter. The fact and the theory were, however, from different points of view both true and even complementary. The repeated conciliar and legislative injunctions concerning tithes, especially in the ninth century, were partly a reaction against the increasing abuse of tithes. Nor was the payment of tithes to monasteries entirely unopposed. Episcopal protests began at least as early as the beginning of the ninth century. In 804 a council at Tegernsee, presided over by Archbishop Arn of Salzburg, adjudicated a dispute over tithes between the bishop of Freising and the abbey of Tegernsee and forced the abbot to return the tithes to the bishop.[2] The matter was again brought up at the council of Salzburg in 807; the Gelasian decree of quadripartition was read; and the abbots agreed to return 'the episcopal portions [of the tithe] to the bishops'.[3] A decree of the council of Chalon-sur-Saône in 813 forbade abbots and bishops to receive tithes from their peasants,

---

[1] *St-Wandrille*, introd. p. cxi. On this type of development, see L. Genicot, 'L'Évolution des dons aux abbayes dans le comté de Namur du Xe au XIVe siècle', *XXXe Congrès de la Fédération archéologique et historique de Belgique: Annales* (Brussels, 1936), pp. 139–42, and Ganshof, in *Camb. Econ. Hist.* I, 287.

[2] MGH, *Conc.* II, 231–3; cf. Hefele–Leclercq, *Conciles*, III. 2, 1239.

[3] See p. 52 and n. 3 above.

who must pay tithes to their baptismal churches.[1] Similar injunctions throughout the century, though less specific, were directed against monastic possession of tithes.

Faced with such opposition, the monks had to defend their holdings of tithes as best they could. Most commonly they relied on the evidence of a gift or long possession, but they also eagerly sought confirmations from both the ecclesiastical and lay authorities and sometimes resorted, when other means failed, to forgery. Lawsuits concerning monastic tithes were increasingly frequent, especially in the East, where the bishops first asserted with vigour their claim to a share in the tithe, and where the special character of the tithing in certain regions, particularly Saxony, Thuringia, Carinthia, and the Slavic East, made the bishops more dependent than elsewhere upon revenues from tithes.[2] The case between Fulda and the bishops of Würzburg will

[1] See p. 38 and n. 6 above.

[2] On this highly disputed question and on the specific controversies mentioned below, see in particular: Friedrich Philippi, 'Zehnten und Zehntstreitigkeiten', *MIÖG*, XXXIII (1912), 393–431, who maintained that the tithes involved were secular rents and not ecclesiastical tithes; Hauck, *Kirchengeschichte*, III, 731 and n. 2; H. F. Schmid, 'Der Gegenstand des Zehntstreites zwischen Mainz und den Thüringern im 11. Jahrhundert und die Anfänge der decima constituta in ihrer kolonisationsgeschichtlichen Bedeutung', *Sav. Zs. Germ. Abt.* XLIII (1922), 267–300, who suggested that in Thuringia the tithes were fixed but not really remitted; Widera, in *A. f. kath. KR*, CX, 75–85; and Erwin Hölk, *Zehnten und Zehntkämpfe der Reichsabtei Hersfeld im frühen Mittelalter*, Marburger Studien zur älteren deutschen Geschichte, II, 4 (Marburg, 1933), pp. 85–7. Thompson, *Germany*, pp. 398, 445, etc., repeatedly maintained that all converts were ruthlessly forced to pay tithes; and Hermann Aubin, in *Camb. Econ. Hist.* I, 363, wrote that 'Agricultural dues were therefore based not on areal units but on the number of ploughs employed. The original way of levying tithe in the Slavonic Church points in the same direction. Normally every tenth sheaf should have been taken from the fields. Instead of this, we find in various places—on the Wendish frontiers, in Pomerania and Poland—a frequent, though not universal, fixed charge in kind, or even in money, imposed on those liable to tithe.' The *Acta Murensia* distinguished between 'given' and 'constituted' tithes in Switzerland in the first half of the eleventh century (*Muri*, pp. 21–2; cf. p. 63 n. 1 above); and a charter from Carinthia in the middle of the eleventh century referred to tithing 'secundum consuetudinem Sclavorum' (*Salzburg*, I, 236): cf. Tremel, in *Zs. d. hist. Vereines f. Steiermark*, XXXIII, 14–18, who discussed the fixed tithe of the Slavs and the efforts of the archbishops of Salzburg in the eleventh century to restore the normal tithe. In the middle of the twelfth century (case VI in Appendix) the archbishop of Magdeburg and the

be discussed later. A dispute between St Gall and the bishops of Constance was settled in 882, when Bishop Solomon II ceded the tithes from certain regions to the monks.[1] And in 891 the great quarrel between the see of Osnabrück and the monasteries of Corvey and Herford began with a protest by Bishop Egilmar to Pope Stephen V that the monks had taken the episcopal tithes.[2] The pope's reply is not known, and the controversy seems to have died down. But it flared up again in the late eleventh century,[3] together with the famous controversies between Mainz and the abbeys of Fulda and Hersfeld and between Hersfeld and the see of Halberstadt over the tithes from the Hessengau and Freisenfeld.[4] The case between the bishops of Treviso and the abbey of St Hilary at Venice, which is described in the appendix, started in the middle of the tenth century—when the bishop claimed the tithes from two estates belonging to the monks—and lasted almost two centuries.

bishop of Halberstadt mentioned in a charter the 'Sclavi decimam non solventes' who cultivated part of an estate in Saxony, but they may have been pagans.

[1] St Gallen, II, 230, no. 621; cf. Widera, in A. f. kath. KR, CX, 75–83.

[2] MGH, Epp. VII, 359–62.

[3] See MGH, Epistolae selectae, II: Das Register Gregors VII., ed. Erich Caspar (Berlin, 1920–3), pp. 156–7 and 587, nos. II, 25 and IX, 10. The forgeries associated with this revival of the controversy in the 1070's were discussed by Michael Tangl, 'Forschungen zur karolinger Diplomen', A. f. Urk. II (1909), 218–250.

[4] In addition to the works cited in p. 73 n. 2 above, see on the Mainz–Fulda–Hersfeld disputes, Thompson, Germany, pp. 133–4 and 218 n. 1; Eduard Ausfeld, Lambert von Hersfeld und der Zehntstreit zwischen Mainz, Hersfeld und Thüringen (Marburg, 1880), who regarded Lambert's account of the dispute as unreliable; Hauck, Kirchengeschichte, III, 731–2 and 736; and Hans Goetting, 'Die klösterliche Exemtion in Nord- und Mitteldeutschland vom 8. bis zum 15. Jh.', A. f. Urk. XIV (1935), 135–8 and 157–68. In this case the root of the trouble lay in the large grants of tithes made to Fulda and Hersfeld in the ninth century and in their independence as missionary Eigenklöster; but the actual controversy, in spite of Lambert's claim that it started in the Carolingian period, seems to have broken out in the middle of the eleventh century, when Mainz sought the support of the emperor against the abbeys, which were supported by the papacy. For the final settlement, well into the twelfth century, see Mainz, I, 397–8 and 505–7. On the Halberstadt–Hersfeld controversy, see Hauck, Kirchengeschichte, IV, 174–5. Discussion and bibliography of some of the forgeries involved in these cases will be found in MGH, Dipl. Louis the German, no. 51 (for Osnabrück) and no. 178 (for Corvey) and Arnulf, no. 3 (for Corvey and Herford) and no. 36 (for Werden).

In the West, in spite of occasional usurpations, as when Louis IV in 936 forced the bishop of Meaux to return some tithes he had taken from the abbey of St Cornelius at Compiègne,[1] the bishops in the ninth and tenth centuries seem to have been less opposed to monastic possession of tithes than in the East. Sometimes they even helped the monks against the clergy and laity. The bishop of Langres in 903, for instance, settled a complicated dispute between St Stephen at Dijon, the little abbey of St John, and several parish priests on the basis that each church or monastery should have the tithes from its own lands.[2] In 916 the bishop of Toul 'in full synod' agreed that the monastery of St Evre was entitled to certain tithes it had held *ab antiquitate*.[3] The archbishop of Lyons in 960/78 threatened to excommunicate the parishioners in Mornant who refused to pay their tithes to the abbey of Savigny.[4] In Poitou in 938/49 the monks of St Cyprien at Poitiers were able to prove their right to the tithes of Clazac, which were claimed by two priests, by producing before the bishop of Poitiers, in his episcopal synod, a charter of Bishop Ingenald (*c.* 860–*c.* 871) assigning the tithes to a chapel that was later given to the monks 'with all its property' by Bishop Frotherius, 'whose allod it previously was'.[5]

In the tenth century the monks also began to look to the papacy for protection of their holdings of tithes. In about 946 Pope Agapitus II confirmed for the nunnery of Essen 'the tithe that, with the permission of the said pope [Zachary] and consent of the bishops of the entire clergy, Archbishop Gunther of Cologne assigned for the support of the nuns'.[6] In 968 John XIII confirmed the tithe-holdings of both St Mary at Arles-sur-Tech

---

[1] *Actes de Louis IV*, pp. 8–13, no. 4 (p. 10 on tithes).

[2] *St Étienne de Dijon*, pp. 31–3, no. 17. This charter includes considerable evidence that was presented to the bishop on the traditional division of tithes.

[3] Mabillon, *Annales*, III, 329 and 646–7.

[4] *Savigny*, I, 92–3, no. 129; cf. 30–1, no. 30.

[5] *St Cyprien*, pp. 118–19, no. 184; cf. Duchesne, *Fastes*, II, 86, on the dates of Bishop Ingenald.

[6] *PL*, CXXXIII, 893; JL 3635. The alleged early date of the original grant and the inconsistency of the dates of Zachary (741–52) and Archbishop Gunther (850–64) throw some doubt on the authenticity of this bull.

and Cuxa.[1] In 973 Benedict VI confirmed the tithes of four churches belonging to Vézelay and forbade the bishops of Autun to disturb the monks on this account or 'to reduce the tithes or transfer them to another parish'.[2] In 990 John XV confirmed the property of Lobbes 'both in possessions and in tithes'.[3] And the confirmation of tithes and first-fruits given by Sylvester II in 999 to a cell of the abbey of Leno was extended by Benedict VIII twenty years later to cover all the churches belonging to the abbey.[4]

When these legitimate methods failed to protect their possession of tithes, the monks might resort to forgery; and monastic chartularies contain many false and interpolated documents concerning tithes dating from the ninth and tenth centuries. The numerous alleged grants of Pepin and Charlemagne for Hersfeld and Fulda,[5] of Charlemagne and Carloman for Ebersheim,[6] and of Charlemagne for St Denis[7] are all forgeries or of dubious authenticity; and the names of later Carolingian kings were freely attached to forged grants and confirmations of tithes.[8] One of the most elaborate cases was that of Fulda, where the monks in 822/3 inserted a clause recognizing their right to 'the tithes of the faithful' into a papal privilege of 751 in order to protect their tithes from the claims of the bishop of Würzburg.[9] Pope Paschal I

[1] *Marca hispanica*, pp. 893-4 and 934-6; JL 3734-5; Santifaller, *Elenco*, pp. 296-7.
[2] *PL*, cxxxv, 1086; JL 3770; Santifaller, *Elenco*, p. 301.
[3] J. Vos, *Lobbes; son abbaye et son chapitre* (Louvain, 1865), I, 437; JL 3837; Santifaller, *Elenco*, p. 311.
[4] *Leno*, pp. 81 and 91, nos. 8 and 12; JL 3901 and 4026; *IP*, VI. 1, 343, nos. 1-2; Santifaller, *Elenco*, pp. 319 and 336.
[5] MGH, *Dipl. Karol.* nos. 32, 104, 105, 121, 129 and 215.
[6] *Ibid.* no. 221; Bruckner, *Regesta*, pp. 132-3, no. 217; and Theodor Sickel, *Acta regum et imperatorum Karolinorum* (Vienna, 1867), II, 224; M² 125; Bruckner, *Regesta*, pp. 133-4, no. 219; and *GP*, III. 3, 45-6. See Bruckner, *Regesta*, nos. 60, 67, 76, 442, 462 and 475 for other tithe-forgeries concerning Ebersheim.
[7] MGH, *Dipl. Karol.* no. 236; Bruckner, *Regesta*, p. 185, no. 295.
[8] Cf. the forgeries cited in case I in the Appendix.
[9] *Fulda*, pp. 25-32, nos. 15-16; cf. Michael Tangl, 'Die Fuldaer Privilegienfrage', *MIÖG*, xx (1899), 210-15; Konrad Lübeck, 'Die Exemtion des Klosters Fulda bis zur Mitte des 11. Jahrhunderts', *SMGBOZ*, LV (1937), 134-41; and Goetting, in *A. f. Urk.* XIV, 107-14.

in 823 recognized that this interpolated version was forged, but it was accepted as authentic by Pope Leo IV in 855 and confirmed by many later privileges.[1] Meanwhile the monks also forged a grant from Pepin the Short incorporating passages from the interpolated version of the 751 bull[2] and a record of a council of Aachen at which Charlemagne recognized the abbey's right to hold tithes despite the protests of several bishops.[3] The need to create these forgeries reveals the weakness of Fulda's claims to tithes, as Lübeck stressed;[4] but they effectively protected the large number of tithes held by the monks.

References to monastic tithes were also inserted into literary and historical texts. In the late tenth or early eleventh century, for instance, a monk at the abbey of St Hubert in the Ardennes wrote a life of the Irish hermit St Monon and included an account of Pepin the Short's visit to the saint's shrine at Nassogne and his gift of his jewelled hat and 'the tithes which he held between the [rivers] Ourthe and Lesse, of which the community at Nassogne still holds a part but has lost the rest owing to the guile of evil usurpers'.[5] The monks of St Hubert later became involved in a

[1] *PL*, cxxix, 999–1001; JE 2605; Santifaller, *Elenco*, p. 256 (dated 850); cf. Tangl, in *MIÖG*, xx, 229 ff.; *Fulda*, pp. 28–32; and Lübeck, in *SMGBOZ*, lv, 141 and 153.

[2] *Fulda*, pp. 39–43, no. 20. This forgery was dated about 809/11 by Tangl, in *MIÖG*, xx, 249, and about the middle of the ninth century (before 843) by Stengel, in *Fulda*. In 943 it was accepted as authentic.

[3] Tangl, in *MIÖG*, xx, 241–8. In this record Charlemagne was said to have cited the charters of Zachary (751) and Pepin and to have decreed 'ut prefati sancti loci videlicet Bonifacii et monachi supra statutam atque necessariam prebendam haberent decimas ex suis villulis...'.

[4] Lübeck, in *SMGBOZ*, lv, 140: 'Bezeichnend für die Rechtsunsicherheit der kirchenzehntlichen Lage Fuldas ist es nun, dass man hier spätestens um 822 das Exemtionsprivileg den Bedürfnissen entsprechend überarbeitete, um es im Kampfe um das Zehntrecht ausspielen und verwerten zu können.'

[5] *Vita s. Mononis*, in *AASS*, Oct. viii, 367–8. This version Vb is shorter than the version Vf printed by Albert Poncelet, 'Passio S. Mononis', *Analecta Bollandiana*, v (1886), 205, but it is probably earlier, according to L. van der Essen, *Étude critique et littéraire sur les Vitae des saints mérovingiens de l'ancienne Belgique*, Université de Louvain: Recueil de travaux publiés par les membres des conférences d'histoire et de philologie, xvii (Louvain–Paris, 1907), pp. 144–9. Poncelet, on the other hand, believed that the longer version (Vf) was earlier and was written in the first half of the eleventh century. The *terminus ad quem*

dispute with the count of Namur over the tithes of Amberloux and invented a legend tracing their origins to the Roman camp at Ambra and supporting their claim to the entire domain of Amberloux. This 'legend' then served as the basis for an alleged grant by Pepin II in 687 and was inserted into the chronicle of St Hubert written in the first half of the twelfth century.[1] In these cases, like that of Fulda, the monks' claims to the tithes in question were certainly ancient and probably justified, though without written evidence; and they serve as a reminder that many forgeries were made to defend authentic rights.

In one way or another many monks were thus able to establish their legal and customary right to tithes, but in theory monastic possession of tithes was still forbidden. Walafrid Strabo and Ralph of Bourges both maintained that tithes might be used to support meditation and prayerful intercession for the whole Christian community, which were performed by monks as well as clerics, but they never asserted the right of monks to receive tithes, and all authorities were agreed in principle that tithes must be paid to the parish priests, even if the bishops later assigned them to monasteries. Many transactions involving monastic tithes, furthermore, were certainly simoniacal. 'God forbid, brethren,' said a priest to the monks of St Denis when they tried to sell him some tithes, probably in the late ninth century, 'that other ecclesiastics and religious men should hear that the monks of the monastery of St Denis sought to sell the tithe in order that they might buy damnation with the proceeds.' He none the less sent two hundred shillings to the abbey for prayers to be said for his memory.[2]

In some areas, such as Italy and England, the rights of the parish

for the forgery is determined by the fact that Nassogne depended on St Hubert from the ninth to the eleventh century. Cf. also Baudouin de Gaiffier, 'Les revendications de biens dans quelques documents hagiographiques du XIe siècle', *Analecta Bollandiana*, L (1932), 127.

[1] Godefroid Kurth, 'Les premiers siècles de l'abbaye de Saint-Hubert', *Compte rendu des séances de la Commission royale d'histoire*, 5th ser. VIII (1898), 15–23; Van der Essen, *Étude*, pp. 113 and 119–20; and De Gaiffier, in *Anal. Boll.* L, 137.

[2] Flodoard, *Historia Remensis ecclesiae*, III, 25, in MGH, SS, XIII, 537–8.

churches seem to have been better protected than in others.[1] In the East the control of the bishop over tithes was also occasionally asserted and even confirmed in royal charters. Bishop Berno of Mâcon in 929 concluded a charter granting several churches with their revenues to Cluny with the statement that 'Those who read or hear this charter should know that our see considers it legal by ancient custom to do this with our tithes'.[2] The Emperor Henry II confirmed 'the free disposition over the tithes in his diocese' of the bishop of Brandenburg in 1010; and in 1013 he confirmed the tithes of the see of Hildesheim and established that, 'no tithes of the diocese shall be taken from the authority of the cathedral and the power of the bishop for the sake of new churches or monasteries'; and in a charter of 1018 he mentioned that the bishop of Liège had consented to a grant of tithes to the abbey of St Adalbert at Aachen.[3] Conrad II in 1025 confirmed that the bishop of Passau held all the tithes in the East Mark north of the Danube,[4] and Henry III and several later emperors helped various bishops in their efforts to recover tithes from the hands of monks.[5]

Even in France, where monastic possession of tithes was probably most extensive in the ninth and tenth centuries, the bishops disapproved in principle of any alienation of tithes,[6] and their

[1] Cf. p. 42 above and Boyd, *Tithes*, p. 81, who said that 'By the end of the ninth century the tithe [in Italy] was recognized as the adjunct of the baptismal font, and any derogations from this rule were known to be exceptions'.

[2] *Cluny*, I, 350–1, no. 373.

[3] MGH, *Dipl.* Henry II, nos. 223, 256b, and 392. The *Fundatio ecclesiae Hildensemensis*, II, in MGH, *SS*, XXX, 943, specifically cited the decree of the council of Mainz in 813 forbidding the transfer of tithes from old to new churches (see p. 40 above).

[4] MGH, *Dipl.* Conrad II, no. 47.

[5] See MGH, *Dipl.* Henry III, no. 61, by which Henry III in 1040 helped the archbishop of Mainz to recover some tithes from Kaufungen, and also some of the controversies cited p. 74 above.

[6] Cf. Imbart de la Tour, in *Rev. hist.* LXVIII, 21, and Thomas, *Droit*, p. 69, who said that 'L'effort principal de la législation ecclésiastique porta surtout contre l'accaparement des oblations et des dîmes par les propriétaires et fondateurs'. In a letter written about 1026 to the archbishop of Sens and the clergy of Paris, Fulbert of Chartres bitterly attacked an archdeacon who had alienated some tithes and oblations to a layman (*RHGF*, x, 477–8).

opposition seems to have come to a head at the council of St Denis in 993.[1] Not much is known about this council, but it was a forum for the growing hostility of the great regional prelates, led by Bishop Arnulf of Orléans, against the monasteries, which were defended by Abbo of Fleury. Abbo's biographer Aimoin of Fleury wrote that the assembled bishops 'talked of nothing but the tithes of the churches, which they tried to take away from laymen and from the monks who serve God, and in this the venerable servant of God Abbo opposed them'.[2] The council ended with an undignified expulsion of the bishops by the supporters of the monks, who were later officially condemned, as Gerbert wrote in a letter to Arnulf of Orléans.[3]

The monks had a strong champion in Abbo of Fleury, however. He spoke for the papacy as well as for the monastic order, and he approached the question of monastic tithes for almost the first time from a theoretical as well as a practical point of view. His exact arguments at the council of St Denis are not known, but in his *Apology to Kings Hugh and Robert of France* he strongly asserted the superiority of the monastic to the lay and clerical orders and implied that monks were entitled to all the privileges of clerics and laymen, though he admitted that an ordained monk 'should not serve in ecclesiastical offices in the manner of the clerical order but should celebrate mass within the congregation

[1] On this council, see Ferdinand Lot, *Études sur le règne de Hugues Capet et la fin du Xe siècle*, Bibliothèque de l'École des Hautes Études, CXLVII (Paris, 1903), p. 88 n. 1; Hefele–Leclercq, *Conciles*, IV. 2, 1403–6; Dumas, in *Histoire de l'Église*, VII, 287; Lemarignier, in *À Cluny*, pp. 307–8 (and the review by Charles Dereine, in *Rev. d'hist. ecc.* XLVI, 767–70); and Patrice Cousin, *Abbon de Fleury-sur-Loire* (Paris, 1954), pp. 131–4 (esp. 132 n. 3, and 134 n. 7, on the date). The council was certainly important, but it is probably an exaggeration to call it the start of systematic episcopal agitation against monastic and lay possession of tithes, as does Ernst Sackur, *Die Cluniacenser* (Halle a. S. 1892–4), I, 285.

[2] *Vita s. Abbonis*, IX, in *PL*, CXXXIX, 396; cf. Ch. Pfister, *Études sur le règne de Robert le Pieux (996–1031)*, Bibliothèque de l'École des Hautes Études, LXIV (Paris, 1885), pp. 314–15.

[3] This condemnation may have taken place at the council of Chelles in 993/4: see *Lettres de Gerbert (983–997)*, ed. Julien Havet, Collection de textes pour servir à l'étude et à l'enseignement de l'histoire, VI (Paris, 1889), pp. 175–8, ep. 190, and Hefele–Leclercq, *Conciles*, IV. 2, 873.

as established by the privilege of [Pope] Gregory'.[1] In his letter to 'G.', however, Abbo went rather further. First he bitterly attacked the fact that laymen used ecclesiastical revenues and that 'By judgement of the bishops, ecclesiastical oblations are of greater use to the horses and dogs of laymen than to pilgrims, orphans, and widows, and to the restoration of churches'.[2] To take away the revenue of a church, he said, is as bad as to divide the two natures of Christ. A bishop in his diocese, like a king in his realm, must preserve the rights of others when controlling the Church's property and tithes, which belong not to him but to Christ. The bishop may keep for himself or give away a quarter or a third of the tithes but may only supervise the distribution of the remainder.[3] Abbo then continued that a monk also may not receive ecclesiastical revenues and oblations 'unless he is promoted to the clerical order' and performs the offices in a church.[4] The word 'unless' here is very important, for although in other respects Abbo's position was a restatement of the traditional doctrine for the distribution of ecclesiastical revenues and a conservative protest against the abuses of the tenth century, on this point he suggested the argument, later much debated, that ordained monks who serve churches were entitled to receive tithes.

These points were doubtless lost on the angry bishops at the council of St Denis, but they show generally the heightened prestige of the monastic order in the post-Carolingian period and specifically the growing opinion that monks might legitimately

[1] *PL*, cxxxix, 463–5; cf. Tellenbach, *Church*, p. 52 n. 1, and Étienne Delaruelle, 'En relisant le "De institutione regia" de Jonas d'Orléans', *Mélanges... Louis Halphen* (Paris, 1951), p. 190.

[2] *PL*, cxxxix, 441; cf. p. 56 and n. 3 above for Abbo's conservative denial of any share of the tithe to the bishops. The identity of the 'G.' to whom this letter was addressed is not certain: cf. Lemarignier, in *À Cluny*, pp. 309–10, who repeated the suggestion of Mabillon that it might refer to Gauzelin, later abbot of Fleury, and Cousin, *Abbon*, s.n. in index, who proposed Abbot Gauzebert of Tours.

[3] Sackur, *Cluniacenser*, I, 286, was of the opinion that Abbo here made use of the contrast between private law (the bishop's possession of his own share) and public law (his control over the use of the remainder).

[4] *PL*, cxxxix, 442: '...scito quod monachus, nisi ad clericatum promotus, ecclesiae retentis ministeriis, deservire, ne quid de reditibus ejus seu oblationibus vivere debeat et possit.' The editor called this passage 'obscurus...locus', but the general meaning seems clear.

receive any revenue normally paid to the clergy or to laymen. By the eleventh century monasteries even in Italy[1] and England[2]

[1] Cf. Gosso, *Vita economica, passim*, and Boyd, *Tithes*, pp. 263–6, citing mostly later examples. The case between Leno and the bishop of Luni, cited p. 87 below, shows that Leno held tithes at least by 960; and the foundation charter of the abbey of the Saviour at Turin in 1006 included a parish church with its tithes in the endowment: *San Salutore di Torino*, p. 2.

[2] W. H. Frere, who has been followed by other scholars, maintained that in England before 1066 all tithes were paid to the local churches and that the Normans introduced the custom of granting spiritual revenues to monasteries: see his 'Some Vicissitudes of English Parochial History', *Church Quart. Rev.* LXXVI (1913), 319, and 'The Early History of Canons Regular as Illustrated by the Foundation of Barnwell Priory', *Fasciculus Ioanni Willis Clark dictatus* (Cambridge, 1909), pp. 199–200. According to his biographical notice in the *ODCC*, p. 528, however, Frere was 'an advocate of "English" rather than "Roman" forms of ceremonial'; and in his historical works he liked to contrast the ecclesiastical purity of the Anglo-Saxons with the continental abuses introduced by the Normans. In fact there is clear evidence that English monasteries held tithes at least a century before the Norman Conquest: see *Anglo-Saxon Charters*, ed. A. J. Robertson (Cambridge, 1939), pp. 74 and 156, nos. 39 (*c.* 963, Peterborough) and 81 (*c.* 1023, Evesham). The 'God's servants' mentioned in the tenth-century text cited p. 42 n. 2 above were very likely monks. William the Conqueror in 1087/94 confirmed the tithes held by the abbey of St Augustine 'at the time when my father was alive and dead [1035], no matter to whom I subsequently gave the lands from which the tithes came': *Regesta regum Anglo-Normannorum*, ed. H. W. C. Davis, Charles Johnson and H. A. Cronne (Oxford, 1913–56), I, 133, no. 57, and R. C. van Caenegem, *Royal Writs in England from the Conquest to Glanvill*, Selden Society, LXXVII (London, 1959), pp. 444–5, no. 64. Frere himself cited a passage from Domesday Book: 'Of Stori, Walter de Aincurt's predecessor, it is said that without anyone's leave he could make for himself a church on his own land and in his own soc and could assign his own tithes where he wished': *Domesday Book*, ed. A. Farley and H. Ellis (London, 1783–1816), I, 280, and F. M. Stenton, in *The Victoria County History of Derby* (London, 1905 ff.), I, 304 and 328. Since Stori was certainly an Englishman, this passage does not support Frere but proves on the contrary that laymen in England had free disposition of their tithes before 1066. It is probable, however, that the number of tithes given to monasteries increased greatly after 1066, as the grants to Belvoir, Lewes, St Gregory at Canterbury, Stoke-by-Clare (a dependency of Bec), Lyre, and many other houses suggest: see *Monasticon*, III, 288–9; *Cluny*, IV, 692, no. 3561; *St Gregory, Canterbury*, pp. 1–3; F. M. Stenton, *The First Century of English Feudalism, 1066–1166*, The Ford Lectures, 1929 (Oxford, 1932), p. 270; F. S. Hockey, 'The Pattern of the Tithes in the Isle of Wight', *Proceedings of the Hampshire Field Club*, XXI (1960), 147–8; etc. According to Reginald Lennard, *Rural England, 1086–1135* (Oxford, 1959), p. 300, 'The Norman landowners exercised a large discretion in the disposal of their tithes and very commonly gave the two-thirds to a monastery either in Normandy or England'.

often owned tithes, and in France and Germany probably most monasteries derived at least some of their income from tithes. The revenues of monks, bishops, priests, and laymen became almost inextricably intertwined; and tithes that had been divided among several owners and passed on by gift, sale, inheritance, and subinfeudation were often impossible to recover for the ecclesiastical patrimony. 'It is now established as law by common usage', as Maiolus of Cluny said in the middle of the tenth century, 'that any ecclesiastical property may be granted for a rent to anyone, even to laymen, by authority of a charter.'[1] The situation of tithes was therefore a perfect microcosm of the confusion of sacred and secular affairs against which the great reform in the eleventh century was directed.

2. THE POLICY OF THE REFORMED PAPACY

During the Investiture Controversy both popes and bishops took up the problem of misused and secularized tithes. Already in the early eleventh century, according to Brooke, local reformers began to work 'on the two principal evils of simony and clerical marriage, and on some of the abuses that resulted from lay patronage, especially over smaller benefices, such as the holding of tithes by the laity'.[2] The pope and cardinals took over this programme with the reform of the papacy in the middle of the century. In the case of tithes and other *spiritualia*, unlike church revenues with no peculiarly sacred character, the issue of simony was even more important than the financial loss to the Church; and the reformers were more concerned with the recovery of tithes from the hands of laymen than with their ultimate disposition. Many recovered tithes were consequently given, often in accord with the wishes of the previous owner, to monasteries rather than to the parish priests to whom they properly belonged.[3]

---

[1] See p. 4 above.
[2] Z. N. Brooke, *The English Church and the Papacy from the Conquest to the Reign of John* (Cambridge, 1931), p. 25.
[3] See p. 66 above.

This practice was also promoted, as Boyd stressed, by the desire of the reformers to assist the monastic order and by the prevailing view that the bishop might dispose of any part of the tithe except the quarter or third owed to the parish priest. It gave rise, however, she said, to some 'strange anomalies [and] aberrations from canon law'.[1]

The first concern of the reformers was to reassert the spiritual nature of tithes, which had been generally disregarded, if not forgotten, in the two previous centuries, and to stress the obligation to pay and the dangers of misusing tithes.[2] Pope Alexander II even maintained that anyone who refused to pay tithes could not be called a Christian.[3] Peter Damian wrote that giving tithes to laymen was like giving them a deadly poison.[4] And Paschal II said that first-fruits, tithes, and oblations belonged exclusively to the Church and that 'to give *altaria* or tithes for money and to sell the Holy Spirit is the heresy of simony',[5] which at this time was accounted not simply a breach of discipline but an aberration of faith.[6] Any purchase or sale of ecclesiastical property might involve this sin. The Church cannot be divided from its property, as Abbo said in the tenth century. And the school of Laon in the twelfth century held that 'Those who purchase ecclesiastical benefices, which are temporal property, also purchase the spiritual things in them, for the temporalities are joined to the spiritualities

[1] Boyd, *Tithes*, p. 119 (and pp. 103–28 generally).

[2] Thomas, *Droit*, p. 88, was of the opinion that 'the idea of the tithe as a spiritual right' appeared only in the twelfth century, but this is certainly much too late.

[3] JL 4577 (a fragment from a letter to Archbishop Siegfried of Mainz in 1065 preserved in the canonical collection of Cardinal Deusdedit).

[4] Peter Damian, ep. IV, 12, in *PL*, CXLIV, 324.

[5] Fragments from two letters of uncertain date from Paschal II are preserved in several canonical collections, including one in *Decretum*, C. I, q. III, c. 14, and printed in *PL*, CLXIII, 436–7; JL 6598 and 6607; cf. Viard, *Dîme*, I, 190–1, and Schreiber, *Kurie*, I, 285–6.

[6] See Jean Leclercq, 'Simoniaca heresis', *Studi Gregoriani*, I (1947), 523–30. Cf. p. 89 n. 4 below, where Gregory VII and Manegold of Lautenbach threatened with eternal damnation any lay possessor of tithes. An anonymous Spanish text from the eleventh century compared a layman who sold tithes to Judas: Guillermo Antolín, 'El Códice emilianense de la biblioteca de el Escorial', *La Ciudad de Dios*, LXXIII (1907), 115.

like the body to the soul, and he who buys or sells one cannot leave the other unbought or unsold'.[1]

This policy was put into effect by a series of papal decrees forbidding lay possession and sale of tithes and enforced by reforming bishops and papal envoys all over Europe.[2] Leo IX touched on the problem at the council of Rome in April 1049.[3] But he seems to have first fully realized the gravity of the situation on his travels north of the Alps later that year, and in October at the council of Rheims he specifically forbade lay possession of ecclesiastical revenues.[4] At the great council of Rome in April 1050, he issued a decree requiring all laymen to return the revenues of churches to their priests and to allow the payment of tithes to the sacramental clergy.[5]

The only evidence for this decree is in two documents issued for the abbey of Marmoutier, probably late in 1050, by the Cardinal Airard, who was abbot of St Paul Outside the Walls at Rome and bishop of Nantes from 1050 until 1059.[6]

Since in France more than elsewhere [he wrote] the wicked custom has grown up that ecclesiastical revenues, tithes, and oblations are usurped

[1] Odon Lottin, *Psychologie et morale aux XIIe et XIIIe siècles*, v: *Problèmes d'histoire littéraire: L'École d'Anselme de Laon et de Guillaume de Champeaux* (Gembloux, 1959), p. 440.

[2] The practical distinction between *spiritualia* and *temporalia* was not always clear: cf. W. E. Lunt, *The Valuation of Norwich* (Oxford, 1926), pp. 75–8, citing examples principally from the thirteenth century; but in spite of some reservations, tithes and oblations were after the eleventh century commonly considered the classical form of *spiritualia*, as was stressed by William Stubbs, *The Constitutional History of England* (Oxford, 1903), II, 179–80. It may be, as Viard, *Dîme*, I, 246–7, suggested, that the absence of lay possession of tithes in the Crusader states was a result of the policy of the papacy in the eleventh and twelfth centuries.

[3] Hefele–Leclercq, *Conciles*, IV. 2, 1008.   [4] *Ibid.* 1019.

[5] *Ibid.* 1040–55, esp. 1052, on this council generally. The evidence cited below leaves little doubt that this decree was issued at this council, though it is not among the published canons.

[6] See René Blanchard, 'Airard et Quiriac, évêques de Nantes (1050–1079)', *Revue de Bretagne, de Vendée et d'Anjou*, XIII (1895), 242; *La chronique de Nantes*, ed. René Merlet, Collection de textes pour servir à l'étude et à l'enseignement de l'histoire, XIX (Paris, 1896), introd. pp. xxxiii–xxxvi; and Basilio Trifone, 'Serie dei prepositi, rettori ed abbati di San Paolo di Roma', *Rivista storica benedettina*, IV (1909), 246–7.

by others than the ministers of the churches to which they rightly belong and sustenance is evilly transferred from the clergy to laymen and from the poor to the rich, the pope of Rome, Leo by name, issued a decree that all laymen must under pain of excommunication give up the revenues of churches to their ministers and allow the tithes of altars to be paid, in accordance with the Apostle, to those who serve them. When word of this decree spread, some men humbly obeyed the apostolic orders, others proudly held back.

At this time Airard became bishop of Nantes, according to his own account, and published this decree 'which had been recently promulgated in a council at Rome', and many tithes and oblations were returned to the Church. In one charter Airard then confirmed the grant of a church to Marmoutier;[1] and in the other he approved a grant of several churches, some to be held directly by the abbey and others in mediate tenure by both priests and laymen, given by Rodald of Pellerin, 'who set an example to others and gave up everything he possessed and left it to me what to do with it, and I gave it all, just as it had been given to me, to St Martin and the monks of Marmoutier...'. He confirmed in advance, furthermore, any future grant or sale to the monks, providing that the synodal due was paid.[2] Rodald's own charter of donation, approved by both his overlord the count of Nantes and by Bishop Airard, laid down the specific terms of the grant, which were omitted in Airard's charter, and stipulated that the bishop and the abbot should arrange jointly for the support of the priests in the churches.[3]

Yet another charter from the diocese of Nantes recorded that Bishop Airard, 'who tried to restore to their proper recipient the tithe taken from the Church in his diocese', threatened to excommunicate a layman named Simon of St Opportune, who had

---

[1] Hyacinthe Morice, *Mémoires pour servir de preuves à l'histoire ecclésiastique et civile de Bretagne* (Paris, 1742–6), I, 402–3. The quoted passage served as a long arenga to this charter.

[2] Mabillon, *Annales*, IV, 680, from which the text of the cited passages is taken; cf. Blanchard, in *Revue de Bretagne*, XIII, 244–5 on these documents.

[3] Morice, *Mémoires*, I, 383–4; cf. Blanchard, in *Revue de Bretagne*, XIII, 243–4. There are two versions of this charter, one witnessed by Airard and the other not.

previously given to the monks of St Aubin at Angers all his altar
and burial dues and half of his demesne tithes from both cultivated
and uncultivated lands in the parish of St Opportune,[1] and who
now 'surrendered to the bishop the half of the tithes which he had
kept in the previous gift; and the bishop restored them to
St Aubin'.[2] Airard's zeal naturally did not endear him to the local
magnates, and in 1059 he was forced out of office and replaced by
a brother of the count of Nantes.[3] His policy clearly shows, however, not only the determination of the reformers at Rome to
recover spiritual revenues from lay hands but also their willingness to grant these *spiritualia* to monasteries.

A more direct statement of papal policy with regard to monastic
tithes is found in a little-known privilege from Nicholas II for the
abbey of Leno in 1060. It includes an account of a case over tithes
between the bishop of Luni, who maintained that 'according to
canon law all tithes are in the power of the bishop', and the abbot
of Leno, who complained that the bishop had taken the tithes
held by his abbey for over a century and who took the case before
a papal council at Rome. After hearing both sides, 'the cardinal-
bishops said that they had attended councils where the late
Popes Leo and Victor had confirmed the statutes of the Fathers
that whoever had held tithes or any ecclesiastical property in
peace for forty or thirty years might for ever hold them securely
on that basis; but they should not in any way take recent tithes
from the bishoprics'. They therefore decided 'that the abbey
should hold the disputed tithe for ever and in peace. For if a
possession of thirty or forty years should be confirmed, a possession
of a century should be yet more secure, so that even if the bishop
thought he had older privileges, the rights of the abbey would be
secured by its intermediate tenure.'[4] This council was attended by
almost all the most influential members of the curia at that time,

---

[1] Morice, *Mémoires*, I, 387–8; cf. Blanchard, in *Revue de Bretagne*, XIII, 245–6.

[2] Blanchard, in *Revue de Bretagne*, XIII, 341.

[3] *Ibid.* 251–4, and *Chronique de Nantes*, introd. p. xxxvi.

[4] *Leno*, pp. 104–6, no. 18; JL 4431 a; *IP*, VI. 1, 344, no. 3; Santifaller, *Elenco*,
p. 391; cf. Hefele–Leclercq, *Conciles*, IV. 2, 1198. The decrees of Leo IX and
Victor II referred to here are not known, but they were probably issued at
councils like that at Rome in 1050.

including Humbert of Silva Candida, Boniface of Albano, Peter of Ostia, John of Porto, Anselm of Lucca, the imperial chancellor Wibert, Desiderius of Monte Cassino, and Abbot Adraldus of Breme; and among the witnesses to the privilege, which was issued by the famous *notarius et sacri palatii scrinarius* Octavian, were the Archdeacon Hildebrand, Peter Damian, Humbert, Desiderius, and Adraldus.[1] Their decision in this case is, therefore, authoritative evidence that the reform party at Rome, while deprecating the further transfer of tithes out of the control of the bishops, definitely accepted in principle the right of monks to hold tithes which they had held for more than thirty or forty years.[2]

This principle was also accepted by local councils inspired by the reformers. In 1068, for instance, Cardinal Hugh Candidus held a series of councils in the south of France and in Spain.[3] At the council of Auch in the summer of 1068,

they decreed that every church in Gascony should give a quarter of its tithe to its bishop, which they had not done previously. When the lord Abbot Raymond of St Orens [at Auch] heard this, he said that he would not allow the churches of the holy confessor, which had remained free so long, to submit to such a yoke. The cardinal heard this ...and decreed...that for love of the said holy confessor, his churches should remain entirely free from this obligation, as they were in the past.[4]

---

[1] Cf. the list of witnesses to the privilege of Nicholas II for St Peter at Perugia, cited p. 95 below.

[2] This was a well-established principle in canon law and derived from Roman practice: cf. W. W. Buckland, *A Text-Book of Roman Law from Augustus to Justinian*, 2nd ed. (Cambridge, 1932), p. 251.

[3] Franz Lerner, *Kardinal Hugo Candidus*, Beiheft 22 der Historischen Zeitschrift (Munich–Berlin, 1931), pp. 26–31; cf. Gerhard Säbekow, *Die päpstlichen Legationen nach Spanien und Portugal bis zum Ausgang des XII. Jahrhunderts* (Berlin, 1931), pp. 14–15, and Theodor Schieffer, *Die päpstlichen Legaten in Frankreich vom Vertrage von Meersen (870) zum Schisma von 1130*, Historische Studien, ed. Ebering, CCLXIII (Berlin, 1935), pp. 74–5.

[4] *Spicilegium*, I, 625; cf. Hefele–Leclercq, *Conciles*, IV. 2, 1267. The council held at Gerona later that year even required the clergy to pay tithes: Mansi, *Collectio*, XIX, 1071; Hefele–Leclercq, *Conciles*, IV. 2, 1268; and San Martín, *Diezmo*, pp. 99–100 and 125–6, who attributed the spread of tithes in Spain in the eleventh century both to the Reconquest and to the growing influence of the papacy.

Here again custom made law, and the monks were allowed to keep all the tithes of their churches.

This indiscriminate confirmation of established holdings of monastic tithes, however, and the grants to monasteries of many tithes recovered from laymen, were prejudicial to the finances and the authority of the bishops, and as time went on the reformers increasingly emphasized the canonical principles of division and of episcopal control over tithes. As early as 1056 a council at Toulouse, presided over by two papal legates, decreed that churches belonging to monasteries and laymen must pay one-third of their tithes, first-fruits, and oblations to the bishop and priests.[1] In 1068 the council of Auch passed a similar decree, and in Italy Pope Alexander II settled a dispute between the bishop of Chiusi and his clergy, who accused him of exacting payment for spiritual services, on the basis that the bishop owed only one quarter of the tithe to the clergy and might himself distribute the other three quarters.[2] Under Pope Gregory VII the reform programme became more rigid and sharply defined in theory, and according to Boyd, 'The most striking feature of Roman legislation of the Gregorian period in regard to the tithes is its emphasis upon episcopal jurisdiction...'.[3] At his Roman synod in 1078 Gregory issued decrees not only against lay possession of tithes, 'which the canons teach have been granted for pious uses',[4] but also against

---

[1] 1056 Toulouse, can. X–XI, in Mansi, *Collectio*, XIX, 847; cf. Hefele–Leclercq, *Conciles*, IV. 2, 1122–3.

[2] *APRI*, II, 108–9; JL 4657; *IP*, III, 233, no. 9; Santifaller, *Elenco*, p. 408.

[3] Boyd, *Tithes*, p. 122; cf. Thomassin, *Discipline*, III, I, 10.5–7, *ed. cit.* VI, 48–50.

[4] *Register Gregors VII.*, p. 404, no. VI, 5b, can. 7 (16) = *Decretum*, C. XVI, q. VII, c. I: 'Decimas quas in usum pietatis concessas esse canonica auctoritas demonstrat, possideri a laicis apostolica auctoritate prohibemus.' For laymen to hold tithes, Gregory went on, is an act of sacrilege and incurs the risk of damnation. Tithes must be paid to the priests and distributed in accordance with the instructions of the bishops. Cf. *Register*, pp. 579–80, no. IX, 5: a letter to the legates Hugh of Die and Amatus of Oléron in which Gregory praised William the Conqueror for forcing laymen to give up their tithes but advised them not to excommunicate laymen who were otherwise well-disposed towards the Church but refused to pay tithes. This suggests that Gregory regarded the recovery of tithes from lay possession as a more pressing problem than non-payment of tithes. Manegold of Lautenbach commented on Gregory's policy

monastic possession without episcopal consent. 'No abbot should hold tithes, first-fruits, or other revenues which belong to the bishops according to canon law without the authority of the pope or the consent of the bishop in whose diocese he lives.'[1] This prohibition was included in the canonical collections of Anselm of Lucca and Cardinal Deusdedit.[2]

Both the causes and the results of this reassertion of episcopal control over tithes were explained in a letter to the abbot of Molesme from the papal chancellor John of Gaeta, the future Pope Gelasius II.

The canons establish that all ecclesiastical property is in the hand of the bishop. But in former times lay rulers were allowed to give even churches to monasteries, and they used this permission so freely that they even sold churches to monks. Pope Gregory VII firmly forbade this, and consequently the bishops began vigorously to despoil the monasteries....Pope Urban [therefore] ordered at the council of Melfi that whatever the rulers had given to the monasteries up to that time should remain firm and untouched, but abbots should refrain from further acquisitions of this sort....By this compromise henceforth both abbots should no longer invade churches and bishops should in no way seek to despoil monasteries.[3]

The actual decree issued by Urban II at Melfi in 1089 forbade any layman 'to give his tithes, church, or any ecclesiastical property to a monastery or house of canons without the consent of the bishop or the permission of the pope. If a bishop withholds his

towards tithes in his *Ad Gebehardum liber*, written probably in the late eleventh century. Manegold was described by Lottin as a 'polémiste violent, défenseur acharné de la politique grégorienne contre l'Empire' (*Psychologie et Morale*, v, 147). But in this respect he denied that Gregory sought to remove all ecclesiastical property from the possession of laymen: 'Nam nusquam beneficiorum mentionem fecit, sed decimas tantum, quas tam sub lege quam sub gratia ad usus tantum pietatis concessas divina testatur auctoritas, a laicis possideri prohibuit, nec diffinita sententia interdixit, sed quantum periculum, quanta dampnatio esset, indicavit': MGH, *Libelli*, I, 399. Manegold was clearly referring here to the decree of 1078, but he definitely weakened its intention. It was repeated by several later councils, including one published in *APRI*, II, 167–8, can. III, as the acts of a Lateran synod in 1097, but which may in fact have derived from the council of 1139, according to Hefele–Leclercq, *Conciles*, v. 1, 453–6.

[1] *Register Gregors VII.*, p. 405, no. VI, 5 b, can. 9 (25).
[2] *Ibid.* p. 405 n. 3.   [3] Mansi, *Collectio*, xx, 726.

consent on account of dishonesty or avarice, the pope should be informed and the grant made with his permission.'[1] At the council of Clermont in 1095 Urban again confirmed episcopal control over tithes. Not all the acts of this council have survived, but the seventh canon decreed 'That *altaria* which have been given to congregations of canons and monks by priests (*per personas*) should return freely into the hands of the bishop when the priests die, unless they are confirmed to them by an episcopal charter or privilege'.[2]

In spite of the safeguard of appeal to the papacy, which was guaranteed by the council of Melfi, it is clear that the bishops tended to abuse these rights of control over tithes and sometimes even forced monasteries to 'ransom' their possessions when the donors died. This practice was the subject of an interesting statute which is attributed in several sources to the council of Clermont, though it is not among the published acts of this council.[3] In a manuscript from Aniane, it appears among the canons of Clermont and says that:

[1] Mansi, *Collectio*, XX, 723. This canon was repeated by the council at Rome in 1099 as canon 15, *ibid.* XX, 963–4, and included in the *Decretum*, C. XVI, q. VII, c. 39. Either the council of Melfi or the council at Piacenza in 1095 may also have repeated the decree of the council of Chalon-sur-Saône in 813 on the payment of tithes by the clergy (see p. 38 above), but the authenticity of this canon has been seriously questioned by Hefele–Leclercq, *Conciles*, V. I, 344–5.

[2] Mansi, *Collectio*, XX, 817 (can. 7). The passage cited in the following paragraph shows that the *personae* here means 'priests'. The purpose of this canon was therefore to prevent the dissipation of parochial revenues without episcopal permission. On the loss of the acts of this council, see Hefele–Leclercq, *Conciles*, V. I, 399.

[3] There are several versions of this text (cf. JL, I, 681, *post* no. 5586), and all are attributed to the council of Clermont: Pierre de Marca, *De concordia sacerdotii et imperii*, 4th ed. (Frankfurt, 1708), pp. 959–60 (from a manuscript of the acts of the council of Clermont at Aniane); *Lérins*, I, 307 and *La Trinité de Vendôme*, II, 119–20, both headed: 'Questum est de episcopis qui altaria monasteriis data frequenter redimi compellebant'; *Decretum*, C. I, q. III, c. 4, with the same heading as in the chartularies except that *pecunia* is added after *redimi*. The canon was re-enacted at the council of Nîmes in 1096 as a statute of Clermont: Mansi, *Collectio*, XX, 933 (can. 1); cf. JL, I, 688, *post* no. 5650. Paschal II also referred to it as a decree of the council of Clermont in a letter written in 1100: PL, CLXIII, 36; JL 5820. On the so-called *rachat des autels*, see L. Compain, *Étude sur Geoffroi de Vendôme*, Bibliothèque de l'École des Hautes Études, LXXXVI (Paris, 1891), pp. 184–6.

Since in France a certain type of simony has long flourished by which churches and tithes (which they commonly call *altaria*), having been given to monasteries, are often through concealed avarice sold by the bishops when the priests (whom they call *personas*) are dead or changed, we expel in the name of God all venality from the property and from the ministers of the Church and by apostolic authority forbid this to be done any more, just as we forbid the sale of prebends. We confirm henceforth for monasteries the peaceful and unmolested possession of any *altaria* or tithes they are known to have held by this sort of transaction for thirty years or more, saving the annual rent which bishops are accustomed to have from these altars.

Both the nature and wording of this decree suggest that it was a modification of the seventh canon of Clermont, and it was issued probably at or soon after the council and re-enacted at Nîmes the following year. It shows that Urban definitely accepted the principle of prescription with respect to monastic tithes and tried to steer a middle course between the dangers of uncontrolled transfers of tithes to monks and the possible abuses of episcopal control.

Urban made a similar attempt in his bull for Cluny in 1095 by setting up the statute of Gregory VII as a dividing line before which he confirmed all altars, churches, and tithes held by the monks, and after which he confirmed only those acquired with the consent of the bishop.[1] Pope Paschal II, who was himself a Cluniac monk, firmly instructed the archbishop of Bologna to prevent the usurpation of churches and tithes by monks without permission either of the diocesan bishop or of the pope.[2] And in a letter to the bishop of Grenoble he confirmed the bishop's authority over both the clergy and the church property, including tithes, in his diocese.[3] The ninth ecumenical council in 1123 even forbade monasteries to establish a right to ecclesiastical property by prescription of thirty years, but this apparently applied only to property acquired since the time of Gregory VII.[4] Later in the

---

[1] *Bull. Clun.* pp. 26–7; JL 5602; Santifaller, *Elenco*, p. 457.
[2] *PL*, CLXIII, 439; JL 6616 = *Decretum*, C. XVI, q. I, c. 9.
[3] *Grenoble*, p. 236, no. C 101; JL 6489 (dated 1100/17).
[4] Hefele–Leclercq, *Conciles*, v. I, 633 (can. 8) and 637 (can. 19).

twelfth century both Gratian and Alexander III lent their high authority to the doctrine that monks might acquire tithes and churches from laymen only by permission of the bishop.[1]

Local councils and individual bishops also tried to keep control over restorations of tithes by laymen and grants to monasteries. Archbishop Rainald of Rheims (1038–96), for example, made every effort, in his own words, 'to restore to ecclesiastical persons the *altaria* which our predecessors negligently granted to laymen and to give them, when they have been freed from the unrighteous bondage to laymen, in accordance with canon law to some servants of God', who included monks as well as priests.[2] A synod at Poitiers in 1100 forbade clerics and monks under pain of excommunication 'to acquire *altaria* or tithes from laymen or priests in return for money'.[3] A council at London in 1102 decreed 'That monks should not accept churches except through the bishops and should not take the revenues of their churches so that the priests who serve them lack what they need for themselves and their churches'.[4] A council at Toulouse in 1119

[1] *Decretum*, C. xvi, q. vii, c. 39; cf. C. xvi, q. i, c. 68 and Alexander III, JL 14015, in Comp. i, iii, 26, 1.

[2] *Cluny*, v, 8, no. 3661, in the arenga to a charter of 1091 granting to Cluny an altar previously held by laymen (cf. *Rev. bén.* lxx, 597). The bishop of Grenoble in the late eleventh century put under interdict any lay possessors of tithes and refused to bury their bodies until their heirs gave up the tithes: *Grenoble*, p. 148, no. B 86 (*c.* 1090). On the efforts of the archbishops of Salzburg and the bishops of Passau to establish their control over the tithes in Styria and Carinthia and in lower Austria respectively, see Tremel, in *Zs. d. hist. Vereines f. Steiermark*, xxxiii, 8–9, and Plöchl, *Zehentwesen*, pp. 29–32. In Belgium in the twelfth and thirteenth centuries there was 'une véritable politique ayant pour but d'obtenir des laïques l'abandon des églises et des biens qui en dépendaient, notamment des dîmes', according to E. de Moreau, *Histoire de l'Église en Belgique*, 2nd ed. (Brussels, 1945 ff.), iii, 384.

[3] Mansi, *Collectio*, xx, 1123 (can. 9); cf. Hefele–Leclercq, *Conciles*, v.1, 470.

[4] David Wilkins, *Concilia Magnae Britanniae et Hiberniae* (London, 1737), i, 383 (can. 22); cf. Hefele–Leclercq, *Conciles*, v. 1, 476–8. Similar decrees forbidding monks and clerics to receive any church, tithe, or ecclesiastical benefice from a layman without permission of the bishop were issued by the council of London in 1125, can. 4, and the council of Westminster in 1127, can. 10: see *The Chronicle of John of Worcester 1118–1140*, ed. J. R. H. Weaver, Anecdota Oxoniensia, iv, 13 (Oxford, 1908), pp. 20 and 25; cf. Hefele–Leclercq, *Conciles*, v. 1, 658 and 667.

forbade anyone to take the quarter of the tithes and oblations that belonged to the bishop.[1] And in 1128 the Cluniac cardinal-legate Matthew of Albano presided over a council at Rouen, held under the auspices of King Henry I, that decreed:

That monks and abbots may not receive churches or tithes directly from laymen (*de manu laicorum*); but the laymen should restore their usurpations to the bishop, and at their request the monks may receive the offerings from the bishop. Because of the papal indulgence they may keep in peace whatever they have previously obtained in any way, but they may not usurp anything more of this sort without the permission of the bishop in whose diocese it is located.[2]

The effects of this policy can be seen in the histories of several individual monasteries. As early as 1070 the abbess of Göss in Styria, probably alarmed by the efforts of Archbishop Gebhard of Salzburg to establish his control over the tithes in his diocese, surrendered to him the tithes of her abbey's lands and other property and then received them back.[3] The abbot of Morigny was worried that his predecessors had acquired churches and tithes by purchase as well as by gift, and he surrendered them into the hands of the cardinal-legate Cuno of Palestrina, who visited Morigny in 1120/1, accompanied by the bishop of Chalon-sur-Saône, and he then received the property back.[4] And in the act of consecration of a parish church belonging to the Cluniac abbey of Arles-sur-Tech, in 1142, the bishop of Elne asserted the principle

[1] De Marca, *De concordia*, pp. 1183–4 (can. 7). The text given in Mansi, *Collectio*, XXI, 227, omitted the reference to the fourth part and the tithes and mentioned only 'part of the oblations'. Cf. *Spicilegium*, I, 635–6; JL, I, 783–4; and Hefele–Leclercq, *Conciles*, V. 1, 570–3.

[2] Ordericus Vitalis, *Historia ecclesiastica*, XII, 48, ed. A. Le Prevost and L. Delisle, Société de l'histoire de France (Paris, 1838–55), IV, 496–7; cf. Schieffer, *Legaten*, p. 230. Cf. also *Thesaurus*, IV, 162 BC, for the statute of an anonymous council, probably in the twelfth century, forbidding any monk or cleric to receive a tithe from the hand of a layman except through the hand of a bishop.

[3] *Steiermark*, I, 80–1, no. 69; cf. Tremel, in *Zs. d. hist. Vereines f. Steiermark*, XXXIII, 9.

[4] *La Chronique de Morigny (1095–1152)*, ed. Léon Mirot, 2nd ed., Collection de textes pour servir à l'étude et à l'enseignement de l'histoire, XLI (Paris, 1912), p. 42; cf. G. Schöne, *Kardinallegat Kuno Bischof von Präneste* (Weimar, 1857), pp. 76 ff., and Schieffer, *Legaten*, pp. 210–11.

of canon law that 'Tithes and first-fruits are in the hand of the bishop'.[1]

In practice, however, this control rarely proved a serious obstacle to the acquisition of tithes by monasteries, and the papacy in particular seems to have encouraged monastic possession of tithes. Pope Nicholas II in 1059 even gave the abbey of St Peter at Perugia the tithes from three papal estates, 'from the fields, vines, woods, olive-trees, herds and all animals that pass under the shepherd's staff and, as St Augustine instructs, the tithes from military service, business, and trade, and the first-fruits of all produce'.[2] Confirmations of holdings of tithes became an almost standard part of papal privileges for monasteries in the late eleventh and twelfth centuries. Leo IX, Alexander II, and, in spite of their emphasis on episcopal control over tithes, Gregory VII, Urban II, and Paschal II all confirmed the possession of tithes by monks.[3] Urban II specified for St Jean-des-Vignes in 1089 that 'If some land from which you are accustomed to receive the tithe should pass into other hands, its tithe should still nevertheless be paid to you'.[4] Even as far away as the Holy Land Paschal II in

[1] Marca hispanica, p. 1290; cf. St Martin des Champs, II, 274 (1159/60).

[2] PL, CXLIII, 1325; JL 4413; IP, IV, 69, no. 18; Santifaller, Elenco, p. 388. This privilege, which cites Lev. xxvii. 32 and Caesar of Arles, serm. XXXIII, which was attributed to St Augustine (see p. 17 n. 4 above), was witnessed among others by Peter Damian, Humbert, and Hildebrand, who also appeared on the privilege for Leno in 1060 cited p. 88 above.

[3] Leo IX in 1049 confirmed a forgery attributed to Hadrian I in 776 confirming the tithes of Nonantola (APRI, II, 22-5 and 76-8; JE†2421 and JL 4168; IP, V, 335-40, nos. 4 and 18) and issued an authentic confirmation for Agaune in 1050 (PL, CXLIII, 666; JL 4246); Alexander II for Fruttuaria in 1063 (PL, CXLVI, 1288; JL 4499; IP, VI. 2, 151, no. 9; Santifaller, Elenco, p. 398) and twice for St Mary at Florence (APRI, II, 119, and PL, CXLVI, 1359; JL 4734 and 4678; IP, III, 27, nos. 1-2; Santifaller, Elenco, pp. 417 and 411-12). Gregory VII in 1078 forbade any bishop to usurp the tithes or first-fruits granted by his predecessors to Leno (Leno, p. 107, no. 19; JL 5069; IP, VI. 1, 344, no. 4; Santifaller, Elenco, p. 426). Urban II in 1096 confirmed for St Sernin at Toulouse the oblations of several churches in spite of the claim of the bishop to a quarter (St Sernin de Toulouse, pp. 475-8 and 194-6; JL 5658 and 5660), and in 1098 gave to the monks of Vallès the tithes 'which your monastery has held by permission of our predecessors for over thirty years' (Marca hispanica, p. 1204; JL 5715). Paschal II in 1113 forbade the bishop to sell any tithes belonging to Nonantola (APRI, II, 206; JL 6354).

[4] PL, CLI, 296; JL 5391; Santifaller, Elenco, p. 437.

1103 granted to the monks of Mt Thabor the tithes from their estates which were for the time being held by crusaders.[1] Both Urban and Paschal more than once confirmed in advance, overruling any possible episcopal opposition, the possession of any tithes which an abbey might recover from lay hands.[2] Later this confirmation usually took the standard form, here cited from the privilege of Innocent II for Paulinzelle in 1136, that 'We also confirm for you the tithes which you legitimately possess and have quietly and peacefully possessed up until this time'.[3]

Pope Calixtus II defended monastic possession of tithes on two more serious occasions. The first was at the council of Rheims in 1119, where the archbishop of Lyons and his suffragans protested vigorously against the number of tithes held by Cluny. Abbot Pontius rested his defence on the privileges granted to Cluny by the papacy. 'Let the lord pope, if he wishes,' he said, 'defend his own church and let him support and guard the churches, tithes and other possessions which he himself entrusted to me.' The pope, speaking through Cardinal John of Crema, replied in terms strongly reminiscent of Gregory VII's privilege for Cluny and took all the property of the abbey under his protection.[4] There also arose at this council the well-known dispute, vividly reported by Hesso Scholasticus, over the terms of the canon forbidding lay investiture. 'Some priests and many laymen', according to Hesso, objected to the original formulation of this canon because

---

[1] APRI, II, 181; JL 5948.

[2] Urban II for Schaffhausen in 1095 (PL, CLI, 520; JL 5580; GP, II. 2, 14, no. 8; Santifaller, Elenco, pp. 454–5) and Cluny (Bull. Clun. pp. 26–7; JL 5602; Santifaller, Elenco, p. 457; cf. Rev. bén. LXX, 603). Paschal II for Weingarten in 1105 (Wirtemberg, I, 337; JL 6017; GP, II. 1, 228, no. 3), which was confirmed with insignificant changes by Innocent II in 1143 (Wirtemberg, II, 21–2; JL 8355; GP, II. 1, 228, no. 5). The privileges for Schaffhausen and Weingarten are almost identical: 'Si quas vero decimas pertinentes ecclesiis quas habetis vel habebitis a laicis, annuente domino, recuperare potueritis, vestris proprie usibus mancipandas absque omni episcoporum contradictione censemus, salva episcopali reverentia.'

[3] Paulinzelle, p. 17; JL 7774. Such confirmations often applied to fractions of tithes, like the bull of Innocent II for Münchsmünster in 1138/43 (APRI, II, 321; JL 8171).

[4] Ordericus Vitalis, Hist. ecc. XII, 21, ed. cit. IV, 385–9; cf. the references in Rev. bén. LXX, 605 n. 1.

it not only forbade investiture 'by a lay hand' of churches and
ecclesiastical possessions but also threatened to deprive the holder
of the honour with which he was so invested. It seemed thus that it
was retroactive and 'that by this canon the pope sought to reduce
or take away the tithes and other ecclesiastical benefices which
laymen had held in former times'. In view of these objections,
the pope revised the canon into a simple prohibition of lay
investiture of bishoprics and abbeys, and this was unanimously
approved by the council.[1] The change in the canon therefore
substituted 'bishoprics and abbeys' for 'all churches and ecclesiastical possessions' and omitted the clause depriving the holder
of any honour held by lay investiture. The significance of this
revision is not entirely clear, but it was surely not intended, as
some historians have suggested, to limit the prohibition of lay investiture to high ecclesiastical offices only, and thus to allow laymen
to keep a hold over churches and tithes.[2] It is more likely that the
change was designed to recognize the distinction between the
spiritual offices and temporal possessions of the church, and in
particular to safeguard previous grants to churches and monasteries, even 'by a lay hand', of minor ecclesiastical property once
held by laymen, and to prevent the bishops from hindering or
invalidating direct grants by laymen to priests and monks.[3]

[1] Hesso Scholasticus, *Relatio de concilio Remensi*, in MGH, *Libelli*, III, 27–8.

[2] Cf. Hefele–Leclercq, *Conciles*, V. I, 589; Tellenbach, *Church*, pp. 122–3;
Augustin Fliche, in *Histoire de l'Église*, ed. Fliche and Martin, VIII, 383; Boyd,
Tithes, p. 127. It is important to note that the priests and laymen feared that the
pope planned to take away the tithes and benefices 'quae antiquitus laici
tenuerant', that is, that laymen had held in former times (but did not still hold).
The potential losers under the new decree, therefore, were not the laymen, as
most scholars have suggested, but the churches and monasteries to which the
tithes and benefices had been granted *per manum laicam*.

[3] There is no evidence in Hesso's account that the bishops objected to the
first form of the decree, which would have given them a powerful weapon to
control lay grants to churches and monasteries. A retroactive prohibition of all
direct grants by laymen would have undermined the entire campaign to recover
tithes and other *spiritualia* from lay hands, since in spite of the canonical prohibitions many grants were made in the twelfth century, as in the past, *per
manum laicam* (see pp. 114–15 below), and even an authority like Gratian
specifically accepted the validity of grants of tithes made to monks *de manu
laicorum* provided that the bishop gave his consent: *Decretum*, C. XVI, q. VII,
dictum post c. 38 (see pp. 183–4 below).

Calixtus II again intervened in favour of a monastery at the Lateran council in 1123, where the bishops renewed their attacks on monastic possession of 'churches, villas, castles, tithes, and the oblations of the living and the dead'. The new abbot of Monte Cassino, Oderisius II, rose to defend the monks and, like Pontius of Cluny four years earlier, appealed to the pope for protection, 'since no one except you, our master, will fight for us'. 'For what will happen', he asked, 'to the monks of Monte Cassino, who night and day ceaselessly invoke the mercy of Almighty God for the salvation of the entire world? What will happen, if the privileges of the popes of Rome are violated?' As before, Calixtus supported the monks and confirmed the property of Monte Cassino.[1]

Faced with this alliance of the papacy and the monasteries, most bishops in the twelfth century gave up their resistance to monastic tithes and tacitly, and sometimes explicitly, relinquished even their right to consent to grants of tithes to monasteries.[2] The bishop of Fréjus confirmed in advance for Lérins the possession of any tithes which it might recover from laymen on a certain estate.[3] And the bishop of Clermont in 1131 specifically granted to Cluny the right to receive tithes in his diocese without his permission.[4] Such a grant was very likely uncanonical, in view of the repeated papal and conciliar decrees requiring bishops to supervise all transactions concerning tithes, but it is clear that by the early twelfth century there were no effective barriers to monastic acquisition of tithes and that the consent of the bishops, in spite of occasional difficulties, had become almost a formality.

[1] Peter the Deacon, *Chronicon Casinensis*, IV, 78, in MGH, SS, VII, 802-3; cf. *IP*, VIII, 170, no. 208, and Herbert Bloch, 'The Schism of Anacletus II and the Glanfeuil Forgeries of Peter the Deacon', *Traditio*, VIII (1952), 174-5, who suggested (n. 57) that 'the pope's reply may be an invention by Peter'; but the precedent at the council of Rheims supports its authenticity.

[2] Cf. Viard, *Dîme*, I, 193-8.

[3] *Lérins*, I, 1.

[4] *Cluny*, V, 380, no. 4023.

3. MONASTIC POSSESSION OF TITHES
IN THE TWELFTH CENTURY

The number of tithes owned by monasteries increased enormously in the late eleventh and twelfth centuries. The methods of acquisition remained much the same as before, but the patterns and proportions tended to change, and new motives and difficulties arose out of the campaign to recover tithes from lay hands and the new importance of monastic tithes in the general economy of the Church. As property rights all over Europe became more clearly defined and laid down in writing, usurpation and tithes from new proprietary churches became relatively less important to monasteries than gifts and sales of tithes and fractions of tithes belonging to established churches or from other lands and revenues. These transactions might simply transfer the tithe from one ecclesiastical institution to another and cost the donor nothing;[1] and tithes were therefore a popular form of gift and endowment for a new house of monks or canons.

A bishop in particular might exercise in favour of a monastery his right to regulate the distribution of tithes in his diocese, or he might simply give the episcopal share, or part of it, or the tithes from his own estates, revenues, and churches. The bishop of Grenoble in 1100 divided between himself and a new house of regular canons the tithes recovered from laymen in a certain parish, except from his own lands and a vineyard belonging to a layman.[2] The bishop of Antibes in 1058 gave the tithes from all his property on the island of Lérins to the abbey there.[3] King Philip I in 1067 confirmed a grant by the archbishop of Rheims to the abbey of St Denis at Rheims of the tithe of all his revenues

---

[1] Cf. Lennard, *Rural England*, p. 316. As a rule, however, laymen in the eleventh and twelfth centuries disposed only of tithes which they themselves owned, though not, as is sometimes said, only from their own demesnes. The viscount of Thouars, for instance, endowed La Chaise-le-Vicomte, which was a dependency of St Florence at Saumur, with the tithe 'quam vicecomiti reddere solebant', in addition to other property: Guérard, *Polyptique*, II, 377.

[2] *Grenoble*, p. 7, no. A 4 (cf. p. 113 n. 2 below).

[3] *Lérins*, I, 94–5.

in the town of Rheims.[1] A bishop might also confirm the possession by a monastery of the tithes from its own proprietary churches[2] or grant it the share otherwise owed to the bishop. Thus the bishop of Tarragona in 1120 gave a church to St Sernin at Toulouse with all its revenues, including 'the third part which belonged especially to the bishop'; and the archbishop of Burgos in 1152 ceded to Oña the episcopal third of the tithes of its churches.[3]

Laymen even more than bishops tended to give either fractions of tithes or tithes from specific regions, products, and revenues both from their own estates and churches and from lands and churches of which they held the tithes alone by usurpation or episcopal grant. Philip I in 1061, for instance, confirmed a grant by his knight Waleran to St Christopher in Halatte of two parts of a certain tithe 'which he held as a fief from the canons of the church of Our Lady at Senlis, with the consent of Bishop Frodland and the clergy, to whom this tithe belonged' and who presumably kept the third part for themselves or assigned it to the priest serving in the church.[4] William of London gave the monks of Hurley his tithe at Egareston, 'that is, a third of the tithe of my demesne grain, two parts of the tithe of money, and the entire tithe of cheese, except for three cheeses, and of wool, linen, apples, horses, calves, pannage, and pennies, and two parts of the piglets'.[5] And in about 1080 a knight whose brother was a monk at St Cyprien in Poitiers gave the abbey a parish church with all the tithes from its own demesne and from the monks' land in the parish and with half the other tithes, 'but he kept half on account of the service owing to his lords'.[6] Occasionally the donor specified the purpose for which the tithes were to be used,

[1] *Recueil des actes de Philippe Ier roi de France (1059–1108)*, ed. M. Prou, CDRHF (Paris, 1908), p. 96, no. 31.

[2] Cf. *St Pierre à Gand*, p. 120 (1117) and Garufi, *Documenti*, I, 36–7, no. 14 (1138), in which the bishop of Cosenza granted the abbey of Our Lady at Josaphat in Palestine the tithes of its churches in Sicily.

[3] *St Sernin de Toulouse*, p. 497; *Oña*, I, 256–7; cf. *St Victor de Marseille*, II, 84–5, in which the bishop of Digne gave half of the tithes 'que ad nostri pertinere videtur episcopii rationem' at Chaudol to the abbey of St Victor.

[4] *Actes de Philippe Ier*, p. 30, no. 9.

[5] *Formulare anglicanum*, ed. Thomas Madox (London, 1702), p. 252, no. 425.

[6] *St Cyprien*, p. 128, no. 195.

as in the elaborate grant to St Sernin in 1092 by several brothers, who gave three churches with their tithes on condition that a church be built at Combei:

for seven years the entire tithe, except for the archbishop's quarter, [is for] the building of the church; but after seven years the canons of St Sernin should have a quarter of the tithes, half of the oblations, and all the burial dues, except for the archbishop's part. The other clergy ordained in that church should receive half of the tithes and oblations.[1]

Similar provisions for the parish priest, either in perpetuity or in favour of an individual incumbent, were often made by bishops and laymen in grants of tithes to monasteries. Rodald of Pellerin in his charter granting several churches and their revenues to Marmoutier in 1050 specified that the bishop and the abbot were responsible for the support of the priests.[2] In the diocese of Salzburg, where episcopal control over tithes was exceptionally strong, Archbishop Gebhard in 1074/87 decreed with the consent of the clergy in a privilege for Admont

that the third part of the tithe which belongs to the parish priests should not be paid to them out of the portion of the monastery, but they should receive their tithes at the same time in specified places elsewhere out of the portion of the archbishop, in order that the usual jealousy and rivalry between the parish priests and monks may not arise out of the division of tithes.[3]

Archbishop Conrad I in 1124 gave three parts of the tithes from certain estates to the abbot of St Peter at Salzburg 'on condition that he distribute them in accordance with justice and canon law, but he kept the priest's quarter in his own power until he decided to whom he would entrust the cure of souls in that place'.[4] In 1144 he reserved the tithes from one estate for the parish priest in a

---

[1] *St Sernin de Toulouse*, p. 496; cf. the grant to Dover priory, cited p. 103 n. 6 below, which was partly to be used for building and maintaining the monastic church.

[2] See p. 86 above.

[3] *Steiermark*, I, 93, no. 77; cf. pp. 184 and 267 for the grants of Archbishop Conrad I in 1139 and 1147 and Jacob Wichner, *Geschichte des Benediktiner-Stiftes Admont* (Graz, 1874–80), I, 37, and Tremel, in *Zs. d. hist. Vereines f. Steiermark*, XXXIII, 11.   [4] *Salzburg*, I, 331.

grant to Frisach,[1] and he gave various tithes to Reichersberg 'except for the canonical portion of the parish priests'.[2] A layman in Burgundy specified in granting a church to Molesme in 1157 that the priest should have half of the tithes and certain other specified revenues.[3] At Athis-Mons in Seine-et-Oise the division was more complex: one-third of the great tithe belonged to the canons of St Victor and two-thirds to William of Chastres, who granted them and all of certain other tithes in three equal parts to two parish churches and to the priory of Longpont; he also gave two-thirds 'of the small tithe, from sheep, calves, eggs, and other small products' to Longpont and one-third to the canons of St Victor.[4] All of these were supposed to be permanent arrangements, but William of Warenne in 1080 endowed the abbey of Lewes with 'the tithes of my lands and those which the priest Richard has for his lifetime, after which they will belong to the monks'.[5] In a confirmation of the foundation of the abbey of St James at Liège in 1134, Lothar III stated that

When this grant was made, the priest serving this church held two parts of the tithe which [the founder] Widichind's mother had given only to him in her lifetime, but future priests of this church should know that after him they will have only a third of the tithes as a prebend and that the two parts will revert to the church of St James and its inhabitants.[6]

As in earlier times, it was common to give monks the tithes of specific products and revenues, especially when the 'great' tithe

[1] *Steiermark*, I, 235. Cf. S.-A. Würdtwein, *Nova subsidia diplomatica* (Heidelberg, 1781–91), VII, 151–2, no. 58, and IX, 351–3, no. 180, for an agreement between the Cluniacs of Seltz and the Cistercians of Neuburg in 1151, arranging for Neuburg to pay nine measures of grain annually to Seltz and three to the priest of Schweighausen in lieu of the tithe of Laubach, which probably represents the earlier division of the tithe between the monks and the priest.
[2] Cited in a letter written by Gerhoh of Reichersberg in 1159/61 in *Salzburg*, II, 432, no. 309. The charter itself is printed *ibid.* II, 331, no. 230. On these two documents, cf. Peter Classen, *Gerhoch von Reichersberg* (Wiesbaden, 1960), pp. 343–4 and 373–4.
[3] Ernest Petit, *Histoire des ducs de Bourgogne de la race capétienne* (Dijon–Paris, 1885–1905), II, 270–1, no. 362.   [4] *Longpont*, p. 212.
[5] *Cluny*, IV, 692, no. 3561. See *Rev. bén.* LXX, 596–9, for a discussion of a grant to Cluny of the *altaria* and tithes of a church in which the *persona* was withheld during the lifetime of the incumbent at that time, whom the donors had appointed.   [6] MGH, *Dipl.* Lothar III, no. 57.

from the principal products of a region was held by a priest or other owner.[1] These specific tithes became more varied and important as economic activity expanded and diversified in the eleventh and twelfth centuries. The index to Round's *Calendar of Documents*, which covers the years from 918 to 1206, lists over fifty kinds of tithes, many from grants to monasteries.[2] They were mostly from agricultural produce of one kind or another, but there were also tithes from mills, ovens, and tanneries, from iron and salt, and often from tolls, market dues, and other revenues in money. In 1079 St Jean d'Angély was given 'half of the tithe of textiles'.[3] In the early twelfth century the monks of Dunfermline in Scotland held the tithes of royal revenues in both cash and kind, of deer and game, and of salt and iron brought to the town for the use of the king.[4] Louis VII in 1143 gave a tithe of the bread 'which is brought to the court of ourselves and our successors whenever we are in Paris' to the nuns of Yerres.[5] Another popular form of special gift to monks was the tithe of fishing. The burgesses of Dover gave Dover priory the tithe of fish 'both in fish and in money from the sale of fish, that is, the tenth fish as they are caught or the tenth penny as they are sold'.[6] There were

---

[1] This type of division was later very common, and in England the great tithe was often called 'rectorial' and the small tithe 'vicarial': see C. S. and C. S. Orwin, *The Open Fields*, 2nd ed. (Oxford, 1954), p. 158 and *ODCC*, pp. 1362 and 1416.

[2] *Calendar of Documents Preserved in France, Illustrative of the History of Great Britain and Ireland*, 1: *918–1206*, ed. J. Horace Round (London, 1899), pp. 679–80.

[3] *St Jean d'Angély*, I, 155, no. 122, cited by L. Bruhat, *Le monachisme en Saintonge et en Aunis (XIe et XIIe siècles)* (La Rochelle, 1907), p. 214, who mentioned a wide variety of tithes held by monasteries in the eleventh and twelfth centuries.

[4] A. C. Lawrie, *Early Scottish Charters Prior to A.D. 1153* (Glasgow, 1905), p. 62, no. 74; cf. p. 71, no. 86. Henry of Lacy in about 1170 gave 'the entire tithe of my hunting, both in flesh and in hides' to the monks of Pontefract (*Pontefract*, I, 34); cf. Stenton, *Feudalism*, p. 77.

[5] Mabillon, *Annales*, VI, 339; cf. Achille Luchaire, *Études sur les actes de Louis VII* (Paris, 1885), p. 134, no. 108.

[6] Avrom Saltman, *Theobald, Archbishop of Canterbury*, University of London Historical Studies, II (London, 1956), pp. 310–14 and 539–41. This grant at first applied only to the fish caught between Michaelmas and St Andrew's day, but it was later extended to cover the entire fishing season. It was confirmed by the pope and by Henry II, and both Thomas Becket (as chancellor) and Henry II issued writs to enforce payment.

in fact probably few products or revenues in the twelfth century from which the tithes were not owned by monks somewhere in Europe.

Monks were also frequently given a set quantity or proportion out of or above a certain tithe or, when the normal tithe had changed from a proportional into a fixed payment, the excess beyond a specified amount. A layman in the eleventh century gave the tithe of his substance in bread, wine, and meat to the abbey of Lérins, 'and from those lands from which he had already given [the tithes] to others, he gave yet another tithe'.[1] Monks might also be given the *redecima*, *retrodecima*, or *reridecima*; the *tractus decimae*, or charge for carrying the tithes; and the *bodium*, which apparently applied in Flanders to the part of a tithe held by a secular lord.[2] As examples of set quantities, the monks of

[1] *Lérins*, I, 271.

[2] For grants of *redecima* and *redecimatio*, see *Vignory*, p. 35 (1052/4); *Lérins*, I, 274 (eleventh century); *St Cyprien*, p. 105, no. 155 (1108/15); *APRI*, I, 180 (JL 8799: Eugene III for St Michael at Verdun in 1145); *Basse-Fontaine*, p. 114, no. 87 (1146); Round, *Calendar*, p. 325, no. 913 (1139/50, for Hambye). For *retrodecima* and *reridecima*, see *St Victor de Marseille*, I, 185 (c. 1040) and 280 (1070). For *tractus decimae*, see *Bibl. Clun.* p. 1391 (1125) and *Longpont*, pp. 59–61 (1152; JL 9559). Scholars are not agreed on the meanings of these terms. The editors of Du Cange, *Glossarium*, s.v., equated the three and defined them as a tenth part of the tithe; and the *Medieval Latin Word-List*, ed. J. H. Baxter and Charles Johnson (Oxford, 1934) s.v., defined *redecima* as a 'second tithe'. Bruhat, *Monachisme*, p. 214, citing *St Jean d'Angély*, II, 258, no. 210, defined the *redecima* more generally as 'des droits perçus en plus des dîmes régulières'. Viard also refrained from strictly defining *redecima* in *Dîme*, I, 233–4; but in *Dîme*, II, 70–1, he followed Du Cange and equated the *redecima* and the *tractus decimae*, computed at a tenth of the tithe or one per cent of the original total. The entire question of the *bodium* and *redecima* in Flanders has recently been examined by L. Voet, 'Bodium—Redecima', *Archivum Latinitatis Medii Aevi (Bulletin Du Cange)*, XX (1950), 207–44, who proposed that the *bodium* was the two-thirds of a tithe held by a layman, in contrast to the one-third (*altare*) held by the parish church, and that the *redecima* referred to 'les dîmes assignées par les seigneurs sur leurs propres revenus qui en principe n'étaient pas décimable' (p. 240). Apart from the fact that seigneurial revenues were in theory tithable, this definition fits the use of the term in the documents in *APRI*, where Eugene III confirmed the possession of a grange 'cum redecimationibus dominicalium comitis', in Round, in *St Cyprien*, where a knight granted 'redecimam mei peatgii', and in Ordericus Vitalis, *Hist. ecc.* III, 2, and VIII, 3, *ed. cit.* II, 37, and III, 281 (cf. v, 186). It does not fit so well, however, with the use of the term in the documents from Vignory, to which the founder granted

Vigeois were repeatedly given two or four measures of grain out of a tithe, of which the donor presumably kept the remainder;[1] and the abbot of Abingdon in 1104/5 agreed to give to the parish church the customary tithe of twenty-four sheaves of grain for each virgate of land out of the tithes given to his monastery by the men of Uffington.[2]

In addition to an existing tithe, whole or partial, great or small, a donor might promise the possession of tithes to monks in the future, either when the present owner died or when they could be recovered from lay hands. Popes and bishops also frequently confirmed such recoveries in advance, as in the grant to Lérins by the bishop of Fréjus. William of Warenne in his endowment of Lewes granted the tithes held by the priest Richard for his life-time and also 'all the tithes which my men have given or will later give to that place'.[3] And in the late eleventh century several donors to the abbey of Gellone withheld the tithes but promised never to dispose of them except to the monastery.[4]

Also of greatly increased importance in the eleventh and twelfth centuries were grants of the noval tithes from the lands that were constantly being opened and cultivated on the frontier in the East and in Spain and even more on the 'internal frontier' of forests, swamps, and moors.[5] These tithes were often given to

'et decimationem et redecimationem clausi mei indominicati', and Basse-Fontaine, which specified that the *redecima* was to be taken from the priest's portions of the great and small tithe (see below, pp. 133-4). These suggest that at least in certain regions the *redecima* may have been a charge above and beyond the normal tithe or, as in Du Cange, the charge for carrying the tithe. Later documents show that in the Forez the *retrodecima* was defined as a tenth part of the tithe and was given in return for collecting the tithe: *Chartes du Forez*, xv, 110-11, cf. 120-1 and 199; and Dubar, *Corbie*, p. 101, remarked that in the thirteenth century the monastic mayor who transported the tithe was entitled to the *carion* or *conroi*, computed at a tenth of the tithe.

[1] *Vigeois*, pp. 54-5 (n.d.), 130 (1092/1100), 186 (1124/64), 224 (c. 1164: cf. p. 131 n. 3 below).

[2] *Abingdon*, II, 94 and 141-6. Production had presumably increased between the time when the tithe was fixed and when it was given to the monks, who collected the difference.

[3] See p. 102 n. 5 above.

[4] *Gellone*, pp. 364, 367, 369, 390, etc.

[5] A guide to the extensive literature on this expansion will be found in vol. 1 of the *Camb. Econ. Hist.*, and in Bryce Lyon, 'Medieval Real Estate Develop-

monasteries by laymen and by bishops, under whose control they were considered to be.[1] A characteristic example of an episcopal transaction concerning noval tithes is recorded in a privilege granted to the abbey of Kaufungen in 1126 by the archbishop of Mainz: 'When we claimed the disposition of these tithes, as of all noval tithes in our archbishopric, and held them at our pleasure for some time, the abbess [of Kaufungen] proved in our regular synod at Fritzlar that all the noval tithes of that forest belonged to her monastery by virtue of a transaction proved by a charter....'[2] A lay grant of noval tithes from a certain forest in Normandy was confirmed by King Philip I of France in 1060, who gave the monks of Marmoutier both the tithe of any honey found in the forest, the terrage and tithe of any crops raised by ploughing new land there, and the tithe alone of any produce raised without ploughing the soil.[3]

The exact amounts and types of tithes held by monks and the

ments and Freedom', *Amer. Hist. Rev.* LXIII (1957–8), 47–50. Archibald R. Lewis, 'The Closing of the Mediaeval Frontier, 1250–1350', *Speculum*, XXXIII (1958), 475–83, has suggested that the expansion lasted from about 1000 until 1250—the 'frontier period' in medieval history—and that later history was deeply influenced by the 'frontier-less existence'. Though not all historians accept this conclusion, most are agreed that there was a widespread opening of land, accompanying the general economic revival and growth of population, in the eleventh and twelfth centuries (cf. Lyon, in *Amer. Hist. Rev.* LXIII, 50). The tithes from these new lands are discussed generally by Viard, *Dîme*, I, 158–60, and esp. Pöschl in *A. f. kath. KR*, XCVIII, 3–51, 171–214, 333–80 and 497–548; see also, on France, the classic work of Léopold Delisle, *Études sur la condition de la classe agricole et l'état de l'agriculture en Normandie au moyen âge* (Évreux, 1851), p. 97 n. 12, and Alfred Maury, 'Les forêts de la France dans l'antiquité et au moyen âge', *Mémoires présentés par divers savants à l'Académie des Inscriptions et Belles-Lettres*, 2nd series: *Antiquités de la France*, IV (1860), 64–5. E. J. Kuujo, 'Das Zehntwesen in der Erzdiözese Hamburg–Bremen bis zu seiner Privatisierung', *Suomalaisen tiedeakatemian toimituksia: Annales academiae scientiarum Fennicae*, Series B, LXII, I (1949), 192–7, remarked that in northern Germany the possession of noval tithes was even more disputed than that of old-field tithes (p. 192). Boyd, *Tithes*, pp. 143–5, discussed noval tithes and said that they were 'mentioned as early as the council of Tribur in 895 but were not important until the twelfth century' (p. 144 n. 1).

[1] On grants of noval tithes to monks, see Delisle, *Études*, p. 392, and Pöschl, in *A. f. kath. KR*, XCVIII, 351–80, who also discussed (pp. 176–80) the special authority of the bishop over noval tithes.

[2] *Kaufungen*, I, 29 (and *Mainz*, I, 447–8).

[3] *Actes de Philippe Ier*, p. 26, no. 8.

methods of acquisition tended to vary regionally according to the goods produced and the degree of control over tithes exercised by the bishops, parish priests, and laymen.[1] All over Europe, however, the number of tithes owned by monks increased enormously in the eleventh and twelfth centuries. 'From about 1150 to 1250', according to Ganshof, '[tithes] were the principal source of wealth of many a religious house'. He also said that 'In the thirteenth century *altaria* and revenues derived from land, of which tithes were by far the most important, occupied a far more important place than land itself in donations to religious houses'.[2] The economic importance of all these proportional dues paid in kind grew steadily in the twelfth century with the increases in production and the rise in prices.[3] Wise abbots everywhere naturally sought to acquire and recover tithes as a protection against rising prices, which reduced the real value of their revenues in money. Abbot Suger of St Denis, for instance, recovered for his abbey some tithes which for a century had been held by some laymen at an annual rent of two shillings, although the yield of twenty to thirty measures of grain was worth many times that sum in the twelfth century.[4] Peter the Venerable estimated that in the first half of the twelfth century Cluny derived about a tenth of her income from tithes;[5] and the Cluniac monk in the *Dialogus inter*

---

[1] In the archdiocese of Hamburg–Bremen, for instance, according to Kuujo, in *Ann. acad. sci. Fenn.* B, LXII. 1, 227, more tithes were acquired by monks from laymen than from bishops before the thirteenth century.

[2] *Camb. Econ. Hist.* I, 313 and 287 (cf. also 556).

[3] Cf. M. M. Postan, in *Camb. Econ. Hist.* II, 165–8. A dramatic example of this rise in prices and of the growth of production is given in case IV in the appendix, where the bishop of Tournai raised the annual rent for the church of Ghistelles, which had been set at eighteen marks early in the twelfth century, to twenty-seven marks in the 1140's and in the late twelfth century insisted on receiving half of the revenues.

[4] *Œuvres complètes de Suger*, ed. A. Lecoy de la Marche, Société de l'histoire de France (Paris, 1867), p. 176. The table of prices in Geoffroi Tenant de La Tour, *L'Homme et la terre de Charlemagne à saint Louis* (Paris, 1943), p. 721, shows that in Limousin in the middle of the twelfth century a measure of grain was worth from five to seven shillings. Germaine Lebel, *Histoire administrative, économique et financière de l'abbaye de Saint-Denis... de 1151 à 1346* (Paris, 1935), p. 145, said that tithes were 'a resource of the first order' for St Denis.

[5] Peter the Venerable, ep. I, 33, in *Bibl. Clun.* p. 700. On the importance of tithes in the budget of Cluny, see Georges Duby, 'Économie domaniale et

Cluniacensem et Cisterciensem monachum, which was written in the
third quarter of the twelfth century, declared at one point that
'The monks of our order hold no possessions more willingly than
tithes'.[1] Tithes also played an important part in the finances of
such great abbeys as Bobbio, Lobbes, Tongerloo, and St Bertin;[2]
and for smaller houses they sometimes constituted the principal
source of income.[3] In England in the later Middle Ages, according to Snape, 'tithe or the income from churches was an important
item in every monastic budget';[4] and although there were

économie monétaire. Le budget de l'abbaye de Cluny entre 1080 et 1155',
Annales. Économies. Sociétés. Civilisations, VII (1952), 155–71, and 'Un inven-
taire des profits de la seigneurie clunisienne à la mort de Pierre le Vénérable',
Petrus Venerabilis, 1156–1956, Studia Anselmiana, XL (Rome, 1956), p. 134, and
my article in *Rev. bén.* LXX, 591–608.

[1] *Thesaurus*, V, 1594. On the author and date of this work see Joseph Storm,
Untersuchungen zum Dialogus duorum monachorum Cluniacensis et Cisterciensis
(Bocholt i. W., 1926), pp. 63–5 (*c.* 1156); P. V. Redlich, review of Storm in
SMGBOZ, XLIV (1926), 224, who suggested Idungus of St Emmeram as
author; André Wilmart, 'Une riposte de l'ancien monachisme au manifeste de
S. Bernard', *Rev. bén.* XLVI (1934), 302–3 (before 1174); Joseph Turk, *Cistercii
statuta antiquissima*, Analecta sacri ordinis Cisterciensis, IV (Rome, 1948),
pp. 82–3 (Irungus of Alderspach not long before 1174); and Kurt Fina, 'Anselm
von Havelberg', *Analecta Praemonstratensia*, XXXII (1956), 200–1 (*c.* 1156, with
further references).

[2] *Bobbio*, II, 275–83 (a statement of the tithes owned by Bobbio in the late
twelfth century); Joseph Warichez, *L'Abbaye de Lobbes depuis les origines jusqu'en
1200*, Université de Louvain: Recueil de travaux publiés par les membres des
conférences d'histoire et de philologie, XXIV (Louvain–Paris, 1909), pp. 212–13;
Hugues Lamy, *L'Abbaye de Tongerloo depuis sa fondation jusqu'en 1263*, in the same
series, XLIV (Louvain–Paris, n.d. [1914]), p. 192; G. W. Coopland, *The Abbey of
Saint-Bertin and its Neighbourhood, 900–1350*, Oxford Studies in Social and Legal
History, IV (Oxford, 1914), pp. 46–8.

[3] Cf. Frere, in *Fasciculus I. W. Clark dictatus*, p. 192; *Newington Longeville
Charters*, ed. H. E. Salter, Oxfordshire Record Society, III (Oxford, 1921),
introd. p. xiii: 'Most of the property of Longeville consisted of the tithes of the
demesnes of the various manors which were in the hands of Walter Giffard
in the county of Buckingham'; Lunt, *Valuation*, pp. 474–524; *St Gregory*,
Canterbury, introd. p. xiii; and *Monasticon*, V, 185 (St Andrew at Northampton,
early twelfth century).

[4] R. N. Snape, *English Monastic Finances in the Later Middle Ages* (Cambridge,
1926), p. 75; cf. Adolf Kopp, *Zehentwesen und Zehentablösung in Baden*, Volks-
wirtschaftliche Abhandlungen der badischen Hochschulen, III, 2 (Freiburg im
Br., 1899), p. 24 (156), who remarked on the number of tithes held by monasteries in Baden.

exceptions to this rule even in England,[1] there can be no doubt that by the end of the twelfth century a considerable proportion of all tithes paid by Christians were given to monasteries.

The principal reasons for this rapid growth in monastic possession of tithes in the late eleventh and twelfth centuries were, first, the efforts of the Church to recover tithes from the hands of laymen and, second, the economic pressure on the owners of the tithes. Many laymen were certainly stimulated to give up their tithes by fear of ecclesiastical censures in this world and of eternal punishment in the next.[2] The long and vigorous arenga in a charter for the abbey of St Maxentius in Poitou in 1126/9 cited the example of Abraham and the law of tithing in the Old Testament and then declared that 'through the weakness of the clergy [the tithe] had been diverted to laymen at the instigation of the Devil, and since all evil should be resisted at all times and in all places, those who lay hands on the holy Church have been excommunicated by God and his ministers and have received as their fitting reward the Devil and the punishment of Hell'.[3] Less flamboyant charters often included a simple recognition of the fact that laymen should not hold tithes. Thus the bishop of Amiens in 1141 gave to St Cornelius at Compiègne some tithes which had been returned to him by 'Ralph Dalfius, a soldier of Montdidier, who wisely heeded divine counsel and the pleas of good men and thought of his ancestors' souls and his own salvation' and who had recovered the tithes from one Adam Batland, who 'unjustly held them from him as a fief by hereditary right'.[4]

---

[1] Cf. R. A. L. Smith, *Canterbury Cathedral Priory* (Cambridge, 1943), pp. 11 and 13, showing that Canterbury held very few tithes even as late as the fifteenth century. According to the list of property in Tenant de La Tour, *Homme et la terre*, pp. 661–726, esp. 723, the abbey of Solignac held almost no tithes in the twelfth century.

[2] Ever since the ninth century conscientious laymen had occasionally returned ecclesiastical property to the Church, especially to monasteries (cf. the references in p. 66 nn. 1–2 above); and according to Boyd, *Tithes*, pp. 125–6 such pious restorations began in Italy in the early eleventh century. But in the second half of the eleventh century ecclesiastical pressure was greatly intensified.

[3] *St Maixent*, I, 313–14, no. 287.

[4] *St Corneille de Compiègne*, I, 107–8; cf. *Conques*, pp. 56–7 (1060/5); Mabillon,

Three successive earls of Leicester felt pangs of conscience concerning the tithes of Sopewich and Ringeston, as Earl Robert II wrote, in a letter to Pope Alexander III in 1168/81:

Ever since the Normans subjugated England, my ancestors were always accustomed to give these tithes to whomever they wished. My grandfather R[obert of Beaumont], count of Meulan [1081–1118], gave them to the monks of Préaux, who after some time were seriously oppressed by the managers of these estates and complained to my grandfather that the violence of his officials made it so difficult to collect the tithes that they derived small benefit from them; and the monks thus complained frequently until my grandfather took the tithes back into his own domain and in their place gave the monks an estate called Expectesberi. For some time my father the late Earl Rob[ert of Leicester, 1118–68] gave these tithes to his managers with his other farms. At last, being a just and devout man, he followed wiser counsel and was unwilling to use them for himself any longer, since he realized that they had once been tithes, although they had become part of his domain by the subsequent exchange for the estate mentioned above; and he gave them to his clerics, first to his doctor, Peter, and then to Adam of Ely. Since he was concerned over recent events, however, and wanted to grant them definitely, he gave the said tithes permanently to the monastery of Lyre and to the monks serving God there, in the presence of myself and many others and at my request, and he confirmed [this grant] in writing and by his seal.[1]

A grant like this was apparently a real gift, motivated by a mixture of fear, piety, and generosity, but most grants of tithes to monasteries were in fact sales or exchanges by owners who either needed ready money or property or simply wanted food, clothing,

---

Annales, v, 25 (1070); *Mâcon*, p. 337 (1080); *Marmoutier (Blésois)*, pp. 80–1 (1095/6, citing the decree of Urban II forbidding lay possession and the sale of tithes); *Marmoutier (Anjou)*, p. 25; and several examples cited by G. d'Espinay, *Les cartulaires angevins* (Angers, 1864), pp. 50–1.

[1] *Thesaurus*, I, 477; also in *PL*, CC, 1390, and Charles Guéry, *Histoire de l'abbaye de Lyre* (Évreux, 1917), pp. 569–70, cf. p. 160 n. 8. See also *The Complete Peerage*, ed. G. E. Cokayne, new ed. (London, 1910 ff.), VII, 523–33, and *English Historical Documents*, II: *1042–1189*, ed. David Douglas (London, 1953), p. 993. The letter is not dated but must have been written between the succession of Earl Robert II in 1168 and the death of Alexander III in 1181.

and shelter in the monastery. In Italy, according to Boyd, 'while no statistical summary is possible, it is almost certain that purchases exceeded gratuitous restitutions in number'.[1] Tithes were a valuable form of property, and few owners had any scruples about holding or disposing of them.[2] Sometimes a grant of tithes was even frankly referred to as 'a sale or purchase',[3] in spite of the patent simony and the numerous canons prohibiting the sale of tithes and other spiritual revenues. The payment of a ransom, the provision of an endowment on entering a monastery, or the expenses of a pilgrimage or crusade, often forced laymen to dispose of their tithes,[4] and only the local monastery might have enough capital to meet the emergency. Even monasteries were sometimes forced to mortgage their lands in order to raise the money with which to redeem some tithes.[5] In 1114 a noble named Bellus-Homo gave some tithes to Sauxillanges in return for 'support and clothing in the cell at Bolnac'—a sort of corrody or annuity—and permission to become a monk at Sauxillanges if he

---

[1] Boyd, *Tithes*, p. 132.

[2] The chartulary of Redon in Brittany, for instance, contains many references to tithes which certain soldiers 'in terris suis, sicut alii milites, jure quodam possidebant' (p. 303, in 1110) and 'quam iure hereditario, ut milites tenere solent, ipse tenebat' (pp. 248–9: grant to the abbey in 1127 of one-third of two-thirds, i.e. two-ninths in all, of a certain tithe).

[3] See case V in appendix and Petit, *Bourgogne*, II, 232–3, no. 283 (*c.* 1143), where a layman sold some tithes to the abbey of St Margaret in the diocese of Autun.

[4] See *Quimperlé*, pp. 154–5 (1066/81): a layman twice sold some tithes to the abbey, once for nine pounds and the next time for sixty shillings and a palfrey, in order to ransom first his lord and then his son. For examples of tithes given as an endowment with new monks, see *Nogent-le-Rotrou*, pp. 148–9 (*c.* 1100); *St Vincent du Mans*, p. 300 (1080/1102); *St Sernin de Toulouse*, pp. 147–8 (1108/37); *St Martin des Champs*, I, 265–7 (1123); *Ste Croix de Bordeaux*, p. 64 (see pp. 113–14 below); and *Vigeois*, p. 224 (*c.* 1164, cf. p. 131 n. 4 below). For tithes sold or mortgaged to monasteries by crusaders and pilgrims, see *Sauxillanges*, p. 257 (n.d.); *Uzerche*, p. 171, no. 201 (1096/1147) and p. 275, no. 493 (1103); *Vigeois*, p. 67, no. 113 (1096/1103), p. 211, no. 313 (1140/3), and pp. 213–14, no. 316 (1147); *Gellone*, p. 366 (1116); *Basse-Fontaine*, pp. 79–80, no. 59 (1145/61); *Aureil*, pp. 76–7, no. 115 (1147); and *St Maixent*, I, 347–8, no. 329 (1147?).

[5] *St Vincent du Mans*, pp. 263–4, which in the early twelfth century mortgaged some land to a priest in order to raise thirty pennies with which to redeem some tithes and first-fruits from a layman.

so desired.[1] Nogent-le-Rotrou received the tithes of two mills from a man who became a monk, but after his death:

his son Ramercius, who first inherited the land, took from the monks the tithe of the mill at Capella; since he was a young man, the monks did not seek justice but awaited his reform, and when he was ill he restored it with the consent of his brother William Rebursus; but when William succeeded to the lands after his brother's death, he did not return [the tithe] until he had to go to Jerusalem, when he came to Nogent and returned the tithe

with the consent of his two younger brothers, who each received thirty shillings and twelve pennies.[2] Over the years, therefore, this transaction involved a characteristic combination of pious and secular motives, including the desire to become a monk, the fear of death, the expenses of a pilgrimage, and the cupidity of the heirs.

The buyers as well as the sellers might take the initiative in such dealings, and many monasteries and churches systematically collected tithes and bought out the interests of rival claimants, sometimes over many years. It took eighteen years, for instance, and a total expenditure of over twenty pounds, plus two lamb-skin coats and a measure of grain, for the abbey of St Martin des Champs to recover the tithe of Orsonville from the hands of the two principal and eight minor owners.[3] Marmoutier paid seventy shillings, in two instalments, to a layman and his family for cer-tain tithes, and ten shillings more to another layman 'in whose

---

[1] *Sauxillanges*, p. 370. Cf. Émile Lesne, 'Une source de la fortune monas-tique: Les donations à charge de pension alimentaire du VIIIe au Xe siècle', *Mélanges de philosophie et histoire publiés à l'occasion du cinquantenaire de la Faculté des lettres de l'Université catholique de Lille*, Mémoires et travaux des Facultés catholiques de Lille, XXXII (Lille, 1927), pp. 33–47, who discussed grants to monasteries in return for *victus* and *vestitus*, which were also called *stipendium praebenda*, or *provenda*.   [2] *Nogent-le-Rotrou*, pp. 135–6.

[3] *St Martin des Champs*, I, 111–13 (covering the years 1079–96): half of the tithe was recovered from Walter of Étampes and his wife for seven pounds and from her brother (40 shillings), with additional payments of 20 shillings to Bouchard of Massy, whose wife claimed the tithe by inheritance, and 40 shillings and two lambskin coats to Wido son of Serlo and his son, who held the tithe from Bouchard's wife. The other half was redeemed for seven pounds from Fulcher of Bullion and his wife, who held it as part of her dowry and whose three brothers had interests in the tithe which were bought out res-pectively for 10 shillings, 10 shillings, and 15 shillings and a measure of grain.

fief the tithe was'.[1] The bishop of Grenoble paid three hundred and forty-nine shillings of Valence to Bernard the Lombard and his family for one-sixth of one half of the tithes of St Ismier and for the entire other half, of which Bernard held two-thirds as an allod and the other third as a fief from three brothers (who dismissed their rights), who in turn held it from three other brothers, who held it from the bishop and surrendered it to him in return for a mule worth a hundred shillings and a grant of some lands illegally usurped by their father. The bishop then joined these seven-twelfths of the tithe to the other five-twelfths, which he already held, and divided the whole reconstituted tithe between himself and the canons of St Martin. But the previous owners and their families kept making trouble and exacting payments from the bishop for another twenty-five years.[2] A monastery might even be put to great trouble and expense to recover the tithes from its own lands or direct possession of tithes previously granted as fiefs.[3]

The recognition of these multiple claims by hard-headed bishops and abbots is the best evidence of the subdivision of the property rights over tithes and the difficulty of redeeming tithes which had been held by laymen for several generations. Inheritance and subinfeudation created claimants whose consent had to be secured for any transaction involving the tithe. A previous owner who had subinfeudated a tithe, or his heirs, were easily overlooked in subsequent transactions and could bring a claim for damages. In 1124, for instance, Gaillard de la Roche complained that certain tithes held from his father had been granted to the abbey of

---

[1] *Marmoutier (Vendômois)*, pp. 19–22 (1066/75).

[2] *Grenoble*, pp. 7–8, no. A 4 (*c.* 1100), pp. 80–4, nos. B 3 (1101), B 4 (*c.* 1101), and B 5 (*c.* 1125), pp. 90–2, nos. B 13 (*c.* 1108) and B 14 (1100), pp. 104–5, no. B 27 (1110), and pp. 175–6, no. B 119 (1108).

[3] Cf. *Gellone*, pp. 18–19 (1051/74); *Marmoutier (Vendômois)*, pp. 19–22 (1066/75); *Redon*, pp. 304–6 (1104: recovery of a series of tithes); *Vigeois*, p. 185 (1111/24: 70 shillings for a *decimarium* held *a feu* from the abbey); *St Cybard*, p. 41 (1142/52: a lay *decimarius* sold two-thirds of his quarter of a tithe to the monks and granted them any tithes they could get from other laymen who had taken them from himself or his parents); *Bobbio*, II, 40–3 (1143: the abbey redeemed the tithe of some of its own demesne from a layman in return for an estate).

Ste Croix at Bordeaux without his consent, and the monks agreed to hold the tithes in future through their cellarer as a fief from Gaillard and his descendants and also to receive him as a monk 'in life and in death...and since the hands of soldiers rarely go empty, he received eighty shillings from the abbey on this account'.[1] A monastery had also as a rule to secure the permission of the bishop, who both had the canonical duty to control the tithes in his diocese and from whom many lay owners ultimately held their tithes. One-sixth of the tithes of St Ismier, which the bishop of Grenoble recovered with such difficulty, were held from the bishop by three brothers, and from them by three other brothers, who had granted it to Bernard the Lombard, who already held another third and sixth of the tithe. Each family had to give its consent before the bishop could recover direct possession of the entire tithe. A grant of tithes to St Martin des Champs in 1123 was described in a charter of confirmation by the bishop of Paris as 'a fief...derived from the right of the bishop and held by the archdeacon Theobald, from Theobald by Gilbert of Montjay, and from Gilbert by the said Milo', who gave it to the monks.[2] And in about 1123 the abbot of Göttweig recovered through the bishop of Passau the episcopal tithes from his abbey's demesne estate at Palt, which the bishop had granted as a benefice to the Marquis Leopold and the marquis had granted to his soldier Gerold.[3]

The proper procedure in cases such as these was for the lay tenant to return the tithe, with the permission of any intermediate tenants, into the hand of the bishop, who then granted it to the monastery. Thus Hugh of Dammartin in 1080 returned the church of St Leu at Essérent, with its tithes and revenues, to the bishop of Beauvais, from whom he held it, 'on condition that he should give it to the church of Cluny'.[4] In fact, however, many

---

[1] *Ste Croix de Bordeaux*, pp. 63–5.   [2] *St Martin des Champs*, I, 266.

[3] *Göttweig*, pp. 46–7, no. 190, and pp. 167–8; cf. *Merseburg*, I, 96–7 (see p. 257 below).

[4] *Actes de Philippe Ier*, p. 266, no. 103. This procedure was also followed by Airard of Nantes (see pp. 85–7 above) and by James of Chacenay in returning the tithes of Vitry (see pp. 133–4 below); and it was prescribed by the council of Rouen in 1128 (see p. 94 above).

tithes were transferred directly by laymen to monasteries, *per manum laicam*, and were occasionally held on conditional tenure and even referred to as fiefs.[1] It may have been for fear of invalidating such direct grants that the proposed canon at the council of Rheims in 1119 was changed.[2] Other tithes were called allods, in the sense that they could be freely disposed of.[3] Part of the tithes of St Ismier in the diocese of Grenoble were held by Bernard the Lombard as an allod. And Fulcran of Nebiano in 1109 returned to Aniane certain tithes 'which I recognize to have been an allod of the Holy Saviour', that is, of the abbey itself.[4] In about 1136 the son of the king of Scotland changed all the property held of him 'in land, tithes, and all other things' by the monks of Daventry from a fief into a grant in free alms owing no secular service.[5]

This feudal terminology clearly indicates the extent to which tithes were still treated as a secular revenue in the twelfth century. Even the recognition of their spiritual character and their return into the possession of the Church could not change their importance as a form of property and their liability, as such, to feudal division of ownership and conditional tenure. Monks themselves treated tithes with little more respect than laymen; and in spite of occasional clauses in their charters prohibiting alienation,[6] they usually granted tithes freely to both clerics and laymen from their own and other lands. In the early twelfth century the abbot of Lérins even approved the grant made by one of his monks of the tithes from a dependency under his charge (except from the labour

---

[1] Richard of Clare in 1173/81 referred to some tithes long held by the monks of Stoke-by-Clare as 'de meo feudo': Stenton, *Feudalism*, pp. 91 and 270; *Marmoutier (Vendômois)*, pp. 19–22 (p. 113 above); *Ste Croix de Bordeaux*, pp. 63–5 (p. 114 above).

[2] See pp. 96–7 above.

[3] Cf. Henri Dubled, '"Allodium" dans les textes latins du moyen âge', *Le Moyen Âge*, LVII (4th ser. VI, 1951), 244–5.

[4] *Aniane*, pp. 258–9.

[5] Lawrie, *Scottish Charters*, p. 87, no. 112.

[6] *Mâcon*, pp. 88 (972/7), 188 (954/86), 192 (971/7), 193 (968/71), 283 (c. 941), etc.; *Cluny*, II, 143–4, no. 1049 (958: cf. *Rev. bén.* LXX, 594); *Scarnafigi*, pp. 241–3 (case III in appendix); *Stavelot–Malmédy*, I, 356 (1140: grant of noval tithes by the archbishop of Cologne with prohibition to alienate); cf. Mollat, in *Rev. hist. de droit fran. et ét.* 4th ser. XXVII, 400–1.

of the monks' own oxen) to the sacristan in return for a good horse.[1] The prior-hospitaller of Vacquiers in 1117/40 received a third of the tithes and other demesne revenues from the monks of St Sernin in return for protecting their estates.[2] In 1132 a church was given to the abbey of Prüm, with the approval of the archbishop of Trier, on the highly improper condition that the tithe should be held by the donor's son, who was himself a monk at Prüm, for his lifetime in return for an annual rent.[3] The abbeys of Cavour, St Peter at Turin, Ste Croix at Bordeaux, and St Sernin at Toulouse all granted tithes as fiefs to laymen in return for property and services, including homage and fealty and occasionally the feudal incident of relief.[4]

Subinfeudation presented a constant threat to the peaceful possession of tithes by monks, especially if they wanted to recover direct possession. The tithe of Hannay, for instance, was granted by Abbot Rainald of Abingdon (1084–97) to a priest for his lifetime and was given by the priest to a knight named Roger, after whose death it was recovered and held by the abbey for four years. It was then granted by Abbot Ingulph (1130–1158/9) to Roger's son Robert, who tried to sell it, and was finally redeemed by the abbey at a cost of seven marks.[5] Wibald of Stavelot in 1146 tried to recover some tithes which had been held by a layman and his son for an annual rent; 'but on account of the evil which abounded in our days and of the agreement made by our predecessors, we were unable to do this [recover the tithe] and decided to re-grant the tithe to Nicholas son of Macharius [son of

[1] Lérins, I, 82.   [2] St Sernin de Toulouse, p. 32, no. 46.

[3] Altluxemburg, I, 545–7.

[4] Cavour, p. 31 (1072: tithes granted iure beneficiario in return for supplying the abbey with horses); Scarnafigi, pp. 241–3 (see case III in appendix); Ste Croix de Bordeaux, pp. 111–13 (see case V in appendix: tithe held for rent and relief); St Sernin de Toulouse, pp. 114 (1145) and 240; cf. Mâcon, p. 361 (eleventh–twelfth centuries: tithe granted as a fief with homage and fealty to the dean). At the request of Archbishop Theobald, the cathedral priory of Canterbury gave some tithes from its demesne lands at Eleigh to Peter the Scribe for his lifetime (Saltman, Theobald, pp. 267–8).

[5] Abingdon, II, 200–2; cf. Monasticon, I, 508, on the abbots' dates. Archbishop Theobald of Canterbury in 1155/9 forced the abbey of Shrewsbury to recover some tithes alienated by the abbot without permission from the monks (Saltman, Theobald, p. 473).

the original holder] for the same rent'.[1] Any grant, as these abbots knew, created a definite property right for the holder and his heirs, and such rights had a market value and were defensible at law.[2] To avoid this situation, the archbishop of Salzburg in 1130 gave some tithes paid by the duke of Carinthia to the monastery of Admont, 'lest he should be forced to grant them as benefices to laymen'.[3]

A second problem for monasteries that held tithes was the difficulty of collection. The regular procedures by which monks gathered their tithes will be discussed later, but there were constant special difficulties to cope with. 'Probably in the collection of no part of their revenue', said Coopland, 'did the monks [of St Bertin] meet with such opposition as in the case of tithes.'[4] Popes, kings, and bishops were all appealed to by monasteries to help enforce regular payment of tithes and to prevent the usurpation of their tithes by local magnates.[5] Frank brigandage and refusal to pay were on the whole comparatively rare,[6] but both were involved in an interesting case settled by the archbishop of Trier in 1154 for the abbey of St Trond.

When the grapes had been harvested on the villa of Brildel, it was customary for the provost and the priest, together with the manager

[1] *Stavelot-Malmédy*, I, 381–2.
[2] See case III in appendix, where the tithes had been granted illegally and without investiture and yet were recovered by the heirs of the holder, and case V, where the monks had to redeem their own property for a large sum after it had been subinfeudated by the holder.
[3] *Steiermark*, I, 139.   [4] Coopland, *St Bertin*, p. 47.
[5] *Aniane*, p. 113, and *EPRI*, p. 111, no. 208 (JL 9663, 1146/53); *The Manuscripts of...the Duke of Rutland*, Historical Manuscripts Commission, XXIV (London, 1888–1905), IV, 149 (Henry I in 1123/7 ordered Hugh of Ropsley to allow the monks of Belvoir to collect their Ropsley tithes at the door of his grange in peace; cf. *Regesta regum Anglo-Normannorum*, II, 212–13, no. 1521); Lawrie, *Scottish Charters*, p. 52, no. 61 (*c.* 1125, King David for Dunfermline) and p. 163, no. 202 (1147/53, King David for Rindelgros); *St Wandrille*, pp. 144–5, no. 81 (1147/8: Archbishop Hugh of Rouen asked the regent Suger to prevent the excommunicated Hugh Brostin of Mantes and Meulan from taking the tithes of St Wandrille); Saltman, *Theobald*, pp. 378–9 (*c.* 1150, for Lewes), 418 (1150/61, for Osney), 497–8 (1151/7, for Tutbury); C. R. Cheney, *From Becket to Langton*, Ford Lectures, 1955 (Manchester, 1956), pp. 187–8 (Henry II for Hurley); cf. Van Caenegem, *Writs*, p. 189 and index, s.v. 'Tithe'.
[6] See *Journal of Ecc. History*, XIII, 175–80.

(*villicus*) and his assistants, to collect from each house the tithe which the parishioners owed. Some paid their tithes joyfully and reverently, as suited the blessing they had received; others gave hardly anything, holding back and arguing; worse were those who blasphemed and gave nothing. Some men who lived outside the parish bought the vineyards of the poor parishioners and, trusting in their strength, gave abuse rather than tithes. We discussed these troubles of the church first with our equals and then with the parishioners and decided at their request that each man must pay what he owes in his own vineyard at the time of the harvest.[1]

The corruption of manorial officials also gave trouble to many monasteries, as to the monks of Préaux, who actually returned some tithes to the earl of Leicester because of 'the violence of his officials'.[2] And the archbishop of Cologne explained in 1135 that a gift of tithes by the abbot of Gladbach to the new nunnery of Neuwerk cost the monks nothing because some of the tithes were held by laymen, others were held by the advocate of the abbey and his sister 'not as a benefice but by the ungrateful grace of the manager', and the remainder were consumed by the manager's servants 'by eating and drinking at the time of the harvest, so it was of no use to the monks or the church'.[3]

A further source of difficulty in the proper collection of tithes arose from their tendency to become a fixed payment in produce or money rather than a proportional due of a tenth. When this happened there might be trouble if the produce increased or changed in type. In some grants the donor in fact specified that the tithe should remain proportional whether the production changed, increased, or decreased.[4] In granting several estates to St Wandrille in 1086, for instance, Roger of Beaumont reserved the right to revert the land to forest and then to give 'only the tithe as from other forests, with no disapproval or complaint'.[5] Sometimes a monastery might benefit from the fixing of a tithe, as at Uffington, where the monks of Abingdon owned all the

---

[1] *Mittelrhein*, I, 641, no. 582 (cf. p. 128 below).
[2] See p. 110 above.   [3] *Gladbach*, I, 10–12.
[4] Cf. *Recueil des actes de Henri II...concernant les provinces françaises et les affaires de France*, ed. L. Delisle and E. Berger, CDRHF (Paris, 1909–1927), II, 152, no. 570 (1174/82).   [5] *St Wandrille*, pp. 95–6, no. 41.

tithes beyond the customary twenty-four sheaves of grain per virgate owed to the parish priest.[1] As a rule, however, the monks suffered. The archbishop of Mainz in 1127 confirmed a grant by his predecessor in 1108 of the tithes from an archiepiscopal manor to the abbey of Disibodenberg, but he excepted the tithes from his own demesne and further specified that:

Justice demands and almost universal custom shows that this tithe must be paid from the fields and vineyards in accordance with the fecundity and sterility of the soil and of the year; but over the years the people, ever ready to neglect justice, took upon themselves by force rather than by choice to pay a certain amount fixed at their pleasure when the crops had been gathered and stored.[2]

Similarly, when vines were planted in place of grain at Cheviré in Anjou, the men there, 'led by avarice and relying on the support and men of their lords', refused to give tithes from the new vineyards to the monks of the abbey of the Trinity at Vendôme, who had owned the tithe of the grain; but in 1146 the court of the count of Anjou decided in favour of the monks that 'for no reason should the tithe of wine be denied to those who held the tithe of grain'.[3] This type of difficulty often arose over the tithes from newly cultivated lands, many of which belonged to monasteries. A synod at Cologne in 1140 confirmed the right of Stavelot to the tithes not only from the pannage at Büllingen, as before, but also from the rich crops that were then being raised on cleared lands.[4]

The most serious threat to monastic possession of tithes, however, was posed by the rival claims of priests, bishops, laymen, and

[1] See p. 105 above.

[2] *Mainz*, I, 342–4 (Ruthard's charter) and 449–50 (Adalbert's charter). The monks had complained for many years before eventually the archiepiscopal court confirmed the proportional nature of the tithe.

[3] *La Trinité de Vendôme*, II, 342–5; cf. *Marmoutier (Dunois)*, pp. 86–8 (1116: see p. 125 below), where the monks established their claim to the tithes from some newly planted grain and vines against a layman who claimed he had given the tithes only from the previous vines; and *Ronceray*, pp. 83–4 (1143): the monks of St Aubin at Angers complained that vines had been planted on some lands from which they shared the tithes with the nuns of Ronceray but they ceded the new vineyard with all its tithes to the nuns in return for the same amount of land with its tithes elsewhere.

[4] *Köln*, I, 510–11, no. 48.

other monks and canons, whose interests were often hurt by the accumulation of tithes by monks. As Viard pointed out, the countless confirmations of the possession of tithes by monks were mostly designed not to enforce payment but to frustrate rival claims,[1] which were often raked up even after many years of peaceful possession by the monks.[2] The terms of the original grants might also be obscure, and supplementary charters were often necessary to establish the exact extent and possession of the tithe.[3] When such rival claims were legitimate, they could usually be dealt with by voluntary compromises and agreements or settled by payments in money or in kind, but they were frequently taken into court. Monastic chartularies are filled with accounts of litigation over tithes.[4] 'If we turn from cases concerning the sacraments to lawsuits over property—whether land or tithes or patronage of churches—', said Cheney, 'we face the central fact of twelfth-century ecclesiastical history in England: the fact that innumerable rights in these things were becoming the endowments of religious houses. Every grant was a potential source of dispute....'[5] These remarks are equally true of the Continent.

The first question in a legal dispute over tithes was to settle the court in which the case would be tried. Officially, since tithes were *spiritualia*, any case in which they were involved belonged in the church courts;[6] but they often came into lay courts both

---

[1] Viard, *Dîme*, I, 169–70.

[2] Cf. case III in appendix and Chénon, *Chapelle-Aude*, pp. 138–9, for examples of laymen reviving claims after more than thirty years; cf. *Molesme*, II, 46–7 (1076/95).

[3] The vague definition of the boundaries, for instance, in the grant of tithes to Reichersberg by Archbishop Conrad of Salzburg in 1144 (see pp. 101–2 above) was a constant source of trouble to the canons, and in 1159/61 the Provost Gerhoh wrote bitterly to the abbot of Admont that owing to a technical flaw they had been deprived of certain noval tithes: *Salzburg*, II, 432–3, no. 309; cf. Classen, *Gerhoch*, pp. 343–4, 347–8 and 373–4.

[4] Cf. Coulton, *Five Centuries*, III, 224–6, and Coopland, *St Bertin*, p. 47. Accounts of nine characteristic legal cases involving monastic tithes will be found in the appendix.   [5] Cheney, *Becket*, p. 50.

[6] See can. 9 of the synod of Ingelheim in 948 (cited p. 56 above); Alexander III in *Appendix ad Concilium Lateranense*, IX, 26, in Mansi, *Collectio*, XXII, 319 (JL 13931); and, among recent works, Viard, *Dîme*, I, 117 and 222–5; Widera, in *A. f. kath. KR*, CX, 38; and Cheney, *Becket*, pp. 96–7.

because tithes were an important form of temporal property and because monks might be able to assert their rights only through an advocate or other layman.[1] The decision in fact seems usually to have lain with the disputants; and it was not uncommon, as with the first three cases described in the appendix, for the same case to come into both civil and ecclesiastical courts. From a legal point of view, Pollock and Maitland wrote that in England, 'From century to century there was a border warfare over tithes between the two sets of lawyers, and from time to time some curious compromises were framed'.[2] Makower pointed out that in spite of William the Conqueror's decree on ecclesiastical courts and Becket's later uncompromising stand, cases concerning tithes were tried in secular courts in every reign from William I to Henry II and that only in the thirteenth century was the sole competence of the church courts in such matters generally recognized.[3] In lower Austria, according to Plöchl, most tithe cases were settled in ecclesiastical courts, but a few, such as the disputes between Zwettl and the parish priest of Polla and between Heiligenkreuz and Melk in 1178, came before the duke.[4] In nearby Styria and Carinthia, on the other hand, most tithe cases after the middle of the thirteenth century were tried in secular courts, largely owing to the declining influence of the archbishops of Salzburg.[5]

Local conditions of this sort often determined the nature of the court, and in the eleventh and twelfth centuries cases concerning monastic tithes were brought before every possible type of

[1] At least half the tithe cases which have come to my attention and in which the nature of the court is known were tried in lay courts.

[2] Frederick Pollock and F. W. Maitland, *The History of English Law Before the Time of Edward I*, 2nd ed. (Cambridge, 1898), I, 127.

[3] Makower, *Kirche*, pp. 446–9; cf. Norma Adams, 'The Judicial Conflict over Tithes', *English Hist. Rev.* LII (1937), 2–4, and Raymonde Foreville, *L'Église et la royauté en Angleterre sous Henri II Plantagenet (1154–1189)* (Paris, n.d. [1943]), p. 419. In Scotland in the twelfth century the royal court also took cognizance of cases concerning churches and tithes: Lawrie, *Scottish Charters*, pp. 146–7, no. 182 (1147/50: see p. 129 below).

[4] Plöchl, *Zehentwesen*, pp. 55–6 and 129–41, who suggested that in the case between Heiligenkreuz and Melk the duke may have served as a papal judge-delegate (p. 133 n. 2), though this seems improbable (see p. 262 below).

[5] Tremel, in *Zs. d. hist. Vereines f. Steiermark*, XXXIII, 40–4.

tribunal: popes, legates, bishops, and archdeacons; emperors, kings, feudal lords and their officials; councils, synods, committees of arbitrators, clerical and lay, and local groups of doomsmen and *boni homines*. On the whole better records were kept by the church than by the lay courts, and the register of a bishop like Theobald of Canterbury gives some idea of the number of disputes over tithes in the middle of the twelfth century.[1] The papacy also became increasingly involved in this litigation, both in cases of the first instance, like that between Leno and the bishop of Luni in 1060, and even more through appeals;[2] and in the second half of the twelfth century the popes made use when possible of legates, local judge-delegates, and the new technique of *appellatione remota* in an effort to cope with the problems of corruption, judicial delay, and repeated appeals.[3] The bishop of Amiens in 1151 settled a dispute over noval tithes between St Cornelius at Compiègne and the collegiate church of St Florence at Roye,

---

[1] Saltman, *Theobald*, index, s.v. 'Tithes' (see also the index to this book, s.v. 'Theobald'). Several of these cases were over tithes claimed by alien monasteries and priories: pp. 325–6 (*c.* 1143: St Martin des Champs *v.* the canons of Exeter), 367–8 (1150/2: St Nicholas at Angers *v.* Llanthony), and 458 (1139/57: St Neot, a dependency of Bec, *v.* the priest of Great Gransden); see also pp. 245–6 (1156/7: Belvoir *v.* Thetford) and 520 (1148/61: Dunstable *v.* Merton).

[2] See pp. 87–8 above, case IX in appendix, for an appeal to Rome, and cases I, IV and VII, all of which were settled or confirmed by papal legates; also JL 5501 (1088/94: St John at la Peña *v.* St Sernin at Toulouse before Urban II), 6095 (1106: Corbie *v.* the chapter of Bruges before Paschal II), 8919 (1146: Lérins *v.* the canons of Ventimiglia before Eugene III), etc. As early as 1059 the archbishop of Tours, the bishop of Angers, and the count of Anjou informed the bishop of Troyes in a joint letter of the decision by a synod at Rome in a case over a proprietary church between St Aubin at Angers and the Trinity at Vendôme (*PL*, CXLVI, 1435–6).

[3] For cases involving papal judge-delegates, see in addition to those cited below, *Basse-Fontaine*, pp. 24–6 (1142/68); *Ronceray*, pp. 14–15 (1147); *Toussaints de Châlons*, pp. 253–4 (1157); *Tiglieto*, p. 236 (1158: cf. *APRI*, III, 193 and *IP*, VI. 2, 281, no. 13). Theobald of Canterbury served as a judge-delegate in the tithe cases between Belvoir and Thetford (see n. 1 above) and between Crowland and the subdeacon Haldanus (1150/3: *PU in England*, III, 222–3). Cf. *The Letters of John of Salisbury*, ed. W. J. Millor, H. E. Butler and C. N. L. Brooke, Nelson's Medieval Texts (London, etc., 1955 ff.), I, introd. p. xxxv, on clauses forbidding further appeal (the earliest example known to the editor was in 1143). It was also used in case VII in the appendix (1152).

which 'had been frequently discussed before the lord pope'.[1] And shortly before 1169 Alexander III and his cardinals confirmed a decision made by the bishops of Winchester and London in a case between the abbey of Ivry and a priest in Norfolk, who had again appealed to Rome after the delegates had found in favour of the monks.[2]

The legal procedure tended to vary according to the court. The church courts usually based their judgements on the evidence either of charters or of long possession. The abbess of Kaufungen established her claim to certain noval tithes by producing a charter before the archbishop of Mainz in a synod at Fritzlar;[3] and in 1112 the archbishop of Bourges awarded the tithes of Saligny to the abbey of Fleury on the basis of a charter and on proof that the lay claimants had already been excommunicated for taking the tithe.[4] Possession, however, was even more important than a charter, as the canons of St Paul at Halberstadt discovered in their controversy with Albert the Bear over the tithes of Gossel.[5] And the nuns of St Peter at Turin relied more on their undisturbed possession for thirty years than on the original grant in laying claim to the tithes of Scarnafigi.[6] In the case between Leno and the bishop of Luni in 1060 the papacy definitely applied the principle of prescription to monastic ownership of tithes, and the ecclesiastical courts in the twelfth century almost always accepted the evidence of the oldest witnesses and defended a long-established possession.[7]

[1] St Corneille de Compiègne, I, 155–6.
[2] Cheney, Becket, p. 60; cf. Alexander's confirmation in 1165 of the decision between St Martin des Champs and the priest of Crespières, cited p. 128 below.
[3] P. 106 n. 2 above.
[4] St Benoît-sur-Loire, I, 278–80.
[5] Case VI in appendix.   [6] Case III in appendix.
[7] Pp. 87–8 above. Case IX in the appendix gives a detailed picture of the procedure in an ecclesiastical court, especially of the taking of oaths and the desire of the losing side to avoid witnessing the oath. Cf. St Victeur au Mans, pp. 22–3 (1135/43), where the archbishop of Tours and the bishop of Le Mans decided in favour of the monks, who had held certain tithes for over thirty years, against a layman who claimed them by inheritance, and Saltman, Theobald, pp. 372–3 (1150/61: see p. 130 below), where Theobald based his decision in a dispute between St Albans and the regular canons of Leeds on the evidence given under oath by three old men on the estate.

Arbitrators and local tribunals also relied heavily on possession and existing practice or made an equitable compromise between the claimants. In 1114 a layman who had several tithe disputes with the monks of Aniane agreed in return for ninety shillings to submit one to the judgement of the local *boni homines*, another to the parishioners, and the third to the bishop and his canons.[1] The controversy between St Severus at Erfurt and the townsmen of Burg-Tonna was adjudicated in 1143 by a committee of seven men who 'named all those who ought to pay the tithe and said what each of them should rightly give'.[2] The case between the priory of St Pry at Béthune and the priest Walter was settled in 1131 by three arbitrators, one each chosen by the two disputants and the bishop of Arras.[3] In the case between Leno and the bishop of Brescia in 1194/5 there seem to have been two fact-finders or mediators.[4]

These procedures based on evidence were often long and expensive, however, and offered endless opportunities for appeals and delays. The royal and feudal courts, on the other hand, sometimes made use, even in cases involving monks and clerics, of the old but speedy techniques of compurgation, ordeal, and judicial duel, which were forbidden in the church courts.[5] In the dispute

[1] *Aniane*, pp. 418–19. On these techniques of arbitration and mediation, see Yvonne Bongert, *Recherches sur les cours laïques du Xe au XIIIe siècle* (Paris, 1949), pp. 103–11 and 159–82.

[2] *Erfurt*, I, 30–1.

[3] *St Bertin*, I, 66–7.

[4] Case VIII in appendix.

[5] On judicial duels involving monasteries, see L. Tanon, *Histoire des justices des anciennes églises et communautés monastiques de Paris* (Paris, 1883), pp. 16–27, who cited various cases from the tenth to the fourteenth centuries which involved Parisian and other houses, esp. St Germain des Prés; Bruhat, *Monachisme*, pp. 338–43, citing *Saintes*, p. 140, no. 218 (1134) and *St Jean d'Angély*, I, 56, no. 29, who said that such conflicts were rare in the Saintonge and Aunis in the eleventh and twelfth centuries; Paul Rousset, 'La croyance en la justice immanente à l'époque féodale', *Le Moyen Âge*, LIV (4th ser. III, 1948), 237; and Bongert, *Cours*, p. 231, who said that after the middle of the twelfth century monks rarely settled their disputes by champions and battle. In case IX in the appendix the lay owner of the land offered to prove the truth of his assertion 'either by divine judgement or by secular duel'. Other examples may be found in D'Espinay, *Cartulaires*, p. 52 (1070/80: ordeal by boiling water in a case between St Nicholas of Angers and the canons of St Maurille); Paul Marchegay,

between the Trinity at Vendôme and Marmoutier over the tithes of Fontaines, the countess of Vendôme in 1087/90 ordered a duel between men chosen from the *familia* of each abbey and 'who had no experience in this'. The monks of Marmoutier, however, presented as their champion a well-known mercenary, 'who hired himself to everybody for such matters', and they would have automatically lost the case unless they had been allowed to choose another champion. But at the last minute before the battle Marmoutier withdrew and ceded the tithes to the Trinity.[1] A few years later the nuns of Ronceray and the monks of St Nicholas at Angers met before Rainald of Châteaugontier to test by oaths the validity of the monks' claim to certain tithes, but the monks refused to accept the nuns' oath-taker and thus lost the case.[2] And in the case between Marmoutier and Gastho of Broico over the tithes from a newly planted vineyard, the court offered Gastho the choice between proving his claim by oath or by battle, but Gastho refused to fight over a grant originally made by himself and accepted the testimony of three witnesses.[3] In each of these three cases cited as examples, one party backed down before putting its claim to the ultimate test of oath or battle, and for this reason it may be that these procedures were less arbitrary in practice than they appear to have been in theory.

The most impressive feature in all these cases is not so much their length and complexity, or the tenacity and unscrupulousness of the litigants, who stooped to perjury and forgery to

'Duel judiciaire entre des communités religieuses. 1098', *Bibliothèque de l'École des Chartes*, I (1839–40), 552–64 (Marmoutier *v.* Talmont and Angles); and Jacques Bouillart, *Histoire de l'abbaye royale de Saint Germain des Prez* (Paris, 1724), p. 89 and *pièce justificatif*, no. 52 (*c.* 1154). Most of the cases cited here and below were in the region of the Loire (involving particularly the abbeys of Marmoutier and St Nicholas at Angers). Outside France I have found no examples of the use of these old judicial techniques in cases involving monks. For other cases tried in secular courts, see *Longpont*, pp. 147–8 (*c.* 1108); *St Martin des Champs*, I, 204–5 (1108/9); and *La Charité-sur-Loire*, pp. 166–7 (1177: see *Rev. bén.* LXX, 608).

[1] *La Trinité de Vendôme*, II, 50–1; cf. Compain, *Geoffroi de Vendôme*, pp. 66–7. On the use of hired champions, see Glanville, *Concerning the Laws and Customs of the Kingdom of England*, II, 3, in *English Historical Documents*, II, 465.

[2] Case II in Appendix.

[3] *Marmoutier (Dunois)*, pp. 86–8 (1116: see p. 119 n. 3 above).

support their claims,[1] as the fact that even in the church courts tithes were treated as a secular revenue and cases concerning tithes were settled in terms not of canon law but of the property interests involved. In the cases described in the appendix, for instance, the decisions were based on custom, long possession, sale, exchange, and grant. Thus the problem in the second case was not whether a laywoman might hold tithes but to which abbey she had given them. No one seems to have questioned the theoretical validity of the grants by the countess to the nuns or by the nuns to a layman in the third case, nor by the abbot to a layman in the fifth case, though all of these were clearly un-canonical. Once grants were made they were defensible at law. The archbishop of Burgos fought for years to establish his right to the episcopal third of the tithes from several monastic churches, but no sooner had he won than he granted the tithe to the abbey in return for some land. The spiritual nature of the tithe was not entirely forgotten in these cases, for the countess forbade the nuns ever to alienate the tithes, and the claim of the archbishop of Burgos was based purely on canon law, but their purpose was to define property rights, not to recover tithes from the hands of laymen or to restore them to the sacramental churches to which they properly belonged.

Partly for this reason, the least dangerous rivals to monks in their claims to tithes were, paradoxically, the canonical receivers of the tithe, the parish priests. The question of the extent to which the growing monastic possession of tithes hurt parochial finances is a matter of dispute. Some scholars hold that the acquisition of tithes by monks deprived the priests of their pay; others, that monasteries were fully entitled to receive tithes.[2] Tithes were of

[1] Cf. the forgeries in case I, the corruption of the abbot and the monk Herbert in case II, and the alleged collusion of the judges and plaintiff in case IX, in the appendix.

[2] Frere, in *Fasciculus I. W. Clark dictatus*, pp. 201–3, denied that the parishes suffered and said that tithes 'might be devoted to such religious objects as the payer of the "tithe" thought best'. From a legal viewpoint, this certainly was not true in the eleventh and twelfth centuries, and even as late as the fifteenth century an English Franciscan was excommunicated for teaching that men could use their personal tithes for the poor rather than give them to the parish

course a very important source of income to many parish priests; but by the eleventh and twelfth centuries their portions had mostly become customary rights, and so many tithes had passed into the hands of other owners that the accumulation of tithes by monasteries probably did less harm to the parish priests than to other monasteries and to bishops and laymen. In addition, some provision was often made for the priests both by bishops and laymen in their grants to monasteries and by the monks themselves, who were responsible for the support of priests in their proprietary churches and in churches on lands from which they held the tithes and other parochial revenues.

Such provisions for the priests, whether made voluntarily or as the result of a legal dispute, usually assigned either a half, third, or quarter of the tithe, or occasionally more or less, to the parish church.[1] Theobald of Canterbury awarded all the tithes of Dengemarsh, except from the monastic demesne, to the priest in his case against the abbey of Battle;[2] but the abbot of Leno gave only a quarter of the tithes from the free tenures to the priests on some of his estates.[3] The abbeys of Redon and Quimperlé in Brittany agreed each to keep one-third of the tithes and other revenues of a church which they owned jointly and to give the remaining third to the chaplains serving in the church.[4] Alternatively the priest might receive all the tithes from certain lands in his

priest: A. G. Little, 'Personal Tithes', *English Hist. Rev.* LX (1945), 67. Cf. also Snape, *Finances*, pp. 75–6, and Cheney, *Becket*, p. 129, who said that 'a benefice might be seriously impoverished...by alienation of tithe in favour of some religious house'.

[1] See the lay and episcopal provisions cited p. 69 (1/5), p. 101 nn. 2 (1/2), 3 (1/3), 4 (1/4), p. 102 nn. 3 (1/2), 4 (2/9), 6 (1/3); *St Bertin*, I, 66–7 (1131: the monks of St Pry at Béthune agreed after arbitration to give the priest Walter half of the revenues of the church at Haut-Bruay and all the 'confessional pennies' and offerings for masses to the dead) and 78 (1143: the bishop of Arras awarded all the land and tithes in a certain parish to St Pry in spite of the claims of the parish priests); *St Martin des Champs*, I, 285–8 (1120/4: see p. 133 below).

[2] Saltman, *Theobald*, p. 242 (1150/4); cf. also pp. 498–9 (1154/61 or 1162/70), where a priest renounced his claim to two-thirds of the demesne tithes at Walsingham (see p. 222 below).

[3] Case VIII in appendix.

[4] *Redon*, p. 302 (1128).

parish,[1] or a set measure of produce out of the tithe, as at Uffington in England and Crespières in France, where the priests received respectively twenty-four sheaves of grain from each virgate and one measure of better grain.[2] On the villa of Brildel in the Rhineland a second tithe was gathered for the priest after the first, which belonged to St Trond.

There is on this estate [according to the charter of 1154] a second tithe after the better one, which was established at one time for ordering and furnishing the church and which the abbot and church of St Trond gave to the pastor of that church on the condition that all the church's needs, both inside and outside, in ornamentation, in books, and binding, and in enclosing the atrium, should be met from this tithe and that they [the monks] should be free from all these things.

This unusual arrangement may partly account for the resistance to tithing at Brildel![3] Finally an abbey might pay a rent in lieu or tithes. The archbishop of Magdeburg, for instance, arranged for the nuns of Our Lady at Magdeburg to pay an annual rent in kind to the priest at Gossel 'in place of the third part of the tithe'.[4] Such allowances were mostly made not as matters of canonical right, however, but as property grants to the priest, whose share or rent might in theory be revoked at any time by the monks.

The claims of bishops, laymen, and other houses of monks and canons could also as a rule be settled by payments in cash or land, by annual revenues, or by divisions. Sometimes a monastery won or lost outright and had to give up the tithe even to a layman.

---

[1] See p. 102 n. 1 above and *Bâle*, I, 330-1, no. 215 (1157), in which the nuns of Sulzburg were to keep the tithes from their own lands in the parish of Rimsingen, the priest was to take the rest, and they were to divide 'the tithes of the inhabitants of adjacent villages'.

[2] See p. 105 n. 2 above and *St Martin des Champs*, I, 232-3 (*c*. 1116: the priest of Crespières received from the monks some land, a measure of grain, two-thirds of the oblations, and all of certain tithes) and II, 287-9 (1165: Alexander III confirmed the revision of this arrangement made by the bishop of Paris and the abbot of St Germain des Prés; JL 11179).

[3] *Mittelrhein*, I, 641, no. 582 (see pp. 117-18 above).

[4] *Unser Lieben Frauen zu Magdeburg*, pp. 7-8 (1136: grant of tithes from the bishop of Brandenburg) and 23-4 (1156: the next bishop claimed a third of the tithes for the priest, and the archbishop arranged for the monks to keep the entire tithe and to pay a rent to the priest).

In the middle of the twelfth century, after a hundred years of ecclesiastical decrees against lay possession of tithes, the abbey of St Stephen at Würzburg gave up its third of the tithes at Gramschatz in return for an annual rent.[1] But the monks usually kept at least part of the tithe under dispute. It is unnecessary to give more examples of rents and payments, which were like the arrangements discussed above;[2] but it may be of interest to look at a few of the compromises arranged by both civil and ecclesiastical courts in order to show how divisions of tithes arose from legal decisions as well as from the older canonical divisions, grants, inheritance, and subinfeudation. The king of Sicily in 1148 settled the almost endless tithe disputes between the bishops of Messina and the dual abbey of Lipari–Patti by dividing the tithes of several churches and fisheries into halves and thirds.[3] The king of Scotland and his barons in 1147/50 awarded the tithes from the royal demesne, both old and new, in the jurisdiction of Stirling to the chapel in Stirling Castle, which belonged to the abbey of Dunfermline, and all the other tithes and burial dues to the parish church of Eccles, which belonged to the bishop of St Andrews.[4] The bishop of Auxerre in 1158 arranged that the monks of La Charité-sur-Loire and the canons of St Satur should own the tithes of their own churches and that the monks should own the tithes of a vineyard which they held jointly with the canons in the parish of the nuns of St Romble, near Sancerre, 'on condition that they would acquire nothing more in the parish by which the half of the tithes belonging to the canons might be reduced'.[5] The

---

[1] *St Stephan in Würzburg*, p. 126 (1143/66).

[2] Cf. *Mainz*, I, 474–5 (1130: St Victor at Mainz and Disibodenberg settled a long dispute in the archbishop's court in return for a grant of land); *St Wandrille*, pp. 109–10, no. 54 (1108: the abbey gave an annual rent of forty shillings to the monks of St Peter of Câtillon at Conches); etc.

[3] *Messina*, pp. 14–15, confirmed pp. 30–2 (1180); cf. the discussion of this case and other documents in White, *Monasticism*, pp. 92–3 and 98–9.

[4] Lawrie, *Scottish Charters*, pp. 146–7, no. 182.

[5] *La Charité-sur-Loire*, pp. 186–9; cf. *St Benoît-sur-Loire*, I, 288–90, in which Louis VI in 1121 confirmed a judgement by which the canons of St-Jean-en-Vallée at Chartres received the great tithe at Mantarville and jurisdiction over tithe disputes and the monks of Fleury received the small tithe, except from the canons' lands, and a rent from the canons, on which see Achille Luchaire, *Louis VI le Gros* (Paris, 1890), pp. 141–2, no. 307.

bishop of Maguelonne decided that the new abbey of Our Lady at Vallecrosa should belong to the bishops of Maguelonne, not to the monks of Aniane, on whose land it was built, but that it should usurp none of the functions or revenues of the churches belonging to Aniane, for whom he decreed that 'Let no one dare to take from your church the oblations, tithes, first-fruits, and other ecclesiastical rights which without official permission belong only to baptismal churches'.[1] Finally, Theobald of Canterbury on the basis of evidence given by three old men awarded the tithes paid by thirteen men at Ringleton to the regular canons of Leeds and the other tithes to the monks of St Albans.[2]

As a result of these elaborate divisions, a monastery might be entitled to only a fraction of the entire tithe of an area, or to all or part of the tithe from specific lands, revenues, products, churches, or even individual tithe-payers, and the difficulties of collection must have been correspondingly multiplied. On the whole, however, very much less is known about the practical administration and collection of tithes than about their possession.[3] The payment of small tithes, as from eggs and vegetables, must have been largely a matter of conscience, unless they belonged to a resident priest who kept a sharp eye on the hen-houses and the gardens. But the collection of the great tithe, which was paid at harvest season,[4] was more strictly regulated, and various details can be gathered from monastic charters.

---

[1] *Aniane*, pp. 260–2.

[2] Saltman, *Theobald*, pp. 372–3 (1150/61); cf. p. 124 above for another case where specific tithe-payers (including the amounts they should pay) were named.

[3] Viard, *Dîme*, I, 150 and 164–7, who said that 'La perception de la dîme est moins bien connue que son assiette'; cf. the chapter on 'Gathering the Tithes' in Boyd, *Tithes*, pp. 196–207, which is largely concerned with Italy in the later Middle Ages, and Lennard, *Rural England*, p. 113, who commented on the difficulty of studying estate management in the twelfth century. A description of later tithing in England may be found in Orwin, *Open Fields*, pp. 158–60. The section on 'Régime des dîmages' in Lesne, *Propriété*, VI, 228, was unfinished at the author's death.

[4] Viard, *Dîme*, I, 166, cited examples of tithes paid in August and September in south-western France and Italy. More generally, Lennard, *Rural England*, pp. 185–9, discussed various rents in kind and money and said that 'These are

The tithes from a given region were known as the *decimarium*, of which the owner, either clerical or lay, was the *decimarius*.[1] The official in charge of collecting the tithe might also be called a *decimarius*, or a *decimator* or *decimanus*, and in return for his services he usually kept a tenth of the tithe, the *tractus decimae*, *redecima*, *retrodecima*, or, as it was later called in France, the *carion* or *conroi*.[2] Many monasteries in the twelfth century used such officials to gather their tithes;[3] and the position of monastic *decimator* was in some regions hereditary and was often held by peasants and even by women.[4] In England, according to Lennard, it was 'a very common practice...to combine a donation of tithe with the assignment to the recipient monastery of a peasant's services' to wearisome details; but the times at which payments fell due must have been matters of intimate concern for those who had to make them; and on the whole the facts seem to suggest that they were determined mainly in the interests of the recipients, though one cannot be sure. Perhaps transport conditions and local facilities for the storage of grain played a part in the temporal allocation of the burdens; but this is mere conjecture.'

[1] See, generally, Sée, *Classes rurales*, pp. 468–9.

[2] For a discussion of these terms and examples of grants to monasteries, see p. 104 n. 2 above. In about 1122, the Cistercians of Bonnevaux bought for three shillings the claims to the tithes from their own produce of one Amedeus, 'qui decimas colligebat'; *Bonnevaux*, pp. 86–7, no. 199.

[3] The abbey of Muri in the twelfth century had a *villicus* to gather and store the tithes, as the author of the *Acta Murensia* said, 'Because anyone who is familiar with the ways of laymen knows that there should be one *villicus* for the tithe of the church and the village, for the welfare and happiness of souls is not served when the offering to God is not properly transported and guarded' (*Muri*, p. 66). Cf. case IX in appendix (eleventh century: *decimatores* of St Timothy); *Conques*, pp. 350–1 (twelfth century: *decimatores* of the abbey and of the lay owner); Bruhat, *Monachisme*, pp. 259–60, citing *decimarius* and *decimator* in Saintes, p. 99, no. 123 (1076) and *St Jean d'Angély*, I, 144, no. 112 (1076); *Cluny*, V, 428, no. 4074 (1142: *decimarius* 'for collecting the tithe'); *Actes de Henri II*, I, 274, no. 154 (1156/61: decimator of St Stephen at Caen) and II, 131, no. 551 (late twelfth century: *decimatores* of Savigny in Normandy); Pierre Tisset, *L'Abbaye de Gellone au diocèse de Lodève* (Paris, 1933), p. 202 (early twelfth century); *Land ob der Enns*, I, 316, no. 73 (1159/61: *decimatores* of Reichersberg and of the archbishop of Salzburg); *Vigeois*, p. 224, no. 336 (c. 1164: grant of tithes mentioning the consent of 'presbyter qui hoc reddet et Petrus del Brol qui decimarius est hujus decime', who may have been either the collector or the overlord of the tithe); *Aureil*, pp. 188–9, no. 253 (1166: three brothers mortgaged some tithes to the monks, and among the *fideiussores* was the bailiff of the tithe, who apparently continued to collect it); *Bobbio*, II, 358–9 (1207); etc.

[4] Tremel, in *Zs. d. hist. Vereines f. Steiermark*, XXXIII, 29.

collect the tithe.¹ The count of Blois in 1157/8 required the
peasants of Roinville to transport the tithe belonging to the monks
of St Martin des Champs to their grange.² At Corbie in the ninth
century, the important tenants had to bring their tithes to the
abbey themselves.³ In the eleventh century the *villicus* at
Quimperlé was required to furnish 'as many sacks as are needed
for collecting the monastery's tithes in the month of August'.⁴
And in a grant of tithes to the abbey of St Cyprien at Poitiers in
1105, the keeper (*serviens*) of the tithe gave up 'whatever he
claimed in the tithe [presumably the *tractus decimae* or a similar
right] so that the prior and monks might appoint whomever
they wished to keep the tithe'.⁵ The tithes from nearby estates and
from an abbey's proprietary churches and lands were usually
gathered by its own manorial officials and priests,⁶ as on secular
manors, where according to an anonymous thirteenth-century
Seneschaucie, 'the bailiff or some one in whom he trusts should be
[present] every year at the selling and tithing of the lambs and at the
tithing of the wool and skins, because of fraud'.⁷

Valuable information on the practical administration of tithes
can often be found in agreements governing the division of tithes
between two or more owners. After the tithes of St Ismier had
been recovered from lay hands and divided between the canons
of St Martin and the bishop of Grenoble, the prior carefully
defined the exact lands from which each owner held the tithes,

---

¹ Reginald Lennard, 'Peasant Tithe-Collectors in Norman England', *English
Hist. Rev.* LXIX (1954), 590 (where the order of the passages quoted is reversed),
and *Rural England*, pp. 360–1.

² *St Martin des Champs*, II, 262–3; cf. *Gellone*, p. 341 (1115), giving to the
abbey 'omnem decimum quem habemus in dominio in parochia Sancti Petri de
Mairois, et fevales illos quem suprascriptum decimum tenent'. The *fevales* here
seem to have been dependent agricultural workers who gathered the tithe.

³ P. 60 above.

⁴ *Quimperlé*, p. 170.

⁵ *St Cyprien*, p. 68, no. 75.

⁶ The priests collected and divided the tithe in the villages of the abbey of
Leno (case VIII in appendix); and on the lands of the abbey of Corbie in the
thirteenth century the provosts had jurisdiction over the tithes, which were
collected and transported by the monastic mayors (Dubar, *Corbie*, pp. 72, 99
and 101).

⁷ Walter of Henley, *Husbandry*, ed. Elizabeth Lamond (London, 1890), p. 95.

and the bishop entrusted the collection of his share, which included half the tithes of the *mansus presbiteralis*, to his agent, the *conversus* Guigo.[1] The abbey of St Martin des Champs in 1120/4 agreed to a division of the tithes of Annet-sur-Marne between its priory there, which held one-third, and Peter the Orphan, who held two-thirds. The agreement specified that (*a*) the *tractores* of the tithe were to swear an oath to the monks and to Peter and were to be chosen jointly: two by Peter and one by the monks if three were needed, one each if two were needed, and by joint agreement if only one was needed;[2] (*b*) Peter might appoint up to three guards for the tithe-barn, of whom the monks should approve one, and the monks might appoint one guard, and all the guards should swear to both Peter and the monks; (*c*) Peter and the monks should be present at the division of the tithes, and the portion of the priest, who was appointed by the monks, should be taken from their third; and (*d*) Peter and his tenants might use the monks' furnace.[3] The abbey of Nogent-le-Rotrou agreed in 1155/64 to divide equally the tithes of Unvarre with a layman and to build the grange for storing the tithe collected by the *decimatores...et tutores segetum*.[4]

A series of documents covering almost a century, in the chartulary of the Premonstratensian abbey of Basse-Fontaine, clearly shows the complexity of the tithing at Vitry-le-Croisé, in the diocese of Langres.[5] In the first half of the twelfth century these tithes were divided between James of Chacenay, a layman, and the parish priest. James owned two-thirds of the great tithe (from all sorts of grain), all the straw, chaff, and incompletely threshed grain, and half of the small tithe (from wine and hemp). The

[1] *Grenoble*, pp. 91–2 and 93–6, nos. B 14 (1100) and B 16 (see p. 113 above).
[2] Cf. *St Jean d'Angély*, I, 144, no. 112 (1076), where the abbey and a layman jointly owned some tithes and the *decimator* swore fealty to both, and *Cluny*, V, 332–7, nos. 3974–6 (1124), where the founder of the Cluniac priory of Bertrée arranged that he should have half the tithes during his lifetime and that 'conductores etiam decimae Sancto Petro et mihi fidelitatem facient'.
[3] *St Martin des Champs*, I, 285–8; cf. *Ste Croix d'Orléans*, pp. 135–6 (1110/11), where the monks and canons arranged for joint collection of some tithes.
[4] *Nogent-le-Rotrou*, pp. 199–200.
[5] *Basse-Fontaine*, pp. 113–14, 116–17, 119–21, and 132–9, nos. 86–7, 90, 93–4, and 102–3 (JL 9250 and 16189).

priest owned a third of the great tithe and half of the small
tithe. James was responsible for transporting all the tithes and
owned the *tractus decimae*. The *redecima* was taken from the
portions belonging to the priest, and the horses which carried the
great tithe were entitled to six measures of grain taken from the
tithe before it was divided. In 1146 James surrendered his share
and rights to the bishop of Langres, who gave them, with some
other tithes, to Basse-Fontaine, 'saving the rights of the bishop of
Langres and of the priests who hold and will hold the parishes of
those estates'; and Popes Eugene III and Clement III confirmed
the abbey's possession of these tithes in their privileges for Basse-
Fontaine in 1148 and 1188. Disputes arose over the division,
however, and in 1223 the pope appointed two delegates to settle
the claim of the priest Raymond, a canon of Langres, to two-thirds
of the great tithe, all the small and noval tithes, and one-third of
the *tractus decimae*. The judges settled that in addition to the
priest's customary share Raymond should receive during his
lifetime a third of the grain, straw, and chaff, the entire tithe of
vegetables, and the *tractus* for a third of the great tithe; and he
might store his share either in the abbot's barn, his own barn, or
some other barn, so long as the division was made in the abbot's
barn. Each party was responsible for transporting his share of
the tithe if it was carried at the same time as the others. No
reference was made in this settlement to the noval tithes, which
were claimed by the priest Nicholas in 1238, after Raymond's
death, when the previous division was again in force; but the
bishop of Langres then applied the same division to noval as to
old-field tithes and therefore awarded the canons two-thirds of
the great and half of the small tithe, on condition that they give
the priest six or seven (the charter is unclear) measures of grain
annually.

These complications, and especially the difficulty of collecting
tithes from distant estates, must have encouraged monks to farm
their tithes for a set annual revenue and to grant them on leases
and as fiefs.[1] Coulton spoke of the farming of tithes by monks

---

[1] On the difference between a farm and a lease, which was usually for a
lump sum or a 'gage of land', see Lennard, *Rural England*, pp. 166–7.

'as early as 1170';[1] but the nuns of Ronceray farmed some tithes to a layman at least a century earlier,[2] and in the late eleventh and twelfth centuries tithes were farmed by monasteries all over Europe.[3] In England, indeed, the practice was so common that some historians have regarded it as peculiarly English.[4] The abbey of Subiaco farmed various tithes to a layman who in turn sub-farmed some of them for specific rents to other laymen.[5] In a sale to the abbey of Aureil of part of the tithe of Eyjeaux in 1142/7, two brothers specified that their man:

who received this tithe...should as long as he is bailiff of this tithe pay to the canons from this tithe either as much as he paid to us or as much as another bailiff would pay from the tithe of Eyjeaux more than other bailiffs to their lords ('quantum alius bajulus de decima d'Esjau plus ceteris bajulis suis dominis redderet'), and jurisdiction over the men of St John should belong not to him but to the canons.[6]

In effect, therefore, the tithe was to be farmed to the bailiff for the highest price. This practice of farming tithes and other ecclesiastical revenues was forbidden by a council probably in the north of France in the twelfth century;[7] but it continued to be popular among monks because it offered them the ease and security of a

[1] Coulton, *Five Centuries*, III, 644 (cf. 185–7).

[2] *Ronceray*, p. 92.

[3] See Viard, *Dîme*, I, 165–6 (Wissembourg, Tournai, Gellone); Warichez, *Lobbes*, p. 211; Lamy, *Tongerloo*, p. 192; Lebel, *St Denis*, pp. 150–2; Guy de Valous, *Le temporel et la situation financière des établissements de l'ordre de Cluny du XIIe au XIVe siècle*, Archives de la France monastique, XLII (Ligugé–Paris, 1935), pp. 110–11 (Cluny, St Martin des Champs); Alfred Hansay, *Étude sur la formation et l'organisation économique du domaine de l'abbaye de Saint-Trond*, Université de Gand: Recueil de travaux publiés par la faculté de philosophie et lettres, XXII (Ghent, 1899), pp. 72–3; and Tremel, in *Zs. d. hist. Vereines f. Steiermark*, XXXIII, 29–30, who said that the earliest reference to farming of tithes in Styria and Carinthia was in 1259.

[4] Schreiber, *Kurie*, II, 12, and David Knowles, *The Monastic Order in England* (Cambridge, 1940), p. 599.

[5] *Subiaco*, p. 89, no. 50.

[6] *Aureil*, pp. 149–50, no. 211; cf. Tenant de La Tour, *Homme*, p. 544, who translated the passage in Latin as 'autant que celui des bailes d'Eyjeaux qui paie à ses Maîtres la plus forte somme'; and *Aureil*, pp. 76–7, no. 115 (1147: also on the tithes of Eyjeaux).

[7] *Thesaurus*, IV, 152 D (from a manuscript at Corbie).

steady revenue in place of the difficulties of collection and the risks of fluctuating production.[1]

For the same reason monastic tithes were often exchanged or commuted into fixed payments in produce and money. In about 1130 the monks of St Lambert in the forest of Lesach in Styria gave various tithes to the abbey of Admont in return for a small estate and a weekly payment in salt.[2] The king of Scotland in about 1142 gave 'the tithe of the land of Brixwald which he held at Atherai' to the abbey of Dunfermline *in escambio* for the tithe from the land in Cambuskinel belonging to the canons of Stirling.[3] The abbot of Muri in Switzerland arranged that 'thirteen talents of the pigments for making mixed wine on the nativities of St Martin and Our Lord' should be given each year in place of certain tithes.[4] Later it was also common to arrange a money payment, called a *modus decimandi*, in lieu of tithes, especially from larger animals, which a small farmer could not easily pay in kind.[5] These arrangements had important economic effects in the long run, as prices and production rose, but it is important to remember, as Lennard stressed with regard to commutations of monastic food rents, that they were the result of 'considerations of need and convenience' rather than of any 'readiness or reluctance to advance from a stage of *Naturalwirtschaft* to one of *Geldwirtschaft*'.[6]

4. OPPOSITION TO MONASTIC POSSESSION OF TITHES

Although by the twelfth century most monasteries gladly received and purchased tithes, a considerable number of monks and canons, especially of the reformed orders, refused to possess them and maintained that no monks or nuns should hold tithes.

[1] Cf. De Valous, *Temporel*, p. 111, and J. Ambrose Raftis, *The Estates of Ramsey Abbey*, Pontifical Institute of Mediaeval Studies: Studies and Texts, III (Toronto, 1957), pp. 81–5, who pointed out that up at least until the twelfth century the farming of monastic lands was often more efficient and flexible than direct exploitation or perpetual lease.

[2] *Steiermark*, I, 139. [3] Lawrie, *Scottish Charters*, p. 110, no. 143.
[4] *Muri*, p. 75 (1110/19). [5] Cf. Orwin, *Open Fields*, p. 159.
[6] Lennard, *Rural England*, p. 140.

They were joined in this opinion, somewhat paradoxically, both by conservative theorists who wanted to reassert the independence of the monastic order and by enemies of the reform movement, who objected to the attacks on lay possession of tithes and to the growing influence of monks in the administration of the Church. This section will be concerned with the attitudes and arguments of these opponents of monastic possession of tithes.

Among the monastic reformers of the eleventh century, the refusal to own tithes was often included in a general prohibition to possess any churches or ecclesiastical revenues. St John Gualbert, who founded the order of Vallombrosa about 1036, forbade his monks to accept churches to be served by themselves, according to his biographer Andrew of Strumi, and 'he said that this was the office of canons, not of monks'.[1] The early monks at Afflighem, which was founded about 1083, also probably refused to own tithes.[2] The reforming Abbot Odo of St Martin at Tournai, who organized his followers first as canons in 1092 and then as monks two years later, was more specific. Many wealthy clerics joined the abbey, wrote its chronicler Herman,

and if we had wished to receive at that time the *altaria* which they held, our church could perhaps have been richer thereby today; but since he [Odo] was determined to accept neither *altaria* nor churches or tithes but to live solely from the labour of their hands, from the land cultivated by their teams, and from the nourishment of their herds, he refused to have any ecclesiastical revenues which they had held and said that such revenues should be owned only by clerics, not by monks. And his determination in this respect conformed to the life and practices of the monks of old.[3]

At about the same time, probably in 1095, according to Ordericus Vitalis, St Robert of Molesme complained to his monks that

[1] Andrew of Strumi, *Vita s. Iohannis Gualberti*, xix, in MGH, SS, xxx, 1085.

[2] Charles Dereine, 'La spiritualité "apostolique" des premiers fondateurs d'Afflighem (1083–1100)', *Rev. d'hist. ecc.* LIV (1959), 60.

[3] Herman of Tournai, *Narratio restaurationis abbatiae s. Martini Tornacensis*, LXVII, in *Spicilegium*, II, 910 (cap. LXVIII, in MGH, SS, XIV, 306); cf. Charles Dereine, 'Odon de Tournai et la crise du cénobitisme au XIe siècle', *Revue du Moyen Âge latin*, IV (1948), 142–3, on the origins of the reform, and 138–40 on the *Narratio*, which though written in 1142 is of high authority.

'We have an abundance of food and clothing from the tithes and oblations of churches, and by skill or violence we appropriate what belongs to the priests. Thus surely we feed upon the blood of men and share in their sins.' He therefore urged his monks to adhere strictly to the rule of St Benedict. 'Let us procure our food and clothing by the labour of our hands....Let us give up tithes and oblations to the clergy who serve the diocese. Thus let us zealously strive to follow Christ in the footsteps of the Fathers.'[1] These sentiments apparently roused little enthusiasm among the monks at Molesme, and a few years later, traditionally in 1098, St Robert left his abbey and founded Cîteaux.

The earliest Cistercian records and legislation adhered strictly to these principles with regard to tithes.[2] One of the canons probably presented to Pope Calixtus II for approval in 1119 laid down that 'The ordinance of our name and order prohibits [the possession of] churches, *altaria*, burial rights, the tithes from the work or nourishment of other men, manors, dependent labourers, land rents, revenues from ovens and mills, and similar [property] which is not in accord with monastic purity'.[3] And the so-called

[1] Ordericus Vitalis, *Hist. ecc.* VIII, 26, *ed. cit.* III, 436; cf. tr. Thomas Forester, Bohn's Antiquarian Library (London, 1853–6), III, 41.

[2] The dates of these documents and especially of the *Carta caritatis* and the *Exordium parvum* have recently been subjected to a searching critique by J.-A. Lefèvre, whose findings were published in a long series of articles (some of which are cited below) and whose conclusions have been accepted, with some reservations, by A. d'Herblay, in the *Rev. d'hist. ecc.* L (1955), 158–64, by F. Masai, in *Scriptorium*, XI (1957), 119–23, and by J. Marilier, in *Annales de Bourgogne*, XXIX (1957), 132. They have been criticized and partially rejected, on the other hand, by Jacques Winandy, in *Rev. bén.* LXVII (1957), 49–76, and by J.-B. van Damme, in *Collectanea ordinis Cisterciensium reformatorum*, XX (1958), 37–60, 153–68, 374–90 and XXI (1959), 70–86 and 137–56, also published as an offprint with consecutive pagination, and a separate pamphlet entitled *Documenta pro Cisterciensis ordinis historiae ac juris studio* (Westmalle, 1959). For the purposes of the present work, all scholars are agreed that the documents under consideration date from the first half of the twelfth century.

[3] This text was published from MS. Trent, Biblioteca comunale, 1711, by J.-A. Lefèvre, 'La véritable constitution cistercienne de 1119', *Collectanea ord. Cist. ref.* XVI (1954), 104, and Van Damme, *Documenta*, p. 28. Lefèvre maintained that this statute was cap. XXIII in the dossier presented to Calixtus II in 1119 and was later incorporated into cap. XIV of the *Exordium parvum* and into the *Instituta generalis capituli apud Cistercium*, both of which formed part of the codi-

Exordium Cisterciensis coenobii or *Exordium parvum*, which may be considerably later in date, explained that since the founders of Cîteaux:

read neither in the rule nor in the life of St Benedict that he had possessed churches, *altaria*, oblations, burial rights, the tithes from other men, ovens, mills, manors, or peasants, or that women had entered his monastery, or that he had buried the dead there, except for his sister, they renounced all these things.... And they said that the holy Fathers had distributed tithes in four portions, one for the bishop, another for the priest, the third for guests coming to the church, for widows, and orphans, and for the poor who had nowhere else to eat, and the fourth for the upkeep of the church. And since in this arrangement they found no reference to the monk, who owns his own lands from which he lives by the labour of himself and his animals, they therefore refused to usurp unjustly for themselves these things which belonged to others.[1]

Other reformed monks were no less rigid in their determination to own no tithes from the labour of other men. The first Carthusian *Consuetudines*, drawn up probably in 1116 by Guigo of La Chartreuse, forbade the possession of fields, vineyards, gardens,

fication of Cistercian records and laws which was approved by Eugene III in 1152: see Canisius Noschitzka, 'Codex manuscriptus 31 Bibliothecae Universitatis Labacensis [Ljubljana or Laibach]', *Analecta sacri ordinis Cisterciensis*, VI (1950), 24 (text of the *Instituta*), and J.-A. Lefèvre, 'Pour une nouvelle datation des *Instituta generalis capituli apud Cistercium*', *Collectanea ord. Cist. ref.* XVI (1954), 251 and 257. Van Damme, on the other hand, considered this statute part of the *Exordium cistercii cum 'Summa Cartae Caritatis' et capitulis*, which was compiled in 1123/4 and included a reworking of the 'authentic' *Carta caritatis* of 1119.

[1] This text was published under the title *Exordium Cisterciensis coenobii* from the incomplete MS. Ljubljana (Laibach), University Library, 31, by Turk, *Statuta*, pp. 33–4, and again, under the title *Exordium parvum*, by Noschitzka, in *Anal. sac. ord. Cist.* VI, 6–16; and from MS. Zürich, Zentralbibliothek, Car. C. 175 (with variants from Ljubljana 31 and Dijon 633) by Van Damme, *Documenta*, p. 13. A similar passage occurs in the so-called *Exordium magnum* printed by Turk, *Statuta*, p. 91. The date of this text is highly disputed. Lefèvre, 'Le vrai récit primitif des origines de Cîteaux est-il l' "*Exordium parvum*"?', *Le Moyen Âge*, LXI (1955), 79–120 and 329–61, said that it was written as part of the dossier presented to Eugene III in 1152. Winandy, in *Rev. bén.* LXVII, 49–76, considered it a reworking, made before 1152, of the *Exordium Cistercii*, which he dated between 1119 and 1148. Van Damme, in *Collectanea ord. Cist. ref.* XXI, 153–5, however, defended the traditional date of before 1119.

churches, cemeteries, oblations, and tithes 'outside the boundaries of their hermitage'.[1] And at their own request the Carthusians of Durbon were forbidden by the bishop of Gap in 1116/21 to own any tithes except from their own lands.[2] The rule of Fontevrault, which was drawn up before 1155, declared 'That they would not receive parish churches or their tithes'.[3] The most extreme expression of these principles is found in the Grandmontine rule, which was approved by Pope Clement III (1187–91) but which was largely based on the teachings of the founder, St Stephen of Muret, who died in 1124.[4] His followers relied completely on the providence of God for their material support and refused to own not only any churches and lands outside the boundaries of their houses (4–5) but also any animals, for which their love might reduce their love of God (6); they were to accept no charters and refused to go to law even to defend their rights (23–4); they were forbidden to build on land belonging to other monks, 'for some of them love you greatly and show you many kindnesses, but the heads of monasteries often change, and some may wish later to recover by frequent claims what others have given away' (33). With regard to tithes, 'You should with pious prayers ask for the tithes of your own labour from the bishop and from the priest in whose parish you live and also from others who possess them. But you should not keep them when they have been given but should

[1] *Consuetudines*, XLI, 1, in *PL*, CLIII, 719–20; cf. A. de Meyer and J. M. de Smet, *Guigo's 'Consuetudines' van de eerste Kartuizers*, Mededelingen van de koninklijke vlaamse Academie voor Wetenschappen, Letteren en Schone Kunsten van België, Klasse der Letteren, XIII, 6 (Brussels, 1951), pp. 13–14, on the date, and p. 39.

[2] *Durbon*, p. 4, no. 3.

[3] Johannes von Walter, *Die ersten Wanderprediger Frankreichs*, I: *Robert von Arbrissel*, Studien zur Geschichte der Theologie und der Kirche, IX, 3 (Leipzig, 1903), p. 194 (cf. p. 79 on the date).

[4] When asked by two cardinals whether he was a monk, a canon, or a hermit, St Stephen replied in the words of Pope John VIII that 'My glory is nothing': *Vita s. Stephani*, XXXII–XXXIII, in *PL*, CCIV, 1021–2. Cf. Rose Graham, 'The Order of Grandmont and its Houses in England' (1924–5), reprinted in *English Ecclesiastical Studies* (London, 1929), pp. 212–15, and Jean Becquet, 'La règle de Grandmont', *Bulletin de la Société archéologique et historique du Limousin*, LXXXVII (1958), 9–36, esp. 16–19 on the poverty of the Grandmontines, which was particularly influenced by St Stephen.

faithfully give them to other poor men' (32).[1] Thus the Grandmontines refused to keep the tithes even from their own labour.

The influence of this view, and especially of the Cistercian
legislation, was felt throughout the monastic world of the twelfth
century. Some preachers went so far as to urge monks to leave any
monastery where the abbot had acquired tithes which the bishop
should have distributed.[2] Archbishop Thurstan of York in his
famous letter to Archbishop William of Canterbury describing
the foundation of Fountains Abbey told how Prior Richard and
other monks at the abbey of St Mary in York had seen 'how
brightly the Gospel shone' in the monks of Savigny and Clairvaux and wished to imitate them rather than to recite the Gospel.
In the list of complaints which he presented to the abbot, Richard
said that:

Concerning the revenues of churches and tithes, for the possession of
which monks are often held greatly to blame, it seems that they
should be held by the legitimate and canonical determination of the
bishops and be spent only for the uses of the poor, pilgrims, and guests.
But he [St Benedict] decreed that monks should live from the lawful
cultivation of the land and use of animals.[3]

The *De claustro animae* by the regular canon Hugh of Folieto,
which was long attributed to Hugh of St Victor, listed the revenues
forbidden to canons, including 'tithes except from those things
which they cultivate in their fields'.[4] And another regular canon,
the Premonstratensian Abbot Philip of Harvengt, speaking of the
revival of monasticism during his own lifetime, praised the example
and especially the desire for poverty of the Cistercian monk, who
'did not seek the tithes of the people but with eager vigour stretched

---

[1] *PL*, CCIV, 1140–51.

[2] Ivo of Chartres, ep. 192, in *PL*, CLXII, 199 (see pp. 168–9 below).

[3] *Memorials of the Abbey of St Mary of Fountains*, ed. J. R. Walbran, I, Surtees
Society, XLII (Durham, etc., 1863), pp. 20–1, and, in a somewhat different
version, in St Bernard, *Opera omnia*, ed. J. Mabillon (Paris, 1839), I, 797; cf.
Knowles, *Mon. Order*, pp. 231–9, for a full account of the affair.

[4] *De claustro animae*, II, 5, in *PL*, CLXXVI, 1053; cf. Barthélemy Hauréau,
Hugues de Saint-Victor: Nouvel examen de l'édition de ses œuvres (Paris, 1859),
pp. 59–66, and Manitius, *Geschichte*, III, 226.

out his hands to work, so that by striving to gain his humble food and clothing in this way he showed that he never forgot his original purpose'.[1]

These texts show that the refusal to own tithes was an important element in the programme for monastic reform and the ideal of apostolic life in the eleventh and twelfth centuries.[2] In the first place, it fitted the desire of the reformers to be poor both communally and individually and to support themselves by the labour of their own hands and animals. Secondly, it was in accord with their frequently expressed ideal of returning to the primitive, pure Church of the apostles, since (as Herman of Tournai, Robert of Molesme, Prior Richard, and the early Cistercians stressed) there were no references to monastic possession of tithes in the rule of St Benedict or in the lives of the early Benedictine monks. Lastly, and in practice perhaps most important, the rejection of other men's tithes kept the reformers from involvement in secular affairs and particularly from litigation, the avoidance of which was an important part of their programme.[3]

Some of the early reformers suffered personally from the claims of other monks to parochial revenues and tithes. The abbey of St Augustine at Limoges, for instance, forced the followers of St Stephen to move, after his death in 1124, from Muret to Grandmont.[4] St Bernard of Tiron had to move first

[1] *De institutione clericorum*, CXXV, in *PL*, CCIII, 836; cf. pp. 158–60 below on Philip.
[2] See the stimulating article of M.-D. Chenu, 'Moines, clercs, laïcs au carrefour de la vie évangélique', *Rev. d'hist. ecc.* XLIX (1954), 59–89, esp. 62–6, reprinted in his *La théologie au douzième siècle*, Études de philosophie médiévale, XLV (Paris, 1957), pp. 225–51, and Ernest W. McDonnell, 'The *Vita Apostolica*: Diversity or Dissent', *Church History*, XXIV (1955), 15–31. According to McDonnell, the *vita apostolica* involved three basic elements: imitation of the early Church, love of the souls of other men, and poverty. Of these the second tended to emerge last historically. Ladner, *Reform*, p. 402 n. 64, discussed the association of the *vita apostolica* with the clerical *vita communis* of the Augustinian Rule, which was 'rediscovered' in the eleventh century.
[3] Dereine, in *Rev. d'hist. ecc.* LIV, 57 n. 4, said that the desire to avoid litigation has not been sufficiently stressed as an aspect of the apostolic spirituality of the eleventh century.
[4] *Vita s. Stephani*, XLVII, in *PL*, CCIV, 1028; cf. Graham, in *English Ecc. Studies*, p. 210.

from Savigny, where his hermitage was too close to the monastery
of St Vitalis, and in 1109 and 1114 from Arcisses and from Tiron,
both of which were given him by the count of Le Perche, owing
to the claims of the Cluniac monks of St Denis at Nogent-le-
Rotrou, who said, according to Bernard's biographer Geoffrey
the Fat, that 'they had the right to the tithes and to [the burial dues
for] the dead bodies on the land given him by the said count. He
was forced by this claim to leave the buildings which his dis-
ciples had built with great labour, and he tried to find another
place where he might live.'[1] This sort of experience quickly
persuaded the reformers to renounce all ecclesiastical revenues and
if possible to live in places where there were no established claims
to such revenues. The choice of an uncultivated and deserted site
for a new monastery was in many cases designed to avoid not
only contact with other human beings but also controversies with
previous owners.

From a more general point of view, the reformers realized that
the possession of tithes by monks and the reassertion of the
spiritual nature of tithes had not changed the practical workings
of the system of tithing in the twelfth century. Indeed, the transfer of tithes from lay to monastic possession tended to bring out
the secular character of the monks more than the religious
character of the tithes. Whether they were owned by monks,
clerics, or laymen, tithes remained a valuable form of property,
and controversies over tithes had long been a source of grave
scandal among monks. St Norbert told the pope in 1119 that
'Our plan is not to seek what belongs to others, never to claim by
legal pleadings or secular judges and complaints what has been
taken [from us], not to bind by anathema anyone on account of
any injuries or damages done to us, but on the contrary, to sum up
everything briefly, I have chosen to live a fully evangelical and

---

[1] *Vita beati Bernardi*, IX, 77, in *AASS*, April, II, 240. Bernard had already been
involved in a long controversy with Cluny over the abbey of St Cyprien,
where he was abbot (*ibid.* pp. 234–6). After his expulsion from Tiron he was
offered lands by both the canons of Chartres and the countess of Blois and
accepted the former because he preferred the protection of Our Lady to 'the
advocacy of some secular person' (*ibid.* p. 240). On these three episodes, see the
introd. by L. Merlet to the chartulary of Tiron, pp. i–xviii.

apostolic life in accordance with a wiser understanding'.[1] Abelard discussed this litigious tendency in a sermon addressed to his monks at St Gildas:

When we pass from secular to ecclesiastical affairs, equal complaints are brought against our ambition. For since we usurp clerical property and obtain parochial revenues, both tithes and oblations, from the bishops by hook and by crook, we often have to buy what we have not seized. On this account we are often drawn to synods and councils and go daily to public lawsuits, and at great expense we bribe judges and lawyers (*oratores*) to gloss over our unjust actions. The frequency of our complaints in these councils clearly shows the great rapacity of our avarice. We rarely see bishops or priests fighting against each other there. Almost all the controversies are either between monks or started by monks.[2]

Similar sentiments were expressed by St Bernard of Clairvaux, who on matters of morals agreed with Abelard more often than is generally recognized.[3] In a letter written jointly with Hugh of Pontigny to the abbot of Marmoutier (whose abbey, significantly, engaged in frequent litigation over tithes), Bernard was amazed that some monks appeared to prefer 'the poor revenues of a single altar [i.e. tithes and oblations] to the glory of the world'. 'We assert', they went on, 'that it is safer for any Christian, and above all for a monk, to own less in peace than more in strife....It is for the clergy to serve the altar and to live from the altar. Our profession and the example of the monks of old prescribe that we should live from our own labours and not from the sanctuary of God.' If monks wished to receive sacramental and parochial revenues, they explained, they must perform pastoral services. 'Otherwise it is hateful to wish to reap where you do not sow, and it is also unjust to gather what another has sown.'[4]

---

[1] *Vita Norberti*, IX, in MGH, *SS*, XII, 678.

[2] Abelard, serm. XXXIII, in *PL*, CLXXVIII, 588. Case IX in the appendix gives a good example of this kind of difficulty and of the use of legal spokesmen by monks.

[3] See, for instance, my article on 'The Second Crusade as Seen by Contemporaries', *Traditio*, IX (1955), 250–1, on the similarity of their views on penance (with references). This similarity did not, needless to say, extend to matters of theology and discipline.

[4] Bernard, ep. 397, *ed. cit.* I, 712–13. Bernard never specifically discussed the subject of monastic possession of tithes, but cf. Viard, *Dîme*, I, 228, and 'Saint

St Bernard here referred to an issue of basic importance in the history of monastic tithes: the distinction between monks and clerics and the right of monks to perform pastoral services.[1] In the early centuries of Benedictine monasticism, the majority of monks were either unordained or in minor orders and took no part in administering the sacraments to the laity.[2] The number of ordained monks was at first very limited, but as time passed it tended to increase because of the need to perform the holy offices for other monks and the prolongation of the liturgy, and by the tenth century, according to Schmitz, over half the monks in many monasteries were in holy orders. 'The results of the transformation were of capital importance', remarked McLaughlin, 'since the custom of ordaining monks was the cause of basic changes in monasticism.'[3] Among these changes one of the most important was the use of monks for pastoral work. As early as the sixth century, of course, monks had served as missionaries, and they had played an important part in the later Irish and Anglo-

Bernard et les moines décimateurs', *Saint Bernard et son temps*, Association bourguignonne des sociétés savantes: Congrès de 1927 (Dijon, 1928–9), I, 292–4. On his attitude towards manual labour, see Maurice Vignes, 'Les doctrines économiques et morales de Saint Bernard sur la richesse et le travail', *Revue d'histoire économique et sociale*, XVI (1928), 547–84, and Hartridge, *Vicarages*, pp. 16–18.

[1] On the performance of the *cura animarum* by monks, see above all the articles by Ursmer Berlière, 'L'Exercice du ministère paroissial par les moines dans le Haut Moyen-âge' and 'L'Exercice du ministère paroissial par les moines du XIIe au XVIIe siècle', *Rev. bén.* XXXIX (1927), 227–50 and 340–64; McLaughlin, *Droit*, pp. 124–8; Schmitz, *Ordre*, I, 264–5 (on the number of monks in holy orders) and 318–22 (with bibliography), and IV, 280–2; and Philipp Hofmeister, 'Mönchtum und Seelsorge bis zum 13. Jahrhundert', *SMGBOZ*, LXV (1955), 209–73. On preaching by monks, which was a special aspect of pastoral work, see the first appendix to my article in *Traditio*, IX, 276–8, and Herbert Grundmann, 'Eresie e nuovi ordini religiosi nel secolo XII', *Relazioni del X Congresso internazionale di scienze storiche*, III: *Storia del Medioevo* (Florence, 1955), pp. 384–6.

[2] Hofmeister, in *SMGBOZ*, LXV, 235–7, maintained against this view that a considerable number of early monks were ordained, both in the East and in the West, and that the works of Gregory the Great show that St Benedict, in spite of his Rule, was not opposed to the performance of pastoral and charitable work by his monks for the laity around their monasteries.

[3] McLaughlin, *Droit*, p. 127; cf. Chenu, in *Rev. d'hist. ecc.* XLIX, 66, on the later effects of the increased number of ordained monks.

Saxon missions on the Continent. But such activity was regarded as unusual, not to say improper, and Delaruelle has even suggested that the reforms of Benedict of Aniane were designed to keep monks in their monasteries and to reassert that prayer rather than evangelism was their principal concern.[1] From the ninth to the twelfth centuries, however, an increasing number of ordained monks performed pastoral work as a result probably both of the shortage of parish clergy and of monastic possession of churches which were more cheaply and easily served by monks than by stipendiary or beneficed vicars.[2] The total number was never very great and may have varied regionally.[3] And the practice was repeatedly forbidden by general and local councils. As late as 1123 the first Lateran council 'totally forbade monks [to perform] anointings, visits to the sick, and public masses'.[4] Berlière was of the opinion, however, that:

In spite of canonical texts, conciliar decisions, and the opposition of certain bishops, the administration of parishes by monks existed in fact, was accepted by bishops, and recognized by papal authority, although before the end of the twelfth century Rome never granted a special privilege for the Benedictines concerning the direct administration of parishes.[5]

Hofmeister also emphasized that the official attitude towards the exercise of pastoral duties by monks changed in the twelfth century and cited numerous examples, especially from Germany,

[1] Delaruelle, in *Mélanges Halphen*, p. 188. Hofmeister, in *SMGBOZ*, LXV, 222–6, however, said that the performance of such work by ordained monks was neither unusual nor improper.

[2] Cf. pp. 61–3 above.

[3] Cf. Knowles, *Mon. Order*, p. 595, who said that before 1216 monks 'took no share whatever in the work of preaching or administering the sacraments to layfolk outside the walls of the monastery'.

[4] Hefele–Leclercq, *Conciles*, v. 1, 636; cf. Hofmeister, in *SMGBOZ*, LXV, 242–9, on this and some provincial synods which accepted the performance of pastoral work by monks. Special privileges to baptize and bury (cf. *Mainz*, I, 412–13: the archbishop of Mainz for Breitenau in 1123) and to preach (cf. *PL*, CXLIII, 610; JL 4170: Leo IX for Fulda in 1049, confirmed in *PL*, CLXXIX, 86 and 328) were occasionally granted to monasteries by bishops and popes.

[5] Berlière, in *Rev. bén.* XXXIX, 351, whose conclusions were based largely on evidence from Germany and the Low Countries.

of monks performing the *cura animarum* both in their own monasteries and in parish churches.[1]

The number of monks in holy orders and their performance of pastoral work was both a cause and, in part, a result of the breakdown in the distinction between monks and clerics. In the Carolingian period monks were commonly regarded as a separate order of society, with special functions and characteristics, distinct from the clergy and the laity.[2] Rabanus Maurus in the ninth century, Abbo of Fleury in the tenth, John of Fécamp in the eleventh, all accepted this tripartite division of society as a matter of course.[3] But there slowly developed a new view which merged the monastic and clerical orders and thus divided society into only two orders, the clergy and the laity. Lanfranc, though himself a monk as well as an archbishop, referred to the catholic church as 'divided into the clerical and lay orders';[4] and the twelfth-century monk Idungus of Regensburg wrote that 'Every catholic is either a cleric or a layman', and said that a monk could be either one.[5] Monks were usually regarded as the regular branch of the clerical order, however. Gratian included in the *Decretum* an apocryphal canon by St Jerome, beginning 'There are two types of Christians', which distinguished the clerics, who were devoted to the service of God and whose tonsure marked their 'abandon-

[1] Hofmeister, in *SMGBOZ*, LXV, 255 and 272.
[2] Cf. Delaruelle, in *Mélanges Halphen*, pp. 185–92, esp. 186–7, who examined this tripartite division in the *De institutione regia* of Jonas of Orléans, which he connected with the council of Paris in 829. The prevalence of this view in the ninth century should be stressed against the later divisions into those who prayed, fought, and farmed, and into simply the clergy and the laity. The bipartite division is found in the Carolingian period principally in the legal and conciliar sources: cf. Ullmann, *Growth*, pp. 125–31 and 183.
[3] See pp. 14–15 above on Rabanus, who called the divisions 'professions' rather than 'orders'; pp. 80–1 on Abbo; and John of Fécamp's letter *Tuae quidem*, in Jean Leclercq and J.-P. Bonnes, *Un maître de la vie spirituelle au XIe siècle: Jean de Fécamp*, Études de théologie et d'histoire de la spiritualité, IX (Paris, 1946), p. 203.
[4] Lanfranc, *Liber de corpore et sanguine domini nostri adversus Berengarium*, IV, in Lanfranc of Canterbury, *Opera quae supersunt omnia*, ed. J. A. Giles (Oxford, 1844), II, 155.
[5] *Argumentum super quatuor quaestionibus*, IX, in *Thesaurus anecdotorum novissimus*, ed. Bernard Pez (Vienna, 1721–9), II. 2, 534; on Idungus, see pp. 177–8 below.

ment of all worldly goods', from the laymen who owned property, married, cultivated the soil, and paid oblations and tithes.[1] Naturally the break between these two views of society was not sudden, and the tripartite view persisted, especially among monks and conservative clerics and canons. Even a canonist like Roland Bandinelli, who later became Pope Alexander III, referred in his *Summa* on the *Decretum* to the *monachicus ordo* as superior to other orders, but he considered that it overlapped with the clerical order.[2] The difference between the monastic and clerical tonsures thus diminished in the twelfth century and, according to Bock, even disappeared, so that tonsure automatically conferred clerical status on monks.[3] This view may be extreme, but the two tonsures were certainly equated by Innocent III.[4] The new emphasis on the mass and the other sacraments linked together all those in holy orders,[5] and even within the clerical order the distinction between ordained and unordained tended to replace that between the secular and regular clerics.[6] The twelfth century therefore not only, as Cheney remarked, 'did much to sharpen the distinction between clergy and laity and to emphasize it legally and theologically',[7] but at the same time greatly reduced the distinction between monks and clerics.[8]

These developments can be discussed here only in passing, but they deeply influenced the history of monastic tithes. Monks who

[1] *Decretum*, C. XII, q. I, c. 7. Stephan Kuttner has kindly informed me that the origins of this canon, which is found in no other canonical collection and is certainly much later than Jerome, are not known.

[2] *Die Summa Magistri Rolandi*, ed. Friedrich Thaner (Innsbruck, 1874), p. 39; cf. pp. 268–70 below.

[3] Columban Bock, 'Tonsure monastique et tonsure cléricale', *Rev. de droit canonique*, II (1952), 373–406, esp. 389–91.

[4] *PL*, CCXVI, 313, cited by Jacques Winandy, 'Les moines et le sacerdoce', *La vie spirituelle*, LXXX (1949), 30.

[5] Cf. Cheney, *Becket*, p. 105.

[6] Cf. Winandy, in *La vie spirituelle*, LXXX, 30–2. In many monasteries today the most conspicuous distinction is between the ordained and unordained monks.

[7] Cheney, *Becket*, p. 104 (cf. p. 156).

[8] These remarks should not be taken to imply that these developments were responsible for all the changes in the structure of the monastic order in the eleventh and twelfth centuries. Lemarignier, in *À Cluny*, pp. 322–3, has stressed the great importance, for instance, of exemption.

performed pastoral work naturally felt entitled to receive for their monasteries the tithes and other revenues normally paid to the parish priest. The progressive assimilation of the monastic and clerical orders also removed some of the most important theological and canonical objections to the payment of tithes to monks and helps to account for the willingness of the reformed popes to grant to monks the tithes recovered from lay possession. Both as parish priests and as members of the clerical order monks were now able to receive tithes.

The possession of parish churches and their revenues by a monastery did not, of course, necessarily entail the performance of parochial services by the monks themselves or the loss of their distinctive position as monks rather than clerics. The abbey of Muri, for instance, claimed all the rights and revenues of the parish church which it had replaced, even though the actual services were performed in the subordinate church of St Goar. Since the altar of the abbey was the principal altar of the place, said the author of the *Acta Murensia*,

Whoever presides over this altar, whether he is a monk or a cleric, should control the endowment, tithe, and all the other rights of the church, since we have never heard of two principal churches and two altars in one place, although it is said (and we do not deny) that a monk neither should nor can be the priest of the people. In order to avoid all disagreement and envy, however, we must maintain and strengthen the settlement and ordinance of our holy predecessors that a cleric should supervise the people at the church of St Goar, since laymen are more properly and firmly instructed and disciplined by secular clerics (*seculares*) than by spiritual monks (*spirituales*), and he should have an endowment and as much of the tithe as the abbot and congregation may give him in the manner of other monasteries and cloisters, which were also built in the places of churches and are much richer and have a larger congregation than us; and all members may thus be at peace.[1]

In later terminology, the abbot here was rector and the priest was vicar, and the distinction between the different functions and natures of monks and clerics was fully maintained.

[1] *Muri*, pp. 58–9.

The reformers who refused to own any churches, *altaria*, or tithes rejected even a compromise like this, however, and radically reasserted the independence of the monastic order.[1] Monks, clerics, and laymen should each be supported by the special means suitable to their orders: monks by the labour of their own hands, clerics by the sacramental revenues, and laymen by the normal workings of the manorial system of agriculture and by other secular activities.[2] Each order should likewise be occupied with its own distinctive functions, and above all monks should not perform the pastoral work and *cura animarum* which were the proper work of clerics, though some of the reformers were not opposed to doing a certain amount of evangelical or apostolic work in the New Testament sense. In the list of charges brought against the Cluniacs, according to Peter the Venerable, the Cistercians asked:

Why do you possess the first-fruits and tithes of parishes, which belong according to canon law not to monks but to clerics? These have been given to those whose office it is to baptize, preach, and administer the other [sacraments] pertaining to the salvation of souls, in order that they need not engage in worldly affairs but may live off the church, since the Lord says that 'The labourer is worthy of his hire'. But why do you usurp this, when you should do none of these things which we have mentioned? And since you do not perform the labour, why do you receive the labourer's hire?[3]

---

[1] This idea was clearly expressed in the works of Joachim of Flora, for instance, who was a Cistercian before starting his own reformed order and whose concept of triads (in history, society, etc.) had a deep influence on later historiography: cf. Bloomfield, in *Traditio*, XIII, 249–311, esp. 266 n. 76.

[2] The reformers particularly objected to the similarity of the economic structures of the three orders of society: see Dereine, in *Rev. du Moyen Âge latin*, IV, 149, and James S. Donnelly, *The Decline of the Medieval Cistercian Laybrotherhood*, Fordham University Studies, History Series, III (New York, 1949), pp. 15–17. The same spirit inspired the celebrated proposal of Paschal II for the clergy to live entirely off spiritual revenues (cf. p. 233 n. 2 below).

[3] Peter the Venerable, ep. I, 28, in *Bibl. Clun.* p. 660. The Cistercian in the *Dialogus inter Cluniacensem et Cisterciensem monachum* also said that tithes should not be held by monks but should be canonically divided into four parts, which greatly alarmed the Cluniac (*Thesaurus*, V, 1593–4).

These accusations clearly show the desire of the reformers to separate the finances of monks, clerics, and laymen.

The refusal to possess tithes was therefore part of a far-reaching plan to reactivate the monastic order and to avoid the engagement of monks in the *cura animarum* and other work in the world. Such work might be meritorious in itself, but it was not suited to the profession of monks. As Bishop James of Faenza stressed in a letter written early in the twelfth century to Bishop Hildebrand of Pistoia, who had been abbot of the Vallombrosan house at Furcule, a monk who travels cannot easily keep fasts, say his psalms, be silent, read, pray, and, in short, perform all the many obligations of his profession.[1] Abelard discussed this point in a letter, probably written after he became a monk in 1118, to a regular canon who had called monasteries 'prisons of penance' and had asserted 'that monks are far below the dignity of clerics', because the dangers and difficulties of clerical life in the world entitled clerics to a higher reward than monks. Abelard replied that on the contrary the dignity of clerics and canons precisely because they worked in the world was below that of monks and that, if the superiority of a way of life depended on its relative difficulty (and Abelard urged his correspondent to test the hardness of the two lives by trying both), 'Why do you yourselves, who are of recent origin and called yourselves recently "regular canons", surround your cloisters with a great circuit of walls, in the manner of monks, and remain separated from the charms and temptations of the world?' Men should shun the world, not seek it, Abelard said; and monks above all, 'who are secluded in monastic cloisters, contemplate the splendour of the highest light more subtly and more perfectly as they are increasingly cut off from the outer cares of the world'.[2]

---

[1] F. A. Zaccaria, *Anecdotorum medii aevi collectio* (Turin, 1755), pp. 257–9, cited by Jean Leclercq, 'Un débat sur le sacerdoce des moines au XIIe siècle', *Analecta monastica*, IV, Studia Anselmiana, XLI (Rome, 1957), pp. 112–13. The letter also contains a series of canonical texts prohibiting the exercise of pastoral duties by monks. James was bishop from 1108 to 1130 and Hildebrand from 1107 to 1133.

[2] Abelard, ep. 12, in *PL*, CLXXVIII, 343–52 (quoted extracts on pp. 351 and 348–9). From its contents this letter might almost have been a reply to the *De institutione*

In many respects this was a conservative position, and it was expressed, from a very different point of view, by some of the supporters of Henry IV in the Investiture Controversy. Bishop Benzo of Alba bitterly attacked the rule of monks over the Church in his *Ad Henricum IV imperatorem libri VII*, written probably in the 1070's. 'Monks and women force bishops to flee as if Hercules were in pursuit', he exclaimed. 'Monks, I say, and what sort of monks? Those defamed by perjury, disgraced by the rape of nuns. These are the creators of popes, to the shame of those who are the rectors of churches.'[1] The episcopal position was exalted in a letter written in 1072 urging Archbishop Siegfried of Mainz, who had become a monk, to return to his diocese. 'Every order, every dignity, every profession is subordinate to the position of apostle [bishop]. Nothing in the world is more eminent or closer to God than the life of a bishop, to whom every monk and recluse, every cenobite and hermit gives way as an inferior.'[2] And Peter Crassus specifically opposed the performance of clerical functions by monks in his *Defensio Heinrici IV. regis*, written in 1084.[3]

Perhaps the most vituperative of all the attacks on monks and on monastic performance of pastoral work and possession of tithes was written by Theobald of Étampes, who was born probably before 1070, was a cleric (or possibly a secular canon),

---

clericorum of Philip of Harvengt (see pp. 158–60 below), but it was probably written earlier and the arguments do not match perfectly. One wonders what Abelard would have replied to Dr Johnson, who once said to an abbess: 'Madam, you are here not for the love of virtue, but the fear of vice', and who argued like the regular canon that merit was in proportion to the possibility for doing wrong.

[1] MGH, *SS*, XI, 672. See also his speech in support of the anti-pope Cadalus of Parma (Honorius II), *ibid.* p. 614; and, on Benzo, Ullmann, *Growth*, p. 392.

[2] *Monumenta Bambergensia*, ed. Philip Jaffé, Bibliotheca rerum germanicarum, v (Berlin, 1869), pp. 81–4 (quoted passage on p. 83), no. 39; cf. Bernhard Schmeidler, 'Anti-asketische Äusserungen aus Deutschland im 11. und beginnenden 12. Jahrhundert', *Kultur und Universalgeschichte: Festschrift Walter Goetz* (Leipzig–Berlin, 1927), pp. 35–52, esp. 48–9 on this letter, and Tellenbach, *Church*, pp. 50–6, who discussed the respective positions of monks and clerics.

[3] MGH, *Libelli*, I, 441.

and taught both at Caen and at Oxford, where he was one of the earliest known masters.[1] In about 1124/33 he wrote a letter to Archbishop Thurstan of York beginning with the provocative declaration that 'The church is one thing and a monastery is another, for the church is the convocation of the faithful but a monastery is the home and prison of the damned, that is, of monks, who have damned themselves in the hope of avoiding eternal damnation...'. He went on to say that monks were inferior to priests, who guard them like shepherds, and might not exercise sacramental offices or rule churches any more than a servant might rule a mistress. If by any chance they did, it was owing to a special dispensation and to the poverty of the clergy, not to a general rule of the Church. Tithes, he said, belong to priests and not to monks, who should pay rather than receive tithes. 'No tithes or churches properly belong to them,' he concluded, 'and there should be none of the strict collections that are used by many monks to extort money; but like the early monks, they should live from the labour of their hands and from the common lot, which is God.'[2]

The attitude of the canons towards this dispute seems to have varied. Traditionally, canons were simply clerics leading a common life under a bishop, provost, or abbot; and they were naturally entitled to exercise pastoral functions and to receive sacramental revenues. St John Gualbert, as seen above, referred to the service of churches as 'the office of canons, not of monks'.[3]

[1] See Hastings Rashdall, *The Universities of Europe in the Middle Ages*, ed. F. M. Powicke and A. B. Emden (Oxford, 1936), III, 16–18; Raymonde Foreville, 'L'École de Caen au XIe siècle et les origines normandes de l'Université d'Oxford', *Études médiévales offertes à M. le doyen Augustin Fliche*, Publications de la Faculté des Lettres de l'Université de Montpellier, IV (Montpellier, 1952), pp. 90–9, and in *Anal. mon.* IV, 9–16. His opponent, whose reply will be studied later, scornfully called him *tantillus clericulus* (*Anal. mon.* IV, 54). In the opinion of Rashdall and Dickinson, *Canons*, p. 188, he may have been a regular canon associated with the house of St Frideswide at Oxford. Foreville, however, called him a secular canon (*Études Fliche*, p. 97) and a 'maître séculier' (*Anal. mon.* IV, 14).

[2] This letter has been edited twice: by T. E. Holland, 'The University of Oxford in the Twelfth Century', *Oxford Historical Society: Collectanea*, II (Oxford, 1890), pp. 153–6, and by Jean Leclercq, in *Anal. mon.* IV, 52–3.

[3] P. 137 above.

An anonymous writer, whose work survives in a twelfth-century manuscript at Rome, said that:

The special and inner life of canons is really to have one heart and one soul; to possess oblations and ecclesiastical property in common and not as individuals; not to give them up or to buy or sell them; and to use them not wilfully but for those leading a common life or those in need; to redeem captives; to restore and decorate churches; to rouse themselves and all men to any good deed of which they are capable; and according to the circumstances to correct daily and discreetly any evil in themselves or in other men.[1]

Many of the new 'regular canons' adhered to this moderate programme, midway between the monastic and clerical programmes, combining a common life of poverty with pastoral service to others. Pope Paschal II in 1116 specifically authorized the Augustinian canons of St Botolph at Colchester both to possess tithes and to preach and administer baptism and penance.[2] Canons of the orders of Springiersbach, St Quentin at Beauvais, Prato, and St Victor at Paris all performed some pastoral work.[3] And various individual houses of canons in Germany, where parish priests were often scarce, were allowed by the diocesan bishops to baptize, bury, and exercise other parochial functions.[4]

The canonical reforms of the eleventh and twelfth centuries are very hard to classify, however;[5] and while the old secular canons were often indistinguishable from clerics and the moderate regular canons resembled the old black Benedictine monks,

[1] *Anal. mon.* IV, 117–18. Some of the occupations here, such as the redemption of captives, hark back to a much earlier period.

[2] *Monasticon*, VI, 106–7; JL 6529; cf. Dickinson, *Canons*, p. 101 n. 2, who defended the substantial authenticity of this bull against the doubts of Löwenfeld and Holtzmann.

[3] *Liber de diversis ordinibus*, XLVII, in *PL*, CCXIII, 837 (see p. 155 below) and Charles Dereine, 'Les coutumiers de Saint-Quentin de Beauvais et de Springiersbach', *Rev. d'hist. ecc.* XLIII (1948), 424 (cf. p. 429).

[4] Cf. *Mainz*, I, 415–17 (1123: Archbishop Adalbert of Mainz for Ilbenstadt) and *Paulinzelle*, pp. 27–30 (1147: Archbishop Henry of Mainz for Ichtershausen).

[5] See in particular Dickinson, *Canons*, pp. 26–58, and Charles Dereine, in *Dict. d'hist.* XII, 353–405, and *Les chanoines réguliers au diocèse de Liège avant saint Norbert*, Académie royale de Belgique: Classe des lettres..., Mémoires in-8°, XLVII. 1 (Brussels, 1952), pp. 15–32.

some of the strict regular canons were in many respects like the new reformed monks.[1] 'Although they claimed a connection with the apostolic and Augustinian tradition,' wrote Dereine, 'the regular canons were newcomers in the church of the eleventh century.'[2] Dickinson also pointed out that although technically the regular canons were not monks, they resembled the reformed monks in that they lived in abbeys under abbots, had 'a clear-cut lay element' in their organization, and claimed to be *pauperes Christi*.[3] A regular canon was even called a *monachus* in a sermon attributed to St Norbert or to Walter of St Maurice.[4] In the *Dialogus inter Cluniacensem et Cisterciensem monachum*, one of the disputants claimed that regular canons 'either are monks or are of no order'.[5] With greater precision, the author of the *Liber de diversis ordinibus et professionibus quae sunt in ecclesia* (which according to Dereine was written about 1125/30 by a regular canon at Liège) distinguished three types of canons and of monks and stressed the similarities between the more austere types of both groups, who lived in solitude, worked with their hands, and refused to own tithes and other clerical revenues.[6] Although there was no specific reference to tithes in the earliest Premonstratensian statutes, which were compiled about 1131/4 possibly under Cistercian influence, the refusal to possess 'altars to which the *cura*

[1] Cf. Winandy, in *La vie spirituelle*, LXXX, 28–30, and Dickinson, *Canons*, pp. 164 ff., who remarked on the similar temperaments of the Augustinian canons and the black Benedictines.

[2] Dereine, *Chanoines*, p. 28.

[3] Dickinson, *Canons*, pp. 80–1 and 198–208, who pointed out in addition that the practical and legal differences were greater between regular and secular canons than between regular canons and monks; cf. Dereine, *Chanoines*, pp. 82, 160, 202, 239–40, and Foreville, in *Anal. mon.* IV, 22–4. See p. 169 n. 3 below on the *pauperes Christi*.

[4] François Petit, *La spiritualité des Prémontrés aux XIIe et XIIIe siècles*, Études de théologie et d'histoire de la spiritualité, X (Paris, 1947), p. 274. Philip of Harvengt, who was himself a Premonstratensian and tended to stress the difference between the clerical and monastic orders (see pp. 158–61 below), also suggested certain parallels between his own order and the Cistercians: *PL*, CCIII, 836–8.

[5] *Thesaurus*, V, 1614; cf. Dickinson, *Canons*, p. 198.

[6] *Liber de diversis ordinibus*, XXXIV, in *PL*, CCXIII, 831; cf. Charles Dereine, 'Les origines de Prémontré', *Rev. d'hist. ecc.* XLII (1947), 359–60 and 375–7, and Dickinson, *Canons*, p. 63.

animarum belongs, unless they can be [made into] abbeys', doubt-less included tithes and other sacramental revenues.[1]

Several recent historians have maintained—in spite of this evidence—that even the strict regular canons were more lenient than the reformed monks in their attitude towards the perfor-mance of pastoral work. Schreiber, for instance, wrote that the Premonstratensians 'were from their origins favourable to pastoral work, since they took charge of parishes and practiced the ministry'.[2] And according to Hofmeister they combined 'saving their own souls (*Selbstheiligung*) in the monastery with pastoral activity'.[3] This view was true only of the moderate orders, however, and for the strict orders it must be revised in the light of the researches of Dereine, Petit, and Dickinson, who said that 'Charters make it abundantly clear that a number of houses of regular canons founded at this time were established on lonely sites where no extensive parochial commitments were to be had and where the prime intention of the community was not to take part in secular worship, but to maintain the contemplative life'.[4] Petit also, after studying the literary sources, concluded that 'In reading the ancient statutes of the order of Prémontré, the historian of spirituality is struck by the lack of provision for apostolic work. The organization is that of a fully contemplative life.'[5] And Dereine repeatedly emphasized that the prime objects of the Premonstratensians were poverty, manual labour, austerity

---

[1] R. van Waefelghem, 'Les premiers statuts de Prémontré', *Analectes de l'ordre de Prémontré*, IX (1913), 45, cited by H. M. Colvin, *The White Canons in England* (Oxford, 1951), pp. 272 n. 3, and, on the date, pp. 13–14. The statute also forbade possession of customs, tolls, serfs, and the advocacies of secular men, and it strongly resembled the early Cistercian and other reformed monastic legislation: cf. Dickinson, *Canons*, pp. 76–9 and 82–8 and esp. J.-A. Lefèvre, 'À propos des sources de la législation primitive de Prémontré', *Analecta Praemonstratensia*, XXX (1954), 12–19.

[2] Schreiber, *Gemeinschaften*, p. 368.

[3] Hofmeister, in *SMGBOZ*, LXV, 210.

[4] Dickinson, *Canons*, p. 73, who went on to say that among many canons the prime object was to maintain a full common life, to which clerical responsibilities (though occasionally undertaken) were recognized as a threat.

[5] Petit, *Spiritualité*, p. 46, cf. pp. 199–200 on contemplation among the early Premonstratensians.

of food and clothing, and a literal application of the rule of
St Augustine rather than pastoral work, even though they occasionally performed it.[1] 'Historians have often presented the
exercise of the *cura animarum*', he said, 'as an essential element in
the profession of regular canons, by which it is distinguished
from monasticism. But a close study of the origins of the canonical
reform shows among its promoters no preoccupation of this sort
and even more no systematic orientation towards preaching or
parochial service.'[2]

From the ranks of the canons, however, came some of the most
astute and vigorous critics of monastic possession of churches and
tithes, since they were anxious to assert and defend the distinctive
nature and prerogatives of their own order, whether or not they
themselves exercised the *cura animarum* and received clerical
revenues, and they joined with enthusiasm in the debate over the
number and relative dignities of the orders within the Church.[3]
'Monks and regular clerics are said to disparage one another',
St Bernard shrewdly remarked in his *Apologia*, 'because they
differ from each other in their own observances.'[4] Arno of
Reichersberg, for instance, wrote his *Scutum canonicorum* in
1146/7 in order to defend the canons against the attacks of monks
and compared the two orders to twins, who are different but not

[1] See Dereine, in *Rev. d'hist. ecc.* XLII, 376–7, and 'Vie commune, règle de
Saint Augustin et chanoines réguliers au XIe siècle', *Rev. d'hist. ecc.* XLI (1946),
365–406, esp. 403, and his reviews of Schreiber, *Gemeinschaften* and Dickinson,
Canons, in *Rev. d'hist. ecc.* XLV, 257, and XLVI, 244. Dickinson, *Canons*, p. 76,
however, said that 'It is doubtful whether or no St Norbert originally intended
his brethren to undertake charge of parishes. They certainly did so from an
early date, but we must beware of regarding evangelism as more than one side
of the Premonstratensian work.' Ernst Werner, *Pauperes Christi* (Leipzig,
1956), p. 79 n. 325, cited against Dereine the example of St Norbert himself;
but neither St Norbert nor St Bernard was the perfect exemplar of the
monastic ideals of his order.
[2] Dereine, *Chanoines*, pp. 30–1, cf. 242–3; cf. Petit, *Spiritualité*, p. 282, and
Grundmann, in *Relazioni*, III, 386–7. The *Liber pancrisis* (cited p. 171 below)
definitely excluded regular canons as well as monks from parochial work
without special permission from the bishop.
[3] See the works of Peter Damian and others cited below, and Tellenbach,
Church, pp. 42–56, and Dereine, *Chanoines*, pp. 93–103 and 'Le problème de
la *cura animarum* chez Gratien', *Studia Gratiana*, II (1954), 311–12.
[4] *Apologia*, III, in *ed. cit.* I (2), 1225 C.

hostile.[1] Theobald of Étampes and the regular canon addressed by Abelard were both inflamed and crude critics of monasticism, calling the monasteries 'prisons of penance' and 'prisons of the damned', but in the works of Anselm of Havelberg, Philip of Harvengt, and Gerhoh of Reichersberg, the monks found more reasoned and weighty criticisms of their exercise of pastoral duties and possession of sacerdotal revenues.

The Premonstratensian canon Anselm, who was bishop of Havelberg from 1129 until 1159, maintained that the canons had a special position between the monastic and clerical orders. 'I am not a monk', he said at one point, and he called himself *clericus et pauper Christi*, showing at the same time that he belonged to the clerical order but sympathized with the ideals of the reformed monks.[2] As an historian, Anselm saw monasticism as the moving power in history and interpreted its influence, according to Bloomfield, 'in mystical and even historical terms'.[3] But he defended the prerogatives of the canons, and in his *Epistola apologetica pro ordine canonicorum regularium*, he replied angrily to a monk, Abbot Ecbert of Huysburg, who had said that regular canons should not hold parishes or exercise the *cura animarum*. Anselm attributed this opinion to hate of the canons rather than to love of truth and replied that all priests should be encouraged to lead a regular life. 'It is clearly the custom of the whole Church', he wrote, 'that in the same way that no monk is received as an archdeacon or an archpriest or in any parish, so likewise no regular canon is excluded from ecclesiastical judgements or synodal cases or from exercising the *cura animarum* or from any ecclesiastical office or dignity.'[4]

The problem was discussed at greater length by Philip of

---

[1] PL, CXCIV, 1521-4; cf. Classen, *Gerhoch*, p. 445, on the date.

[2] PL, CLXXXVIII, 1120D; on Anselm and his attitude towards monasticism, see the series of articles by Fina, in *Anal. Praem.* XXXII (1956), 69-101 and 193-227; XXXIII (1957), 5-39 (esp. on the *cura animarum*) and 268-301, and XXXIV (1958), 13-41.

[3] Bloomfield, in *Traditio*, XIII, 281, and Johannes Spörl, *Grundformen hochmittelalterlicher Geschichtsanschauung* (Munich, 1935), pp. 18-31, esp. p. 27. Other works are cited by Ladner, *Reform*, p. 413 n. 52.

[4] PL, CLXXXVIII, 1128-9; see Fina, in *Anal. Praem.* XXXII, 84-5 on the date.

Harvengt, abbot of the Premonstratensian house of Bonne Espérance, in Belgium, in the fourth book of his *De institutione clericorum*,[1] where he answered Rupert of Deutz and others who defended the right of monks to receive parochial revenues on the grounds that the clerical status was determined by holding clerical office and exercising clerical functions and could therefore be combined with the monastic status.[2] Philip based his refutation of this view on three arguments drawn from the history, relative dignities, and exclusive natures of the two orders. He began with an interesting account of early monasticism. The monks in Egypt, he said, did not preach, rule churches, or exercise the *cura animarum*; and they 'did not presume to seek the oblations of the people nor deserve to be oppressed with a foreign burden by usurping what was not theirs (*indebitum*)'. At that time, he remarked later, 'It was not the custom, I think, for monks in monasteries to be ordained as commonly as is done in our days'.[3] He then explained why monks ceased living from their own labour and accepted grants of ecclesiastical revenues and how they gave up poverty and became rich (cap. 85). Advancing to his second point, however, he said that the dignity of an ecclesiastical order is not established by personal sanctity, way of life, or wealth; and he regarded the superiority of clerics to monks as clearly established both by the Bible, backed by the opinions of the Fathers, and by the relatively greater difficulty of clerical life. 'To flee from the middle of Babylon and to be saved is, therefore, as much safer as it is easier; but to be crowned victor in the middle of Babylon is as much grander as it is harder; so that monastic perfection, though commendable for merit, is considered as much lower as it is easier than clerical [perfection].'[4]

Philip then came to his principal point: that a man's place in

---

[1] On Philip of Harvengt, see A. Erens, in *Dict. de théol. cath.* XII. 1, 1407–11, who dated the *De institutione clericorum* after about 1158, when Philip became abbot of Bonne-Espérance (p. 1409); De Ghellinck, *Littérature*, I, 202–3; Petit, *Spiritualité*, pp. 129–66; and P. Delhaye, 'Saint Bernard de Clairvaux et Philippe de Harveng', *Bull. de la Soc. hist. et arch. de Langres*, XII, no. 156 (1953), 129–38.

[2] See pp. 161–5 below.

[3] *PL*, CCIII, 771–8 (quoted extracts on 773 and 777).   [4] *Ibid.* 802.

society is determined by his status, what he is, not by his occupation, what he does, and that the two must not be confused. A man's order is thus settled by his profession, in the technical sense, not by whether he performs pastoral work, owns tithes and oblations, can read or write, or fights and fornicates. If he changes from one order to another (Philip was not quite clear how this was done), he entirely loses the character of the former. Many laymen and nuns own tithes and are literate, he pointed out, yet they are not clerics. Many clerics fight and fornicate, and some are illiterate and serve no altar, but they remain clerics. Similarly, a monk remains a monk even if he rides, fights, fornicates, and (if ordained) performs pastoral work. For Philip, the term *clericus* did not simply apply to anyone who was ordained and literate and who served an altar. And he likewise held that 'Unless I am mistaken, a monk cannot properly be called either a husband, a knight, or a cleric, nor in reverse can any of these properly be called a monk, although one performs the office of another so often that none of them is considered content with his own functions'.[1] He later repeated that although monks were granted the right to serve altars, which was originally reserved for clerics, they remained monks. 'A monk therefore does a cleric's work but is not a cleric.'[2] Philip thus joined the monastic reformers in asserting the distinction between the orders of society and the independence of the monastic order. He did not actually forbid monks to exercise the *cura animarum* and to receive clerical revenues, and he even appeared to accept that many monks in fact performed the work of clerics; but his remark that the early monks did not take 'what was not theirs' and his admiration for the manual labour and refusal to accept tithes of the Cistercians[3] show where his sympathies lay, and that in his view monks should ideally live apart from the world, supported by their own labour, and should leave pastoral work and clerical revenues to the clergy.[4]

[1] *PL*, CCIII, 823. In cap. cx he mentioned a learned nun who referred to herself as a *bonus clericus* in the masculine.

[2] *Ibid.* 835.   [3] *Ibid.* 836 (cited p. 155 above).

[4] Philip did not discuss the status of his own order of canons, but he definitely regarded himself as a cleric rather than a monk: see Delhaye, in *Bull. de la*

The practical importance of this position is shown by two interesting legal pleadings or briefs presenting the opposite sides in a presumably hypothetical case before a judge and his assessors, probably in the Lowlands during the pontificate of Alexander III.[1] A canon, who had run away from school at the age of fourteen or fifteen and had entered a monastery, was trying to recover his canonry. He had been a minor, he claimed, when 'he allowed the larger crown to be made upon him...and allowed himself to put on the monastic dress'; and since he had not been a monk at heart, he remained a canon and should never have been deprived of his canonry. His lack of learning should not prejudice his right to the canonry, he argued, because there were other members of the chapter 'with no more and much less learning'. The canons answered his claim by pleading that at fourteen he was old enough 'to enter into a contract and to take an oath'. 'Did he not show that he gave up his canonry', they asked, 'by the very fact that he assumed the monastic tonsure and habit?' The decision in this case is not known—if, indeed, one was ever made—but Philip of Harvengt reported a somewhat similar case concerning two men who made professions as clerics in their youth and then returned to lay status, and who were required by a synod to be clerics. 'For someone is judged to be a cleric,' Philip commented, 'not on account of the orders by which he serves at the altar but on account of the profession which he has assumed.'[2] In these two cases there seems to have been no question that the orders concerned were mutually exclusive, and the plaintiff in the first case apparently never considered that even as a monk he might still hold the canonry.

Boto of Prüfening, unlike Philip of Harvengt, who was at heart a reformer, tended to look back wistfully to the good old days when monks knew their place in society. He belonged to the conservative theological circle which included Rupert of Deutz

---

Soc. hist. et arch. de Langres, XII, 132 n. 18, and 135 n. 27. But he called the house he entered after living as an unordained cleric a 'monastery': *PL*, CCIII, 828 C.

[1] Published from a manuscript at Liège by Hubert Silvestre, 'Dix plaidoiries inédites du XIIe siècle', *Traditio*, X (1954), 376–9.

[2] *De institutione clericorum*, CXVIII, in *PL*, CCIII, 827.

and Honorius of 'Autun', though he differed from them on the issue of monastic performance of pastoral work.[1] In his *De statu domus Dei*, written about the middle of the twelfth century, Boto complained that 'those in the monastic order who accepted the *cura animarum*' not only introduced individualism into monasteries by setting their own good above that of all but also neglected the orders of God and the boundaries established by the Fathers. Under the pretext of avoiding laziness and doing good works, Boto said, the present leaders of the Church were devoted to building up the new and destroying the old, much of which should be preserved. Physical labour in monasteries was of use only to promote contemplation, since monks should always progress from the material to the immaterial. 'For the monastic life is devoted not to practical cares but to theoretical studies.' Now that levity has replaced gravity in monastic life, however, especially owing to the introduction of new feasts into the monastic liturgy, monasticism has ceased to be 'the column and foundation of religion'.[2]

Another member of this conservative circle in Germany was the celebrated Provost Gerhoh of the Augustinian house of Reichersberg.[3] He was a prolific writer and a zealous reformer, although he has been accused of being temperamental and vacillating;[4] and he expressed himself strongly on the issue of monastic and lay possession of tithes in a series of works written during a period of over thirty years.[5] Above all in the *Opusculum de edificio Dei*,

[1] On Boto, who lived from about 1103 until about 1170, see J. A. Endres, 'Boto von Prüfening und seine schriftstellerische Thätigkeit', *NA*, xxx (1904–5), 603–46, who disproved the name 'Potho of Prüm' (pp. 605–18) and considered the *De statu domus Dei* one of Boto's earliest works (pp. 626–7).

[2] *Maxima bibliotheca veterum patrum* (Lyons, 1677), xxi, 489–513 (quoted extracts on pp. 501–2), where the work is dated 1152.

[3] On Gerhoh, who lived from 1093 to 1169, see Classen, *Gerhoch*, and (on some of the aspects discussed here) J. A. Endres, *Honorius Augustodunensis: Beitrag zur Geschichte des geistigen Lebens im 12. Jahrhundert* (Kempten–Munich, 1906), p. 83.

[4] Cf. Hauck, *Kirchengeschichte*, iv, 215, and G. W. Greenaway, *Arnold of Brescia* (Cambridge, 1931), p. 173.

[5] Cf. Classen, *Gerhoch*, pp. 42, 45, and 177, who stressed Gerhoh's attacks on episcopal misuse of tithes and his belief that only those who did pastoral work

which he wrote in about 1128/9 and revised in 1138, Gerhoh defended a strict canonical division of tithes and attacked both the possession of tithes by monks and laymen and their misuse by bishops. Quadripartition, he explained, which has replaced the Spanish tripartition, allows only one quarter of the tithes to the bishop, who should use it not for soldiers but for pilgrims, guests, and the poor, or he may assign it for his lifetime to a baptismal church or to a monastery. Any permanent alienation would damage the rights of his successors and is illegal according to both divine and secular law, so that the giver and the receiver, whether a monastery or a layman, will both be condemned. Men must redeem the inheritance of God, Gerhoh said, 'so that not only the quarters for the clerics, the poor, and the upkeep of churches are restored to their old and proper uses but also the episcopal quarter is recovered from monks and especially from soldiers and is spent by him [the bishop] as it should be'.[1] To the argument that monks made better use of tithes than bishops and priests, Gerhoh replied that monks and 'cloistered canons' must serve the churches from which they collected the tithes, and he applied to them the decree of Pope Urban I prohibiting private possession of ecclesiastical property.[2] He allowed monks to hold the tithes from their own labour, 'unless they are lay and illiterate monks who need clerical ministry', and he interpreted the decree of Gregory VII requiring the permission of the pope or diocesan bishop for monastic possession of tithes as applying only to their own tithes and not to the tithes of other men. 'No authority confirms or can confirm that they should possess by perpetual right the tithes which according to the firmest evidence of the Fathers must be brought to the baptismal churches.'[3] Monks may

should receive tithes, and Erich Meuthen, *Kirche und Heilsgeschichte bei Gerhoh von Reichersberg*, Studien und Texte zur Geistesgeschichte des Mittelalters, VI (Leiden, 1959), pp. 159–60.

[1] MGH, *Libelli*, III, 192.

[2] *Decretales Ps.-Isidorianae*, Ep. Urbani I, c. 4, *ed. cit.* p. 145; cf. *Decretum*, C. XII, q. I, c. 26 (see p. 45 n. 3 above).

[3] MGH, *Libelli*, III, 196. See pp. 89–90 above on Gregory VII's decree in 1078. Gerhoh referred with scorn to the 'learned monks' who cited this canon in support of their possession of other men's tithes. In fact, Gerhoh's own interpretation was wrong, and the canon was certainly designed not only to

not receive tithes even from their own peasants, far less from other men, and are liable to excommunication for resisting 'the bishop who is exacting his right (*iusticiam*) of tithes', or for seeking to avoid this obligation from which even the pope cannot free them.[1] Also in his *Liber de simoniacis*, written in about 1135 and dedicated to St Bernard, Gerhoh cited the decree of Urban I and called episcopal grants of tithes to laymen both simoniacal and sacrilegious.[2]

Gerhoh always maintained his opposition to lay possession of tithes, but over the years he became less hostile to monastic tithes, owing, perhaps, to the fact that his own abbey owned tithes and encountered various difficulties in keeping them. In the *Liber de novitatibus huius temporis*, written in 1156 and dedicated to Pope Hadrian IV, besides attacking lay possession of tithes he called on the pope to protect monks and regular canons from being forced to pay tithes from their own fields, vineyards, and animals to laymen and to secular clerics.[3] In the *Liber de laude fidei*, which he wrote in 1158/9 at the request of the Cistercian Cardinal Henry of SS. Nereo e Achilleo, Gerhoh used another passage from the letter of Urban I, forbidding alienation of church property,[4] and again attacked the rich men who usurped the patrimony of the poor of Christ and even forced them to pay tithes from their own produce, 'when on the contrary the need of these poor men ought to be alleviated from the legitimate tithes given by the faithful populace'.[5] Finally, in his great *De investigatione Antichristi*, of which he prepared a revised version in 1160/2, he repeated his complaints that the bishops often gave laymen benefices consisting of 'the tithes and other oblations of the faithful which were given for the uses of those serving God and above all of

---

allow monks who required no clerical services to keep their own tithes but to establish papal and episcopal control over monastic possession of other men's tithes.

[1] MGH, *Libelli*, III, 198.   [2] *Ibid.* 251.   [3] *Ibid.* 291–2 and 298.

[4] *Decretales Ps.-Isidorianae*, Ep. Urbani I, c. 3, *ed. cit.* p. 144; cf. *Decretum*, C. XII, q. I, c. 16 (see p. 45 n. 3 above).

[5] Gerhoh of Reichersberg, *Opera inedita*, I, ed. D. and O. van den Eynde and A. Rijmersdael, Spicilegium pontificii Athenaei Antoniani, VIII (Rome, 1955), 207–8.

those leading a common life and of the other poor men of the church of God'.[1] The *pauperes ecclesiae Dei* here presumably included monks, and it therefore seems that towards the end of his life Gerhoh was prepared to accept and even favour monastic possession of tithes. But his earlier view, common among the reformers, was that monks should own the tithes only from their own labour and from churches where they themselves performed the *cura animarum*. For monks to possess other tithes was to disregard canon law, history, and the purity of their profession and thus to permit a serious threat to the stability and independence of the monastic order.

5. THE DEFENCE OF MONASTIC POSSESSION OF TITHES

The case against monastic possession of tithes did not go unanswered, and some of the most influential writers of the twelfth century, including Ivo of Chartres, Anselm of Canterbury, Peter the Venerable, and Gratian, took up their pens to refute the arguments of the radicals and reactionaries and to justify the right of monks to receive tithes from the labour of other men. Broadly speaking, the defence of monastic possession of tithes followed one of two courses: one, more moderate, attempting to establish a limited right of monks to perform pastoral work and to receive the tithes of the churches which they served and the other, more radical, seeking to establish generally the right of all monks to own tithes.

In the eleventh century the principal approach was along the more moderate course. Already at the end of the tenth century, Abbo of Fleury suggested in his letter to G. that an ordained monk who served a church was entitled to its oblations and revenues, although in his *Apology* he maintained that monks should celebrate mass only within their own monasteries.[2] The reformed papacy also supported this argument. In 1050 Pope Leo IX, whose efforts to recover tithes from laymen and to allow monks to hold tithes by prescription have been mentioned above,

---

[1] MGH, *Libelli*, III, 347.   [2] See p. 81 above.

permitted the monks of St Ponziano at Lucca to receive and bury the dead, to administer penance, and to visit the sick; and he stated that he did so 'the more willingly because the monastic order is seen to adhere more devotedly to God'. The right of this monastery to bury and to receive alms from the living and the dead was confirmed by Gregory VII in 1074.[1] Such a grant of sacerdotal duties to monks was evidently unusual, and the abbey later forged an elaborate justification attributed to Leo IX, citing the examples of St Martin and Gregory the Great and saying that St Benedict never forbade his monks to perform pastoral work.[2] Peter Damian defended the right of monks to administer the sacraments in his *Apologeticus monachorum adversus canonicos*, written in 1058, and cited two apocryphal decrees attributed to Gregory the Great and Boniface IV permitting monks to exercise sacerdotal offices.[3] In 1059 and 1060 he witnessed the grant of papal tithes to the abbey of St Peter at Perugia and the conciliar confirmation of the tithes belonging to Leno.[4]

At about the same time in Germany, Otloh of St Emmeram at Regensburg went to Fulda and wrote his *Vita s. Bonifacii*, in the preface to which he bitterly attacked the failure of the bishops to distribute the tithes in the four portions prescribed by canon law, and defended the possession of tithes by monks, who used them properly. 'Was not St Boniface', he asked, 'able to give tithes to monks or to the poor by the same authority with which modern bishops are accustomed to give tithes to soldiers and other

---

[1] *APRI*, II, 72 and 124; JL 4228 and 4864; *IP*, III, 446, nos. 3 and 5.

[2] *APRI*, II, 81–2; JL 4324; *IP*, III, 446, no. 4; cf. Paul Kehr, 'Papsturkunden im westlichen Toscana', *Nachrichten der königl. Gesellschaft der Wissenschaften zu Göttingen*, Phil.-Hist. Klasse (1903), pp. 594–5, who called this charter 'eine freie Fälschung ohne echte Vorlage'.

[3] *PL*, CXLV, 511–18. On the forged decretals of Gregory the Great (JE 1951) and Boniface IV (JE 1996), which were composed probably in Italy in the middle of the eleventh century and were much used by those who supported the right of monks to perform pastoral work, see: Berlière, in *Rev. bén.* XXXIX, 233–4; Jean Leclercq, in *Analecta monastica*, II, Studia Anselmiana, XXXI (Rome, 1953), 137–8 (with references to earlier literature); Dereine, in *Studia Gratiana*, II, 308 and 313–18; and J. J. Ryan, *Saint Peter Damiani and his Canonical Sources*, Pontifical Institute of Mediaeval Studies: Studies and Texts, II (Toronto, 1956), pp. 54–8.

[4] See pp. 87 n. 4, and 95 n. 2 above.

laymen?'[1] Bernald of St Blaise, on the other hand, appealed to history rather than canon law in his *Apologeticae rationes contra scismaticorum obiectiones*, which was written probably after 1086 and addressed to Provost Adalbert of Speyer, who had clearly criticized monks for preaching. Bernald replied that permission to preach had not been given to monks in the past because they were not ordained and like laymen were forbidden to preach. 'But since modern monks are ordained,' he continued, 'what harm can be done [and] why when they are so ordered should they not exercise the offices of their ranks, especially since they are the same as clerics in their reception of consecration?' He went on to specify that monks 'should not preach unless they have been ordained and should obey the bishop unless they have been freed by the apostolic see'.[2] Similar arguments were used by the monks of Molesme in their answer to the reforming programme of St Robert:

The tithes and oblations of the faithful are by common consent given to the clergy and the ministers of God for their support.... Thus the Lord has ordained that those who preach the Gospel should live by the Gospel. We are clerics both by our order and by our office, and we offer clerical service to the High Priest, who has entered the heavens, in order that with his aid we may receive the lot of heavenly inheritance. We therefore have a right to possess ecclesiastical benefices and are determined by common consent to hold [them] for ever.[3]

These monks were not lax in their discipline, but they adhered to the old monastic ideal and supported the view which tended to merge the clerical and monastic orders and to regard ordained monks as entitled to all the privileges and revenues of clerics.

The great canonist Ivo of Chartres embraced several points of view on this subject. In his canonical writings, although he cited

[1] Otloh of St Emmeram, *Vita s. Bonifacii*, ed. W. Levison, MGH, SS in usum schol. (Hanover–Leipzig, 1905), pp. 115–16; cf. Wattenbach, *Geschichtsquellen*, II, 65–6. Otloh wrote this life of St Boniface soon after coming to Fulda in 1062.   [2] MGH, *Libelli*, II, 98.

[3] Ordericus Vitalis, *Hist. ecc.* VIII, 26, ed. cit. III, 441; on Molesme and its ascetic origins, see *Abbayes et prieurés de l'ancienne France*, XII: *Province ecclésiastique de Lyon*, 3: *Diocèses de Langres et de Dijon*, ed. Jacques Laurent and Ferdinand Claudon (Ligugé–Paris, 1941), pp. 290–305, esp. pp. 301–2.

the apocryphal decree of Boniface IV granting ordained monks 'the power and office of binding and loosing', he tended to oppose the performance of pastoral work and the possession of tithes by monks.[1] In an early letter to Bishop Peter of Poitiers in about 1094 he maintained that true monks should live in solitude and find their highest honour in humility and obedience, and he supported this assertion of the independence of the monastic order with the classical quotations from St Augustine and St Jerome that 'a good monk scarcely ever makes a good cleric' and that 'a monk has the office not of teaching but of weeping'.[2] In a letter written in about 1098 to Walter the provost of the Augustinian abbey of Lesterps, however, although he still said that regular clerics should live in seclusion, Ivo allowed that they need not be altogether excluded from 'the rule of parishes and the confession of penitents', and he advised Walter to present a few suitable canons to the bishop of Limoges 'in order that they may receive from him the *cura animarum*'.[3] In a letter to Bishop John of Orléans in 1096/1116 he again defended the right of regular canons to perform pastoral work by asserting the desirability of a regular and common life for all priests, both in towns and in the country.[4]

These letters both referred to canons or to clerics leading a common life, but in his long and famous letter to the monks of Coulombs Ivo defended and justified the possession of tithes by monks in new and general terms. His anger had been roused by certain preachers who had urged monks to leave any monastery which owned tithes uncanonically.

Let these subtle students of divine judgements tell me whether it is better for monks to remain cenobites, obedient to their superiors... and

---

[1] Ivo of Chartres, *Decretum*, VII, 22, and (for canons applying episcopal control and quadripartition to tithes) *Panormia*, II, 57–62, in *PL*, CLXI, 1093–6; cf. Dereine, in *Studia Gratiana*, II, 311 and 315, and the canons from Gratian cited p. 183 below.

[2] Ivo of Chartres, *Correspondance*, ed. Jean Leclercq, I, Les classiques de l'histoire de France au Moyen Âge, XXII (Paris, 1949), 146–52, ep. 36 (the citations are from St Augustine, ep. 60, and St Jerome, *Contra Vigilantium*, XVII).

[3] *Ibid.* pp. 304–8, ep. 69.

[4] Ivo of Chartres, ep. 213, in *PL*, CLXII, 216–17; cf. Gams, *Series*, p. 593.

to live off the tithes and oblations of the faithful, which by the law of charity the Church can give not only to monasteries but also to hospices, the sick, and pilgrims, or whether they should become Sarabaites, so as to live as they please in private places and to support themselves on substance seized from the poor and on the profits of merchants. For although tithes and oblations are owed principally to the clerical army, the Church can hold everything it has in common with all the poor. How much the more with those poor who have given up their own goods, carry the cross of Christ voluntarily, and follow Christ in his poverty? The abbots and provosts of monasteries should not be spared, however, in my opinion, if they accept tithes and oblations from laymen, to whom they do not belong, if they acquire them methodically from various people, [or] if they transgress the old boundaries, that is, if they reduce or take for themselves the stipends of priests which were established long ago.[1]

This letter shows not only Ivo's preference for orderly and established forms of monastic life[2] but also his ability to work out common-sense solutions to practical dilemmas. In principle, he was not particularly well disposed towards monastic possession of tithes, as his earlier letters and the concluding remarks in this one show; but he realized the impossibility of restoring all tithes to their canonical owners and therefore combined the ancient concepts of the Church's responsibility to support the poor, of tithes as the sustenance of the poor, and of monks as the poor of Christ,[3]

[1] Ivo of Chartres, ep. 192, in *PL*, CLXII, 199–200.
[2] Cf. Germain Morin, 'Rainaud l'Ermite et Yves de Chartres: Un épisode de la crise du cénobitisme au XIe–XIIe siècle', *Rev. bén.* XL (1928), 99–115, and Dereine, in *Rev. d'hist. ecc.* XLIII, 417–21.
[3] There is an extensive bibliography on this topic in Werner, *Pauperes*, pp. 209–18, which itself contains much of interest but (*a*) is written from a Marxist point of view, (*b*) concentrates on the renewal of religious life at the turn of the twelfth century, and consequently (*c*) devotes little attention to the history of the idea of 'the poor of Christ', besides mentioning that the term had been applied to monks and nuns since the ninth century (p. 19). The idea of *pauper pauperem Christum sequi*, which was used by Ivo, and the closely related *nudus nudum Christum sequi* in fact went back to Patristic sources: cf. Matthäus Bernards, 'Nudus nudum Christum sequi', *Wissenschaft und Weisheit*, XIV (1951), 149. Peter Damian in his *Apologeticum de contemptu saeculi* (which was not cited by Werner) referred to monks as those 'qui amore perfectionis pro Christo effecti sunt pauperes' (*PL*, CXLV, 254).

and he so established what was in effect the first general theory justifying the payment of tithes to monks.[1]

The early scholastic theologians tended to be cautious in allowing monks to perform pastoral work and receive sacramental revenues. St Anselm of Canterbury was fearful of simony in transactions concerning tithes and adhered closely to the canonical decrees on monastic tithes in his reply to Abbot Gelduin of Anchin (1103-10), who had asked whether he might recover the tithes belonging to his church from the laymen who held them.

It is assuredly allowed, in accordance with the papal privilege, for you to redeem from others any ecclesiastical property that came into the possession of your church by grant of the bishop. And you should not grant whatever you have so that any layman holds tithes, churches, or

---

[1] The idea that monks as *pauperes Christi* might own and use tithes was clearly in the air in the eleventh and twelfth centuries. It appears in a letter in the Tegernsee collection, written about 1101/2: 'We feel fraud everywhere, alas, alas, in the tithing which we ought to give with a charitable hand to the poor of Christ (*Christi pauperibus*) for the Church of God and the souls of the blessed,' *Die Tegernseer Briefsammlung*, ed. Karl Strecker, MGH, Epistolae selectae, III (Berlin, 1925), p. 64, ep. 54. Paschal II used the similar concept of monks as the voluntary poor as a reason for freeing them from paying tithes (see p. 231 below). Georg Ratzinger, *Geschichte der kirchlichen Armenpflege* (Freiburg im Br., 1868, 2nd ed. 1884), cited by both Schreiber, *Kurie*, I, 288-9, and Coulton, *Five Centuries*, III, 155-6, apparently traced back to Pseudo-Isidore the idea that voluntarily poor monks, nuns, and canons had a right to charity; but as early as 829 the council of Paris urged the bishops to devote their share of the tithes 'to the uses of the churches and of the *pauperes Christi*', by which it may have meant monks, since another share was properly allocated to the involuntarily poor (see p. 53 above). Coulton said that Ivo 'laid down the principle that the *pauperes Christi*, in the truest sense, are monks', citing this letter (*Five Centuries*, III, 191); and Schreiber, *Gemeinschaften*, p. 350-1, found in the work of Hugh of Amiens, who also said that monks as the true poor were entitled to tithes (see pp. 172-3 below), 'a completely new basis' for monastic possession of tithes, which replaced 'the older and Germanic form of lordship over the church (*Kirchherrschaft*)'. A letter attributed to Fulbert of Chartres (or by Dickinson, *Canons*, p. 206 n. 3, to Fulcher of Chartres) said that the Church was responsible for supporting those 'qui sunt pauperes Christi, scilicet monachis, et canonicis regularibus, vel religiosis quibusque communiter viventibus' (*RHGF*, XI, 496). And in 1140 Archbishop Arnold of Cologne cited his duty 'to bear more readily the care of our brothers and poor men' as a reason for confirming the tithes and other property of Stavelot, which was hardly a poor abbey! (*Köln*, I, 510-11, no. 48, cited p. 119 above).

altaria as a fief from you. As to whether you should refuse or accept if someone wishes, with your knowledge but without your arranging it by word or reward, to redeem some ecclesiastical property for the use of your church, it seems to me that you should be permitted to accept this with the consent and grant of the bishop.[1]

Like Ivo, therefore, St Anselm opposed any direct or systematic acquisition of tithes by monks. His pupil Anselm of Laon was equally conservative on the subject of monastic performance of sacerdotal work. A sentence in the *Liber pancrisis* taught 'that to hold a parish or to have any ministry is forbidden as much for a regular canon as for a monk. But a bishop may with due consideration make either of them an archdeacon or a priest provided that each remains in his order.'[2]   At the end of a long letter to Abbot Heribrand of St Laurence at Liège, written probably before 1113, Anselm of Laon again discussed the respective functions of clerics and monks and said that clerics should live off tithes rather than possess land. 'Clerics are chosen to preach and to instruct those who are under them,' he wrote, 'but monks [are chosen] to pray; for clerics cannot be free for constant prayer on account of the distractions of their office and business. But when necessary monks often assume the office of preaching and teaching at the command of the bishop.'[3] This part of the letter may be a later addition,[4] but it agrees with the sentence in the *Liber pancrisis* and reflects the conservative tendency of the school of Laon, which in this respect resembled the monastic reformers in maintaining the distinction between the clerical and monastic

---

[1] Anselm of Canterbury, ep. III, 163, in *PL*, CLIX, 198; cf. *Dict. d'hist.* II, 1523, on the dates of Gelduin.

[2] Lottin, *Psychologie*, V, 67. See Jean Leclercq, in *Analecta monastica*, II, Studia Anselmiana, XXXI (Rome, 1953), pp. 139–40, for a copy of this text, attributed to Ivo of Chartres, in a twelfth-century manuscript at Berne.

[3] *PL*, CLXII, 1590.

[4] Ludwig Ott, *Untersuchungen zur theologischen Briefliteratur der Frühscholastik*, Beiträge zur Geschichte der Philosophie und Theologie des Mittelalters, XXXIV (Münster in W., 1937), p. 40 n. 2, said that the part of the letter following the words 'prudenter intendere' (*PL*, CLXII, 1588 A) were 'lose aneinandergereihte theologische Fragmente über verschiedene Gegenstände', cf. Dickinson, *Canons*, p. 214; Dereine, *Chanoines*, pp. 93–4 and 246; and Lottin, *Psychologie*, V, 175–8.

orders and in subjecting monastic performance of pastoral work and possession of tithes to the strict control of the diocesan bishop.

A more spirited defence of the prerogatives of the monastic order naturally came from the monks themselves. Even a reformer like Bernard of Tiron, while on a preaching tour in Normandy early in the twelfth century, vigorously asserted the right of monks to preach and to exercise 'the pastoral rule in churches' when he was criticized by the archdeacon of Coutances, who asked 'why he who was a monk and dead to the world preached to the living'.[1] Hamelin of St Albans in his *Liber de monachatu*, written about 1100, argued that monks might possess tithes and oblations because 'according to papal decrees monks should and can be placed canonically in the offices of clerics', because 'the oblations of the faithful are paid not only to monasteries of canons and to parish priests but also to wandering clerics', and because monks are no less worthy than clerics to receive alms and in their own way serve the Lord, who said in Malachi, 'Bring ye all the tithes into the storehouse, that there may be meat for the servants in mine house'.[2] The functions, dignity, and nature of monks were also cited as proof that they might own tithes by the influential Cluniac Hugh of Amiens, who became successively prior of St Martial at Limoges, prior of Lewes, abbot of Reading, and lastly archbishop of Rouen, and whose *Dialogues* were addressed to his friend Matthew, prior of St Martin des Champs, who in 1126 became cardinal-bishop of Albano.[3] 'No one becomes a monk unless he has previously been a cleric', Hugh said; and clerics who are monks are superior to those who are not monks and are ideally suited:

[1] *AASS*, April, II, 235 AB.

[2] *Thesaurus*, V, 1455–6; cf. T. D. Hardy, *Descriptive Catalogue of Materials Relating to the History of Great Britain and Ireland*, Rolls Series, XXVI (London, 1862–71), II, 93, and Schreiber, *Gemeinschaften*, pp. 351–3. In the Vulgate, Malachi iii. 10 reads 'Inferte omnem decimam in horreum, et sit cibus in domo mea'; but here and in the anonymous reply to Theobald of Étampes (see p. 181 below) it reads: 'Apportate [Inferte *in the reply*] omnem decimationem [meam] in horreo meo, ut sit cibus servientibus in domo mea', which changes the meaning considerably.

[3] Cf. Ursmer Berlière, 'Le cardinal Matthieu d'Albano', *Mélanges d'histoire bénédictine*, IV (Maredsous, 1902), 11.

by virtue of their more perfect lives...to preach the kingdom of God to the people, to reprove sinners, and to receive, loose, and bind penitents. They should serve altars diligently and live off oblations and tithes. Tithes indeed belong to the poor, but the true poor are those who in accordance with the Gospel are poor in spirit, because there are those who give up not only their possessions but also their wills to their fathers. Cenobites do this by their public profession. By virtue of their true poverty, therefore, and by their rejection of property, the true poor of Christ should live off oblations and tithes....

Anchorites, on the other hand, who live as they please and gather property, must, according to Hugh, pay tithes and oblations to the altar.[1]

Several of these points were examined at greater length in the works of Rupert of St Laurence at Liège, who in 1119/20 became abbot of Deutz, near Cologne,[2] and who belonged, in the opinion of Ott, 'among the great representatives of the traditional and conservative tendency in theology in the early twelfth century, who knew how to combine deep speculation with mystic intensity'.[3] Hauck remarked that 'He was a monk and thought and felt as a monk',[4] and he strongly defended the rights of monks. He drew up a brief account of a debate between himself and a cleric named Nopertus (Norbert?) on the subject of whether monks were allowed to preach.[5] Philip of Harvengt also mentioned this

[1] *Thesaurus*, V, 972–3; cf. Schreiber, *Gemeinschaften*, pp. 350–1; D. van den Eynde, 'Nouvelles précisions chronologiques sur quelques œuvres théologiques du XIIe siècle', *Franciscan Studies*, XIII (1953), 74–7, who dated the two editions of the *Dialogues* in 1126 and 1130/4 respectively, and C. H. Talbot, 'The Date and Author of the "Riposte"', *Petrus Venerabilis*, pp. 72–80, who defended against the doubts of Jean de la Croix Bouton the attribution of the 'Riposte' to Hugh of Amiens made by Wilmart, in *Rev. bén.* XLVI, 296–344.

[2] On Rupert and his many writings, see Hauck, *Kirchengeschichte*, IV, 432–43; Manitius, *Geschichte*, III, 127–35; De Ghellinck, *Littérature*, I, 118–20; and Wattenbach–Holtzmann, *Geschichtsquellen*, pp. 657–66, with bibliography.

[3] Ott, *Untersuchungen*, p. 73; cf. Martin Grabmann, *Die Geschichte der scholastischen Methode* (Freiburg im Br., 1909–11), II, 100–1, who said that 'Abt Rupert von Deutz...gehört zu den tiefsinnigsten Theologen des 12. Jahrhunderts in deutschen Landen'; and Chenu, *Théologie*, *passim*, esp. pp. 323–5, where he stressed Rupert's conservative reaction against the methods of early scholasticism.   [4] Hauck, *Kirchengeschichte*, IV, 434.

[5] *PL*, CLXX, 537–42, entitled *Altercatio monachi et clerici quod liceat monacho praedicare*, and Clm 27129, f. 116v, entitled *Conflictus Ruodperti Coloniensis*

debate, with specific references to Rupert's work, in his *De institutione clericorum* and said that the cleric was very learned in secular letters, especially in Porphyry and Aristotle, but not in sacred letters, and conceded victory to his adversary after consulting the masters at Laon.[1] According to Rupert's own account he forced the cleric to recognize the right of monks to preach, by arguing, like Hugh of Amiens, that there was no opposition or mutual exclusion between the *monachatus* and the *clericatus*. 'Those who serve at the altar are therefore clerics,' he said, 'and the *clericatus* indicates nothing more than the office of the altar.' By this definition, he said to the cleric, 'You are only a cleric; I am both a monk and a cleric'. And he claimed for himself all the rights of clerical status.[2] Rupert or his disciple Wazelin used the same argument to prove the superiority of the monastic to the clerical order in a letter written in about 1130 to the canon Liezelinus.[3] In another letter, to Abbot Everard of Brauweiler, Rupert argued that Jerome's dictum that monks should weep and not teach applied only to unordained monks and that ordained monks might preach, baptize, absolve, and celebrate the mass.[4] And in a separate treatise on the *Quaestio utrum monachis liceat praedicare*, Rupert applied another famous dictum of St Jerome— that monks should be dead to the world—to secular work only, and he said that literate and ordained monks had the right and duty to perform pastoral work. 'Just as it is permitted to all priests without distinction to celebrate mass,' he wrote,

abbatis...cum Noperto clerico: Si liceat monacho predicare an non, which suggests the debate took place after Rupert became abbot of Deutz. It may, however, have been a result of the letter from Anselm of Laon to the abbot of St Laurence at Liège, where Rupert was a monk. Rupert is known from his commentary on the rule of St Benedict, cap. I (*PL*, CLXX, 482–3), to have gone to Laon to debate with William of Champeaux and Anselm of Laon: cf. Chenu, *Théologie*, p. 323.

[1] Philip of Harvengt, *De institutione clericorum*, CIII, in *PL*, CCIII, 807.

[2] *PL*, CLXX, 539–40.

[3] *Ibid.* 663–8; cf. Ott, *Untersuchungen*, pp. 78–9, and Dereine, *Chanoines*, pp. 97 and 100–1, and in *Studia Gratiana*, II, 315 n. 42, who suggested that this letter might be by Abbot Wazelin of St Laurence, though it shows the influence of Rupert.

[4] *PL*, CLXX, 541–4; cf. Ott, *Untersuchungen*, p. 79.

'so also it is permitted to all priests of whatever profession to preach, baptize, and perform other offices of the ecclesiastical order.'[1]

A twelfth-century manuscript from Ottobeuren includes both a copy of Rupert's debate with the cleric Nopertus and an unpublished anonymous treatise entitled *Ratio quod liceat monachis predicare, baptizare, et penitentiam iniungere*. The author of this work denied that there was any rigid separation between the active and contemplative lives, which he compared to the two loves of one's neighbour and of God, and cited the examples of Elijah and John the Baptist as evidence that monks and hermits might engage in active pastoral work. Monks indeed are closer to God and more suited for his work, he argued, because they have given up the goods and pleasures of this world. God sends both priests and monks, but 'if every priest [is] an angel, a monk-priest [is] certainly an archangel'. He further maintained that St Benedict in chapter four of the Rule allowed his monks to visit the sick, bury the dead, and perform other work in the world. At the end of the treatise he cited six decretals concerning monastic possessions and the performance of pastoral work and the payment of tithes by monks: the letters of Gregory the Great to Marinianus of Ravenna and Augustine of Canterbury, with an addition prohibiting the exaction of tithes and first-fruits from monks; an alleged decree of Gregory the Great on the consecration of monks, authorizing them to baptize, preach, give communion, and absolve penitents; the apocryphal decree of Boniface IV asserting the superiority of monks to priests and allowing them to exercise sacerdotal offices; and two forged decrees forbidding the exaction of tithes from monks.[2]

A treatise on whether monks might preach was also written by the so-called Honorius of Autun, who lived from about

---

[1] Published by Endres, *Honorius*, pp. 145–7 (quoted extract on p. 146), with discussion on pp. 82–6; cf. Ott, *Untersuchungen*, p. 79 n. 57, who doubted the authenticity of this work, and Dereine, *Chanoines*, p. 98, who accepted the attribution to Rupert.

[2] Clm 27129, fos. 114r–116v. See pp. 304–5 below on the forged canons concerning monastic payment of tithes, which suggest that this work was written in the second half of the twelfth century.

1090 until 1156, perhaps as a hermit near Regensburg, and was another important representative of the conservative monastic theology in Germany.[1] He defended the right of monks to preach in terms of two dualisms: first, that there were two offices in the Church, clerical and lay, which were concerned respectively with spiritual and secular affairs; and second, that there were two religious professions, monastic and regular, which were represented by the Benedictine monks and the Augustinian canons. These professions, Honorius said, 'are titles of merit, not of office, since they signify contemptors of the world'; and either a monk or a canon might hold clerical or lay office and, if he was a cleric, might preach 'not from his rule but from his office'. He conceded with St Jerome that a monk 'has indeed the office of weeping from his profession, but he has the office of teaching from his sacerdotal ordination'. Anyone who had the major duty of celebrating the mass might perform the minor duty of preaching. And he ended with an assertion of the superiority of monasticism over other forms of religious life.[2] A work entitled *De vita vere apostolica*, which has been variously attributed to Rupert, Honorius, and a Victorine canon, also sought to demonstrate the superiority of monks over canons and emphasized among other things the right of monks to exercise the *cura animarum*.[3]

---

[1] *ODCC*, p. 653, including a good bibliography, to which should be added Romuald Bauerreiss, 'Honorius von Canterbury (Augustodunensis) und Kuno I., der Raitenbucher, Bischof von Regensburg (1126–1136)', *SMGBOZ*, LXVII (1956), 306–13, who argues that Bishop Cuno was responsible for bringing Honorius from Canterbury to Regensburg.

[2] Published by Endres, *Honorius*, pp. 147–50, with a discussion on pp. 85–6; cf. E. M. Sanford, 'Honorius, *Presbyter* and *Scholasticus*', *Speculum*, XXIII (1948), 411–12, who mentioned the circumstances under which this treatise was written, and Ullmann, *Growth*, pp. 414–19, on Honorius's hierocratic view of society.

[3] *PL*, CLXX, 609–64, esp. 637; cf. Manitius, *Geschichte*, III, 129 and 135, who questioned the attribution to Rupert; Ott, *Untersuchungen*, p. 79 n. 57; Charles Dereine, 'L'Élaboration du statut canonique des chanoines réguliers spéciale-ment sous Urbain II', *Rev. d'hist. ecc.* XLVI (1951), 550 n. 2; Dereine, *Chanoines*, pp. 97–8, and in *Studia Gratiana*, II, 313, who suggested Honorius as author; and Chenu, in *Rev. d'hist. ecc.* XLIX, 62 n. 1, who dated the treatise after 1121 and cited Morin's support of the attribution to Rupert, though other scholars attribute it to a Victorine.

Even more elaborate distinctions and combinations than those
of Honorius were made by the monk Idungus of Regensburg in
his *Argumentum super quatuor quaestionibus*, which was written
about the middle of the twelfth century and shows the influence
both of Rupert of Deutz and of Honorius.[1] Like Rupert, Idungus
discussed the idea that monks should be dead, but he distinguished four types of death: of the body, of the spirit, of sins (as
in baptism), and 'dead to the world', *mortuus seculo*, which he
further divided into death by complete separation from other
men, which is the mark of hermits, and death to secular but not
to ecclesiastical affairs, which should mark all clerics and monks.
He therefore distinguished two basic types of monks: the anchor-
ite, who lived in complete isolation, and the cenobite, who was
dead to secular affairs (as Rupert also said) but might engage in the
ecclesiastical work of teaching and writing.[2] Like Rupert and
Honorius, and in direct contrast to Philip of Harvengt, Idungus
maintained that the *monachatus* and *clericatus* were different but
not opposite and might be combined in the same person.[3] He
recounted with glee that at a synod in the diocese of Regensburg
in 1123 some priests objected to the presence of monks, who were
supposed to be dead men, but that in 1126 a monk named Cuno
became bishop of Regensburg.[4] He cited with approval Lanfranc's division of the church into clerical and lay orders and
commented that 'this division would be very pernicious unless a
monk might be either a cleric or a layman'. A monk was a cleric
if he had been ordained to any clerical grade and was a layman,
'whom custom calls a *conversus*', if he held no clerical order. The

---

[1] The *Argumentum* was addressed to Herbord of Michelsberg, the author of
several hagiographical works, before he became a monk in about 1160: cf.
Pez, in *Thesaurus anec. nov.* II. 1, introd. pp. xxxi–xxxiii; on Herbord, see
Wattenbach, *Geschichtsquellen*, II, 187–8; Manitius, *Geschichte*, III, 596–8; and
De Ghellinck, *Littérature*, II, 192.
[2] *Argumentum*, VIII, ed. cit. pp. 529–32.
[3] *Ibid.* II, ed. cit. pp. 510–12, and IX, 534. In cap. III, 512–14, he cited St Bernard and (somewhat oddly) Anselm of Laon to support his view of the superiority of the monastic order.
[4] *Ibid.* VIII, ed. cit. pp. 528–9; cf. Endres, *Honorius*, pp. 82–3, and Gams,
Series, p. 304. The date of the synod is given by Idungus's statement that
Bishop Hartwich died three years later.

prohibitions of monastic preaching by St Jerome and several popes applied only to lay monks, in the opinion of Idungus. An ordained monk, however, was 'both a cleric and a monk: a monk because he has made the monastic profession, a cleric because he holds a clerical office'; and by the nature of his ordination he might celebrate mass and preach, though he should seek the permission of the parish priest, and he should be called a priest and 'live from the benefice which should provide the stipend for his office, that is, from the tithes and oblations of the faithful'.[1] Idungus even claimed that these monks were more suited to receive tithes than simple priests, who might inherit property, because God ordained that tithes were to be paid to the Levites, who had no inheritance, 'as if he had said: these are my tithes which I wish only those whose portion I am, that is, who have nothing on earth except me, to have'.[2]

In the *Liber de diversis ordinibus et professionibus quae sunt in ecclesia*, the distinctions were drawn within the orders of monks and canons, and the author explained that some members of each order were entitled to receive the sacramental revenues which other members refused to own.[3] He divided both monks and canons into three corresponding types. The first type was that which included the Cistercian monks and the strict regular canons, who lived apart from men, supported themselves by their own labour and, as he said of the canons, 'do not exact from the faithful the tithes or revenues which belong to the priests, canons, or clerics'.[4] The second type lived near to and in association with other men, and the third or 'secular' type actually lived among other men. Monks of this last type made no profession and led no regular life, and the canons served churches and administered the sacraments to laymen from whom they were fully entitled to collect tithes and other clerical revenues. The real question of the

---

[1] *Argumentum*, IX, ed. cit. pp. 533–5 (quoted extracts on 534 and 535); see p. 147 above on Lanfranc. In cap. X, 536–9, Idungus further justified monastic holding of parishes by analogy with monastic bishops holding dioceses, which are large parishes.   [2] *Ibid.* IX, ed. cit. p. 535.

[3] This work is unfortunately incomplete and deals only with monks, canons, and hermits. Cf. p. 155 above.

[4] PL, CCXIII, 814 (on monks) and 830 (on canons).

propriety of owning alms, ecclesiastical revenues, and tithes
therefore arose in connection with the second type of monks and
canons, such as the Cluniacs and the canons of the orders of
St Quentin, Prato, and St Victor, who lived near but not among
laymen. On this point the author wrote:

Now if I am asked, as many people often ask, why these [monks and
canons] live off revenues and tithes, which were assigned by the Lord
through Moses for the support of the priests and Levites, I simply
reply, with apologies to those who may disagree with me, that whoever
serves the altar should share with the altar and whoever undertakes the
work of priests and Levites...should not be entirely deprived of the
reward of the priest and Levite. For I see their churches attended by
the faithful, whether they want it or not, and I see them assiduously
singing masses, frequently preaching the Gospel, being forced to give
a sermon in the church, touching the sins of the people with the coal
from the holy altar, and announcing to the people their sins.[1]

He also distinguished in the second type of canons, whom he
compared to the Gershonites, those who stayed 'in the cloister to
serve God within its walls', those who remained in the cloister to
take care of their brothers and of guests and pilgrims, and those
who were sent to distant dependencies and parishes and who performed pastoral work, 'so that they may live from the revenues
and tithes of the faithful and bring back what is over to their
brothers at the church as to the priests and ministers at the tabernacle.... There should be no question concerning the tithes which
they receive, because like the Levites and the priests they demand
what is theirs.'[2]

A less sophisticated historical approach is found in an anonymous commentary on the rule of St Augustine in a twelfth-century
manuscript at Vienna. In the preface the author asserted the
superiority of the canons over other types of observance, all of
which he traced to the primitive community of the apostles.
The monks went and lived entirely apart from other men while
the canons, for whom St Augustine wrote his rule, continued to

---

[1] *PL*, ccxiii, 817.
[2] *Ibid.* 836–7. In the text, the final sentence comes before the preceding
quotation.

serve churches and to preach. They were consequently alike in their lives, their professions, and their origins; and 'the difference between a monk and a cleric…is understood to lie more properly in whether or not they have the cure of souls than in whether they wear different costumes'.[1] The argument is not very clear, and the author implied that a monk who exercised the *cura animarum* might be a cleric rather than a monk; but like Rupert, Honorius, and Idungus he held that the two orders were similar and compatible rather than different and exclusive and that a monk or regular canon might perform the functions of a cleric.

Meanwhile in France, Peter the Venerable wrote an official reply, probably about 1127, to the Cistercian charges against the Cluniacs, including the accusation concerning the possession of first-fruits and tithes.[2] He made no use of the point, which the author of the *Liber de diversis ordinibus* cited specifically in favour of the Cluniacs and which replied directly to the accusation, that his monks performed pastoral work and were therefore entitled to sacramental revenues, presumably because the monks at Cluny, as in any strictly organized monastery, were not allowed to exercise the *cura animarum* for the laity. Instead, he rested his defence on three points. First, like his predecessor Abbot Pontius at the council of Rheims in 1119, he cited the papal privileges and confirmations for Cluny.[3] Second, he made the point, later also made by Idungus, that monks, like the Levites, had no worldly inheritance and persisted night and day in divine services, by which they accomplished as much for the salvation of the faithful as did the clergy by their pastoral work. Third, he cited two canons, probably from the *Decretum* of Ivo of Chartres, allowing a bishop to turn a parish church into a monastery and to grant to any church the episcopal third of parochial revenues. From these Peter argued that a monastery might receive all the

---

[1] Vienna, Nationalbibliothek, 2207, fos. 11r–16v (quoted extract on 14r). The author also mentioned the origins of anchorites and of so-called secular clerics, of whom he disapproved. In the prologue (fo. 11r) he admitted that Augustine had not certainly written the rule attributed to him.

[2] Peter the Venerable, ep. I, 28, in *Bibl. Clun.* pp. 678–9; cf. p. 150 above and, on Cluniac tithes generally, *Rev. bén.* LXX, 591–608.

[3] Cf. pp. 96–7 above and *Rev. bén.* LXX, 602–4.

revenues of a parish.[1] He concluded that 'In accordance with this and similar [authorities] which are too long to cite here, we therefore possess freely, justly, and canonically the churches and all their goods which bishops have granted to us without sale'. Peter discussed the matter again in the two letters written probably in 1135/7 to Pope Innocent II and the Cardinal-chancellor Haimeric in connection with the controversy over tithes between the Cluniac priory of Gigny and the Cistercian abbey of Le Miroir. Here he cited the long possession and 'numerous and ancient' papal privileges confirming Cluniac holdings of tithes, and he also used the legal argument, later widely used to protect established holdings of tithes, that the new houses which refused to pay tithes were founded on lands belonging to Cluny 'without our consent and against canon law'.[2]

Several of these arguments were also used in a long, angry, and confused reply to Theobald of Étampes written by an anonymous monk, probably in England, in about 1123/33.[3] He urged above all that monks were clerics and were entitled to perform pastoral work and receive the reward of this work. 'For not all clerics are monks or canons,' he said, 'but every monk and genuine canon is certainly a cleric.... And whoever is ordered to work in the church at the same time to save himself and others may with justice be supported from that work.'[4] He cited the apocryphal version of Malachi iii. 10, which was also used by Hamelin of St Albans, to prove that God ordered men to bring their tithes into the storehouse in order that there might be food for the servants in his house,[5] who included monks. He even maintained

---

[1] Ivo of Chartres, *Decretum*, III, 168 (= *Decretum*, C. XII, q. II, c. 73) and 171 (only in Ivo), in *PL*, CLXI, 236–7; cf. Paul Fournier, 'Un tournant de l'histoire de droit, 1060–1140', *Nouvelle revue historique de droit français et étranger*, XLI (1917), 166 on the influence of Ivo on this letter of Peter the Venerable, which he dated 1123. Abbo of Fleury in the tenth century stressed the opposite or Peter's point: that the right of the bishop to dispose of part of the tithe did not entitle him to dispose of it all (*PL*, CXXXIX, 441).

[2] Peter the Venerable, epp. 1, 35–6, in *Bibl. Clun.* pp. 704–8; see pp. 276–7 below and *Rev. bén.* LXX, 610–14.

[3] Published by Jean Leclercq, in *Anal. mon.* IV, 54–111 (see pp. 152–3 above on Theobald's attack on monks).

[4] *Anal. mon.* IV, 62 and 67 (cf. also p. 89).   [5] See p. 172 n. 2 above.

monasteries (39), but again stressed that with the consent of the bishop monks might receive both churches and 'tithes evilly owned by laymen...from the hand of the laymen (*de manu laicorum*)' and might hold them 'with permanent security'.[1]

Gratian thus threw the weight of his great authority, which later became part of the law of the Church, on the side of a limited right of monks to possess tithes in so far as they performed pastoral duties and received grants of ecclesiastical revenues, and always subject to the control of the bishop.[2] He was followed in this opinion by the influential school of the Decretists, of whom one of the earliest was Roland Bandinelli, who as Pope Alexander III later exercised a profound influence on the history of monastic tithes. In his *Stroma* or *Summa* on the *Decretum*, which was written in 1142/8, he explained Gratian's meaning and particularly emphasized that not all monks were priests, that not all monks who were priests were entrusted with congregations, and that both the sacerdotal *ordo* and the episcopal *licentia* were required for a monk to administer the sacraments.[3]

This point of view approximately corresponded to that of the conservative theologians in Germany and the Lowlands, such as Rupert of Deutz, Honorius of 'Autun', Idungus of Regensburg, and the author of the *Liber de diversis ordinibus*, who, without

---

[1] *Decretum*, C. XVI, q. VII, *dictum post* c. 38.

[2] In the second question of the sixteenth case Gratian also insisted on episcopal control over institution to parish churches and cited in particular the canons of Urban II prohibiting institution by abbots or monks. Baluze discussed this point in De Marca, *De concordia*, pp. 961–4, and cited a letter from Eugene III to monasteries in the diocese of Narbonne, in which he asserted the right of the bishop to institute priests in parish churches belonging to monasteries, explained that the priest is responsible to the bishop for the cure of souls and to the abbot for the temporalities in the parish, and required the monks to pay the canonical portion of the tithes and oblations to the archbishop and not to baptize, give penance, or say mass themselves (JL 9721); cf. *St Pierre à Gand*, pp. 115 (1108), 116 (1100), 117 (1111), 126 (1123), etc.; *St Martin de Tulle*, pp. 622–5 (1113); *Bibl. Clun.* pp. 1389–90 (with corrections in *Cluny*, V, 341, no. 3985) (1125) for examples of episcopal charters reserving the right to present the *cura animarum* in churches belonging to monasteries. An abbey might be able to escape this control, however, if the abbot himself was 'rector' of the church and received the cure of souls from the bishop and then chose a 'vicar' to serve the church, as at Muri (see pp. 62–3 above).

[3] *Summa mag. Rolandi*, pp. 36–45; cf. Pacaut, *Alexandre*, p. 64.

laying as much stress on episcopal control as the canonists, strongly defended the right of ordained monks who served in churches to receive tithes. Even some of the opponents of monastic possession of tithes, such as Gerhoh of Reichersberg and the Cistercian critics of Cluny, directed their attacks primarily against the possession by monks of clerical revenues which they had not earned and implied that monks who exercised the cure of souls might legitimately receive tithes. Historically, this moderate position, whether of approval or of opposition, depended on the increased number of monks who were ordained and performed pastoral work, on the new importance of the sacraments, especially the mass, and on the gradual merging of the clerical and monastic orders. It recognized, though occasionally with disapproval, that the status of a monk could be combined with the status, or at least with the functions, of a cleric or priest.

The extremists at both ends rejected this reasoning and argued along different lines. The strongest opponents of monastic possession of tithes reasserted the primitive distinction between the natures, functions, and finances of the monastic and clerical orders and claimed that under no circumstances could a monk properly exercise the *cura animarum* or receive any clerical revenues. The extreme defenders, on the other hand, attempted to establish a general right of monks to own tithes, whether or not they performed pastoral work. Their reasons were often confused and repetitive, but broadly speaking they fell into three categories. One argument was that all monks were *ipso facto* clerics and as such entitled to all clerical rights and revenues (even without episcopal permission, according to the reply to Theobald of Étampes). Another was that monks had at least as good a right to tithes as clerics on account of their services to the Church as a whole, as distinct from a single congregation, or, more crudely, on account of the superiority and purity of their lives. The third, and historically probably the most interesting and important argument, was that monks were the *pauperes Christi*, the true poor to whom tithes should be given, or, as Idungus and Peter the Venerable suggested, the real heirs to the Levites, to whom the Lord in the Old Testament ordered that tithes should be paid.

6. THE END OF THE OPPOSITION

From a theoretical point of view, the arguments of the opponents of monastic possession of tithes were probably stronger than those of the defenders. There can be no question that early monks in the West owned no tithes, that canon law before Gratian recognized no right of monks to receive tithes, and that in practice the possession of tithes often involved monasteries in secular affairs and lawsuits. The arguments for the defence, on the other hand—that monks as *ipso facto* clerics or as parish priests might canonically receive tithes and oblations—were weak, because monasteries often claimed more than the quarter or third assigned to the parish priest and because even this fraction belonged not to any cleric but only to priests who exercised the cure of souls. The argument that monks were the poor of Christ was also weak because most monks who owned tithes, though individually poor, were collectively rich and because many really poor monks refused to own tithes. Some of the early canonical texts, especially those of St Jerome, were sadly twisted by the defenders of monastic tithes; Gratian relied almost exclusively on forgeries, or canons of doubtful authenticity; and even their strongest arguments— long possession, papal and episcopal grants, and the occasional performance of pastoral work by monks—were either weak in theory or entitled the monks at most to a fraction of all the tithes they held.

In practice, however, the refusal of the monastic reformers to accept any clerical revenues was unrealistic and radical in the strict sense of the word. Their economic principles were aimed, as Hoffmann remarked of the Cistercians, not towards the future but towards a golden vision of the past,[1] on which they hoped to base a new and revivified monastic life. Their efforts to set back the clock and to restore an earlier type of monastic economy had no more chance of success than the proposal of Paschal II to base the finances of the Church exclusively on spiritual revenues. It is

[1] Eberhard Hoffmann, 'Die Entwicklung der Wirtschaftsprinzipien im Cisterzienserorden während des 12. und 13. Jahrhunderts', *Historisches Jahrbuch*, XXXI (1910), 702.

impossible to trace here the history and extent of the failure for each order and individual house, partly owing to the difficulty of clearly distinguishing in the charters between tithes from their own and tithes from other men's labour; but it is certain that within a comparatively short period, certainly not over half a century, almost all the reformers accepted the tithes which they had at first refused.

Already before the end of the eleventh century, the reforming Abbot Odo of St Martin at Tournai was persuaded 'that like other religious abbots he should not refuse to accept them if someone for the sake of his soul wished without simony to give *altaria* to our church'.[1] The abbey of St Martin accepted many clerical revenues from this time on. The monks of La Grande Chartreuse were before 1129 given the tithes and parochial rights in the parish of St Laurent-du-Desert by the abbey of St Chef, and although this parish may have been within the boundaries of their hermitage and the lands worked by the monks, as the editor suggested, it is unlikely that they expelled all the previous inhabitants.[2] The Templars also, although they are not known for certain ever to have refused tithes, in spite of the part played by St Bernard in their origins, were specifically authorized either by the council of Troyes in 1128 or by the patriarch of Jerusalem in 1130 to accept tithes both from bishops with the permission of their chapters and from laymen with the permission of the bishops on the grounds that they lived a common life and had voluntarily given up riches.[3]

---

[1] Herman of Tournai, *Narratio*, LXXIII, in *Spicilegium*, II, 911–12.

[2] *Chartreuse*, p. 40, no. 15 (included in a general confirmation of several grants by the bishop of Grenoble).

[3] Gustav Schnürer, *Die ursprüngliche Templerregel*, Studien und Darstellungen aus dem Gebiete der Geschichte, III, 1–2 (Freiburg im Br., 1903), p. 151, cap. LXIV, cf. pp. 87–8 attributing this statute to the definitive redaction in 1130. Patrice Cousin, 'Les débuts de l'ordre des Templiers et saint Bernard', *Mélanges Saint Bernard* (Dijon, 1954), p. 43, however, associated this statute with the council of Troyes, which was attended by St Bernard. For the French version, written about 1140, see Henri de Curzon, *La règle du Temple*, Société de l'histoire de France (Paris, 1886), pp. 59–60, cap. LVIII. The versions and dates of this rule are far from clear: see the introd. by Mabillon to his edition of Bernard's *De laude novae militiae* (ed. cit. I. 2, 1250–1); Elphège Vacandard, *Vie de Saint*

With regard to the Grandmontines, Gerald of Wales wrote in his *Speculum ecclesiae* that:

With the passage of time the dispensing advice of older and more mature men tempered the statutes which had been made at the beginning without discretion or consultation and with excessive harshness. So that at present they are allowed to possess, like the Cistercians, as many ploughs and tools, cattle and sheep, broad lands and pastures as they need. They also accept with gratitude the ecclesiastical benefices given them by the faithful with charitable generosity, but not the cure of souls, which they renounce and refuse on account of the accompanying dangers. In this they resemble both the Cluniacs and the Carthusians, just as they differ greatly from the Cistercians in the said excessive quantity of both movable and unmovable property. And they are neither ashamed nor afraid to possess churches, which it [their order] previously refused and feared with greater devotion and religious perfection, just as in recent times the order of Cîteaux, desiring at last to return to its vomit, not without grave scandal, resembles both the Cluniacs and the Grandmontines in this matter.[1]

The regular canons also accepted tithes at an early date:

Little need be said of the Austin canons [remarked Ganshof] beyond the fact that the wealth of their houses seldom consisted in landed property on any scale....By far the greater part of their patrimony consisted in tithes and *altaria*....The organization of the estates of the Praemonstratensians, or Norbertines, was somewhat different. Tithes, which they were at pains to acquire or to collect together again where they had been divided, and appropriated churches certainly played an important part in their economy, but so also did land....[2]

These remarks apply especially to the later Middle Ages, but the developments they describe began in the twelfth century. Even those historians who emphasize most strongly the contemplative ideals of the strict regular canons and their resemblance to the

---

Bernard (Paris, 1895), I, 233; and Hefele–Leclercq, *Conciles*, v. I, 671 n. I. It seems unlikely, however, that St Bernard took part in allowing the Templars to receive tithes.

[1] Gerald of Wales, *Speculum ecclesiae*, III, 21, in *Opera*, ed. J. S. Brewer, J. F. Dimock and G. F. Warner, Rolls Series, XXI (London, 1861–91), IV, 256.
[2] *Camb. Econ. Hist.* I, 313–14.

reformed monks are agreed that they soon conformed to the standards of the more moderate canons and often owned parish churches and revenues even if they were unwilling to perform pastoral work themselves.[1] In Germany in the second quarter of the twelfth century Anselm of Havelberg, who was a close associate of St Norbert, even defended the right of regular canons to exercise the *cura animarum*, and several houses in the diocese of Mainz were granted the right to perform various parochial functions.[2] Although this may have been unusual among the strict canons, the possession of clerical revenues soon became common. St Norbert himself in 1121 accepted from the count of Namur as part of the endowment for a new Premonstratensian house two churches at Floreffe, of which both held tithes and one also held the *nona* from the count's demesne lands, that is, from land certainly not to be worked by the canons themselves.[3] The canons of Reichersberg, even under the reforming provost Gerhoh, performed pastoral work and received tithes in the middle of the twelfth century.[4] Tithes were also included in the original endowment of the Premonstratensian abbey of Basse-Fontaine in 1143, and the first papal privilege in 1148 confirmed its possession of many tithes, including those of Vitry-le-Croisé, which were given to the abbey in about 1146 in the presence of St Bernard by the Cistercian Bishop Godfrey of Langres, who justified the grant on the grounds that 'It is proper that we should restore to God what belongs to God'.[5] Even the monastic

---

[1] Cf. pp. 153–7 above and Dickinson, *Canons*, pp. 229–31, 239 and 241, who said that 'there was never any intention that the early inmates should undertake the care of most or all of the parishes given to them' and that 'the vast majority of houses of regular canons probably originally served only a few of their cells'; see also the works of Dereine cited p. 157 nn. 1 and 3 above and *Chanoines*, pp. 195 and 243, who mentioned the acquisition of parish churches but doubted that they were served by regular canons in the twelfth century.

[2] See p. 146 n. 4, and p. 158 above.

[3] *Namur*, pp. 9–10, no. 2.

[4] Classen, *Gerhoch*, p. 72.

[5] *Basse-Fontaine*, pp. 1–5, 132–4, and 86–7, nos. 1–2, 102 (JL 9250), and 86–7 (see pp. 133–4 above). The abbey shared the tithes with the church of Vitry and never owned the church or nominated the priest. Over a quarter of the 119 documents in the chartulary of Basse-Fontaine from 1143 until 1297 were concerned in one way or another with tithes.

reformers, therefore, regarded regular canons as suitable recipients of churches and tithes. And Colvin remarked in his book of the Premonstratensians in England that 'By the middle of the twelfth century this rule [against the possession of churches] seems to have been a dead letter, and in England there is no evidence that churches were ever rejected'.[1]

The case of the Cistercians is complicated by several factors. First, the Cistercians usually established their houses in deserted places and held land which either had never been cultivated or from which they had expelled the previous inhabitants, and this simplified the task of avoiding parochial responsibilities and revenues.[2] Second, they often owned the tithes from their own lands, which they worked themselves, and thus they paid no tithes to anyone else. It is sometimes very hard to distinguish these tithes, which they were eager to own, from the tithes of goods produced by other men, which they rejected at first. Third, they persisted longer and more firmly than the regular canons and most of the reformed monks in refusing to accept tithes from other men. In 1133, for instance, Louis VI gave some tithes to the Cistercians of Ourscamp, who arranged through the bishop of Soissons to give the tithes to the monks of St Leger in Bosco in return for a field 'because the institution of the Cistercian order altogether refused to hold this revenue'.[3] Fourth, some abbeys which owned tithes before joining the Cistercian order did not give them up.[4] The chief offender in this respect was the order of Savigny, which not only kept its privileges, churches, *altaria*, and tithes but even continued to acquire them after joining the

---

[1] Colvin, *White Canons*, p. 272; cf. Berlière, in *Rev. bén.* XXXIX, 344.

[2] Cf. Delisle, *Études*, p. 394; Maury, in *Mémoires présentés...à l'Académie*, 2nd ser. IV, 64–5; Henri Dubled, 'Aspects de l'économie cistercienne en Alsace au XIIe siècle', *Rev. d'hist. ecc.* LIV (1959), 765–82, esp. 776–7, and R. A. Donkin, 'Settlement and Depopulation on Cistercian Estates during the Twelfth and Thirteenth Centuries, especially in Yorkshire', *Bulletin of the Institute of Historical Research*, XXXIII (1960), 141–65, esp. 143–9.

[3] *Ourscamp*, pp. 75 and 283–4; cf. Luchaire, *Louis VI*, pp. 238–9, no. 521. The Cistercians of Old Wardon owned no chapels or churches, in contrast to neighbouring Benedictines and Augustinians: *Old Wardon*, p. 7.

[4] Cf. Hoffmann, in *Hist. Jb.* XXXI, 707, and Donnelly, *Laybrotherhood*, p. 41 n. 18.

Cistercians.[1] The abbey of Orval also owned some tithes, according to a charter of 1124, before it became Cistercian in 1132.[2] And a fifth complication, which was not unique to the Cistercians among those who refused to own tithes, was the presence in the order of nuns who were physically unable to support themselves by their own labour and were forced to rely on other types of revenues, which might easily include tithes.

Already in the second quarter of the eleventh century a few Cistercians began to accept tithes from the labour of other men. The earliest example that has come to my attention was in 1130, when the archdeacon of Xanten, with the permission of his congregation, gave to the Cistercian abbey of Camp, 'in consideration of the voluntary poverty of the monks', all the noval tithes in his archdeaconry, which the archbishop of Cologne had recently given to him and his church.[3] The monks of Byland, who were Savigniac in name but Cistercians at heart and who still refused to accept three churches in about 1143, accepted from Roger of Mowbray in the late 1130's 'the entire tithe of the food of his household' and deputed a lay brother to collect the tithe daily and either to send it to the abbey or, when Roger was far away, to sell it and send the proceeds to the abbey. This arrangement proved difficult, however, and in 1140 Roger gave the monks some land in place of the tithe.[4] The Cistercians of Walkenried, who were responsible for draining and bringing under cultiva-

---

[1] Jacqueline Buhot, 'L'abbaye normande de Savigny, chef d'Ordre et fille de Cîteaux', *Le Moyen Âge*, XLVI (3rd ser. VII, 1936), 115 and 121, who stressed the acquisition of tithes by Savigny before joining the Cistercians, and 178–90 and 255–60; cf. C. H. Haskins, *Norman Institutions*, Harvard Historical Studies, XXIV (Cambridge, Mass., 1918), p. 323 (1154/8); Donnelly, *Laybrotherhood*, p. 58; and *Vaux de Cernay*, I, 15–19 (1156/7) on later claims and acquisitions by Savigny.

[2] *Orval*, p. 8. The nunnery of Rifreddo, which became Cistercian in 1244/9, had and kept large holdings of tithes: see Catherine Boyd, *A Cistercian Nunnery in Mediaeval Italy*, Harvard Historical Monographs, XVIII (Cambridge, Mass., 1943), pp. 123–38.

[3] *Xanten*, pp. 10–11.

[4] *Monasticon*, v, 350; cf. Stenton, *Feudalism*, pp. 72–3, and Knowles, *Mon. Order*, pp. 249–50 and 355 (on Byland and its refusal to possess churches). An interesting account of the troubles caused to the monks by this grant of tithes is given in the *Historia fundationis* of Byland.

tion the 'Golden Fields' in Thuringia, owned the tithes from various lands apparently not in their possession in the 1140's.[1] The bishop of Noyon in 1147 gave some tithes to the Cistercians of Longpont with permission 'to exchange it with any church for the two sesters of grain and twelve pennies' which they owed annually to the church of St Mary at Noyon.[2] After 1150, examples of Cistercian possession of tithes are common, particularly in England. The monks of Flaxley were given 'each year the tithe of the chestnut trees at Dene' by the future King Henry II in 1151/4; the founder of Greenfield, before 1153, included 'the tithe of my mills' in the endowment; and in 1158/61 Archbishop Theobald of Canterbury confirmed the possession by Quarr Abbey of a chapel with its tithes and other revenues.[3] In 1158 the abbot of Staffarda in Piedmont gave the tithe of some lands near Saluzzo, 'which tithe he held from the lord William, who held it from St Mary at Testona for a rent of three pennies', to a layman in return for some land and payment of the rent.[4]

The Cistercian leaders seem at the same time to have felt less strongly on the subject of monastic performance of pastoral work and possession of clerical revenues. In 1138/47 the abbot of Pontigny witnessed a grant by Bishop Godfrey of Langres, who had previously been prior of Clairvaux, of some tithes and the right to nominate a priest to the monks of St Germain at Auxerre.[5] St Bernard himself witnessed the grant of tithes to Basse-Fontaine in 1146.[6] The archbishop of Mainz arranged in 1147 that the

[1] *Walkenried*, I, 14–15, no. 11 (1148), which seems to have applied to lands not owned by the monks, whereas no. 8, pp. 10–11 (1144) gave them the tithes of goods produced by themselves on the swamp-lands given them by the count of Rothenburg and was not a real exemption from tithes, as claimed by Thompson, *Germany*, p. 570; cf. Richard Sebicht, 'Die Cistercienser und die niederländischen Kolonisten in den goldnen Aue', *Zeitschrift des Harz-Vereins für Geschichte und Altertumskunde*, XXI (1888), 39, who said that the abbey held only the tithes and not the land.

[2] *Héronval*, pp. 3–4. The fact that the monks might dispose of the tithes shows that they were from the labour of other men.

[3] *Monasticon*, V, 590 and 579–80, and Saltman, *Theobald*, pp. 425–6; cf. *Monasticon*, V, 317.

[4] *Staffarda*, I, 30. References to tithes from lands not worked by the monks also occur in *Gimont*, pp. 12 (1167), 50–1 (1167), 89 (1158), etc.

[5] *Yonne*, I, 332.   [6] See p. 134 above.

provost of the new Cistercian nunnery at Ichtershausen should be
an Augustinian canon chosen by the community and that 'since
the salvation of the people living there requires it' he and other
brothers should have the power to preach, baptize, visit the sick,
bury the dead, and perform other pastoral work for which, presumably, they were entitled to receive tithes and other clerical
revenues in the name of the community.[1]

Most impartial historians have accepted these conclusions, but
they have usually been dated in the second half of the twelfth
century or even later.[2] Hoffmann, for instance, who relied principally upon evidence from north-east Germany, divided the
economic history of the early Cistercians into three phases: the
first, up to about 1150, was marked by adherence to their original
principles; the second, from about 1150 to 1208, by the emergence
of a distinctive type of Cistercian economic activity and organization; and the third, up to 1278, showed increasing similarity with
the economic organization of other monks and of laymen. With
regard to tithes, however, as Hoffmann admitted, this third phase
really began in the twelfth century; and tithes are a guide to the
changes in the economic principles and organization of the
Cistercians during the first century of their history.[3] Svoboda also
remarked that the foundation charters and early history of the

---

[1] *Paulinzelle*, pp. 27–30.

[2] See Viard, *Dîme*, I, 202–3 and II, 100–2, and in *St Bernard et son temps*, I,
292–4; Pöschl, in *A. f. kath. KR*, XCVIII, 376–7, who said that the Cistercians
often converted their holdings of tithes into fixed rents; Canivez, in *Dict. d'hist.*
XII, 921; Coulton, *Five Centuries*, III, 179–80; Knowles, *Mon. Order*, p. 355;
Ganshof, in *Camb. Econ. Hist.* I, 314–15; Mahn, *Ordre*, pp. 116–18; Kuujo, in
Ann. acad. sci. Fenn. B, LXII. I, 226–32, who stressed that the Cistercians in the
archdiocese of Hamburg–Bremen bought many tithes in the thirteenth century;
and Hofmeister, in *SMGBOZ*, LXV, 268–70, who mentioned the performance
of pastoral work by Cistercians in the late twelfth century. In addition to the
works on individual monasteries mentioned above, see E. de Moreau, *L'Abbaye
de Villers-en-Brabant aux XIIe et XIIIe siècles* (Brussels, 1909), pp. 175–6, and
Hans Muggenthaler, *Kolonisatorische und wirtschaftliche Tätigkeit eines deutschen
Zisterzienserklosters im XII. und XIII. Jahrhundert*, Deutsche Geschichtsbücherei,
II (Munich, 1924), pp. 28 ff. (on Waldsassen). The distinction between the
labour of the monks themselves and of other men is not always sufficiently
emphasized in these works.

[3] Hoffmann, in *Hist. Jb.* XXXI, 700 and 715.

MONASTIC POSSESSION OF TITHES

Cistercian abbeys in eastern Germany showed that the rule against possession of churches and tithes was rarely observed.[1] Duby said that after about 1160 the monks of La Ferté, which was one of the first four daughters of Cîteaux, acquired not only, as previously, tithes from their own lands and herds but also 'tithes which came from neighbouring lands and which provided them with grain and wine without any labour'; and he also remarked that 'From this time on the patrimony of La Ferté differed less clearly from the neighbouring landed seigneuries'.[2] Thoma's analysis of the possessions of the Cistercian abbey of Leubus in Silesia indicated, according to Donnelly, 'that the abbey did not differ from a Benedictine house in respect of secular entanglements'.[3]

It is easier to establish the fact than the cause of this change in the practice and attitude of the reformers towards the possession of other men's tithes. Broadly speaking, the question can be seen either in moral or in economic terms. Most contemporaries, including those who were sympathetic to the monastic reform, tended to consider the acceptance of clerical revenues by the new monastic orders, especially the Cistercians, as a sign of avarice and moral decline. As early as 1159 Pope Alexander III showed in several letters his concern over the change in the economic practices of the Cistercians; and in his bull *Inter universas mundani turbinis* in 1169, of which a section was excised by the Cistercians at an early date and only recently has been republished, he bitterly criticized them for seeking and owning many types of property which they had at first refused, and he even threatened to withdraw their privileges unless they reformed their ways.[4] These

[1] Hanno Svoboda, *Die Klosterwirtschaft der Cistercienser in Ostdeutschland*, Nürnberger Beiträge zu den Wirtschaftswissenschaften, XIX/XX (Nuremberg, 1930), p. 36.   [2] *La Ferté*, p. 21.

[3] Walter Thoma, *Die colonisatorische Thätigkeit des Klosters Leubus im 12. und 13. Jahrhundert* (Leipzig, 1894), pp. 88–137, cited by Donnelly, *Laybrotherhood*, p. 41 n. 17; cf. Franciscus Hanus, *Die aeltere Geschichte der Zisterzienser-Abtei Leubus in Schlesien bis zur Mitte des 14. Jahrhunderts* (Breslau [published in U.S.A.], 1947), index, s.v. 'Zehnt'.

[4] Jean Leclercq, 'Épitres d'Alexandre III sur les Cisterciens', *Rev. bén.* LXIV (1954), 68–82, and 'Passage supprimé dans une épitre d'Alexandre III', *Rev. bén.* LXII (1952), 149–51. The only complete edition of *Inter universas* (JL 11633) is in André Duchesne, *Historiae Francorum scriptores* (Paris, 1636–49), IV, 478–80.

views were shared by several influential Cistercians, including Gilbert of Holland, abbot of Swineshead, who died in 1172 and wrote a long letter to Roger, abbot of Byland, deploring the cupidity of his age and especially of his order,[1] and Abbot John of Ford, who in his life of the hermit Wulfric of Haselbury, which was written in about 1185/6, compared the Cistercians to the angels and praised them in all things except 'that in the possessions that are given to them they use their right too freely and pay more attention to what is permitted than what is suitable...'.[2] Joachim of Flora while he was still abbot of Corazzo in 1186/7 sadly commented on how few abbeys maintained the economic ideals of the early reformers.[3] Gerald of Wales told the tale of how King Richard I, when he was accused of pride, luxury, and avarice, replied that 'I have already married off those three daughters: the first and most ancient, that is pride, to the Templars; the second, that is luxury, to the black monks; and the third and last, that is avarice, to the white monks'.[4] Towards the end of the century these charges became so pressing that the Cistercians sought to remove their cause by limiting their wealth and re-enforcing the restrictions on the types of property to be held by their abbeys.[5] More recently, the historian Viard accepted this interpretation when he wrote that the original renunciation of tithes by the reformers was done 'in a moment of fervour and dis-interestedness which did not last for long, because if the spirit was willing the flesh was weak'.[6]

[1] *PL*, CLXXXIV, 276–88.

[2] John of Ford, *Wulfric of Haselbury*, cap. XLVIII, ed. Maurice Bell, Somerset Record Society, XLVII ([Cheddar], 1933), p. 66.

[3] Cited by Leclercq, in *Rev. bén.* LXIV, 81 n. 2.

[4] Gerald of Wales, *Speculum ecclesiae*, II, 12, ed. cit. IV, 54. He told a different version in his *Itinerarium Kambriae*, I, 3, ed. cit. VI, 44. Cf. Odo of Cheriton, fable 153, in Léopold Hervieux, *Les fabulistes latins depuis le siècle d'Auguste jusqu'à la fin du moyen âge*, IV: *Eudes de Cheriton et ses dérivés* (Paris, 1896), p. 325.

[5] *Statuta capitulorum generalium ordinis Cisterciensis*, ed. J. M. Canivez, I, Bibliothèque de la Revue d'histoire ecclésiastique, IX (Louvain, 1933), pp. 86–7; cf. the passages from MS. Laon 471 (from Vauclair) cited by Leclercq, in *Rev. bén.* LXIV, 74–82. On the changes in Cistercian economic organization in the second half of the twelfth century, see Hoffmann, in *Hist. Jb.* XXXI, 704; Mahn, *Ordre*, p. 111; Gosso, *Vita economica*, pp. 145–57; and *La Ferté*, pp. 14–16.

[6] Viard, *Dîme*, I, 202.

Most historians have rejected this moral interpretation, however, and have seen the change in more objective economic or historical terms. Hoffmann, for instance, emphasized the difficulty of maintaining a small natural or enclosed economy in surroundings where money was increasingly used.[1] The Cistercian economy, furthermore, never really was self-sufficient and always used certain amounts of money. Schreiber said that Cîteaux was drawn to the side of Cluny in the possession of *decimae aliorum hominum* by 'the nature of things', among which he included the economic necessity of accepting theoretically prohibited revenues, the character of Germanic property and land transactions, and the inclusion in the order of older monasteries which already owned other men's tithes.[2] Buhot in particular stressed the importance of the permission given to former Savigniac houses to own revenues forbidden to other Cistercians and even said that Cîteaux herself first acquired tithes 'doubtless under the influence of Savigny'.[3] Hamilton Thompson and Pöschl both remarked that the incorporation and appropriation of parish churches by the Cistercians led to the acquisition of tithes and other parochial revenues, especially in the later Middle Ages.[4] Duby also pointed out that many of the lands given to La Ferté in the twelfth century were already occupied by peasants paying rents and that this prepared the monks to receive regular dues in kind.[5] Perhaps even more important was the acquisition by the Cistercians as time went on of uncultivated lands which were either too extensive or too distant to be cultivated by the monks or lay-brothers themselves and which were therefore granted to peasants in return for rents in money and in produce.[6] Since as a rule the Cistercians owned the

---

[1] Hoffmann, in *Hist. Jb.* XXXI, 708 and 726.   [2] Schreiber, *Kurie*, I, 257 n. 3.
[3] Buhot, in *Moyen Âge*, XLVI, 260 and 268–9.
[4] Thompson, in *Camb. Med. Hist.* V, 676, said that 'the appropriation of churches and tithes was less eagerly sought by the Cistercian order than by others'; Pöschl, however, in *A. f. kath. KR*, CVIII, 36, maintained that 'Besonders häufig begegnen Zisterzienserklöster, männliche wie weibliche Konvente, als Begünstigte bei Inkorporationen'.   [5] *La Ferté*, pp. 19–21.
[6] Cf. Ganshof, in *Camb. Econ. Hist.* I, 315, who said that 'Like the other ecclesiastical lords, the Cistercian monasteries were to become first and foremost landlords, *rentiers* of the soil', especially after the system of lay brothers broke down in the fourteenth century.

tithes from their own lands, these inhabitants also often paid their tithes to the monks.

The acceptance of tithes and changes in economic organization may also have been influenced by the shift in the ideals of the reformers about the middle of the twelfth century. Like all reform programmes, theirs was made up of old and new elements, and in the second half of the century the radical reformers tended less and less to seek their fulfilment within the traditional frame-work of monasticism, with its ideal of separation from the world, to which they had given in their early years a new content and intensity. They now increasingly sought to lead a distinctively apostolic life based on communal poverty and on proselytism, pastoral work, and service to others 'in the world'.[1] At the same time many of the more conservative reformers returned to the old ideals of the strict black monks like the Cluniacs, who emphasized regularity of monastic observance and accepted clerical revenues while refusing to perform any pastoral work which would dis-turb their *clausura*. These inner developments in monasticism thus influenced their economic principles and may help to explain the change in attitude towards the possession of other men's tithes and the fact that by the end of the twelfth century, in spite of early theory and canon law, almost all monastic communities freely owned and accepted tithes.

[1] Cf. Chenu, in *Rev. d'hist. ecc.* XLIX, 69–80.

CHAPTER III

MONASTIC PAYMENT OF TITHES

THE question of by whom tithes were paid has technically no connection with to whom they were paid, but in fact the payment of tithes by monks was closely associated with monastic possession of tithes, since historically the right to keep or distribute their own tithes, that is, the tithes from their demesne lands, was often the first step towards paying no tithes at all. The canon lawyers, indeed, usually regarded freedom from tithes as an indirect form of possession,[1] and Schreiber suggested that both freedom from tithes and possession of tithes, by monks and by laymen, were parallel expressions of Germanic proprietary church law and that the 'passive freedom' of the lay lord, who paid no tithes because he owned the local church or at least its tithes, corresponded to the possession by monks of the tithes from their own lands and to their later freedom from tithes of goods produced by themselves or for their own use.[2] This view tends to exaggerate the influence of purely Germanic institutions, but it confirms the fact that the question of payment of tithes cannot properly be separated from the questions of their use and possession.

In theory all Christians had to pay tithes. Neither position nor means was ever officially recognized as a reason for excusing anyone from tithes. Only the sacramental clergy, the legitimate receivers of the tithe, were in practice not required to pay.[3] From an obligation of this nature there could be no dispensation, exemption, or immunity in the strict senses of these terms. Dispensation applied to laws made by the Church itself.[4] Exemp-

[1] Viard, in St Bernard et son temps, I, 293.
[2] Schreiber, Kurie, I, 270–3.   [3] See pp. 14–16 and 31–4 above.
[4] R. Naz, in Dict. de droit can. IV, 1284–5, and ODCC, pp. 406–7. On dispensation from divine commandments see Roland Bainton, 'Interpretations of the Immoralities of the Patriarchs', in his Collected Papers in Church History, I (Boston, 1962), pp. 122–33. Bernard of Clairvaux, in De praecepto et dispensatione, III, 6, said that no man could dispense from divine decrees, such as the Ten Commandments.

tion applied to ecclesiastical authority, usually the immediate superior, and, in the case of monks, almost always the diocesan bishop.[1] Historically, exemption was closely connected with papal protection of monasteries,[2] and the term was first used in the twelfth century in the meaning of 'the freeing of a monastery from the jurisdiction of the diocesan bishop and its direct subordination to the pope'.[3] It therefore guaranteed the freedom or *libertas* of a house, subject to papal control only, in such matters as monastic elections, control over temporal property, and episcopal visitation and discipline.[4] Immunity, finally, applied to secular burdens and jurisdiction and was a denial of subordination rather than an emancipation from any recognized superior.[5] An immune monastery was thus free from any secular control or obligation and, in the eleventh and twelfth centuries, especially from any lay proprietary rights or advocacy.[6] Exemption, immunity, and simple protection in fact often overlapped and were concerned with a wide range of rights and privileges,[7] but not properly with payment of tithes. 'Because they were a matter of divine law,' Thomassin said,[8] 'it was considered impossible to mitigate any particular without gravely prejudicing those

[1] E. Fogliasso, in *Dict. de droit can.* v, 646. According to modern canon law, an exempt order is 'Religio sive votorum sollemnium sive simplicium a jurisdictione Ordinarii loci subducta' (*ibid.* p. 651).

[2] See Otto Lerche, 'Die Privilegierung der deutschen Kirche durch Papsturkunden bis auf Gregor VII.', *A. f. Urk.* III (1911), 160, who called the distinction between protection and exemption quantitative rather than essential, and Willy Szaivert, 'Die Entstehung und Entwicklung der Klosterexemtion bis zum Ausgang des 11. Jahrhunderts', *MIÖG*, LIX (1951), 287–8, who tended to distinguish protection from exemption more sharply.

[3] Goetting, in *A. f. Urk.* XIV, 105; cf. Szaivert, in *MIÖG*, LIX, 286, on the date of the term.

[4] Cf. Karl Weiss, *Die kirchlichen Exemtionen der Klöster von ihrer Entstehung bis zur gregorianisch-cluniacensischen Zeit* (Basel, 1893), pp. 80–1; Lerche, in *A. f. Urk.* III, 151; and Szaivert, in *MIÖG*, LIX, 273–82.

[5] Fogliasso, in *Dict. de droit can.* v, 637.

[6] See in particular Stengel, *Immunität*, and Hirsch, *Klosterimmunität*, who followed Lamprecht and Dopsch in regarding regulation of the advocate's rights as the prime feature of monastic immunity in Germany after the Investiture Controversy (cf. Eng. tr., pp. 144 and 161) and who said that in spite of the efforts of the church 'the old Eigenkirchenrecht was transformed into the advocacy' (*ibid.* p. 171). [7] Stengel, *Immunität*, p. 553.

[8] Thomassin, *Discipline*, III, 1, 9.9, *ed. cit.* VI, 42.

whom it was planned to spare.' Beginning in the twelfth
century, these terms were very occasionally loosely applied to
tithes,[1] but their use in a technical sense became common only in
the thirteenth century, when tithes were increasingly subjected to
the control of the ecclesiastical and even secular authorities. It is
anachronistic to refer to exemption or immunity from tithes
before the twelfth century,[2] and it is wiser to speak simply of
freedom from tithes.

Such freedom was a constant source of worry to ecclesiastical
theorists and canon lawyers, because tithes were not recognized as
being within the dispensing authority of any earthly power.
Attention will have to be given in this chapter as in the last,
therefore, to the development of theory and to the slow changes
in the nature of tithes as well as to the practical stages by which
many monks in the twelfth century won the right to pay no
tithes from the goods produced *propriis manibus et sumptibus.*

[1] The earliest official use of *immunes* in reference to tithes seems to have been
by Paschal II in 1109/10 (see p. 230 below); it was also used in a charter of
Bishop Walter of Langres in 1163 (see p. 259 below), by Alexander III in his
letter to Archbishop Roger of York (see pp. 295–6 below), by Peter of Blois in a
letter to Alexander III in about 1180 (see p. 292 below), and in the rubrics to
the collection known as the *Appendix concilii Laterani*, in Mansi, *Collectio*,
XXII, 256, which was compiled probably in England during the pontificate of
Lucius III (1181–5): see Stephan Kuttner, *Repertorium der Kanonistik (1140–1234)*,
Studi e Testi, LXXI (Vatican City, 1937), pp. 290–1. Gerhoh of Reichersberg
in his *Liber de novitatibus huius temporis*, written about 1155, referred to an
episcopal dispensation allowing monks to keep their demesne tithes (MGH,
Libelli, III, 291), but this clearly meant the episcopal control over tithes.
Alexander III also used the term dispensation broadly, without special application to tithes, in the preface to his letter to Thomas Becket in 1162/70 (see p. 301
below). In his letter to Alexander III, Peter of Blois referred to the tithe-
privileges as both 'exemptions' and 'immunities', showing that even a trained
administrator and canonist used these terms imprecisely in referring to tithes.
[2] Viard's frequent use of the term 'exemption' with regard to tithes was
based principally on usage in the thirteenth century (cf. *Dîme*, II, 54–8); and he
admitted that exemption from tithes differed from normal monastic exemption
in that it did not apply to the diocesan bishop (*ibid.* p. 42 n. 2). Jean Imbert,
Les hôpitaux en droit canonique, L'Église et l'état au Moyen Âge, VIII (Paris,
1947), p. 88, mentioned the later canonical theory of exempting charitable
institutions from tithes; and see Viard, *Dîme*, II, 32–59; Adams, in *Eng. Hist.
Rev.* LII, 17 ff.; and Kopp, *Zehentwesen...in Baden*, p. 36 (168), on later legal
grounds (e.g. poor land, non-claimance for thirty years) for non-payment of
tithes.

I. MONASTIC PAYMENT OF TITHES
BEFORE THE TWELFTH CENTURY

During the long period from the first references to tithing in the West until the end of the eleventh century, comparatively little is known about the payment of tithes by monks. The works of the Carolingian theologians and legislators show that monks were definitely expected to pay tithes,[1] and probably no theorist would have accepted that monks could in any way be formally freed from paying tithes. In fact the vast majority of monasteries presumably paid tithes in some form or another, but it is clear that as time went on an increasing number were entitled to distribute, use, or keep their own tithes and that a very few may even have been allowed to pay no tithes at all.

The practice of monks distributing the tithes from their own produce and revenues seems to have been tolerated from the earliest times on account both of their religious character, although they were not the proper recipients or distributors of tithes, and of the prevailing theory that tithes belonged to God, not to the clergy, and were to be used for charitable purposes. In the seventh century, for instance, St Philibert used the tithes of his abbey for the redemption of captives and the support of the poor, and Eadberct of Lindisfarne apparently gave his tithes directly to the poor.[2] In the monastic capitulary of 817 monks were specifically instructed to give tithes 'to the poor from everything that is given in alms both to the church and to the brothers'.[3]

It was a short step from distributing their tithes to the needy to giving them to the monastic *hospitium* or *porta*, where guests were cared for.[4] In the expanded version of Chrodegang's *Regula canonicorum*, the canons were required 'to give tithes very freely both from their crops and from all the charitable oblations

---

[1] See the works of Rabanus and Agobard cited pp. 14–15 and 32–3 above.

[2] See pp. 22–3 above.

[3] See p. 33 above. This statute was included in the customary of Monte Cassino: see Bruno Albers, *Consuetudines monasticae*, III: *Antiquiora monumenta maxime consuetudines Casinensis inde ab anno 716–817 illustrantia continens* (Monte Cassino, 1907), p. 131.

[4] Cf. Lesne, *Propriété*, VI, 116–26 and 173–4.

to the guest-house for the use of the poor'.[1] The commentary
on the rule of St Benedict attributed to Paul the Deacon decreed
that 'From everything that comes to the monastery, that is, from
gold, silver, copper, iron, labour, wine, fruit, animals, and the
rest, we should give tithes only to the guest-house of the poor, so
that no others, such as servants and nobles, but only the poor are
fed, for so it is written in the law and no poor man should be
without these tithes'.[2] The statutes of Adalhard of Corbie, which
were promulgated in 822, also show that at Corbie the tithes of
the abbey's income were used for guests and that a number of
specific revenues were tithed for the benefit of the gate where food
was distributed to the poor.[3]

Many charters in the ninth and tenth centuries granted monks
the right to use for their guest-houses and *portae* the tithes both
from their own demesne lands and occasionally also from lands
which they had granted as benefices.[4] Charles the Bald in 847
gave the tithe from the demesne villas of the abbey of St Amand
to the gate and hospice of the monks.[5] Lothar II established in
862 that all the tenants of Stavelot had to pay the tithes from their
demesne lands to the monastic guest-house.[6] The diet of Pistes held
by Charles the Bald in 864 ordered 'that the tithes from all the

---

[1] *Spicilegium*, I, 574; cf. p. 49 n. 3 above.

[2] Paul the Deacon, *Commentarium*, p. 418. The attribution of this commentary to Paul the Deacon has recently been questioned by Wolfgang Hafner,
*Der Basiliuskommentar zur Regula S. Benedicti: Ein Beitrag zur Autorenfrage
karolingischer Regelkommentare*, Beiträge zur Geschichte des alten Mönchtums
und des Benediktinerordens, XXIII (Münster, 1959), who suggested that it
derived from lectures given by Hildemar of Corbie at Civate in about 845 (cf.
the review by Anselm Biggs, in *Speculum*, XXXV, 461).

[3] Adalhard, stat. 8, 14 and 15, ed. Guérard, II, 322–3 and 333–4, and ed.
Levillain, pp. 369–70 and 384–5; cf. Lesne, in *Rev. d'hist. ecc.* XIII, 659–73 on the
regime of tithing at Corbie; and Dubar, *Corbie*, p. 41, showing that centuries
later the hospitaller at Corbie still disposed of many of the tithes from the abbey's
estates.

[4] Cf. Lesne, in *Rev. d'hist. ecc.* XIII, 487, who pointed out that monks unlike
bishops usually tithed their entire demesne, not only specific estates, for the
benefit of the poor but who also believed that the tithes used for their guest-
houses came from their demesne lands only (XIII, 501 and 667).

[5] *Actes de Charles II*, I, 250, no. 92; cf. *Speculum*, XXXV, 246.

[6] *Stavelot-Malmédy*, I, 85; M² 1296; confirmed by MGH, *Dipl.* Louis the
German, no. 147 (873).

other properties of the monastery [of St Germain at Auxerre], which are held either by demesne right or by the custom of benefices, should in their entirety be brought to the hospices of the rich and of the poor, as was previously established'.[1] Archbishop Hincmar in 870 assigned to the guest-house of the abbey of St Vaast at Arras several manors and 'a fifth of all the tithe which comes to the door'.[2] Charles the Fat in 886 confirmed an arrangement by which the bishops of Tours and Angers held an estate from the abbey of St Aignan in return for paying both an annual rent and 'the tithe from the demesne labour and the demesne vines and from the *corvée* to the canons of St Aignan for the hospice of the saint'.[3] When Zwentibold returned the little abbey of Salonne to St Denis in 896, he gave all its demesne tithes for the use of the poor and of guests 'as is done in the entire abbey of St Denis'.[4] Berengar I in 903 forbade the bishop and priests in the diocese of Piacenza to exact tithes from any goods produced by the monks of Tolla or their servants and gave the tithes 'to the guest-house of the monastery, as is just, for the poor'.[5] Similar arrangements were made or confirmed for Monte Amiata by Louis II in 853,[6] for St Martin at Tours and St Médard at Soissons by Charles the Bald in 862 and 866/70,[7] for Farfa by Louis II, Charles the Bald, and

---

[1] *Yonne*, I, 89; cf. Hefele–Leclercq, *Conciles*, IV. 1, 353. In 877 Charles the Bald gave the guest-house (*hospitale*) of the abbey of Nivelles the *villula* of Monstreux and 'the entire tithe of the whole abbey both from the demesne land and from the property of the brothers and sisters and from the benefices, except for those estates which render tithe to the almshouse (*matricula*) and one vineyard at Berzy in the county of Soissons' (*Actes de Charles II*, II, 467–8, no. 433); and in 897 Zwentibold confirmed that 'the tithe which is given in the *districtum* of this monastery belongs especially to the [charitable] work of that congregation without interference from anyone' (MGH, *Dipl.* Zwentibold, no. 16). These charters seem to show conclusively, against Lesne (cited p. 202 n. 4 above), that the tithes assigned to guest-houses occasionally came from more than the demesne lands of the monks.

[2] *St Vaast d'Arras*, p. 28; cf. also De Marca, *Concordia*, pp. 313–14, dated 866.

[3] MGH, *Dipl.* Charles III, no. 143.

[4] *Ibid.* Zwentibold, no. 7.

[5] Schiaparelli, *Diplomi*, II, 113; confirmed with a few changes by Kings Hugh and Lothar in 935 and by Henry II in 1014; Schiaparelli, *Diplomi*, III, 124, and MGH, *Dipl.* Henry II, no. 297 (and again, from the original charter, in MGH, *Dipl.* IV, 421–3).

[6] See p. 208 below.   [7] See *Speculum*, XXXV, 247, on these charters.

Berengar I in 872, 875 and 920,[1] for Lobbes by Arnulf in 889,[2] for
Cluny by Pope John XI and King Louis IV in 931 and 939,[3] for
Leno by Berengar II, Otto I, and Otto II in 958, 962 and 981,[4]
for St Peter at Metz by Otto I in 960,[5] for Cornelimünster by
Otto III in 985,[6] and subsequently for many other monasteries.[7]

This privilege was soon sufficiently important to appear in
forgeries, some of which were confirmed by authentic charters.
In a heavily interpolated privilege, probably based on a genuine
original, Arnulf in 888 gave the monks of Werden 'what has also
been granted to other monasteries...that wherever they have
demesne lands...we grant the tithes (which the bishops otherwise take) to the gate of the monastery and...they should not be
forced to give them elsewhere (but they should be for ever at the
disposition of the abbot of that monastery) in order that it may be
devoted to the pilgrims and guests who come there....'[8] Early
in the tenth century the abbey of Corvey forged a charter attributed to Louis the German and dated 873, together with a
confirmation by Arnulf in 888, granting 'that the tithes from
the demesne farms of the monastery should not be given to
bishops but to the gate of the monastery...to provide the
supplies for ministering to the pilgrims and guests who are
never absent from the monastery'.[9] Otto I in 956 confirmed

---

[1] *Farfa*, III, 12, no. 307 (M² 1254: 'ad portam monasterii'); *Actes de Charles II*,
II, 395, no. 401; and Schiaparelli, *Diplomi*, II, 325.

[2] MGH, *Dipl.* Arnulf, no. 64. After the monks gave up regular life, Arnulf
gave half of their property to the bishop of Tongern and Liège, at whose
request the monks were allowed to keep all their demesne tithes for the gate
and guest-house.

[3] See *Rev. bén.* LXX, 605, on these charters granting the demesne tithes to the
hospice.

[4] Schiaparelli, *Diplomi*, III, 323: 'omnes decimas desuper totam abbatiam in
usus pauperum et hospitum'; MGH, *Dipl.* Otto I, no. 240 and Otto II, no. 243
(also in *Leno*, pp. 69, 72 and 78).

[5] MGH, *Dipl.* Otto I, no. 210, granting the demesne tithes to the poor,
pilgrims, and guests.

[6] MGH, *Dipl.* Otto III, no. 18, granting the demesne tithes to the gate of the
monastery for the poor and guests.

[7] Cf. MGH, *Dipl.* Conrad II, no. 257 (1038), etc.

[8] MGH, *Dipl.* Arnulf, no. 36.

[9] MGH, *Dipl.* Louis the German, no. 184 (M² 1498, cf. M² 1768).

a series of forged charters for the monks of St Maximin at Trier granting 'the demesne, which are commonly called salic, tithes in whatever diocese, parish or region of our realm they may be situated, for the use of the hospices of the pilgrims and of the poor'.[1]

Perhaps the most famous of these frauds was in several early charters for Fulda, which are now recognized as interpolated or forged but were long considered authentic, and which misled Lesne, Perels, Viard, Schreiber, and other scholars into believing that Fulda was freed from paying tithes in the late eighth or early ninth century.[2] It is true that in the ninth century Fulda's position with regard to the diocesan bishop was exceptional, and the success of its forgeries confirming the possession of other men's tithes has already been discussed,[3] but it was never formally freed from paying tithes from its own revenues. The first authentic permission to control the use of its own tithes appeared in the charter of Louis the German in 875,[4] which was, according to Stengel, the earliest undoubted privilege of this sort east of the Rhine.[5] It was remarkable in allowing the monks to use their tithes for themselves, their buildings, and the lighting of their churches as well as for pilgrims and the poor; but it was consistent

---

[1] MGH, *Dipl.* Otto I, no. 179. This privilege also appears in charters of Arnulf in 893, Zwentibold in 897, and Charles the Simple in 912, but it was probably interpolated into these documents about the middle of the tenth century and was then authenticated by Otto: Harry Bresslau, 'Über die älteren Königs- und Papsturkunden für das Kloster St Maximin bei Trier', *Westdeutsche Zeitschrift für Geschichte und Kunst*, v (1886), 31-2. Otto's privilege was subsequently confirmed by Henry II in 1023, Henry IV in 1065, and Henry V in 1111: MGH, *Dipl.* Henry II, no. 502 and *Altluxemburg*, I, 428 and 494.

[2] Cf. Lesne, in *Rev. d'hist. ecc.* XIV, 490-1 and 491 n. 1: 'Par l'effet d'un privilège qui est sans doute une conséquence de l'exemption dont ils jouissent vis-à-vis du pouvoir épiscopal, les moines de Fulda sont donc dispensés de payer au prêtre de l'église la dîme de leur *dominicum*'; Ernst Perels, *Die kirchlichen Zehnten im karolingischen Reiche* (Berlin, 1904), p. 88; Viard, *Dîme*, I, 133 and 188 (who expressed some doubt of its authenticity); Schreiber, *Kurie*, I, 248.

[3] Pp. 76-7 above; Weiss, *Exemtionen*, pp. 40-1, and Szaivert, in *MIÖG*, LIX, 291-2, who said that before the Cluniac reform Fulda was the only exempt monastery in Germany.

[4] MGH, *Dipl.* Louis the German, no. 162 (with bibliography).

[5] Stengel, *Immunität*, p. 563 n. 3.

with contemporary ideas about the use of tithes[1] and was thus an extension of the privilege permitting monks to use their tithes for their gates and hospices.

The tithe which a monastery devoted to charitable uses might sometimes be supplemented by a second tithe, or ninth.[2] The commentary on the Benedictine rule attributed to Paul the Deacon, after decreeing that monks should devote their tithes to the guest-house for the poor, went on:

But since the Lord says in the Gospel, 'unless your justice abound more than that of the scribes and Pharisees, you shall not enter into the kingdom of Heaven', the justice of the scribes is to give tithes from all things; for we should give two tithes in order that we may enter the kingdom of Heaven;...that is, when we give tithes, we will then give a ninth part. For we should give this ninth part to the hospice for the rich, whatever it will be, and from this we should cater to the needs of the rich.[3]

There are several examples of pious clerics and laymen adding a *nona* to their *decima*, although this had no connection with the secular *nona et decima* paid as a rent by holders of church lands granted as *precaria verbo regis* by the kings to their vassals. At the abbeys of St Amand in the region of Tournai, at St Martin at Tours, St Médard at Soissons, and at St Caprasius at Aulla it was apparently customary in the ninth century for a ninth to be gathered for charitable uses from the demesne lands of the monks in addition to the tithe for the guest-house of the pilgrims and the poor.

The strictly charitable use of these tithes was entirely in accord with the early theory of tithing and shows that the monasteries in question were in no way freed from paying tithes. On the contrary, they devoted at least a tenth and sometimes a fifth of their incomes to their hospices and other charities. The purpose of these grants was not to abolish tithes but to change their

[1] See, for instance, the letter of Pope Zachary in 748 (cited p. 27 above), who allowed tithes to be used for priests and for building and decorating churches as well as for purely charitable uses.

[2] On this entire paragraph, see *Speculum*, xxxv, 246-8.

[3] Paul the Deacon, *Commentarium*, pp. 418-19.

destination,[1] and in effect they made the monks into the recipients and distributors of their own tithes.

One can therefore conclude [Lesne said], that the exemption of the *indominicatum* of cathedrals and monasteries with respect to the parish churches corresponded to the tithing of this portion of the ecclesiastical demesne in favour of the hostelry or *mensa*. This tithe was not an exception to the general law. It was only part of the ordinary ecclesiastical tithe, a reserved part, which was taken from the parish church and assigned to another destination owing to the ecclesiastical quality of the person whose revenues were tithed.[2]

Even here, the use of the term 'exemption' may be misleading, since the monks were still obliged to devote their tithes to a charitable use. Indeed, the influence of the early idea of tithing was occasionally so great that tithes from lands not belonging to the monks and even the secular *nona et decima*, which had no connection with the ecclesiastical tithe, were explicitly assigned to the guest-house or some other charitable use.[3] A monastery might thus find a significant restriction placed upon part of its income.

From the point of view of the monks, however, control over their own tithes offered the double advantage of avoiding possible extortions and oppression by episcopal and parochial officials and of allowing them either to give greater support to their own charities or to use revenues previously devoted to charity in other ways. In fact it often led to the absorption of the tithe into their general economy and the disappearance of any specific payment of tithes. Especially when there was a monastic *mensa*,

---

[1] Cf. F. W. Maitland, *Domesday Book and Beyond* (Cambridge, 1897), pp. 272–3, who pointed out that the object of a fiscal immunity was not to free anyone from paying a due but to change the beneficiary to whom it was paid, i.e. the king granted some customary revenue to the church.

[2] Lesne, in *Rev. d'hist. ecc.* XIV, 494; also 490–1, where he stressed that the monks were required by the bishops to pay tithes like everyone else unless they were specifically allowed to pay them to their own guest-house or *mensa*.

[3] In 917, for instance, Charles the Simple specified that various tithes which had been given without any apparent restriction on their use to St Cornelius at Compiègne in 877 (see p. 66 n. 4 above) should be given only to the hospice for the poor: *Recueil des actes de Charles III le Simple*, ed. P. Lauer, CDRHF (Paris, 1940 ff.), I, 208, no. 91; on the *nona et decima*, see *Speculum*, XXXV, 248.

incorporating and dividing the entire income of the monastery, certain specific revenues, rather than the tithe of all revenues, were usually set apart for charity and hospitality.[1] Even when no formal *mensa* was established, most monks seem to have taken very lightly their obligation to devote their tithes to the *porta* or guest-house, and, like the clergy, they clearly regarded guests, travellers, and the poor as a charge upon their general income rather than specifically on their tithes.

The development of this attitude and the change of the right to distribute their tithes into a right to pay no tithes can be traced in several series of charters and confirmations. The monks of Lobbes, for instance, who were granted in 889 the right to devote the tithes from their demesne lands to their gate or guest-house, were given by Otto II in 973 'all the demesne tithes from the entire abbey, both from beneficed churches (*ecclesiis beneficiatis*) and from those deputed for their own support'.[2] The history of this privilege can also clearly be seen in the charters of the abbey of Monte Amiata,[3] which was given by Louis II in 853 'all the tithes and revenues from protection and jurisdiction and every composition and public tax from all the inhabitants on the above-mentioned cells and estates... to be brought for ever to the gate of the monastery to be used as alms for supporting pilgrims...'.[4] The Emperor Guy of Spoleto in 892, the bishop of Chiusi in 911, Berengar I in 915, Kings Hugh and Lothar in 937, and Otto I in 962 all confirmed the right of Monte Amiata to the tithes from its demesne lands.[5] Also about the middle of the tenth century a

---

[1] See Lesne, in *Rev. d'hist. ecc.* XIV, 105–12.

[2] MGH, *Dipl.* Arnulf, no. 64 (see p. 204 n. 2 above) and Otto II, no. 53, which was confirmed by Henry V in 1101: see *Gesta abbatum Lobbiensium*, XII, in MGH, *SS*, XXI, 316.

[3] According to Harry Bresslau, in MGH, *Dipl.* IV, 103, many skilful forgeries were made at Monte Amiata in the eleventh and twelfth centuries, but recent editors have accepted the authenticity of most of the charters cited here.

[4] A. Fanta, 'Unedierte Diplome, II', *MIÖG*, V (1884), 386, see 407–15 on the authenticity of this charter, which was accepted as genuine in M² 1194 and by Schiaparelli and Kehr in their editions of later charters for Monte Amiata.

[5] Schiaparelli, *Diplomi*, I, 46; Ughelli, *Italia sacra*, III, 616–17; Schiaparelli, *Diplomi*, II, 276–9 and III, 138; MGH, *Dipl.* Otto I, no. 237. The terms of the privilege varied somewhat in these charters.

clause granting the abbey's tithes to the hospice for the pilgrims was interpolated into a forged version, dated 896, of an authentic privilege from Arnulf.[1] Finally in 996 Pope Gregory V granted a charter to the monks confirming their right to the first-fruits and tithes of their lands and workers and permitting them to baptize in two churches.[2] These privileges were naturally galling to the bishop of Chiusi, who consequently refused to consecrate any churches belonging to Monte Amiata or to St Antimo, which also owned 'the tithes and first-fruits from all its lands'.[3] In 1007 the two abbeys therefore lodged a complaint against the bishop before the Emperor Henry II at Neuburg:

When the bishop came and the king carefully asked him why he refused to bless and consecrate the churches in his diocese, he replied [that it was] because the above-mentioned abbots denied to himself and his canons the tithes of their abbeys. The king then asked the abbots themselves whether they had any authority by which their monasteries could protect and claim the tithes for their side. When the abbots showed the very old charters of the monastery, it was then discovered and proved by the evidence of those who were around that from the foundation of the monastery and from the times of the lord king Charlemagne and all his successors, the abbots and monks had held those tithes and all the predecessors of Bishop Airard had allowed them to hold in complete peace. And since everyone had agreed that this should remain unchanged for ever, the lord king Henry agreed and confirmed and made the bishop be content and silent.[4]

[1] MGH, *Dipl.* Arnulf, nos. 140 and 189.
[2] Ughelli, *Italia sacra*, III, 618; JL 3864; *IP*, III, 239, no. 5; Santifaller, *Elenco*, p. 315. It was confirmed by Leo IX in 1050: *PL*, CXLIII, 651; JL 4232; *IP*, III, 240, no. 10; Santifaller, *Elenco*, p. 362. The privileges of Celestine II and Anastasius IV for Monte Amiata, on the other hand, included no such references to tithes (*APRI*, III, 48–9 and 121–3; JL 8498 and 9748; *IP*, III, 241–2, nos. 12 and 16).
[3] *APRI*, II, 52–3; JL 3842 (and 3860); *IP*, III, 248, no. 6. It was confirmed by Anastasius IV in 1153: *PL*, CLXXXVIII, 994, and *APRI*, III, 124–5; JL 9754; *IP*, III, 249, no. 8.
[4] MGH, *Dipl.* Henry II, no. 129; cf. Bresslau, *Urkundenlehre*, I, 500 n. 2. In settling a dispute between the bishop and clergy of Chiusi in 1068, Pope Alexander II specifically protected the rights of Monte Amiata and two other monasteries: *APRI*, II, 109; JL 4657; *IP*, III, 233, no. 9; Santifaller, *Elenco*, p. 408.

C M T

This decision was made in the presence of the abbots of Cluny and Farfa (both of which held the tithes from their own lands) and other leading churchmen, and it shows that in contemporary opinion a grant to an abbey of its tithes for the gate or guest-house freed it in effect from paying any tithes.

Simple grants to monks of their own tithes, without specifying their use, were much rarer than grants for the gate or guest-house, and their very rarity tends to throw suspicion on the earliest examples. King Sigebert was said to have given to Abbot Remaclus of Stavelot, who died in 669/79, 'the tithes from the estates surrounding the monasteries, which [tithes] the inhabitants of these monasteries are known to have possessed up until the present time'.[1] There is no reference to tithes in Sigebert's charter for Stavelot in 651, however,[2] and the passage was probably inserted into the later life of Remaclus in order to justify a subsequent claim. Coville has shown that the alleged testament of Archbishop Aunemundus of Lyons, which was dated 652/8 and referred to his grant to the abbey of St Peter at Lyons of various tithes, including those from all its own vineyards, was forged in the twelfth or thirteenth century and that references to the testament and the tithes were inserted probably at the same time into a letter written in 813/14 by Archbishop Leidrad of Lyons to Charlemagne.[3] The grant of King Cunibert in 686 to the monks of St Fridiano at Lucca of 'their tithes in that place' may, however, be authentic.[4]

In the ninth century it was less uncommon for monks to keep their tithes for their own use. The council of Chalon-sur-Saône in 813 even authorized abbots to have the tithes from their own demesne lands brought to their churches.[5] The abbey of Corbie in

---

[1] MGH, SS. Merov. V, 111; cf. MGH, SS, VII, 187; the passage may represent the form written by Notker in 972/80 or the eleventh-century version of the Vita.   [2] MGH, Dipl. in fol., I, 23-4, no. 23.

[3] Alfred Coville, Recherches sur l'histoire de Lyon du Vme siècle au IXme siècle (450-800) (Paris, 1928), pp. 401 and 407-11. For Leidrad's letter, see MGH, Epp. IV, 543, and Lesne, in Rev. d'hist. ecc. XIV, 490, who accepted the references to tithes as authentic.

[4] Mabillon, Annales, I, 650, and Carlo Troya, Storia d'Italia del medio evo (Naples, 1839-55), IV: Codice diplomatico longobardo dal DLXVIII al DCCLXXIV, III, 12, no. 352.   [5] See p. 38 above.

the early ninth century apparently forced its more important tenants to pay their tithes to the monastery rather than to the parish churches.[1] In 830 a council at Langres approved a grant to the monks of Bèze of the tithes from certain vineyards given to them by their founder, but this record is found only in a later manuscript from Bèze itself and may have been fabricated to assist the abbey in a dispute over tithes with the canons of Langres.[2] Even in the tenth century authentic grants of this sort were unusual. In a charter for the abbey of St Peter in Ciel d'Oro at Pavia in 929, King Hugh said that the founder King Liutprand had given the monks the tithes from all their possessions.[3] In 998 Otto III added to his confirmation of Otto I's privilege for St Zachary at Venice (963) a clause 'that all the peasants on these estates should pay their tithes to the monastery'.[4]

In the late tenth and early eleventh century, the papacy began granting and confirming for monks possession of their own tithes. Already in 950 and 951 Pope Agapitus II gave to Cuxa and to Ripoll the tithes and first-fruits from their own lands.[5] John XV in his charter for St Peter at Pavia in 986 confirmed its possession of lands 'with the tithes and first-fruits' and forbade any disturbance of the monks on this account.[6] The grants of John XV for St Antimo in 992 and of Gregory V for Monte Amiata in 996 have been cited above, together with the decision of King Henry II in favour of the abbeys against the bishop of Chiusi.[7] Gregory also confirmed the grant to St Peter at Pavia.[8]

---

[1] See p. 60 above.

[2] MGH, Conc. II, 682; cf. Hefele–Leclercq, Conciles, IV. 1, 82, and p. 215 below on the dispute with the canons of Langres.

[3] Schiaparelli, Diplomi, III, 57. The abbey was founded in 722.

[4] MGH, Dipl. Otto III, no. 272, confirming Otto I, no. 258.

[5] Marca hispanica, p. 864; JL 3651; Santifaller, Elenco, p. 287; and Marca hispanica, p. 867; JL 3655. On the early history of Cuxa and its domain, which as early as the tenth century constituted the largest holding of lands in the counties of Cerdagne and Conflent, see the articles by Pierre Ponsich, in Études Roussillonnaises, II (1952), 7–19 and 67–100.

[6] Historiae patriae monumenta, XIII: Codex diplomaticus Langobardiae (Turin, 1873), pp. 1450–1, no. 829; JL 3826; IP, VI. 1, 193, no. †2; Santifaller, Elenco, p. 309.   [7] See pp. 208–9 above.

[8] Cod. dip. Lang. p. 1619, no. 920; JL 3871; IP, VI. 1, 194, no. 4; Santifaller, Elenco, p. 316; see pp. 208–9 above.

In a privilege for Arles-sur-Tech in 1011, Pope Sergius IV confirmed the abbey's possession of several parishes with their tithes, oblations, and first-fruits, and decreed that within certain boundaries all these dues must be paid to these parishes.[1] In 1019 Benedict VIII confirmed for Leno the tithes and first-fruits of all its dependants and of its parish church 'as was granted and confirmed by order of its founder and his successors the kings and emperors and by our predecessors the pontiffs of the holy Roman church'.[2]

The earliest known privilege allowing monks to pay no tithes at all was in the papal bull of 643 for Bobbio, in which Pope Theodore forbade the diocesan bishop to infringe the rights of the abbey 'and to lay claim for himself in any way to its baptismal churches or tithes'.[3] Bobbio is known to have enjoyed remarkable privileges at that time,[4] and this formula, which was not uncommon in later bulls, was repeated and confirmed in a royal privilege in 929.[5] But in the seventh century it is unique, and it may well be a later interpolation. Even if genuine, it is ambiguous and may have applied to tithes paid by other workers on the abbey's lands, in which case the monks would still have been expected to pay tithes even if the bishop was forbidden to take them for himself. The freedoms from tithes in the charters of Carloman and Charlemagne for St Denis were almost certainly later interpolations.[6] But in 792 Charlemagne conceded to the church of Aquileia that its men and serfs (*servientes*) 'wherever they may be should at no time pay in public any tithe either from

---

[1] *Marca hispanica*, p. 991; JL 3977.

[2] *Leno*, p. 91, no. 12; JL 4026; *IP*, vi. 1, 344, no. 2; Santifaller, *Elenco*, p. 336. The grants mentioned by Benedict are the royal charters giving the abbey its tithes for the use of guests and the poor, cited p. 204 n. 4 above, and the bull of Sylvester II in 999 (*Leno*, pp. 81–2, no. 8; JL 3901; *IP*, vi. 1, 343, no. 1; Santifaller, *Elenco*, p. 319), which applied only to a cell of Leno. Sylvester's bull is the first known papal privilege for Leno, but it refers to earlier lost papal charters.

[3] *Bobbio*, i, 110; JE 2053; cf. Bresslau, *Urkundenlehre*, ii, 195 n. 1, who considered this charter interpolated.

[4] Cf. Szaivert, in *MIÖG*, lix, 291. The earliest charter of exemption for Bobbio was issued in 628.

[5] Preserved in the *Miracula s. Columbani*, which was written in the third quarter of the tenth century: *Bobbio*, i, 299, and MGH, *SS*, xxx, 1009.

[6] MGH, *Dipl. Karol.* nos. 46 (769) and 93 (775).

their crops or from their cattle'.[1] This exceptional privilege was doubtless granted on account of the personal friendship between Charlemagne and the Patriarch Paulinus, and it applied to a cathedral and not to a monastery; but it may be the first authentic freedom from tithes granted to any ecclesiastical institution and shows the influence and initiative of Charlemagne in the matter of tithes.

Such grants remained very rare, however, throughout the ninth and tenth centuries. Experts in the study of documents have expressed doubts about the prohibition of Charles the Bald in 850 to gather tithes from the lands of the abbey of Cormery,[2] the grant of Charles the Fat in 886 'that neither tithe nor anything except the annual rent should any more be exacted' from the nuns of Cusset,[3] and the privilege of 894 for Gigny from Pope Formosus saying that 'You have asked concerning tithes, however, because payment from your own goods has been required of you. If so, we forbid this to be done, above all since it is written that priests should not be forced to give tithes.'[4] The only undoubted freedom from tithes in the ninth century was for the monks of Montiéramey in a bull issued in 878 by Pope John VIII, whose importance in the development of papal protection of monasteries is well known.[5] 'At the time we celebrated a synod at Troyes for

[1] MGH, *Dipl. Karol.* no. 174. It is possible that the tithe referred to here was a secular due of a tenth. There may be some interpolations in the list of possessions in this charter, but it was frequently confirmed and was accepted as authentic by Walter Lenel, *Venezianisch-Istrische Studien*, Schriften der wissenschaftlichen Gesellschaft in Strassburg, IX (Strasbourg, 1911), pp. 186 and 188 n. 1; cf. Heinrich Schmidinger, 'Die Besetzung des Patriarchenstuhls von Aquileja bis zur Mitte des 13. Jahrhunderts', *MIÖG*, LX (1952), 341–2, and *Patriarch und Landesherr: Die weltliche Herrschaft der Patriarchen von Aquileja bis zum Ende der Staufer*, Publikationen des österreichischen Kulturinstituts in Rom, I, I (Graz–Cologne, 1954), pp. 23 n. 6 and 26.

[2] *Actes de Charles II*, I, 344, no. 131, cited by Lesne, in *Rev. d'hist. ecc.* XIV, 502. [3] MGH, *Dipl.* Charles III, no. 187.

[4] PL, CXXIX, 846; JL 3499: 'Clausula est vitiosa'; cf. Bresslau, *Urkundenlehre*, I, 210 n. 4.

[5] Hans Hirsch, 'Untersuchungen zur Geschichte des päpstlichen Schutzes', *MÖIG*, LIV (1941–2), 387, and Heinrich Appelt, 'Die Anfänge des päpstlichen Schutzes', *MIÖG*, LXII (1954), 103, who stressed the importance of the entire period from Nicholas I to John VIII in the development of the theory of papal protection.

the affairs of all the churches of God,' wrote the pope, 'we recognized your reverence for God and ordained by apostolic authority that no bishop and no public minister or his agent should ever exact tithes from this monastery or from any of its estates.'[1] In 909 Charles the Simple granted to the monks of Psalmodi 'that they should pay no tithes or taxes to anyone'.[2] Pope John XIII in 972 forbade anyone 'to exact tithes or tribute' from the abbey of Breme;[3] and John XVIII in 1006 granted a privilege to the monks of Fruttuaria forbidding anyone 'to exact from them the revenue of tithe, either from demesne lands hitherto cultivated for fields, meadows, vines, or any crops or animals, or from all the uncultivated lands which are or will be cultivated by their industry either at Fruttuaria, where the monastery is located, or at any place where they own anything by the right of the monastery'.[4] Pope Benedict VIII confirmed the privileges of Breme in 1014,[5] and of Fruttuaria in a synodal decree of 1015, after the abbot explained that his abbey was founded 'in a deserted place, where no bishop had ever been known to have the revenue of tithes or of any other sort'.[6]

Even in the second half of the eleventh century, however, when the reformed papacy actively promoted monastic possession of tithes from the labour of other men, most monks were still expected to pay tithes from their own products and revenues, and only a few were allowed to keep their own tithes, or effectively freed in any

[1] *Montiéramey*, p. 9, and H. d'Arbois de Jubainville, 'Bulle inédite du pape Jean VIII en faveur de l'abbaye de Montiéramey', *Bibliothèque de l'École des Chartes*, xv (1854), 280–3; JE 3185; Santifaller, *Elenco*, p. 268; cf. Bresslau, *Urkundenlehre*, i, 214 n. 5, and, on the council of Troyes in 878, Hefele–Leclercq, *Conciles*, iv. 2, 666–78. The authenticity of this charter seems to be unimpeachable, although the privilege is unique and the bull is not included in the register of John VIII, which is known, however, to be incomplete for his trip to France in 878: see E. Caspar, in MGH, *Epp.* vii, introd. p. xiv.

[2] *Actes de Charles III*, i, 135, no. 61.

[3] *Breme*, p. 20; JL 3761; *IP*, vi. 1, 234, no. 2; Santifaller, *Elenco*, p. 299; cf. Gosso, *Vita economica*, pp. 196–7.

[4] *PL*, cxxxix, 1485; JL 3950; *IP*, vi. 2, 149, no. 1; Santifaller, *Elenco*, p. 324. It was confirmed in similar terms in MGH, *Dipl.* Henry III, no. 338 (1055).

[5] *Breme*, pp. 58–9; JL 4002; *IP*, vi. 1, 234, no. 3; Santifaller, *Elenco*, p. 331.

[6] Ughelli, *Italia sacra*, i, 157; JL 4007; *IP*, vi. 2, 150, no. 4; Santifaller, *Elenco*, p. 332.

other way from paying tithes to the bishops and priests. Leo IX was one of the few popes who took an active interest in the tithes paid by monks.[1] In July 1050 he granted the abbey of the Saviour at Isola in the diocese of Siena a privilege, which was later confirmed by Nicholas II and Alexander II, 'decreeing by apostolic decision under a solemn charge of divine judgement that no man should ever...exact any tithe from the goods of the monastery or turn the hospice to any secular use'.[2] In September of 1050 Leo confirmed the right of the monks of Monte Amiata to the first-fruits and tithes from their lands and men.[3] In October of the same year he was at Langres, and an interesting account of his visit there was given in the chronicle of Bèze, written by the monk John about a century later. While at Langres, he wrote, Leo consecrated the new bishop and settled several disputes, among them a case between the monks of Bèze and the canons of Langres, who claimed the tithes from a vineyard belonging to the monks.

When Pope Leo heard the case, he spoke out and explained what he had seen on this matter in the papal archives and said that 'By the authority of the Holy Fathers who preceded me in the see of Rome, it was permitted that no church founded in honour of St Peter, the prince of the Apostles, should pay a rent or tithes to another church'. The canons were subdued by the weight of his reason and authority, and they remained silent.[4]

This privilege is not known to have been authenticated by a charter, and the reason given seems improbable, although certain popes unquestionably felt a special concern for churches dedicated to St Peter and a considerable number of the early papal privileges

---

[1] See pp. 85–6 above on Leo's opposition to lay possession of tithes.

[2] *APRI*, II, 72; JL 4231; *IP*, III, 310, no. 1; Santifaller, *Elenco*, p. 362. The wording here suggests that the monks were to use the tithes for their hospice. Cf. *APRI*, II, 90–1 (1060) and 96–7 (1062); JL 4427 and 4493; *IP*, III, 310–11, nos. 2–3.   [3] See p. 209 n. 2 above.

[4] *Antiquum Besuensis abbatiae chronicon authore Johanne monacho*, ed. E. Bougaud and J. Garnier, Analecta Divionensia, IX (Dijon, 1875), p. 337. On Leo's visit to Langres, see Georges Drioux, 'Un diocèse de France à la veille de la réforme grégorienne: Le pape Léon IX et les évêques de Langres Hugues et Hardoin', *Studi Gregoriani*, II (1947), 39–40.

concerned with monastic payment of tithes were in fact granted to monasteries dedicated to St Peter, such as Bobbio, Breme, Cluny, Gigny, and Montiéramey.[1] Even if Leo's wording is not correct, however, the general meaning of the record may be authentic.

Leo's successors continued the policy without enthusiasm. Alexander II issued, in addition to the confirmation for Isola, a similar privilege in 1070, forbidding the exaction of any tithes, for the abbey of the Trinity at Torre, also in the diocese of Siena.[2] No grant of this sort is known to have been made by Gregory VII, whose pontificate marked in other respects an important stage in the development of formulas of monastic privileges.[3] Urban II in 1089 granted a charter to the Cluniac priory of St Jean-des-Vignes, in the diocese of Soissons, forbidding anyone to exact tithes from its noval lands which were cultivated by or for the monks themselves; but the formula relating to tithes may be a later interpolation.[4] In 1092, however, Urban decreed for the Augustinian house at Raitenbuch 'that the tithes from the noval lands of the canonry should belong to itself, saving the rights of the neighbouring churches',[5] and he also permitted his old master and adviser St Bruno and his friend Lanvinus to use 'the tithes from the labour of yourselves and of your monks' on the wild land in Calabria given them by the Count Roger.[6] These three grants were all conservative, however. The

---

[1] Nicholas II in his privilege for St Peter at Perugia in 1059 said that he gladly granted what he could as a gift to the saint 'because your monastery belongs especially to St Peter and is marked by his name': *PL*, CXLIII, 1325; JL 4413; *IP*, IV, 69, no. 18; Santifaller, *Elenco*, p. 388.

[2] *APRI*, II, 111; JL 4670; *IP*, III, 228, no. 1; Santifaller, *Elenco*, p. 410.

[3] Cf. Lerche, in *A. f. Urk.* III, 127, who pointed out that the development of monastic privileges during Gregory's pontificate was relatively greater in France and England than in Germany, which is not surprising.

[4] *PL*, CLI, 296; JL 5391; Santifaller, *Elenco*, p. 437. The formula 'Sane novalium vestrorum quod propriis manibus vel sumptibus colitis decimas nemo praesumat exigere' was not commonly used in papal bulls until half a century later (see pp. 242–4 below), and it seems too technical to have been hit upon here by chance.

[5] *PL*, CLI, 339; JL 5459 (dated 1092); *GP*, I, 375, no. 2; Santifaller, *Elenco*, p. 444.

[6] *PL*, CLI, 353; JL 5468; Santifaller, *Elenco*, pp. 445–6.

fact that Bruno and his followers were opening new lands, from
which no tithe had previously been paid, the protection of
established rights of other churches in the grant to Raitenbuch,
and the restrictions to noval tithes in the grants to St Jean-des-
Vignes (if genuine) and Raitenbuch, although an interesting
anticipation of later policy, all show the reluctance, even in pro-
monastic circles, to disturb the existing system of tithing and to
free monks in any way from the obligation to pay tithes.

Beyond a negative conclusion of this sort, it is difficult to
estimate the real effect of the privileges concerning monastic
payment of tithes before the twelfth century. It is not even
always certain that the *decima* in question was the ecclesiastical
tithe, although the nature of the due and the references to bishops
and priests usually rule out the possibility of a secular due of a
tenth. In judging the authenticity of the references, the very
rarity of the privilege may too easily be used as an argument
against them, and the reasoning can easily become circular. The
inclusion of such a privilege, for instance, has been used to throw
suspicion on the charters for Bobbio, Cormery, Gigny, and
St Jean-des-Vignes;[1] and Werminghoff, who accepted the
authenticity of the acts of the 830 council at Langres allowing
Bèze to keep the tithes from its own vineyards, doubted the
authenticity of the acts of the so-called council of Fleury in 839
partly because it allowed monks to use their tithes for alms and
their guest-houses.[2] In most of these cases the documents are in
fact suspicious for other reasons, but it is possible that if enough
authentic examples of this privilege were found to create a
supposition in its favour, some of the charters which are questioned
on this account might be considered genuine.

---

[1] See, for instance, Lesne, in *Rev. d'hist. ecc.* XIV, 502 n. 4, who used various
charters of doubtful authenticity but who was suspicious of the grant by
Charles the Bald to Cormery 'car au IXe siècle, les diplômes d'immunité
n'ont jamais été employés...à établir l'exemption d'un monastère en matière
de dîmes'; and *Actes de Charles II*, I, 344: 'Dans la formule d'immunité, la
clause "ad causas audiendas" est anormalement remplacée par les mots "ad
decimas percipiendas".' Cf. also Pardessus' criticism of the grant to the abbey of
Our Lady at Le Mans, cited p. 58 n. 5 above.
[2] MGH, *Conc.* II, 854.

The dates of the undoubted documents show that the distribution by monks of their own tithes, their use for the monastic gate or hospice, the possession by a monastery of its tithes without specifying their use, the prohibitions for anyone to exact tithes from a monastery, and the permissions to pay no tithes at all were not historical stages leading one to the other. The fact that they overlapped also suggests that their effects should not be too strictly distinguished, and it should be remembered that for the later canonists any freedom from tithes was an indirect form of possession. In fact, only the privileges for Aquileia (792), Gigny (894), Psalmodi (909), and Bèze (1050), of which the second and fourth are suspect, decreed that no tithes need be paid, and it is probable that the other types of privilege envisaged that the monks would set aside and use their own tithes. Even abbeys which were entitled to keep their demesne tithes, such as Fruttuaria and Cluny, sometimes paid tithes to other men and institutions,[1] and the principal effect of all the grants was probably to authorize the monks to supervise their own tithing and to pay tithes or not as they saw fit.

The dates further suggest that the decisive period in the development of these grants was the second half of the ninth century, which saw not only the beginning of the series of royal grants to monasteries of the right to use their tithes for their *portae* and guest-houses but also the first undoubted papal privilege prohibiting the exaction of tithes from a monastery.[2] It is hard to say whether or not the apparent distinction between secular grants of permission for monks to use their own tithes, and ecclesiastical grants of possession of their tithes and of permission

---

[1] See pp. 222 and 225-6 below.

[2] Cf. Stengel, *Immunität*, p. 563, who remarked in his discussion of the ancillary rights and privileges in immunity charters in Germany that 'The position of the general tithes-privileges, which can be found since the last quarter of the ninth century, is of the same sort, although it was concerned not with the grant of an imperial but with a purely ecclesiastical revenue'. Of the documents cited on p. 555 to support this view, however, at least two are forged (M^2 1768 and M^2 1801), two are from the suspicious series of charters for Corvey, and two were concerned with the tithes of episcopal churches (MGH, *Dipl.* Henry II, nos. 223 and 256b). The remainder mostly authorized monks to use their tithes for charitable purposes.

to pay no tithes is significant.[1] But it is certain that in this matter the papacy did more than simply confirm the privileges granted to monasteries by secular authorities, as some scholars have asserted,[2] and that after the ninth century the popes cautiously led the way in generalizing these grants, both by guaranteeing for monks possession of their own tithes without specifying the use and particularly by prohibiting the exaction of tithes and allowing monks to pay no tithes. Perhaps even more significant in the long run were the reasons for the grant given in two papal charters. Formosus in his privilege for Gigny (894, if genuine) specified that priests, among whom he evidently included monks, should not be forced to give tithes; and Benedict VIII in his confirmation for Fruttuaria (1015) pointed out that the abbey was built on lands from which no tithe had ever been paid. Admittedly the total advance in both the theory and the practice of freeing monks from the payment of tithes was not very great in the ninth, tenth, and eleventh centuries, and Pope Urban II was almost more cautious in his grants than his predecessors two centuries before. But a slim precedent had been established for the developments in the twelfth century.

[1] With the exception of the grants of Hincmar for St Vaast and John XI for Cluny, all the grants of tithes for the use of pilgrims, guests, and the poor were from secular rulers. Even the papal confirmations for Monte Amiata and Leno omitted any reference to the use of the tithes. On the other hand, a great majority of the grants of their own tithes, prohibitions to exact tithes, and permissions to pay no tithes were in papal privileges. The investigation and publication of more charters might, however, blur this apparent distinction between the types of grant made by the secular and ecclesiastical authorities.

[2] Cf. Stengel, *Immunität*, pp. 372, 384, 388, etc., and Hirsch, *Klosterimmunität*, pp. 16–18, who characterized Leo IX as a 'süddeutscher Dynast' whose privileges confirmed the claims of the former owners of the monasteries. This may be true of certain types of rights, but not of payment of tithes, which was not under the control of secular rulers. The character of the 'general tithes-privileges' mentioned by Stengel (cited p. 218 n. 2 above) is not quite clear, but they were not usually included in grants of immunity. The papal confirmations of secular tithe-privileges for Monte Amiata and Leno both extended the privilege, and in the cases of Cluny and Fruttuaria the papal grants seem to have been confirmed in the royal privileges.

2. THE GROWTH OF MONASTIC FREEDOM FROM TITHES IN THE FIRST HALF OF THE TWELFTH CENTURY

The period from Pope Paschal II to Pope Alexander III was of key importance in the history of monastic payment of tithes, as of monasticism generally and its relations with the outer world.[1] It has been said that the preceding period of Leo IX, Gregory VII, and Urban II was even more important in forming relations between the papal curia and monasteries, but for the internal development of monasticism the twelfth century was decisive. 'This period', said Brackmann, 'saw the breakdown of the old form of monastic organization and the rise of the new orders.'[2] Many of these new monasteries were either formally freed from paying tithes or were granted possession of their own tithes. Tithing increasingly became a matter not of divine law and moral obligation but of human law, ecclesiastical discipline and finance, and even of private-property relationships. In the early years of the century Paschal II formulated for the first time a reasonable doctrine, which was later endorsed by Gratian, for excusing monks from the payment of tithes. And Innocent II first applied this policy on a large scale for the benefit not only of individual monasteries but also of entire congregations. More bishops exercised their control over the distribution of tithes in favour of monasteries, and under ecclesiastical pressure more laymen gave monks the tithes from their own lands. By the middle of the

---

[1] The most important work on this subject is Schreiber, *Kurie*, of which the third section (1, 246–94) is concerned with monastic tithes. It contains a wealth of valuable detail, but in judging its conclusions the reader should bear in mind its chronological limits and the author's adherence to several points of view not now universally accepted, such as the alliance between the reformed papacy and monasticism, the unity and continuity of the policy of the reformed papacy, and the contrast between Roman and Germanic institutions in the medieval Church. There is nothing very useful on tithes in the series of Greifswald dissertations on the monastic policies of the reformed popes written between 1910 and 1913 under the direction of Ernst Bernheim by Carl Korbe, Gregor Ender, Paul Adamczyk, and Wilhelm Reichert, but I have been unable to find G. Wieczorek, *Das Verhältnis des Papstes Innocents II. zu den Klöstern*, which is cited in the *Dict. d'hist.* xii, 905.

[2] Brackmann, in the *Göttingische gelehrte Anzeigen*, CLXXV, 277.

century these developments had created a severe economic situation, in addition to theoretical and political problems, and the final section of this chapter will examine the solution of these difficulties by Hadrian IV and Alexander III.

In this period as previously, much less is known about the payment than about the possession of tithes, since chartularies were by their nature more concerned with assets than with obligations. But there is evidence that throughout the twelfth century monks had to pay tithes in some form or another unless they had been explicitly freed or given the tithes in question. 'The abbeys were legally subject to this impost', wrote Viard. 'Otherwise the exemption from tithes granted to monasteries would have had no raison d'être.'[1] The numerous grants to monks of their own tithes also prove that in the absence of such grants the monks were expected to pay the tithes. Several spokesmen for both the old and the new monks in the twelfth century fully recognized this obligation. In his defence of monastic possession of tithes, for instance, Hugh of Amiens asserted that anchorites who observed no rule must pay tithes and oblations.[2] Gerhoh of Reichersberg, who on the whole opposed monastic possession of tithes, said that the diocesan bishop had a right to the tithes from a monastery's dependants and that even the pope could not free monks from this obligation. He also said that 'lay and illiterate monks who need clerical ministry' should pay tithes from their own labour, but he apparently regarded ordained monks who performed their own services as entitled to keep their own tithes, like other clerics.[3]

The sermons of Caesar of Arles, some of which were attributed to St Augustine, helped to spread the doctrine of the universality of tithing in monastic circles in the twelfth century.[4] They influenced among others St Stephen of Muret, who pleaded eloquently that tithes should be paid to God who gave to man the land, the seed and animals, the strength of his arm, the sun and rain, and the wind to blow away the chaff, and yet who asks not for nine-

[1] Viard, Dîme, I, 163 (cf. 106 n. 6).
[2] See p. 173 above and the passage by Peter the Venerable cited p. 16 above.
[3] See p. 163 above.   [4] See pp. 13, 17, and 18 above.

tenths but only for a tithe.[1] Geoffrey of Auxerre spoke in similar
terms, urging all men to pay tithes to the Giver of all things, in a
sermon on the anniversary of the death of St Bernard.[2] These
works were both addressed to monks and show that they were
definitely regarded as subject to the universal burden of tithes.

The actual obligation to pay tithes to other men naturally
rested more heavily on old and rich abbeys which owned extensive
lands not worked by their own monks and from which the tithes
belonged to some other institution or individual, either clerical
or lay. The annual sum of tithes paid by the monks of St Denis,
according to Lebel, was five times as great as they received
from their own lands.[3] And Peter the Venerable in his letter to
Pope Innocent II protesting against the refusal of the Cistercians
to pay tithes explained that in spite of their privilege to keep the
tithes from their own parishes and demesne lands the monks of
Cluny 'humbly and modestly paid tithes from both their peasants
and their serfs not only to monks and canons but also to all
kinds of clergy, priests, soldiers, and robbers'.[4] Specific references
to such payments can be found in the charters of several monasteries. In the sixth case cited in the appendix, the abbey of Our
Lady at Magdeburg was forced to pay tithes from its lands at Mose
to the vassals of Albert the Bear of Saxony, whose rights the
monks finally bought off in 1145. In the eighth case, the tithes
from various lands belonging to Leno at the end of the twelfth
century were held by laymen. Archbishop Theobald of Canterbury settled an interesting case in which two-thirds of the demesne
tithes of Walsingham were ceded by a priest to the monks of
Stoke-by-Clare, who then granted them to the prior of Walsingham in return for an annual rent.[5]

Not infrequently monks paid tithes to other monks and to

---

[1] Stephen of Muret, *Liber sententiarum*, CXXII, in *PL*, CCIV, 1135–6. Cf. the
remarkably similar passages in Caesar of Arles, serm. XXXIII, 2 and XXXIV, 3,
in *CC*, CIII, 145 and 148.
[2] Bernard, *Opera*, II(6), 2548–9.
[3] Lebel, *St Denis*, p. 158.
[4] Peter the Venerable, ep. I, 33, in *Bibl. Clun.* p. 700; cf. *Rev. bén.* LXX,
609–617.
[5] Saltman, *Theobald*, pp. 498–9 (1154/70); cf. p. 127 n. 2 above.

canons. The monks of Tiron (whose founder Bernard was more than once driven from his hermitage by the demands of nearby monks for tithes) agreed in about 1130 to pay to the monks of St Peter at Chartres all the tithes except the small tithes from their own animals, but including the tithes from animals belonging to their dependants, on the lands they held from St Peter's at Bois-Ruffin.[1] The Cluniacs at La Charité-sur-Loire agreed in about 1139 to pay to the Augustinian canons of St Satur 'like other parishioners, the tithes of the vineyards which the monks held in the parishes of the canons...and part of which [tithe] the monks had been accustomed to keep'.[2] In about 1142 the monks of Dunfermline gave up the tithes from some lands belonging to the canons of Stirling in return for some other tithes given them by the king of Scotland.[3] Of these tithes paid by monks, probably the most important part was that owed to the bishop, whose rights were repeatedly confirmed by the papacy in the twelfth century and who was entitled to a quarter or a third, and occasionally to more, of the tithes even in parishes belonging to a monastery.[4]

Indirect evidence for the payment of tithes by monks is also furnished by the grants to monasteries of fractions of their own tithes, of which they were still expected to pay the remainder,[5] and by occasional charters specifically excluding tithes from grants to monasteries. Examples of such withholding of tithes, either permanently or for the lifetime of the donor, are found in the eleventh and twelfth centuries among the charters of Aniane, Gellone, St Victor at Marseille, Vigeois, Jumièges, Cluny, and

---

[1] *Tiron*, I, 156; on Bernard of Tiron's difficulties, see pp. 142–3 above.

[2] *La Charité-sur-Loire*, p. 183; cf. the later agreements by which Cistercian monks promised to pay tithes to La Charité, cited in the *Rev. bén.* LXX, 608 n. 1, and p. 289 n. 3 below.

[3] Lawrie, *Scottish Charters*, p. 110, no. 143 (cf. p. 378).

[4] See case VII in appendix and the bull of Eugene III cited p. 184 n. 2 above. Two grants to the bishop of Grenoble in 1080/1132 and in 1092 included tithes 'supra monasterium sancti Laurentii': *Grenoble*, pp. 113–14, nos. B 38–9; cf. p. 133 above, where the bishop of Grenoble also collected tithes from the *mansus presbiteralis* of the parish priest. The prior of La Charité-sur-Loire wrote in a letter to Abbot Suger of St Denis that the bishop of Auxerre took his dues 'et in decimis et in ecclesiis' from the lands of La Charité: *Thesaurus*, I, 420–1.

[5] See pp. 248 ff. below.

St Jean d'Angély.[1] In Poitou it seems almost to have been the custom for donors to exclude tithes from grants to monasteries. Some allods given to St Cyprien in 1090, for instance, were described as free of all debts to any lord 'except for the tithe'.[2] In 1094 the abbey of St Maxentius was given a church by the bishop of Poitiers and bought from some laymen the land belonging to the church, a small fief, and a house near the church, which were described as 'free from all service to them, except that as in other parishes the soldiers kept for themselves the tithes of the men's animals'.[3] In 1111 a layman returned a salt-pan to the abbot of St Maxentius but kept the tithe for himself 'just as I have done in others'.[4] The reason usually given for withholding the tithe, as in some of these examples, was that it belonged to a powerful church or layman who refused to give it up or that the donor held it as a fief. Cluny was thus given a church with all its property 'except the tithe, which the soldiers have up to now held in their power'.[5] The abbey of St Martin at Cologne owned the tithes from a certain vineyard belonging to the canons of Rolduc, who held most of their lands 'with the right of tithes'.[6] In 1139 a family gave an allod to Bobbio 'except for the allod's tithe, which we hold as a fief and which we cannot give'.[7] In such cases, of course, the monks were often able to gain possession of the withheld tithes at a later date;[8] but in the meantime they had to

[1] *Aniane*, pp. 354 (1026: life interest), 263 (1100), and 422 (1117); *Gellone*, pp. 70 (1051/74), 364 (1081), 323 (1097), 152 (1101), 153 (1110) (cf. p. 105 above); *St Victor de Marseille*, II, 62 (1069); *Vigeois*, p. 42 (1092/1110); *Jumièges*, I, 127–8 (eleventh century); *Cluny*, V, 332–7, nos. 3974–6 (cf. p. 133 n. 2 above); *St Jean d'Angély*, I, 374, no. 308 (cited by Bruhat, *Monachisme*, p. 212).

[2] *St Cyprien*, p. 232, no. 377.

[3] *St Maixent*, I, 215, no. 182: the charter specified that the church was not invested with the land belonging to it.

[4] *St Maixent*, I, 272, no. 245.

[5] *Cluny*, IV, 218, no. 3025 (1049/1109).

[6] *Annales Rodenses*, s.a. 1118, in MGH, SS, XVI, 699; cf. Dereine, *Chanoines*, pp. 169 ff. on Rolduc.

[7] *Bobbio*, II, 25.

[8] Abingdon thus acquired in 1110/35 part of the tithes of Nuneham which had previously been withheld, and they were paid to the almoner: *Abingdon*, II, 52–3.

pay tithes even if the land in question formed part of their demesne.

Even those houses which were not required to pay any tithes outside their walls might still use the tithes from their demesne lands, whether they were worked by the monks or by lay dependants, and from other revenues for charitable uses, especially for the gate and guest-house.[1] The customs of William of Volpiano for Fruttuaria and for St Benignus at Dijon show that the tithes of certain revenues were given to the almoner, presumably for distribution to the poor, but that 'Nothing from that which the chamberlain receives from the cultivation, rent, and revenue of the abbey's land and property is customarily tithed as alms for the poor'.[2] The tithes from many of the estates belonging to Corbie were given to the hospitaller, infirmarian, and almoner of the abbey.[3] Abingdon in the twelfth century used various tithes from its own lands for the poor and for sick monks.[4] The abbey of St Mary at Josaphat in the Holy Land devoted the tithes from all its goods to the hospice for pilgrims and the poor.[5] The nuns of Eschau used 'the tithes of all their profits and payments coming to their cell' for a guest-house 'on the Roman road'.[6] And late

[1] Cf. pp. 201–6 above. Even when tithes had been incorporated into a *mensa*, they might be assigned to the almoner or hospitaller for charitable uses so long as they were paid separately by the workers on the monastic lands.

[2] Bruno Albers, *Consuetudines monasticae*, IV: *Consuetudines Fructuariensis* (Monte Cassino, 1911), p. 143, nos. II, 8 and 11; cf. Bruno Albers, *Untersuchungen zu den ältesten Mönchsgewohnheiten*, Veröffentlichungen aus dem kirchenhistorischen Seminar München, II, 8 (Munich, 1905), pp. 71–85, and, on the influence of these customs, Kassius Hallinger, *Gorze-Kluny*, Studia Anselmiana, XXII–XXV (Rome, 1950–1), index, s.v. 'Consuetudines von Fruttuaria'. Fruttuaria had been freed by the papacy in 1006 from paying demesne tithes to anyone else.

[3] Dubar, *Corbie*, pp. 41–3; cf. *APRI*, I, 181 (JL 8799) in which Eugene III confirmed for St Michael at Verdun in 1145 the possession of various churches and lands with their tithes and 'the tithes which the almoner possesses for the use of the poor'.

[4] *Abingdon*, II, 33 (1087/1100), 52–3 (see p. 224 n. 8 above), 146 and 169.

[5] *Josaphat*, p. 48, no. 19 (1130/45); Reinhold Röhricht, *Regesta regni Hierosolymitani* (Innsbruck, 1893), no. 135.

[6] Würdtwein, *Nova subsidia*, VII, 128–9, no. 49; also in *GC*, V, instr. 482; Paul Wentzcke, *Regesten der Bischöfe von Strassburg bis zum Jahre 1202* (Innsbruck, 1908), no. 500 (confirmation by the bishop of Strasbourg in 1143).

in the century the abbot of Glastonbury gave 'the tithes of our demesne at Sturminster Newton and Marnhull for providing our monastery with bread, wine, and fish, and the remainder as alms for the poor each year on the day of our anniversary'.[1]

The law of tithing was also respected by the new orders of monks and canons, many of whom tithed their revenues for the benefit of charity even though they owned little property, worked new lands, refused to possess the tithes of other men, and sought by owning their own tithes to pay no tithes to other men themselves. The founders of Afflighem, for instance, settled in 'a wooded and uncultivated wilderness' and resolved to support themselves entirely by the labour of their own hands.[2] They laid down in the *Statute on Tithes*, which was drawn up towards the end of the eleventh century perhaps as a protest against the growing property and worldliness of the monks, that 'Since the land and its produce belong to the Lord, who gives seed to the sower and bread to the eater, we decided of our own will that we would give a tenth of all our crops and possessions for the use of his poor'. The almoner therefore received tithes, according to the *Statute*, from all the monks' animals, grain, and agricultural produce, including the hay from fields both belonging to the monks and held by them as security, from all money, oblations, gifts of precious metals, and gifts for building, 'since the support of his building is more pleasing to God than the raising of walls', and from any possessions brought by a new monk, sent by a dependency, or found on the abbey's lands, unless it was known to belong to the monks already. Even the bread bought with money that had been tithed should be tithed again, since the almoner was instructed to receive all comers. The only explicit exceptions to

---

[1] *Glastonbury*, III, 706, no. 1308 (cf. introd. pp. ccxxxvi–ccxxxviii; *c.* 1180).
[2] Afflighem was founded in 1083, and it was noted during its early years for its fervour. The monks later adopted the customs of Cluny, received from Anchin, and their accumulation of wealth led to some internal dissension in the community: cf. *Chronicon Affligemense*, in MGH, *SS*, IX, 407–10; Berlière, in *Dict. d'hist.* I, 672; De Moreau, *Église en Belgique*, II, 427–30; and Dereine, *Chanoines*, pp. 120–1, 136, 240, and esp. *Rev. d'hist. ecc.* LIV, 41–65, who defended 1083 as the foundation date (p. 46 n. 2) and doubted whether the original customs were Cluniac, as suggested by Sabbe (pp. 48–9).

this rule were hay that had been bought, a few clothes belonging to a new monk, wax, and ornaments and utensils for divine services, including those of precious metals. By these comprehensive regulations the monks sought to banish envy and strife from their abbey.[1] The rule of Grandmont, whose founder St Stephen so earnestly urged the payment of tithes and warned against worldly possessions, decreed that the tithes from the monks' own labour, after being respectfully requested from the bishop, priest, or other owner, should be given to the poor.[2] The Templars were also instructed to give a tithe of all their bread daily to their almoner for distribution to the poor.[3]

The regular canons likewise tithed their income even when they paid no tithes to other men. The chronicler of the Augustinian house of Rolduc described under the year 1122 how the guesthouse received 'the tithes of all things: of the rents, the wine, and the crops, except for the food of the horses and the seed of the field and anything spent to buy an allod. And anything given as alms in this place is tithed for the house of the poor'.[4] Arno of Reichersberg in his *Scutum canonicorum* also praised the canons because they fed guests and the poor 'from the tithes of the monastery's provisions and from the leavings of the brethren'.[5]

While they satisfied the moral obligation of tithing by thus devoting a tenth of their income to charities within their walls, many of the reformers in the twelfth century sought to avoid the legal necessity of paying tithes by obtaining grants of the tithes from their own lands from the previous owners and privileges permitting them to keep their own tithes, prohibiting others to

[1] H.-P. Vanderspeeten, 'Monachorum Afflighemiensium et imprimis B. Fulgentii primi coenobii abbatis statutum de decimis rerum omnium in eleemosynas expendendis', *Analecta Bollandiana*, IV (1885), 253–5, and *Afflighem*, pp. 8–11; cf. Dereine, in *Rev. d'hist. ecc.* LIV, 53.
[2] See pp. 140–1 above.
[3] Schnürer, *Templerregel*, p. 138, cap. XV. The editor attributed this statute to the version of the rule drawn up in 1130, rather than that of 1128, because it was incompatible with the principles of St Bernard, who attended the council of Troyes which approved the earlier version. Cf. De Curzon, *Règle*, p. 38, cap. XXIX.
[4] *Annales Rodenses*, in MGH, SS, XVI, 702; cf. Dereine, *Chanoines*, pp. 195–6.
[5] *PL*, CXCIV, 1513.

collect tithes from their lands, or even formally freeing them from tithes. Arrangements of this sort first became a matter of papal policy during the pontificate of Paschal II, who alone granted, although the total number was still far from large, more privileges concerning monastic payment of tithes than all his predecessors put together. Over a period of twelve or thirteen years, beginning in 1102, Paschal granted new privileges to the monks of San Salvatore Maggiore at Pavia, San Salvatore in Settimo, St Walburg, Cheminon, Polirone, San Salvatore in Moxi, Chaumouzey (twice), St Mary at Florence, St Peter at Luco, Dietramszell near Freising, Lambach, St Mary of Josaphat, the hospital of St John at Jerusalem, Baumburg, St Vanne at Verdun, and Montmajour, and a confirmation for Cluny.[1] The formulas relating to tithes in these bulls were not fixed, though they incorporated elements from earlier tithe-privileges. Those for the Saviour at Pavia, Cheminon, Chaumouzey, Lambach, St Mary of Josaphat, and Montmajour explicitly forbade the exaction of tithes either from the revenues of the abbey or from the goods produced by the monks or for their use or, in the case of Lambach alone, from the noval lands cultivated by or for the monks themselves. The other privileges authorized the monks to keep their own tithes or, at Dietramszell and Baumburg, their noval tithes, and of these four specified that the tithes should be used for the hospice (St Walburg and Jerusalem) or for pilgrims and the poor (the Saviour at Settimo and Cluny, which had already received the right to use its demesne tithes for its hospice from John XI and Louis IV in the tenth century). There also was no consistency in the houses to which the privileges were granted: some were rich, others were poor; some were old, others were new; some were

[1] JL 5853 (dated 1100; *IP*, VI. 1, 205, no. 4), 5895 (*IP*, III, 54, no. 5), 5916, 5921, 6012 (*IP*, VII. 1, 332–3, no. 16), 6091 (*IP*, III, 378, no. 1), 6125 and 6229 (both for Chaumouzey: see pp. 231–2 below), 6170 (*IP*, III, 28, no. 3), 6171 (*IP*, III, 69, no. 1), 6179, 6231, 6336, 6341 (*Hospitaliers*, I, 29, no. 30), 6434 (*GP*, I, 76, no. 1), 6393 (see p. 231 below), 6443 (see pp. 229–30 below), and 6046 (*Cluny*, V, 195; no. 3836; see p. 231 below). In 1113 Paschal granted to the abbey of St Nicasius at Rheims 'the entire tithe of the food from the manor (*curtis*) of the monks', together with three parts of the tithe of a certain church: *Reims*, I. 1, 262 (JL 6347); and this may have had the same intention as the other tithe-privileges.

famous, others were obscure. San Salvatore in Moxi was so obscure that Paschal's bull is the only evidence that it existed at this date.[1] Cheminon, Chaumouzey, and Baumburg were houses of regular canons. The others were mostly Benedictine houses, both independent abbeys and members of reformed congregations, though there is no evidence that the privileges ever applied to more than the individual houses to which they were granted.[2] They were also widely scattered geographically, but it may be significant that the three grants which applied only to noval tithes were to houses east of the Rhine, where episcopal control over tithes was probably stronger than elsewhere.

Paschal justified his new practice in two important statements, one from an unidentified letter and the other in his privilege for Montmajeur, which became part of canon law as the decretals *Novum genus* and *Decimas a populo*. In the former he wrote that 'It is a new form of exaction for clerics to exact from clerics the tithes of crops and animals. We have never read in divine law that this was ordered or allowed. For the Levites are not said to have received or exacted tithes from the Levites. Assuredly [only] those clerics who receive the labours of spiritual ministry from clerics owe tithes to them.'[3] In the privilege for Montmajour he said that:

The authority of divine law ordained that tithes must be paid by the people to the priests and Levites. But no reason allows that soldiers, bishops, or any person should receive tithes from the labour and food of monks or of clerics leading a common life. Therefore by the present decree we forbid any soldiers, bishops, or other persons to extort or exact from you [the tithes] of your labour or animals and from any monks or clerics leading a common life the tithes of their own labour

---

[1] *IP*, III, 377–8.

[2] Schreiber, *Kurie*, I, 252, claimed that the grant to St Peter in Luco covered the entire order of Camaldoli, but Paschal's later privilege for Camaldoli itself (JL 6357) included no such grant. The privilege for the knights of St John, allowing them to keep for their hospice the tithes from produce gathered in any place for their own use and by their labour, also seems to have applied only to their house in Jerusalem (*Hospitaliers*, I, 29, no. 30).

[3] *PL*, CLXIII, 437; JL 6605, which refers to the many canonical collections including this canon. Cf. Viard, *Dîme*, II, 39–41, on its later use.

and food. For when the blessed Gregory spoke about dividing the fruits of the tithes in his instructions to Augustine bishop of Canterbury, he said 'But why need we talk about the making of portions or the showing of hospitality or fulfilling of mercy to those who live a common life, since any surplus should be used for pious and religious causes, as the Lord [and] Master of all things teaches, "That which remaineth, give alms; and all other things are clean unto you".'[1]

Paschal discussed the argument of *Novum genus* at greater length in a letter written about 1109/10 to the bishop of Noyon–Tournai complaining that the clerics of Tournai had oppressed the monks of St Martin by exacting tithes and forbidding burials and that both the bishop himself and the bishops of Arras and Thérouanne, to whom the dispute had been referred, had failed to do justice. Paschal took the case into his own hands and decided in favour of the monks. He supported this decision with a brief reference to Gregory's letter to Augustine of Canterbury and principally with two passages by Leo IV. The first, in which Leo ordered laymen to pay tithes, first-fruits, and oblations to the churches of God, was used to prove 'that tithes are ordered to be paid not by monks but by laymen, for since many monks either are Levites or priests or enjoy other ecclesiastical orders and by God's grace serve in the sacred ministry, they should be considered immune (*immunes*) from exactions of this sort'. The second passage was taken from Leo's letter to the bishops of Brittany and was used by Paschal to show that 'tithes should be paid by the people for the sake of baptism, the eucharist, penance, and other offices performed by priests, in all of which no service is done by clerics in the convents of monks'.[2] The point that monks as priests should not be forced to pay tithes had already been made

---

[1] *EPRI*, p. 75, no. 152, and, with minor differences, *Decretum*, C. XVI, q. I, c. 47. Gregory's letter (JE 1843) is in Bede, *Hist. ecc.* I, 27, *ed. cit.* I, 49. In the bull for Montmajour (not in the *Decretum*), the citation from Luke xi. 41 has 'cetera' in place of 'ecce'.

[2] *APRI*, I, 101–2; JL 6254. To support the permission of monks to bury, Paschal cited other texts. On Leo's letter to the bishops of Brittany, see p. 36 n. 5 above and *Decretum*, C. XVI, q. I, c. 45. Friedberg in his edition of the *Decretum* (pp. 773–4, n. 400) apparently missed the quotation of this canon in Paschal's letter.

in the privilege for Gigny in 894 and depended historically on the steadily increasing numbers of ordained monks.[1] Paschal may not have been aware that at the time Leo was writing in the middle of the ninth century the number of ordained monks was comparatively small, but he evidently realized that in his own day most monasteries did not need clerical services from priests outside their walls, though in *Novum genus* he carefully stipulated that any clerics who used the spiritual services of other clerics must pay tithes.[2]

The reason given in *Decimas a populo* was probably originated by Paschal, who seems to have been the first person to use Gregory the Great's letter to Augustine of Canterbury as evidence that those who lead a common life and devote all they can spare to charity need not pay tithes. This idea was based on the early theory that tithes should be used exclusively in charitable works and was related to the argument used by the defenders of monastic possession of tithes, that monks were the true poor, the *pauperes Christi*, and were entitled to receive tithes.[3] In his confirmation for Cluny in 1105 Paschal justified the possession by the monks of their demesne tithes on the grounds that they used 'not only parts of the tithes but almost everything that can be spared for pilgrims, brothers and the poor', where the wording clearly derived from Gregory's letter and the Bible.[4] In his privilege for St Vanne in 1114 he said that 'Neither does reason approve nor does the authority of the holy canons allow that tithes or first-fruits should be exacted from those who distribute everything they have in pious works'.[5]

In the *Primordia Calmosiacensia* Abbot Seher of Chaumouzey gave an interesting account of the circumstances leading up to the

---

[1] Cf. pp. 145–7 and 213 above.

[2] In his letter in 1113 to the bishop of Arras, he insisted that 'those parishioners who receive baptism, instruction, and burial from the mother [parish] church' must pay first-fruits, tithes, oblations, and other parochial dues, 'For it is fitting that material things should be reaped from those in whom spiritual things are sown': *PL*, CLXIII, 333–4; JL 6360.

[3] Cf. p. 170 n. 1 above. Ivo of Chartres applied this idea to monastic possession of tithes at almost exactly the same time.

[4] *Bull. Clun.* p. 211.   [5] *APRI*, I, 108.

privilege for his abbey, which was the result of the claim of the canonesses of Remiremont to tithes and parochial rights on the lands of the canons, who brought the case before Paschal and a council of cardinals at Langres in 1107. The pope at once ordered 'the decree of Gregory the Great clearly forbidding the exaction of tithes from those who lead a common life' to be read aloud in the council, and after the cardinals had declared in favour of the canons, he issued the bull, which he repeated in 1109, recording that 'it is added to the same judgement and established by the decree of St Gregory that they should not be required to pay tithes or first-fruits from their plough-lands, labour, or food either to that parish church or to any others'.[1]

These texts supplied the theory upon which the entire policy of freeing monks from tithes was later based. Gratian in particular relied heavily on *Decimas a populo*,[2] and *Novum genus* was the only canon used by Thomas Aquinas in the *Summa theologica* to support his point that clerics who performed pastoral work need not pay tithes from ecclesiastical property.[3] In the long run, indeed, these texts were probably more important than Paschal's application of the new policy. The relatively small number of his grants and his stipulation that clerics who required the *cura animarum* from outside must pay tithes show that he had no idea of freeing all monks from tithes. His references to the charitable work of those leading a common life and to the use of monastic tithes for hospices and the poor show that he expected even monks who owned their own tithes to devote as much as they could to charity. There is no evidence to support Schreiber's view that Paschal had grandiose plans to exalt the power of the papacy and to reward the monastic supporters of reform by freeing monks

---

[1] Seher of Chaumouzey, *Primordia Calmosiacensia*, in MGH, *SS*, XII, 338–9, and in *Documents rares ou inédits de l'histoire des Vosges*, ed. L. Duhamel (Paris–Épinal, 1868–82), II, 38–40. On the eremitical origins of Chaumouzey and its subsequent organization into a house of regular canons (in 1094), see Dereine, in *Dict. d'hist.* X, 597–8, and 'Saint-Ruf et ses coutumes aux XIe et XIIe siècles', *Rev. bén.* LIX (1949), 161–82. The original of Paschal's bull is in the Bibliothèque nationale at Paris, according to Dereine, and has *nutrimentis* (food) in place of *jumentis* (animals), which is found in PL, CLXIII, 206.

[2] See pp. 265–6 below.

[3] *Summa theologica*, II. 2, q. LXXXVII.

from tithes or that 'The legislative will of the curia insisted that all monasteries and orders be drawn into freedom from tithes'.[1] On the contrary, it is reasonable to accept from the evidence of his actions that his own stated motives were sincere and that in view of his known sympathy for monasticism and his devotion to the ideals of poverty and charity he genuinely wished to free from the burden of paying tithes those monks who owned no private property, gave all they could spare in charity, and who ministered to their own spiritual needs.[2] Poor monks who supported themselves by their own work had long been regarded as suitable recipients of charity,[3] and in the early twelfth century the idea was widespread in monastic circles that monks were by their nature the truest poor and the most suitable objects of charity. The fact that Paschal did not apply the policy more widely may be attributed to its novelty, to the difficulties of his position, and partly perhaps to a cautious desire to grant freedom from tithes only to monks who really deserved it.[4]

---

[1] Schreiber, *Kurie*, I, 250 and 252.

[2] On monastic influence in the curia under Paschal II, see H.-W. Klewitz, 'Die Entstehung des Kardinalkollegiums', *Sav. Zs.* Kan. Abt. xxv (1936), 115–221, reprinted in *Reformpapsttum und Kardinalkolleg* (Darmstadt, 1957), pp. 11–134, esp. 98–111, who worked out that of the cardinals whose backgrounds are known just a third were monks. The most celebrated example of Paschal's unworldliness (or impracticality, depending on the point of view) was his proposal in 1111 that the church should give up its feudal holdings and live off its 'hereditary possessions' and off tithes and oblations: MGH, *Const.* I, 141, no. 90 (JL 6289) and p. 150, no. 100; cf. Z. N. Brooke, in *Camb. Med. Hist.* v, 102. This proposal may have derived from the desire of the monastic reformers to separate the finances of the three orders of society. Hayden V. White, 'Pontius of Cluny, the *Curia Romana*, and the End of Gregorianism in Rome', *Church History*, xxvii (1958), 215 n. 24, said that in his so-called *Tractatus*, 'Paschal presents poverty as the rule of the Church in all its orders, enjoins the hierarchy to live the "apostolic life", and admonishes the priest to seek for himself nothing more than food and clothing, the necessities of life'. Partly on this account, White regarded Paschal as 'a deviation from the type of pope which the Gregorians had traditionally considered necessary to the proper implementation of the Gregorian program' (p. 198).

[3] See, for instance, the Life of Leofgyth (Leoba), abbess of Tauberbischofsheim, by Rudolf of Fulda, c. 17, in MGH, *SS*, xv. 1, 129, for the dispositions of Boniface for Fulda; cf. Levison, *England*, p. 76 n. 2.

[4] The fact that the three grants in Germany were limited to noval tithes suggests that Paschal was aware of the possible repercussions of his policy.

Paschal's immediate successors were in many ways men of a different stamp. While they continued his policy of occasionally freeing monks from tithes, they did not advance it in any significant way apart from defining more clearly its practical effects. Gelasius II gave the tithes of its own lands to the abbey of St Mamiliano on the island of Montecristo in 1118.[1] Calixtus II confirmed Paschal's privileges for Cluny, the Saviour at Pavia, Turrita, St Walburg, the Saviour at Settimo, the hospital of St John at Jerusalem, and Polirone, and he granted new privileges to Marbach, Springiersbach, Hugshofen (Honcourt), and Balerne.[2] His successor Honorius II issued confirmations for St Walburg and Baumburg and new grants to St Mary at Brisach, Fontevrault, St Mary at Luxemburg, St Peter in the Black Forest, and Prüfening.[3] For over a dozen years, therefore, the average of new grants was less than one a year. As before, they show no uniformity in the wording of the formula, nor in the type or location of the houses to which they were granted, except that they were relatively recent foundations. The privileges for St Peter in the Black Forest and the three Augustinian houses of Marbach, Springiersbach and Brisach used substantially similar terms, granting possession of the tithes from their own produce and animals 'which are cultivated or raised for your use or by your labour on all your possessions' and forbidding the diocesan bishop or anyone else to disturb them on this account. The privileges for Hugshofen,

---

[1] JL 6654. St Mamiliano was the only ancient foundation to receive a new grant in this period.

[2] Ulysse Robert, *Bullaire du pape Calixte II* (Paris, 1891), I, 210 (JL 6821; *Cluny*, v, 299, no. 3945), 247 (JL 6842; *IP*, VI. 1, 206, no. 8), 287 (JL 6869; cf. Urban's grant to St Bruno, cited p. 216 above, which was now expanded to include 'the tithes from the labour of yourselves and your villeins' in place of 'your monks'), 318 (JL 6891), and II, 31 (JL 6967; *IP*, III, 54, no. 6), 89 (JL 7005; *Hospitaliers*, I, 61, no. 68), and 326 (JL 7157; *IP*, VII. 1, 334, no. 21). For the new grants, *ibid.* I, 119 (JL 6763; *GP*, II. 2, 288, no. 3), 142 (JL 6778), and II, 283 (JL 7130) and 347 (JL 7170).

[3] JL 7212 and 7397, and, for the new grants, 7218, 7270, 7302 (*Altluxemburg*, I, 538), 7385 (*GP*, II. 1, 190, no. 2, in which the tithe-privilege is incomplete but can be reconstructed by comparison with similar grants), and 7395 (*GP*, I, 296, no. 2). The grant for Aniane (JL 7330) should probably be attributed to Hadrian IV rather than to Honorius II (see p. 282 below).

Balerne, Fontevrault, St Mary at Luxemburg, and Prüfening
simply specified that the monks should not be forced to pay tithes
from their demesne lands. Calixtus II mentioned the letter of
Gregory the Great in his bulls for Springiersbach and Hugshofen,
and Honorius II said in the bull for St Mary at Luxemburg that
'the tithe should for ever be devoted to the uses of the monks
serving God in that place'.[1]

Owing to their novelty and the vagueness of their wording, the
practical application of these grants was not always clear, and the
two series of charters and confirmations for St Walburg and
Polirone help to explain the real meaning of the privilege. The
original grant for the monks of St Walburg in 1102 permitted the
monks simply to keep the tithes of their crops and animals for
their guest-house, and this was confirmed by Calixtus II in 1121.
Honorius II in 1125, however, specified that 'in accordance with
the decision of our predecessor Pope Calixtus, you should have
the tithes of your animals [and] crops which you gather by your
labour and for your use throughout the land of the Holy Forest
[of Haguenau], [without] any opposition from the monks of
Seltz or other men; but your peasants (*rustici*) should pay their
tithes to the priests of their parish'.[2] In the charters for Polirone
the original grant of 'the tithes of your demesne lands' in 1105
was extended by Calixtus II to 'the tithes of your crops which you
cultivate in any place and for your use'. This was confirmed by
Innocent II and Eugene III as 'the tithes of your produce which
you cultivate for your own use'.[3] In his confirmation for Cluny,
furthermore, Paschal II carefully defined 'the tithes of your
produce...which they call demesne [tithes and] which are

---

[1] *Altluxemburg*, I, 538.

[2] *PL*, CLXIII, 98; *Bull. de Calixte II*, I, 318; and *PL*, CLXVI, 1236. In 1139
Innocent II confirmed this privilege in almost the same form as Honorius II:
'You should have in peace the tithes of your crops and animals, which you
cultivate or gather by your own labour or for your own use throughout the
land of the Holy Forest and in other places, without opposition of the bishops or
their officials or of the monks of Seltz or other men; but your peasants should
freely pay their tithes to the priests in whose parishes they are': *PL*, CLXXIX,
416–17; JL 7965.

[3] *APRI*, II, 185; *Bull. de Calixte II*, II, 326; *APRI*, II, 268 (JL 7574); *APRI*,
III, 106 (JL 9488); on the entire series, see *IP*, VII. 1, 332–5.

cultivated for your use by the dependants (*clientes*) of your monastery and cells'.[1] Paschal and Calixtus specified the produce and food in their grants to Balerne and Chaumouzey, and Honorius included the gardens and the orchards in his grant to Prüfening. From this evidence it is clear that the grant applied exclusively to the monastic demesne, that is, as it was later defined by Richard fitz Nigel, 'those [lands] which are cultivated for the use or by the labour of the owner',[2] and did not apply to land tilled by tenants on their own account and still less to monastic lands granted as benefices, from which tithes had to be paid as usual to the parish priest.

The term *labor* in the privilege referred not only to work but to 'the produce from work' and even to the land itself;[3] and the term *sumptus* meant 'use' or 'consumption', as its occasional replacement *nutrimen* shows, rather than 'expense' or 'under the immediate direction', as some authors have suggested.[4] Perhaps the most confusing terms were *decimas animalium*, which were mentioned in several grants by Calixtus II and Honorius II,[5] and the later *decimas de nutrimentis animalium*. Schreiber argued that the second term referred literally only to the food of the animals, whereas Viard claimed that 'The true meaning of *nutrimen animalium* is not "food of animals" but "animals"'.[6] It may also have been intended to extend the application of the privilege to the food produced for the monastic animals as well as for the monks themselves. Be this as it may, the terms of the privilege

---

[1] *Bull. Clun.* p. 211; cf. *Bull. de Calixte II*, I, 210.

[2] Richard fitz Nigel, *Dialogus de Scaccario*, XI, ed. and tr. Charles Johnson, Nelson's Medieval Texts (London–Edinburgh, 1950), p. 56: 'Noueris autem dominia cuiuslibet hec dici que propriis sumptibus uel laboribus excoluntur....' The similarity of the terms used here and in the papal bull for Cluny shows that *propriis sumptibus et laboribus* meant the same as *dominicaturus*.

[3] Cf. Gosso, *Vita economica*, pp. 204–5, who stressed that the bounds of *proprius labor* corresponded to the old Benedictine *dominium* and that *labor* was used as a synonym for agricultural produce and land; cf. also Imbert, *Hôpitaux*, p. 89.

[4] Such as Rose Graham, *S. Gilbert of Sempringham and the Gilbertines* (London, 1901), p. 112; Viard, *Dîme*, II, 42; *Dialogus de Scac.*, ed. cit. p. 56.

[5] Cf. the privileges for Marbach, Springiersbach, St Walburg, Brisach, and Fontevrault.

[6] Schreiber, *Kurie*, I, 291, and Viard, *Dîme*, II, 56 (cf. I, 102 and 152).

together clearly covered not only the agricultural produce on the monks' demesne but also the annual increase of their flocks and herds.

By the time Honorius II died, in 1130, therefore, the theory and the terms of the papal grants freeing monks from tithes were well established, but the total number of such privileges was still comparatively small. The figures given above are certainly far from complete, but it may be doubted whether more than fifty houses all over Europe enjoyed the formal right either of paying no tithes or of keeping the tithes from the monastic demesne. The first pope to distribute this privilege on a liberal scale was Innocent II, who reigned from 1130 to 1143 and who both perfected the formula for the grant and included it in at least a hundred charters for individual houses and several entire monastic orders.[1] It is naturally impossible to examine individually each of these privileges, but a brief survey of their dates and recipients may help to show the direction and significance of Innocent's policy.

Chronologically these charters fall into roughly three groups, dating respectively from June 1130 to July 1132, from the end of 1136 to the beginning of 1137, and from November 1138 until Innocent's death in 1143, with a few scattered grants in between. The first group included new privileges for Vallombrosa, Beaulieu near Roanne, Aniane, Beaulieu-sur-Aube, Bellevaux, Abelard's convent of the Paraclete near Troyes, Cîteaux, Clairvaux, Tiron, and Tiglieto and confirmations for St Vanne at Verdun, Beaulieu near Roanne, the Saviour at Pavia, and Polirone.[2] From the middle of 1132 until 1136 the rate seems to have slackened, but a few grants were made, including new privileges for Marturi at Poggibonsi in Tuscany (which may not be authentic)

---

[1] This figure is based principally on the charters printed in *PL, APRI, PU*, and a few chartularies and cannot be considered complete.

[2] JL 7414; *PU in Frankreich*, III, 22; JL 7432, 7448; *PU in Frankreich*, I, 30; JL 7513, 7537, 7544, 7557 and 7587, and (confirmations) JL 7504; *PU in Frankreich*, III, 24; JL 7570 and 7574. The bull attributed to Innocent II and dated 4 March 1130 in *St Maixent*, I, 315–16, no. 289, must be assigned to Innocent III on the basis of both content and style: see Léopold Delisle, *Mémoire sur les actes d'Innocent III*, offprint from *Bibliothèque de l'École des Chartes*, XVIII–XIX (Paris, 1857), p. 61.

and St Peter at Ghent and confirmations for the Saviour at Settimo and the hospital of St John at Jerusalem and also of an episcopal grant of noval tithes for Ilsenburg.[1] Towards the end of 1136, however, the number increased, and the second group included new grants to Acquanegra, La Colomba, and L'Aumône, confirmations for Prüfening and Fontevrault, and a revision of the privilege for the hospital of St John.[2] This small group was followed by a period of a year with no known grants, and the full flood of privileges began at the end of 1138, following Innocent's victory over his rival Anacletus II and the healing of the schism which had lasted eight years. Already in the last two months of 1138 Innocent issued new grants to St Zeno at Verona, Sept-Fontaines-en-Thiérache, Gottesgnaden, St Mary in Portu at Ravenna, and, on 21 December, to six individual Premonstratensian abbeys and to the entire order of Prémontré.[3] In 1139 he made new grants to Mallersdorf, Biburg, Heiligenkreuz, the Knights Templar, Lützel (Lucelle), Mehrerau (Bregenz), Vangadizza, Kastel, St Stephen at Dijon, Camp, Averbode, Pöhlde, Selbold, Ramsey, and Chiaravalle at Bagnolo and renewed the privileges for St Walburg, Baumburg, Prüfening, and Bellevaux.[4] In 1140 the abbeys of Salem, Bellefontaine in Franche-Comté, Altenberg, Zwettl, Miseray, Josaphat (twice), Bessa, Schäftlarn, and Himmerod received grants; and in 1141, Thame, Orval, Bithaine, St Pierremont, Yerres, Riéval, Wessobrunn, and Corneux received new grants and Ramsey a confirmation.[5] In 1142 the number increased and included new privileges for Mortemer-sur-Eaulne, Longpont, Berchtesgaden, Reichersberg, Münchs-

[1] JL 7628, 7700, 7637; *Hospitaliers*, I, 95–6, no. 113; and JL 7751 (cf. pp. 240 and 243 below).
[2] JL 7788, 7822, 7826, and (confirmations) 7792; *PU in Frankreich*, NF v, 116; JL 7823.
[3] JL 7911, 7912, 7921, 7922, 7924–7 and 7929–31.
[4] JL 7938, 7939; *Heiligenkreuz*, p. 4; *Ordre du Temple*, p. 377; JL 7953, 7966, 7967, 7975, 7988, 7997, 8000, 8010, 8014, 8016a, 8052; and (confirmations) JL 7965, 7969, 7972 (and again 8046); and *PU in Frankreich*, I, 31.
[5] JL 8073; *PU in Frankreich*, I, 39; JL 8078, 8079, 8088, 8095, 8096, 8105, 8110, 8112; *PU in England*, III, 158; JL 8134; *PU in Frankreich*, I, 41, and NF I, 223; JL 8139, 8143, 8160; *PU in Frankreich*, I, 43; and (confirmation) JL 8124a.

münster, Bobbio, Bellelay, Ebrach, Pforte, Grandselve, Stromberg, Arnstein, Varlar, Rott-am-Inn, Les Roches, and Pontigny and confirmations for Bellevaux (twice) and Beaulieu near Roanne.[1] In the last year of his pontificate Innocent gave new privileges to Neustift near Freising, Rheno, Seckau, and Mont-Cornillon at Liège and renewed the grants to Springiersbach and Balerne.[2] In addition he issued undated privileges for Bonne-Espérance and Old Wardon.[3]

This tedious list, which could doubtless be extended, gives some idea of the number, geographical range, and character of Innocent's grants of freedom from tithes. Most of the houses were poor and relatively new, and a privilege concerning payment of tithes was very rarely found in conjunction with the standard rights of monastic exemption regarding visitation, the election and apparel of the abbot, the blessing of holy oil, and the right of burial which appear in the privileges for many old and powerful houses.[4] Of the privileges listed above, twenty-six were for Cistercian, twenty-two for Premonstratensian, and ten for Augustinian houses; eight more were for houses of military orders and of Fontevrault and Vallombrosa. Most of the grants to black Benedictine monks were for houses founded in the previous half century, and only a few were for rich and old houses like Aniane, St Vanne, Bobbio, and St Stephen at Dijon. This fact alone strongly suggests that the purpose of the grants was to help poor and obscure houses rather than to win the support of the entire monastic order, especially since many older monasteries stood to lose heavily from the privilege now granted to more recent houses.

The purpose given by Innocent in several of his bulls closely

---

[1] *PU in Frankreich*, NF II, 72, and NF IV, 114; JL 8193, 8194, 8198, 8208, 8211, 8213, 8214, 8219, 8235, 8239, 8241, 8250, 8258, 8259, and (confirmations) *PU in Frankreich*, I, 45 and 46 and III, 25.

[2] JL 8342, 8345, 8349, 8362, and (confirmations) 8346 and *PU in Frankreich*, I, 49.

[3] JL 8271 and *PU in England*, III, 164.

[4] Cf. Schreiber, *Kurie*, I, 115–245, and Knowles, *Mon. Order*, pp. 585–6. Tremel, in *Zs. d. hist. Vereines f. Steiermark*, XXXIII, 33, said that in Styria freedoms from tithes were never granted to old and rich monasteries.

resembled that given by Paschal II in his bull for Montmajour, which formed the basis for the decretal *Decimas a populo* and was cited almost verbatim by Innocent in the long *arenga* to his general privilege for Prémontré in 1139.[1] In eight other bulls granted between 1136 and 1139 he justified the privilege more briefly on the grounds that monks and other religious men who lived a common life should be supported by the gifts and alms of others and should pay no tithes from their own produce. In his privileges for Cîteaux in 1132 and the Cistercian abbeys of Les Roches and Pontigny in 1142 he further cited the letter of Gregory the Great freeing those who lived a common life, and who gave all they could as alms, from any obligation to divide their incomes.[2] The revised privilege for the Hospitallers in 1137 gave as a reason 'because all your goods should be devoted to the support of the poor and pilgrims and should not therefore be applied to other uses'.[3] In the privilege for the Templars in 1139 Innocent even said that 'Since those who defend the Church should live and be supported by the goods of the Church, we entirely prohibit the exaction of tithes against your will from your movable or moving property or from anything belonging to your venerable house'.[4] Also in 1139 he gave the privilege to the Cistercians at Bagnolo near Milan simply 'in order that you may be able to serve God more securely and freely'.[5] Innocent thus adhered fairly closely to the theory of *Decimas a populo* in these bulls, and he seems never to have used the idea of *Novum genus* that monks as priests should pay no tithes.

Although Innocent did little to develop the theory of monastic freedom from tithes, he made an important advance by winning conciliar approval of the policy. The council of Pisa in 1135 decreed that 'monks and regular canons should not in future be

---

[1] *PL*, CLXXIX, 386–7.

[2] See the privileges for Fontevrault, La Colomba, L'Aumône, Gottesgnaden, Clairefontaine, Sept-Fontaines, Prüfening, and Ramsey: *PU in Frankreich*, NF v, 116; *PL*, CLXXIX, 311, 317, 377, 390, 392, 425; *Ramsey*, II, 144; and *PL*, CLXXIX, 123, 613–14, and 615. Viard, *Dîme*, I, 188, attributed to Innocent II a passage from his confirmation of Paschal's bull for St Vanne at Verdun.

[3] *PL*, CLXXIX, 313.

[4] *Ordre du Temple*, p. 377.   [5] *PL*, CLXXIX, 486.

required to give tithes from the goods which they produce by their own work or for their own use'.[1] Innocent referred to this decree in several subsequent bulls and letters. In October 1136, for instance, he forbade the bishop of Regensburg to exact tithes from the monks of Prüfening and explained that he had confirmed the policy of freeing monks and regular canons from paying tithes from their demesne lands 'at the council which, by the grace of God, we recently held at Pisa'.[2] He wrote similarly to the bishop of Passau in 1139/40 prohibiting the exaction of tithes from the canons of Reichersberg and Berchtesgaden and saying that 'It was established by the holy fathers long ago and renewed by us in general councils, with the assent of many discreet and wise men, that religious men should not be forced to pay tithes to anyone from the goods which they produce by their own work or for their own use or from the food of their animals'.[3] He used almost the same words in a letter written in 1141/3 to the bishops of Auxerre, Langres, and Autun in support of the monks of Reigny.[4] He also referred to the conciliar decree freeing monks from tithes in his bulls of 1139 for St Stephen at Dijon and in 1141 for Wessobrunn.[5]

A second important innovation by Innocent was to grant general privileges freeing an entire order of monasteries from paying tithes. There is no evidence that any previous tithe-privilege applied to more than one house, but in his grant for Cîteaux in 1132 Innocent extended the freedom to include 'the tithes of the goods which you and the brothers of your entire

---

[1] Ernst Bernheim, 'Ein bisher unbekannter Bericht vom Concil zu Pisa im Jahr 1135', *Zs. f. Kirchenrecht*, XVI (1881), 149; cf. Viard, *Dîme*, I, 198, and II, 42 n. 3, who used the inaccurate abbreviation in JL, I, 865.

[2] *PL*, CLXXIX, 291; JL 7793.

[3] *Land ob der Enns*, I, 284, and II, 188; JL 8119. It was repeated in a letter of 1142, in *ibid.* I, 285, and II, 190–1; JL 8195. Cf. Classen, *Gerhoch*, pp. 99, 336 (no. 19) and 338–9 (no. 25); and also the tithe-grant to the bishop of Passau by Conrad II in 1025: MGH, *Dipl.* Conrad II, no. 47 (see p. 79 above).

[4] *PU in Frankreich*, V, 40. The similarity between this and the preceding letter suggests that they should both be dated 1141.

[5] *PL*, CLXXIX, 440 and 559. It may be significant that these were both old Benedictine houses, which sought a statement of conciliar approval for an innovation in their privileges.

congregation produce by your own hands and for your own use'.[1] Soon after in a privilege for Clairvaux he likewise forbade anyone to exact tithes 'from you or from any monastery subject to Clairvaux'.[2] And his privilege for Prémontré in 1139 was addressed 'to our beloved sons the abbots, provosts, and other brothers, and those who are professed both now and for ever in the future into the order of Prémontré'.[3] Unless the general character was thus specified, it is probable that even privileges for the chief monasteries of other orders, such as Cluny and Vallombrosa, were still regarded as specific. The general grants, however, were probably on the whole less effective than individual privileges. Long after his general grants for the Cistercians and the Premonstratensians, Innocent continued to include (and occasionally to omit) the privilege in his charters for their individual houses and to confirm specific holdings of tithes from their own lands, which was still apparently considered the most secure basis for freedom from tithes. In his charter of 1138 for the Cistercian nuns of Pforte, for instance, Innocent confirmed their possession of two granges, presumably part of their demesne, 'with all the appurtenances and tithes', but he included no formula freeing them from tithes, which appeared for the first time for Pforte in his charter of 1142.[4] In spite of these limitations, however, the general privileges in theory extended freedom from paying tithes to a large and growing number of unspecified monasteries in addition to those which received individual grants.

Innocent also developed a standard diplomatic formula for freeing monks from tithes, which began *Sane laborum* and forbade any cleric or layman to exact tithes from the goods which were produced by the monks or for their use or from the food of their animals. The terms of the grant had previously varied, as has been seen, and had occasionally been a source of confusion. There was still considerable variation during the first decade of Innocent's pontificate. The terms of the grants to Aniane and Beaulieu-sur-Aube in 1130 were like the later formula forbidding

[1] PL, CLXXIX, 123.   [2] *Clairvaux*, p. 6, no. 4.

[3] PL, CLXXIX, 386.

[4] *Pforte*, pp. 2–3 and 12; JL 7868 and 8214.

anyone to exact tithes from the monastic demesne,[1] but other contemporary grants adhered to the old pattern of giving monks possession of their own tithes. The confirmation for the Saviour at Pavia in 1132 even changed a prohibition to levy tithes into a grant of possession.[2] Of the three charters for Beaulieu near Roanne, on the other hand, the first in 1130 gave the nuns their own tithes, the second in 1132 forbade any exaction of tithes, and the third in 1142 used the new standard formula of prohibition.[3] In 1135 Innocent confirmed for the Hospitallers the earlier grant of their demesne tithes to the hospice, but in 1137 he changed the formula to a more conventional form freeing them from paying tithes of goods produced for their own use.[4] The grant to St Peter at Ghent in 1135 restricted the freedom to the abbey's estates in France and to produce other than crops, that is, to small tithes only.[5] The grant to Camp in 1139, although it was a Cistercian house, applied only to tithes from uncultivated lands and from cattle.[6] In his charter for Vangadizza in 1139, Innocent granted separately the tithes from the *curtis abbatiae* and other estates, from which the monks were apparently accustomed to receive the tithes in their entirety, and the tithes from goods produced on other lands by the monks or for their use.[7] Also in 1139 he redefined the privilege for St Walburg.[8] These variations probably represent for the most part experiments and adaptations for special cases rather than real changes in policy or in the general purpose or application of the privilege. Meanwhile, Innocent was working out the standard formula, which he seems to have used for the first time in 1139 in his confirmation for the monks of Baumburg, who had previously been granted freedom only from noval tithes.[9] Later in the same year it was used with slight

---

[1] *Aniane*, p. 97, and *PL*, CLXXIX, 75.

[2] *PL*, CLXXIX, 138 (cf. p. 237 above).

[3] *PU in Frankreich*, III, 22, 24, and 25.   [4] *PL*, CLXXIX, 313.

[5] *St Pierre à Gand*, p. 134; cf. pp. 141–2 and 149–50, where the restriction was dropped in charters of Eugene III in 1145 and Hadrian IV in 1156.

[6] *PL*, CLXXIX, 444–5; cf. his grant to the chapter of St Omer, in *PU in Frankreich*, NF III, 68.

[7] *PL*, CLXXIX, 420–1; JL 7967; *IP*, V, 196, no. 3.

[8] *PL*, CLXXIX, 416; JL 7965.   [9] *PL*, CLXXIX, 423 (cf. p. 238 above).

variations in the bulls for Averbode, Pöhlde, and Prüfening, and after 1140 it regularly appeared both in new privileges and in confirmations of old grants.[1]

Innocent's policy was continued almost without change by his four immediate successors, Popes Celestine II, Lucius II, Eugene III, and Anastasius IV, and the total number of monasteries freed from paying tithes steadily increased. Occasionally the formula *Sane laborum* was slightly altered or the reason for the grant was given. Lucius in his privilege for Luxeuil in 1144 specified that those who lived a common life not only should live off the alms and gifts of others but also should possess their property without trouble or damage.[2] The wording of Eugene's confirmation in 1152 of the early privilege of 1070 for the abbey of the Trinity at Torre reflected the original terms forbidding any ecclesiastical or secular person to exact tithes from the goods of the abbey.[3] Sometimes, as before, *novalium* was put in place of *laborum* in the formula, and the privilege was thus limited to the produce from newly cultivated lands.[4] And the grant to Savigny by Lucius in 1144 may have applied to the entire order.[5] As a rule, however, the privileges applied to single monasteries and to all the produce from their demesne. The Cistercian Pope Eugene alone granted at least a hundred individual privileges and often added to his confirmations of earlier charters for monasteries a clause freeing

---

[1] See the confirmations in *Ramsey*, II, 156 (1141, JL 8124a) and *PU in Frankreich*, I, 45 (1142, for Bellevaux), and, more generally, Comp. I, III, 26, 12. The statement by Dubled, in the *Rev. d'hist. ecc.* LIV, 779, that the formula varied according to the congregation to which the monastery belonged is based upon charters of widely differing dates and represents a later change in papal policy rather than, in the 1140's, a difference in the treatment of houses of different orders.

[2] *PU in Frankreich*, I, 57.

[3] *APRI*, III, 112; JL 9572; *IP*, III, 228–9, no. 4. It is based on a lost intermediate charter of Innocent II, not directly on the privilege of Alexander II cited p. 216 above.

[4] See JL 8490 (Celestine), 8731, 8790 (see p. 280 below), 9008, 9128, 9250, 9273, 9355, 9417 (Eugene), 9773, and 9872 (Anastasius). A forged bull of Eugene also confirmed the freedom from noval tithes granted by Innocent II to Ilsenburg: *Ilsenburg*, I, 19 and 23; JL 7751 and †9199 (cf. p. 264 n. 2, and p. 280 below).

[5] *PL*, CLXXIX, 917; JL 8673; cf. Buhot, in *Moyen Âge*, XLVI, 108.

the monks from tithes.[1] In April 1147, for instance, at the specific request of St Bernard, he added the formula *Sane laborum* to the privilege for the Cistercian nuns at Bourbourg, who had not received an explicit freedom in their charter from Innocent II in 1138.[2] Three days later Eugene added the same privilege to his confirmation of Innocent's charter for the Augustinian canons of St Lupus at Troyes.[3]

It should not be thought, however, that these popes invariably adhered to the policy of freeing monks from tithes or entirely discarded the ancient principle of episcopal control over tithes. Innocent II in his bull of 1133 raising the ancient abbey of Brugnato (near the modern La Spezia) to a bishopric, decreed that the new bishop should like any bishop 'hold and dispose of the tithes, oblations, and other [revenues] both in temporalities and spiritualities'.[4] Privileges for old and rich houses, furthermore, rarely included formulas of freedom from tithes or possession of their own tithes. It is true that the privilege for Cluny was renewed even at the height of its dispute with the Cistercians over payment of tithes,[5] but an abbey like Molesme, which enjoyed many exceptional privileges, received no freedom from tithes in its great charter of 1145,[6] and the first known papal grant of freedom from tithes for La Grande Chartreuse was in 1184.[7] These examples are reminders that even in the middle of the twelfth century monastic freedom from tithes was still in theory an exception to the rule and was reserved in principle for new and needy houses.

The total number of grants nevertheless shows that during the twenty-five years between the accessions of Innocent II and Hadrian IV an important change had occurred in the papal

---

[1] This figure, like that for Innocent II, is based solely on the bulls printed in the *PL*, *APRI*, *PU*, and a few chartularies. Cf. also his defence of monastic freedom from tithes at the council of Rheims in 1148, cited p. 278 below.

[2] *Bourbourg*, pp. 37–8 and 44; JL 7888 and 9016.

[3] *St Loup de Troyes*, pp. 18–22 and 35; JL 7761 and 9019.

[4] *PL*, CLXXIX, 179; JL 7621; *IP*, VI. 2, 369, no. 4.

[5] Cf. *Bull. Clun.* pp. 53 and 56; JL 8621 and 8859.

[6] *Molesme*, II, 355–8; JL 8792; cf. *Molesme*, introd. I, 162, on the favour shown by Eugene III to Molesme.

[7] *Chartreuse*, p. 112, no. 39; JL 15141.

attitude towards monastic freedom from tithes and an occasional practice had been turned into an established policy. Most historians have tended to see this development as a natural outgrowth from the earlier policy of monastic exemption from episcopal control. Viard, Vendeuvre, Monod, and Mahn all considered freedom from tithes as an element or consequence of exemption in general and as part of the effort of the reformed popes to free monasteries from onerous obligations to the local bishops.[1] In the opinion of Schreiber, Paschal II wanted to reward the monks for their support and to undermine the entrenched power of the bishops, and Innocent II continued and extended this policy. 'We are therefore faced', he said, 'with a papal policy on tithes which continued uniformly from Paschal to Innocent II and which granted complete freedom from tithes to each monastery in its turn, if not explicitly in a document, at least with the full intention and in principle.'[2] He therefore regarded both the general grant for Cîteaux in 1132 and the decree of the council of Pisa in 1135 as continuations and amplifications of existing policies. This opinion of Innocent's policy was shared by Hoffmann, Gosso, and Mahn.[3]

This interpretation fails to take into full account, however, either the nature of monastic exemption, the monastic policy of the reformed popes, or the radical increase in papal grants of freedom from tithes in the second quarter of the twelfth century. Monastic exemption was common long before monastic freedom from tithes. Properly speaking, it applied to episcopal authority, as seen above, and not to tithes, of which the bishop was entitled to at most a third or a quarter. The very fact that the early Cistercians sought freedom from tithes while opposing monastic

---

[1] Viard, Dîme, I, 187–8; Jules Vendeuvre, L'Exemption de la visite monastique (Dijon, 1906, and Paris, 1907), p. 126; Bernard Monod, Essai sur les rapports de Pascal II avec Philippe Ier, Bibliothèque de l'École des Hautes Études, CLXIV (Paris, 1907), p. 116; Mahn, Ordre, p. 102.

[2] Schreiber, Kurie, I, pp. 251–8 (quoted extract on p. 255).

[3] Eberhard Hoffmann, 'Die Stellungnahme der Cisterzienser zum kirchlichen Zehntrecht im 12. Jahrhundert', SMGBOZ, XXXIII (1912), 426: 'Innocenz II. bei der Privilegierung der Cisterzienser aus dem Rahmen der gesamten päpstlichen Zehntpolitik nicht herausgetreten ist'; Gosso, Vita economica, p. 198 n. 11, speaking of Innocent's privilege for Breme; Mahn, Ordre, p. 104.

exemption is a warning against including tithes in the normal scope of exemption.[1] Only in the broad sense of exemption as 'the last and most articulate stage in that evolution of privileged rights and jurisdictions, civil and ecclesiastical, which had gone on for centuries',[2] can freedom from tithes be considered part of exemption in general. Second, from the point of view of papal policy, the majority of tithes in the twelfth century were not owned by the bishops, and a great number belonged to parish priests and to monks, whom the popes had no desire to antagonize by depriving them of part of their income.[3] Third, it appears to have been no accident that the great growth of tithe-privileges coincided with the so-called 'New Reformed Papacy' in which the reformed monastic orders played a very important role.[4]

Recent research has increasingly shown the significance of the pontificate of Innocent II in the history of monasticism.[5] Innocent is the first pope who can be said to have had a definite policy of freeing monks from tithes. The motives of this policy are not entirely clear, but it is probable that he used freedom from tithes as a weapon to win the support of the new monastic orders, especially the Cistercians, in his struggle against Anacletus II, who is not known to have granted any freedoms from tithes and may indeed have feared that such privileges would be displeasing

---

[1] On the opposition of the early Cistercians to any exemption from the authority of the diocesan bishops, see Monod, *Essai*, pp. 98–9 and 109; Vendeuvre, *Exemption*, pp. 139–41; Mahn, *Ordre*, pp. 135–6; and Bernard Jacqueline, 'À propos de l'exemption monastique', *Bernard de Clairvaux*, Commission d'histoire de l'ordre de Cîteaux, III (Paris, 1953), pp. 339–44.

[2] Knowles, *Mon. Order*, p. 575.

[3] Graham, *Gilbert*, p. 113: 'This indulgence pressed hard on the parish priests.'

[4] Cf. the important article by H.-W. Klewitz, 'Das Ende des Reformpapsttums', *Deutsches Archiv für Geschichte des Mittelalters*, III (1939), 371–412, reprinted in *Reformpapsttum und Kardinalkolleg*, pp. 209–59, and Bloch, in *Traditio*, VIII, 159–74.

[5] Cf. Hirsch, *Klosterimmunität*, pp. 64–5 and 106, who discussed the distinction in Innocent's privileges between those *ad indicium protectionis* and those *ad indicium libertatis* and said that papal protection of monasteries re-entered canon law during his pontificate; David Knowles, 'Essays in Monastic History, IV: The Growth of Exemption', *The Downside Review*, L (1932), 426, remarked on the increase of papal privileges after 1130; Goetting, in *A. f. Urk.* XIV, 140, said that curial influence reached a high point in Germany under Innocent II; and Pöschl, in *A. f. kath. KR*, XCVIII, 357.

to the conservative interests whose support he sought. The decree
of the council of Pisa in 1135 was certainly more pleasing to the
supporters of Innocent than those of Anacletus. The number of
Innocent's grants before 1138, however, does not seem sufficiently
large clearly to establish ecclesiastical politics as their motive.
On the contrary, the majority of his privileges were granted after
his victory over Anacletus, and they seem to have been the result
of a genuine sympathy for the new monastic orders, though
whether on the part of the pope himself, of influences in the curia,
or of outside pressures it is impossible to say. The Second Lateran
Council in 1139 renewed the decrees against lay possession of
tithes, which were to be given 'for the use of piety'.[1] And an
anonymous elaboration of this decree, first published as a canon
of a Lateran synod in 1097/9, 'firmly forbade laymen to hold or
possess in the future the tithes from the lands of churches which
the churches cultivate for their own uses'.[2] From a broad point of
view, the policy of freeing monks from tithes may thus be seen
as part of the papal effort to restore tithes to their proper uses as
well as to assist new and poor monasteries.

A papal privilege was not the only way in which monks could
avoid the obligation to pay tithes from their demesne, and many
monasteries preferred to obtain grants of their own tithes from
the institutions or individuals to whom they belonged. These
grants are not always easy to distinguish from grants of tithes
paid by other men, but the documents show that in the first half
of the twelfth century many monks were given all or part of the
tithes from their demesne lands, which they would otherwise
have had to pay, and were thus in effect freed from paying tithes.[3]
In the late eleventh or early twelfth century, for instance, a layman
gave Cavour 'two-thirds of my tithe which I hold in the field

---

[1] Hefele–Leclercq, *Conciles*, v. 1, 728; JL, I, 885; cf. also the letter against lay
possession of tithes written by Innocent to the bishop of Regensburg in 1132/43:
EPRI, p. 94, no. 185; JL 8290.

[2] *APRI*, II, 167 (as of a Lateran synod in 1097/9); cf. Hefele–Leclercq,
Conciles, v. 1, 455, who associated it with the Lateran council in 1139. The use
of the terms *propriis sumptibus* on the whole supports this suggestion.

[3] Cf. *St Cyprien*, p. 128, no. 195 (*c.* 1080, quoted p. 100 above); *St
Victor de Marseille*, I, 159 (late eleventh century), granting a third of the

which is worked by the hands of the monks of the said church, on
condition that half is for the servants of the church and the other
half is for guests'.[1] Four brothers gave a church to Sauxillanges
but kept for themselves three-quarters of the tithes and burial
dues except from one *mansus* 'which the monks worked in
demesne [and] from which they [the brothers] would take no
tithe either from the produce or from anything, and no burial
dues from their men whom they [the monks] fed and clothed,
nor would they take the tithe from their animals'.[2] The monks of
St Peter at Chartres were given an estate by the king of France
from which the tithes belonged to the cathedral of Orléans, and
asked the canons to remit half the tithes. 'We did not at once
agree to their request,' wrote the canons in a charter of 1110/11,
'but finally we took into consideration that at great expense and
labour they had cultivated the land, which had been deserted...
and realized in addition that the tithes would be more faithfully collected and stored by them, and we consented to their request....'[3]
In this case the lands may not have been entirely worked by or for
the monks themselves, but in the settlement of a dispute between
the abbey of St Victor at Marseille and the cathedral there the
distinction between 'their own' and 'other men's' tithes was
clearly brought out. At the request of Pope Gelasius II, the archbishop of Arles settled this case in 1119 and decided that 'The
monks should have and hold the tithes from these and from other
lands which they cultivate with their own oxen and implements
throughout the diocese of Marseille', except at three places
'where we wish everything to be held as it is today', and that the
canons should possess the tithes of their own churches 'except for
the demesne of the monks, as said above, and if the monks
increase their demesne they should have the tithes from that

---

tithes in bread and wine from the monks' demesne on a certain estate; *St Martin
des Champs*, I, 181–2 (1106), granting the monks of Acy the tithe 'of all the
animals which they have in demesne at Acy and Avilly and which they use for
their own purposes...' (cf. *Acy*, p. 50); *Sauxillanges*, pp. 504–5 (1112), granting
part of the tithe from a vineyard held by the monks and from some land
'which the monks cultivate by working'.

[1] *Cavour*, p. 42.   [2] *Sauxillanges*, p. 432 (undated).
[3] *Ste Croix d'Orléans*, pp. 135–6.

increase and if they decrease it and give it to labourers, the clerics should have [the tithes]'.[1] It was also common, especially in Germany, for bishops to grant to monasteries the tithes of new lands opened by their own monks.[2]

These grants to monks of their own tithes conveyed no formal freedom from tithes. They were grants of property, like the more numerous grants of other men's tithes discussed above, but their effect, although limited in scope, was much like that of a papal tithe-privilege. Practically speaking there was little difference between a papal prohibition to levy tithes from the produce and animals of a monastery and a lay grant, as to the monks of Molesme in 1102/11, of 'the tithe from their own fields which they ploughed...and from the animals in all their herds', except that the papal grant technically applied to the entire monastic demesne and the private grant only to specific lands.[3] Likewise, the episcopal confirmation for San Venerio del Tino of all its lands 'with the tithe of its demesne' presumably had the same effect as the papal grant to Polirone of 'the tithes of your demesne', which was later changed into a standard papal formula.[4] In many cases, indeed, the private grants were probably less subject to controversy than the papal privileges and therefore more desirable to the monks.

In the first half of the twelfth century these grants were

[1] St Victor de Marseille, II, 340; cf. St Bertin (alt.), pp. 237–8 (1106), granting decimas proprias atque communes to a colony of lepers, who had their own church, cemetery, and priest, on the lands of St Bertin and St Omer, which were to recover the tithes if the lepers left the land (cf. Imbert, Hôpitaux, p. 88, on tithe-privileges for lepers, which he attributed to sanitary rather than to charitable purposes); and St Martin des Champs, II, 109 (1139), granting the monks of Acy the tithes of their garden behind the church 'even if it can be enlarged to a greater capacity', in return for an annual rent (cf. Acy, pp. 52–3).

[2] Ilsenburg, I, 15 (1119), granting the monks the tithes from noval lands in all places where they owned the old tithes and from propria novalia at Hedersleben, which may have been part of the monastic demesne (confirmed in papal privileges cited p. 244 n. 4 above); Mainz, I, 457 (1128, for Hilwartshausen) and 532 (1137, for Fredelsloh); Heisterbach, p. 102, no. 6 (1176). The bishop of Reggio in 1140 granted to the monks of Polirone the tithes of all lands cleared by themselves or their men: Liber grossus antiquus comunis Regii, ed. F. S. Gatta (Reggio nell'Emilia, 1944–63), II, 298, no. 263.

[3] Molesme, II, 149.

[4] San Venerio del Tino, I, 46 (1125, by the bishop of Luni).

especially sought by members of the new monastic orders, who refused to possess tithes from the labour of other men and often also to pay tithes from their own produce. They hoped thus to avoid a serious charge on their usually slender resources and to escape the worldly involvements and disputes which the payment of tithes entailed.[1] The early Grandmontines were thus instructed to ask for the tithes of their own labour from the bishop, priest, or other owner. And at the same time as the bishop of Gap forbade the Carthusians at Durbon, at their own request, to take tithes from other men, he issued another charter granting them 'all the tithes, first-fruits, and ecclesiastical dues from the entire hermitage which they have acquired in that place and also from any land which they may acquire anywhere in the surroundings'.[2] In this way a new or small community of monks could relatively easily avoid any obligation to pay tithes from their own produce, particularly from lands which they had opened themselves and from which no tithe had previously been paid.[3]

The early Cistercians appear to have regularly asked for the tithes from any land which they were given, whether or not tithes had previously been paid, and grants of this sort are found among the early charters of many Cistercian houses.[4] In 1120, for example, various monks, clerics, and laymen gave to the monks of Bonnevaux the tithes from some of their own lands at the request of Pope Calixtus II and Abbot Stephen Harding of Cîteaux.[5] Such grants were usually made, as was proper with any trans-

---

[1] Cf. pp. 142 and 150–1 above.

[2] *Durbon*, pp. 3–4, nos. 2–3 (cf. p. 140 above). Honorius II in 1125/6 confirmed a grant by the bishop of Grenoble early in the twelfth century to the monks of Chalais of the tithes from goods produced by themselves in the parish of Racin: *Chalais*, I, 3 and 70, no. 5; and in 1136 Peter the Venerable granted the Carthusians of Meyriat the tithes from their own produce that had previously belonged to the Cluniacs of Nantua: *Lyon*, I, 32–3, no. 22.

[3] Dubled, in *Rev. d'hist. ecc.* LIV, 777–82, stressed that the new lands worked by the Cistercians in Alsace were mostly freed from tithes, in contrast to the new lands worked by black monks. The later papal grants of freedom from tithes on newly opened lands, however, were granted to all types of monks and not (as Dubled suggested) especially to Cistercians.

[4] Cf. Mahn, *Ordre*, pp. 103–4.

[5] *Bonnevaux*, p. 17, no. 19; cf. Ulysse Chevalier, *Regeste Dauphinois*, I, (Valence, 1912–13), no. 3238 on the date.

action concerning tithes, by the hand, or at least with the permission, of the bishop,[1] who occasionally exacted some con-
cession in return, such as an annual rent for the parish priest.[2]
Sometimes the donor specified that the grant was valid only so
long as the land was worked by the monks or lay-brothers themselves, or by their dependents, and for the monks' own use. In
about 1119 the bishop of Autun granted to Cîteaux the tithe
from its land at Moisey, which had previously been held by two
priests and several laymen, 'so long as it shall come from the
produce of the monks or lay-brothers or of their ploughs or hired
labourers'. He went on to specify that 'If some peasants should
cultivate this land for the use of the monks, the tithe will belong to
the monks; but if by permission of the monks other men should
cultivate this land for their own use, those who have a right to
the tithe should receive it'. He then forbade the priest of Moisey
to continue exacting tithes from the monks.[3] In a charter for
Morimond in 1126, the bishop of Langres listed those who had
given tithes to the abbey and granted to the monks 'all other
tithes of their produce and animals'.[4] The archbishop of Sens in
1127 confirmed for Pontigny 'all the tithes of your entire produce throughout our diocese...that is, the tithes which the
previous owners have granted and will in the future grant to your
monastery'.[5] Again, in 1128, the bishop of Langres decreed that

[1] Cf. *Yonne*, I, 274-5, where the archbishop of Sens gave some tithes from
the labour of the monks of Vauluisant, which had been surrendered to him by
their lay owner, to the abbey in 1130; but cf. *La Ferté*, p. 172 (grant directly
to the abbey by two laymen in 1120/1).

[2] *Preuilly*, pp. 6 (1121/2), 12 (c. 1130), 21 (c. 1142); *Steiermark*, I, 235-6,
where the archbishop of Salzburg in 1144 protected the interests of the parish
priests in two grants to Frisach and Reichersberg.

[3] Petit, *Bourgogne*, I, 472-3, no. 190; cf. also 479 (no. 196) and 465 (no. 179),
where the dean and canons of Autun in 1119 granted various tithes to Cîteaux
on condition that they would revert to the legitimate owners if the land was
not worked by or for the monks. The abbot of St Chef in 1127 specified that
various tithes given to the monks of Chalais would revert to the parish or
St Laurence if the land was worked by other men: *Chalais*, I, 71, no. 6.

[4] *Exordium Cistercii cum Summa Cartae Caritatis et fundatio primarum quattuor
filiarum Cistercii*, ed. T. Hümpfner (Vác, 1932), p. 25.

[5] *Yonne*, I, 261 and 270; cf. 270-1 (1127: grant of the bishop of Auxerre to
Pontigny).

the monks of Clairvaux should have their tithes from any land in the diocese worked by themselves or their *familia* and that 'They should hold these tithes from the bishop of Langres, to whom the distribution of tithes properly belongs, for the support and assistance of their poor'.[1] St Bernard also obtained several individual grants of tithes from lands worked by the monks of Clairvaux, including one from Abbot Pontius of Cluny, which was later confirmed by Peter the Venerable, one from the abbot of St Claude, who specified that the grant would be annulled 'if this monastery, in conformity with other monasteries, becomes less regular', and another, in 1136, from the abbot of Molesme, who specified that it applied to all goods produced for the use of Clairvaux either by the monks, lay-brothers, or hired workers.[2]

Such grants remained a standard element in Cistercian privileges even after the general papal tithe-privilege in 1132 and as the order grew steadily in size, wealth, and influence. Bishops, priests, monks, and laymen all over Europe rivalled one another in their generosity to the new monasteries.[3] St Bernard encouraged both papal and private grants to Cistercians of their own tithes and witnessed among other charters a grant in 1139/43 by the Cistercian Bishop Godfrey of Langres remitting to the monks of La Crête 'the tithes of their labour by both their hands and their ploughs...not only from crops but also from animals and other things of which tithes are given to the priests', who consented to

---

[1] *Clairvaux*, p. 2, no. 1 (confirmed in 1135: *ibid.* p. 35).

[2] *Clairvaux*, pp. 3–4, 8, and 14, nos. 2, 5, and 7. In 1127/31 Peter the Venerable granted to the Cistercians of Trois-Fontaines the tithes that they had previously paid to the Cluniac priory of Baudivillard: *GC*, x, instr. 168–9 (panchart of Bishop Geoffrey of Châlons-sur-Marne). In his grant for Meyriat (cited p. 251 n. 2 above) Peter the Venerable specified that Nantua should recover its rights if the Carthusians moved or changed their rule.

[3] Cf. *Ourscamp*, pp. 248–9 (1133, by the bishop of Noyon and Tournai) and 41 (*c.* 1147, by the abbot of Chauny); *GC*, I, instr. 179 (1136: Bonnefont granted the tithes of all its lands in foundation charter) and xv, instr. 139 (1138, by the bishop of Lausanne for Hauterive); *Altluxemburg*, I, 574 (1139: the archbishop of Trier gave Himmerod the tithe which he had owned from a certain vineyard when it was worked by peasants); Petit, *Bourgogne*, III, 515, no. 1499 (before 1142, by the duke of Burgundy for Maizières); *Vaux de Cernay*, I, 8–9 (1142/54: Louis VII gave the tithes of a vineyard given to the abbey by a canon of Étampes).

the grant.[1] Occasionally lands given to Cistercians were actually declared free of tithes for one reason or another. The abbey of Neuburg in Alsace, for instance, was given in about 1133 an estate which had long been uncultivated because of a dispute over its possession but on which stood a chapel 'free from all authority of another parish and to which the tithes of those fields entirely belonged'. The monks were therefore under no obligation to pay tithes when they converted the estate into a grange worked by themselves.[2] In 1138 the abbey of Staffarda in Piedmont was given an estate by some laymen 'in such a way that it will give no tithe, first-fruits, or anything at all to anyone at any time'.[3] As time went on more and more of these transactions were in fact business arrangements, since they involved a valuable form of property. If the generosity of the owners of the tithes proved deficient, the monks might buy the tithes from their lands either for money or property or in return for permission to enter the monastery, in the same way that black monks acquired the tithes from lands worked by other men.[4]

These private grants of tithes from specific lands and products were entirely different in character from the papal privileges prohibiting the exaction of any tithe or granting to a monastery the tithes from its entire demesne. The practical difference was not very great, and a monastery which had private grants covering all its demesne lands was probably in at least as strong a position with regard to paying tithes as a monastery which had received a general privilege from the papacy. But the theoretical difference

---

[1] Petit, *Bourgogne*, IV, 479–80, no. 3024. At the same time a knight and his family gave the abbey his share of the tithes of their produce in the same parish. Cf. *ibid.* II, 223, no. 265 (1136) and 239–40, no. 297 (1147).

[2] Würdtwein, *Nova subsidia*, VII, 80–1, no. 30; cf. on the later history of this estate the document of 1201 in Paul Wentzcke, 'Ungedruckte Urkunden zur Geschichte der Strassburger Bischöfe im 12. Jahrhundert', *MIÖG*, XXIX (1908), 590–2, no. 11, and Dubled, in *Rev. d'hist. ecc.* LIV, 770–1. In 1157 Neuburg was again given a chapel and land 'sine omni decimarum exactione': Würdtwein, *Nova subsidia*, IX, 356–7, no. 183.

[3] *Staffarda*, I, 15.

[4] Cf. pp. 271–2 below and Petit, *Bourgogne*, II, 283–4, no. 384, where Fontenay in 1162 acquired some tithes from land worked by its monks in return for a hundred shillings and two places in the abbey.

was immense, because the private grants were transfers of property belonging to the donor, whereas the papal privileges were
the sovereign acts of an ecclesiastical authority which claimed
general supervision over all matters pertaining to the welfare and
revenues of the Church, but which had no proprietary right to the
tithes from which the monks were freed.

Historians have long been puzzled by the relation of papal and
private initiative in granting privileges to monasteries. The
tendency of recent research, especially in Germany, has been to
emphasize the initiative of the local authorities and patrons.[1]
Brackmann pointed out in his study on the influence of the curia
in the archdiocese of Salzburg that in the first half of the twelfth
century only thirteen out of the forty-five monasteries belonging
to the bishop received papal privileges and that these as a rule
confirmed the grants and wishes of the local patrons. From this
he concluded that the curia had relatively little success in exercising influence over the episcopal monasteries, which remained
essentially under the control of the bishop, and that even the
monasteries which paid a *census* to the papacy received no privileges which basically changed their legal position. The monks
both sought and obtained papal privileges concerning tithes,
particularly noval tithes, but the curia took little initiative in the
matter.[2] Hirsch also emphasized that for the reformed monasteries
in southern Germany independence, guaranteed by papal protection, was the main point, and that they had no desire to substitute
submission to Rome for submission to the laity.[3] In the diocese
of Liège, according to Dereine, the monasteries in the tenth and
eleventh centuries looked for protection towards the emperor
rather than the pope and even in the twelfth century exemption
was unknown and the bishop exercised full control over the
monasteries.[4] Speaking generally of the position of monasteries
in the twelfth century, Schreiber, who was not inclined to under-
estimate papal influence, said that 'the practical relationships of

[1] See pp. 6–7 above.
[2] Brackmann, *Kurie*, pp. 60, 64 and 75–7.
[3] Hirsch, *Klosterimmunität*, Eng. tr., II, 142.
[4] Dereine, *Chanoines*, pp. 48–50 and 244.

diocesan life and associations proved themselves stronger than the will of papal privileges'.[1]

This opinion is based largely on evidence from east of the Rhine, where monasteries were as a rule more dependent upon local powers than in the West, where papal influence was stronger. Hirsch himself admitted that 'The subordination of protected houses to the Holy See was stronger in the Romanized lands and consequently the conception of a system of papal proprietary churches is more strongly accentuated there'.[2] Even in Germany, however, there is little evidence that the kings, bishops, and other monastic patrons took the lead in granting monastic freedom from tithes, which was never a normal part of the privileges of exemption and immunity. There was no precedent in 'the framework of formulas of immunity', as Stengel claimed, for the tithe-forgeries of Corvey, Werden, and Osnabrück.[3] The privileges of Conrad III for Zwettl and Salem, which were cited by Hirsch as evidence of the efforts of the Hohenstaufens to establish a general advocacy over all Cistercian houses in the empire, included no references to payment of tithes, and both houses were granted freedom from tithes by the pope rather than the emperor.[4] Of the thirteen monasteries in the archdiocese of Salzburg cited by Brackmann as receiving papal privileges, only seven were granted freedom from tithes in the first bull and two more in later bulls. The fact that four houses received no such grant in any privilege in the first half of the century suggests that at least in this respect the curia was not subservient to the wishes of the recipients and their local patrons.[5]

---

[1] Schreiber, *Kurie*, I, 77; cf. Brackmann, in *Göttingische gelehrte Anzeigen*, CLXXV, 278.

[2] Hirsch, *Klosterimmunität*, Eng. tr., II, 144 n. 46 (tr. slightly revised).

[3] Stengel, *Immunität*, p. 564.

[4] Hirsch, *Klosterimmunität*, pp. 108–9; JL 8073 and 8079, granted by Innocent II in 1140, in *Salem*, I, 3, and *Zwetl*, p. 37.

[5] Brackmann, *Kurie*, pp. 59–60. The monasteries which received freedom from tithes in the first privilege were Seckau (1143), Viktring (1146: see p. 259 below), Reichersberg (1142), Schäftlarn (1140), Neustift (1143), and Biburg (1149). The general privilege for Raitenhaslach dated 1147 (JL 8997: dated 1142 in Brackmann) is a forgery, but in 1147 Eugene III ordered the bishop of Regensburg to exact no tithes from the lands of the monks in his diocese

Private grants to monks of their own tithes almost invariably applied to specific tithes belonging to the donor or granted through his hands. Neither kings nor bishops could freely dispose of tithes or grant to one institution or individual the property of another. Occasionally they may have appeared to do so, but closer study usually shows that they either owned the tithes in question or were taking part in a transaction which involved the owner. The Cistercian abbey of Raitenhaslach, which was cited by Brackmann, offers a good example. In the foundation charter dated 1146 the archbishop of Salzburg recorded that he had given to the monks 'our ancient church of Raitenhaslach, which was vacant at that time... with its tithes, endowment, and dependents'. The bishop of Regensburg, however, required the monks to pay tithes from their property in his diocese. In 1147 Eugene III wrote forbidding him to exact any tithes from the monks, and in 1152 the bishop issued a charter in the presence of the archbishop of Salzburg accepting the papal mandate 'because we recognize that it was reasonably constituted' and freeing the monks from paying tithes in his diocese.[1] The bishop of Liège indemnified the previous owners for the tithes which he gave to regular canons in his diocese in order to free their lands from all obligations.[2] The bishop of Merseburg had previously received the tithes from the lay owner when in 1174 he freed (*relaxavimus*) 'from all further payment of tithes' a villa belonging to the monks of Pegau.[3]

Kings and bishops only very rarely granted general freedoms from tithes and so disposed of revenues over which they had no legitimate authority. Bishop Cuno of Strasbourg in 1109 con-

---

(*Raitenhaslach*, pp. 9–12, nos. 6–7). Prüfening received freedom from tithes in 1136 and in subsequent privileges, but not in 1123, and Mallersdorf in 1139 but not in 1131. Suben, Herrenchiemsee, St Zeno at Reichenhall, and Rohr, all Augustinian houses, received no grant in the cited privileges before 1150. MGH, *Dipl*. Lothar III, no. 4 (1125) included no reference to tithes, although it may in other respects have served as a basis for Innocent II's privilege in 1136, as Brackmann said.

[1] *Raitenhaslach*, pp. 5–8, 11–12, and 14–15, nos. 4, 7, and 9.
[2] Dereine, *Chanoines*, pp. 92 and 159.
[3] *Merseburg*, I, 96–7 (cf. the wording of the grant to Neuburg, cited p. 254 n. 2 above).

firmed the foundation of the abbey of St Leonard at Börsch in Alsace and decreed that the surrounding lands cleared as fields and vineyards by the monks should be 'free and quit from all payment of tithes, just as we hold established by the blessed Gregory and other pontiffs of the holy church of Rome, since it is highly improper that priests of God and the poor of Christ should be forced to give a tithe of their produce to any priests, especially when they are not in need, on account of which tithes were established (*contracte sunt*) for the use of priests'.[1] Soon after his deposition in 1125 Cuno also granted 'freedom from the exaction of any *census* or tithe' to the abbey of Baumgarten, which became Cistercian in 1148.[2] In making these grants Cuno was clearly following the example of the papacy, as he showed by citing the precedents of Gregory the Great and other popes and by justifying the privilege on the grounds that monks were priests and the poor of Christ. It is improbable that Cuno himself was in touch with Paschal II, since he was a friend and adviser of Henry V; but he may have seen one of the papal bulls, or perhaps heard of Paschal's decision at Langres in the case of Chaumouzey in 1107, and have been glad to show by his imitation his sense of equality with the bishop of Rome.

[1] Würdtwein, *Nova subsidia*, VII, 20–4, no. 11; cf. Wentzcke, *Regesten*, no. 382 for other editions of this charter. The monastery of Börsch, which is not mentioned in the *Gallia christiana* or by Cottineau, *Répertoire*, was founded in 1109 near Rosheim, south-east of Strasbourg: see MGH, *SS*, xv, 1000–2 for an account of its foundation. The present grant seems to have applied only to tithes from lands cleared by the monks, that is, to noval tithes, but the entire monastic demesne may have consisted of new lands. In 1134, however, Bishop Gebhard of Strasbourg exacted an annual rent of twenty pounds of wax in return for the tithes from certain lands belonging to the monastery: *Strassburg*, I, 64–5, no. 83; Wentzcke, *Regesten*, no. 452.

[2] This charter (Wentzcke, *Regesten*, no. 426) is known from the confirmations by Bishop Gebhard in 1133, which granted 'exceptionem decimarum de suis novalibus et propriis laboribus tam de fetibus quam de seminalibus et emancipationem totius censualis vel decimalis exactionis ex tunc imperpetuum' (Würdtwein, *Nova subsidia*, VII, 78–80, no. 29; Wentzcke, *Regesten*, no. 450) and by Bishop Burchard in 1155/6, which referred to it as 'emancipatio censualis vel decimalis exactionis' (Würdtwein, *Nova subsidia*, VII, 167–71, no. 65; Wentzcke, *Regesten*, no. 558). The freedom from tithes may therefore have been interpolated into Cuno's grant subsequently. On Baumgarten, see *GP*, III. 3, 48.

In 1136 the bishop of Passau gave to Heiligenkreuz, at the request of the Marquis Leopold, 'the entire tithe from the agriculture of the said venerable abbot and his monks and from all new lands'; and in 1139 the archbishop of Hamburg gave various tithes to the monks of Neumünster and allowed them to receive 'the tithes both in crops and in animals from everything which the monks produce by themselves or by their peasants anywhere in the woods or swamps'. But these grants seem to have applied either to tithes already owned by the bishop or lay donor or to noval tithes, over which the bishops in the East exercised a special control.[1] The archbishop of Salzburg in 1143, however, gave the Cistercians in the new abbey of Viktring, at the request of the count of Spanheim, 'the entire tithe...which they can obtain from their own labour, so that nothing of use should be exacted from them either as tithes or in place of tithes in the name of the bishop or of the parish priest'. Pope Eugene III mentioned this grant in his privileges of 1146 and 1147, which included the standard formula *Sane laborum*, and it is possible that in this case the diocesan bishop and the lay patron took the initiative in granting a general freedom from tithes to a monastery.[2] Bishop Godfrey of Langres was also said, in a charter issued by his successor in 1163, to have granted to the monks of Clairvaux 'immunity and liberty from all tithes, so that no one shall presume to exact from them tithes from their lands and granges'.[3] These two charters, however, were later than the general papal grants to Cîteaux and Clairvaux, which they partially resemble in language, and they should probably be interpreted as local applications and confirmations of papal policy rather than independent episcopal grants of general freedom from tithes.

General grants by kings were also very rare. Roger II of

---

[1] *Heiligenkreuz*, p. 3, and *Schleswig-Holstein*, I, 33 and 35 (repetition in 1141).

[2] *Die kärntner Geschichtsquellen, 811–1202*, ed. August von Jaksch, Monumenta historica ducatus Carinthiae, III (Klagenfurt, 1904), pp. 299, 316–17, and 320–1, nos. 754, 816, and 824; JL 8958 and 8998; GP, I. 1, 110–11, nos. 1–2; cf. August Jaksch, *Geschichte Kärntens bis 1335* (Klagenfurt, 1929), II, 294–6, and Tremel, in *Zs. d. hist. Vereines f. Steiermark*, XXXIII, 32.

[3] Petit, *Bourgogne*, II, 291, no. 399; the original charter by Godfrey is lost.

Sicily, who enjoyed exceptional ecclesiastical powers within his
kingdom, decreed in 1132 that the Augustinian canons of Cefalù
should pay no tithes.[1] And Frederick Barbarossa in 1156 inserted
into his confirmation of Conrad III's privilege for the Cistercian
abbey of Lützel in Alsace a clause prohibiting 'by imperial
majesty, following the canonical and apostolic authority, that
tithes should be exacted from you or your monks from the produce
which you raise by your own hands and for your own use or
from your food'. This passage derived from the papal privilege
for Lützel in 1139 (not from the later privilege, of 1147, in which
the standard formula Sane laborum was used) and simply replaced
the words 'auctoritate apostolica' by 'canonum apostolicamque
auctoritatem sequens imperiali maiestate'.[2] Presuming it is
authentic (which is not certain), this charter was probably drawn
up at Lützel itself, or at least outside the imperial chancery, and
was later authenticated by the emperor.[3] It may be a sign, there-

[1] Giuseppe Spata, *Le pergamene greche esistenti nel grande archivio di Palermo*
(Palermo, 1862–4), p. 430: '...de terra nullam decimam tribuant'. In 1130 the
antipope Anacletus had raised Roger to a king and assured his control over
ecclesiastical affairs in Sicily.

[2] The four documents concerned are printed in *Bâle*, I, 272 (JL 7953), 278–80
(Stumpf 3388), 304 (JL 9097), and 329 (Stumpf 3737), nos. 181, 184, 199 and
213; cf. *GP*, II. 2, 259, nos. 1–2. Alexander III used the standard formula in his
privilege for Lützel in 1179 (JL 13482).

JL 7953	Stumpf 3737
Porro de laboribus quos propriis	Porro de laboribus quos propriis
manibus aut sumptibus colitis,	manibus aut sumptibus colitis,
sed etiam de nutrimentis vestris,	seu de nutrimentis vestris,
a vobis vel fratribus vestris	a vobis vel fratribus vestris
decimas exigi auctoritate	decimas exigi, canonum apostolicamque
apostolica interdicimus.	auctoritatem sequens imperiali
	maiestate interdicimus.

[3] The two charters of Conrad and Frederick both survive in alleged originals.
According to Stumpf, Conrad's charter was considered a forgery by Pertz,
Hidber, and Scheffer-Boichorst, and Frederick's charter was called 'dubious'
by Hidber and 'alleged' by Pertz on account of the irregularity in the date:
see B. Hidber, *Schweizerisches Urkundenregister* (Bern, 1863–77), I, 557–8, and
II, 123–4, nos. 1734 and 2034. Julius Ficker, *Beiträge zur Urkundenlehre* (Innsbruck, 1877), I, 290–1, pointed out that the witness lists were authentic and that
the charters were therefore either forged on the basis of authentic exemplars or,
more probably, drawn up outside the papal chancery and later authenticated;
and he was followed by Paul Scheffer-Boichorst, 'Diplome Friedrichs I. für

fore, of the monks' desire to secure an imperial confirmation of
their privileges at a time when the influence of Rome was waning
in the empire, and also of Frederick's desire to express his rivalry
with the pope and to enhance his own prestige.[1] But the previous
papal grant and the specific reference to the authority of the pope
and the canons show that even the emperor followed the lead of
the pope in granting freedom from tithes.

This leadership was explicitly recognized and accepted in
several private charters and confirmations. The dean of Grammont,
for instance, gave up his claim to tithes from the monks of
St Peter at Ghent 'when he realized the truth of the opposite side
and saw the privileges in which the supreme pontiff freed them
from tithes of this sort'.[2] In his privilege for the abbey of Acquanegra in 1137, Lothar III mentioned 'the grant of the lord
Pope Innocent' in confirming possession of the tithes from its
demesne.[3] The archbishop of Trier in 1131/45 granted some
tithes, which had been given up in turn by several laymen, to the
abbot of Orval 'so that, in accordance with the terms of the
privilege granted to the church of Cîteaux by the Roman church,
he may have the same courtesy and right over this tithe in our

Cisterzienser-Klöster, namentlich in Elsass und Burgund' (1888), reprinted in
Zur Geschichte des XII. und XIII. Jahrhunderts, Historische Studien, ed. Ebering,
VIII (Berlin, 1897), pp. 149–62, who pointed out that the two charters derived
independently from Innocent's bull of 1139 (p. 155). More recently, both
charters were accepted as authentic by Hans Hirsch, 'Die Urkundenfälschungen
des Abtes Bernardin Buchinger für die Zisterzienserklöster Lützel und Pairis',
MIÖG, XXXII (1911), 15–16 and 18 n. 5, and Brackmann, in *GP*, II. 2, 256.
None of these critics drew attention to the inclusion of the tithe-privilege in
Frederick's but not in Conrad's charter or to the extreme rarity of such a grant
in any imperial charter.

[1] It may also have been a result of the efforts of Hadrian IV to limit the
freedom to noval tithes only.

[2] *St Pierre à Gand*, p. 129 (undated). The papal privilege is dated 1135
(JL 7700). Cf. *Xanten*, pp. 24–5 (1154) where the provost of Xanten confirmed
that the Premonstratensians of Cappenberg should pay an annual rent to the
parish priest in return for certain tithes but recognized that the canons were free
'from all exaction of the small tithe, which used to be paid from the food of
animals, in accordance with the decree of Pope Eugene'.

[3] MGH, *Dipl.* Lothar III, no. 124; JL 7788 (1136); *IP*, VI. 1, 355, no. 1. The
words *decimas omnium reddituum et...dominicatorum quae* in Lothar's charter
derived directly from the papal bull.

diocese as other abbots of this order in the dioceses of their bishops'.[1] Otto of Freising in 1155 gave to the canons of Reichersberg the tithes of their demesne lands in his diocese in the same way that the pope had given them a general grant, and the following year the bishop of Passau confirmed their possession of various demesne tithes which they held *ex auctoritate apostolica*.[2] The decision of Duke Leopold of Austria in 1178, awarding certain estates to the abbey of Melk in return for the tithes 'which the monks of Heiligenkreuz have not paid for almost forty years on account of the privilege of Pope Innocent II', has been used by several historians as evidence for the legal authority of the papal tithe-privileges even when they were not confirmed by the local secular or ecclesiastical powers.[3]

The influence of the papacy in promoting grants to the Cistercians by local authorities is also shown by an interesting charter from Archbishop Arnold of Cologne in 1138 for the Cistercian abbey of Altenberg:

In accordance with the request of the most venerable lord Pope Innocent and of the reverend Cardinals Haimeric the chancellor, Gerard, Octavian, and many other religious men, I gave annually...to the poor of Christ in that monastery twenty marks from the money which according to my arrangement was given to the poor people of the populace...on condition that when I, God willing, or one of my successors shall give to the said monastery of Altenberg a suitable and useful estate paying twenty marks of tested money of Cologne in legal rent...the other twenty marks will be returned to the bishop for the previous uses of the church.[4]

---

[1] *Orval*, p. 10. The papal privilege referred to may either be the general grant for Cîteaux in 1132 or the specific grant for Orval in 1141 (JL 8134).

[2] *Land ob der Enns*, II, 274–5 and 282–3, nos. 184 and 189; cf. Classen, *Gerhoch*, pp. 361–2 and 367, and also the grant by the bishop of Regensburg for Raitenhaslach in 1152, cited p. 257 above.

[3] *Heiligenkreuz*, pp. 11–12 (and 4–5 for the papal grant of 1139); cf. Oskar von Mitis, *Studien zum älteren österreichischen Urkundenwesen* (Vienna, 1906–12), p. 51; Lerche, in *A. f. Urk.* III, 209–16; and Plöchl, *Zehentwesen*, p. 133 n. 2, who suggested that the duke was acting as a papal delegate (see p. 121 above).

[4] *Altenberg*, p. 2; on the economic position of Altenberg and its fight for freedom from tithes, see Gerhard Kallen, 'Altenberg als Zisterzienser-Kloster in seiner Stellung zur Kirche und zum Reich', *Jahrbuch des kölnischen Geschichtsvereins*, XVIII (1936), 296.

This diversion of ecclesiastical funds from the *pauperes vulgi* to the *pauperes Christi* was fully consistent with the policy of the papacy under Innocent II and reflected the same attitude as the grants freeing the *pauperes Christi* from tithes.

A final indication of the practical importance of the papal grants is the number of forgeries made in the twelfth century. The great controversies over the tithes of Corvey, Herford, Fulda, Hersfeld, and Werden all involved forged grants of freedom from tithes,[1] and forgeries were made in the twelfth and thirteenth centuries for Monte Amiata, Prüfening, St Peter in Ciel d'Oro at Pavia, and other important houses.[2] Many of these included obvious anachronisms, such as a clause granting freedom from tithes in an alleged bull of Pope Zachary in 748 for Monte Cassino and the formula *Sane novalium*, which was not used before the middle of the twelfth century, in a bull for St Bartholomew at Ferrara attributed to John XIII in 967.[3] Others are very hard to detect, and many, needless to say, were accepted as genuine and even authenticated by genuine confirmations. These forgeries all relied implicitly on the authority of the papacy and occasionally referred to specific papal authorization. Two forgeries for Reinhardsbrunn, for instance, which were probably made in 1152/68 and purported to be charters of Archbishop Ruthard and Adalbert of Mainz in 1105 and 1116, granted to the monks 'the tithes of all their demesne lands and of all their adherents, which they originally recognized [as belonging] to God and ourselves...' at the alleged request and desire of Pope Paschal.[4]

Taken together this evidence shows that during the first half of the eleventh century the papacy was generally recognized as the sole authority competent to grant a general freedom from tithes

---

[1] Cf. pp. 73–4 above and Lesne, in *Rev. d'hist. ecc.* XIV, 497–8. The dates of many of these forgeries are uncertain.

[2] See p. 208 n. 3 above on Monte Amiata; MGH, *Dipl.* Lothar III, no. 126 (pp. 214–15) on Prüfening; *APRI*, II, 221–2, JL†6841, and *IP*, VI. 1, 198–9, no. 16, on St Peter at Pavia; *Raitenhaslach*, pp. 9–11, no. 6 (JL 8997); Schmid, in *Sav. Zs.* Germ. Abt. XLIII, 281–4 on other forgeries.

[3] JE†2281 and *IP*, VIII, 121–2, no. 22; *APRI*, II, 48, JL†3711, and *IP*, V, 232–3, no. 1.

[4] *Mainz*, I, 328 and 372–3.

and that all other grants were restricted to specific tithes.[1] The popes never confirmed a general grant by a lay or lesser ecclesiastical authority,[2] of which the few known examples were clearly inspired by the papal policy. The two types of grant remained separate in theory and complementary in practice. The popes often confirmed monastic possession of demesne tithes acquired by gift or purchase; and episcopal and private grants to a monastery of part or all of its demesne tithes were made, like those to Orval, Raitenhaslach, and Reichersberg, as a result of a papal grant. The true position of an individual monastery with regard to paying tithes, therefore, depended not on any single privilege or set of privileges originating in either papal or local initiative but on the total effectiveness of all its privileges, both private and papal. An abbey with no papal grant, like La Chartreuse, might still pay no tithes by virtue of its private charters; and some monasteries with general freedoms, such as Cluny, in fact still paid tithes.[3] Private grants continued to be sought as reinforcements for general privileges and as the easiest and most secure way for a monastery to avoid paying tithes from specific lands worked for its own use, but it still had to approach the papacy for a general right to pay no tithes.

The exceptional nature of this right was fully recognized and even stressed by Gratian and the early Decretists. It has been seen

---

[1] Cf. Viard, Dîme, II, 36. Even the later private grants which imitated the language of the papal privileges usually applied to specific tithes: see Ourscamp, p. 190 (1156), where two brothers granted 'ut de omnibus terris quas fratres de Ursicampo in toto territorio quod Tuletel dicitur, quomodocumque acquirere possent, et proprio labore suo excolerent, ab omni decima liberi et absoluti in perpetuum permanerent...', and St Sernin, pp. 471–2 (1173): the bishop of Toulouse granted to Grandselve 'omnes decimas et omnes primicias omnium laborum vestrorum quoscumque facitis vel facturi estis propriis sumptibus atque manibus in grangia Delasela et in omnibus pertinenciis ejus', in return for an annual rent of three shillings to St Sernin and a rent in kind to the chaplain of La Selle if he served the church.

[2] The closest approximations to papal confirmations of episcopal general grants were in the privileges of Innocent II and Eugene III for Ilsenburg, which applied only to noval tithes (see p. 244 n. 4 above) and in Eugene's two privileges for Viktring, in which the episcopal grant was cited but changed (see p. 259 above).

[3] Cf. p. 187 on La Chartreuse and p. 222 on Cluny.

that in the first question of the sixteenth case in the *Decretum* Gratian accepted within definite limits the right of monks to perform parochial functions and to possess tithes,[1] and in the fourth section of this question he cautiously broached the matter of monastic payment of tithes and asked:

Should those who are within a monastic cloister and who exercise no rule over the people give or receive tithes? Here a distinction should be made whether they keep for themselves the tithes from the fields and vineyards which are cultivated for their own use. For if tithes were paid by the people to the sons of Levi because of the ministry of serving the Lord in the tabernacle by offering sacrifices and holocausts for the sake of the people, it is clear that monks should not be required to pay tithes from their own fields any more than other priests. But it is said that before the fields came into the possession of the monks, whether they were bought for a price or given for the salvation of souls, they paid first-fruits and tithes to baptismal and other churches [and] that these churches cannot be deprived of their right.

He then cited four ninth-century decretals protecting the tithes of established churches and continued that:

If, therefore, no one may take the income of tithes from the previous church to which it was assigned, if the right of an old church should not be given to new ones, and if tithes may be given only to baptismal churches, it is clear that monks may be required to pay tithes from their own fields. But the council of Mainz spoke of the seller and the giver and established that he who sells or gives may not take the income of tithes from that church to which it was formerly properly assigned. Monks, however, hold tithes not by the authority of a sale or gift but by the authority of this same council and of Pope Paschal, who established that monks should not pay tithes from their own fields.

He then cited the decree of the council of Chalon in 813 allowing the demesne tithes of bishops and abbots to be brought to their own churches and the decretal *Decimas a populo* of Paschal II and entitled them respectively that 'Abbots and bishops should not pay tithes from their own fields' and that 'Monks and canons should certainly not be required to pay tithes from their own

[1] Cf. pp. 182–4 above.

produce'.[1] Gratian rested his case on these two texts and made no use either of the decrees of Gregory the Great and Leo IV, which were cited by Paschal II, or of Paschal's own *Novum genus*, which was widely used by later canonists. In his own *dicta* Gratian in effect admitted the weakness of the case for freeing monks from tithes and principally argued that they might possess the tithes from their own fields.[2]

The same point arose in the twenty-fifth case, which was concerned with the power of the papacy to change the established laws of the Church. Here Gratian posited that the papacy had at one time granted all the tithes in a parish to the baptismal church and had subsequently granted to a monastery the right to pay no tithes from its own fields. The monastery then acquired some land within the parish of the baptismal church, and a conflict over the tithes arose between the clergy and the monks. Gratian examined the issue in two questions: first, whether the first privilege entitled the clergy to claim all the tithes of their parish and, second, whether the second privilege might impair the first. To both these questions he answered yes. He thus maintained that in spite of various authorities supporting the inviolability of established canons, the papacy had the right to grant special privileges contrary to, or rather interpreting, the general laws, in this case the rule of quadripartition of tithes. To support this he attributed to the pope the principle of Roman law that the emperor had the power to modify and interpret the laws. He therefore held that the clergy might claim all the tithes of their parish on the basis of their privilege unless the bishops were forced by very great need to demand their quarter. By the same

---

[1] *Decretum*, C. XVI, q. I, pars IV: cc. 42 (922 council of Coblenz, attributed by Gratian to the council of Mainz: see pp. 40, 56 above), 43 (813 and subsequent councils of Mainz, attributed by Gratian to the council of Chalon: see p. 40 and n. 6 above), 44 (803 capitulary of Salz, attributed by Gratian to the council of Worms: see p. 37 and n. 6 above), 45 (letter from Leo IV in 847/8: see p. 36 and n. 5 above), 46 (813 council of Chalon-sur-Saône, attributed by Gratian to the council of Mainz: see p. 38 and n. 6 above), and 47 (see pp. 229–30 above).

[2] In the apocryphal canon of St Jerome mentioned pp. 147–8 above (*Decretum*, C. XII, q. I, c. 7), Gratian divided laymen, who pay tithes, from clerics, but he did not specifically call monks clerics or even say that clerics need not pay tithes.

token, the privilege might later be modified. Thus a monastic privilege might either affect no existing interest, as when monks were not required to pay tithes from noval lands, from which no one received tithes, or it might impair an existing interest, if it was necessary to relieve the poverty of the monks and if the baptismal churches were not ruined by the growth of monastic possessions.[1]

Gratian dealt indirectly with the same problem and came to a significantly different conclusion in his discussion of the fixity of the income from tithes at the beginning of the thirteenth case of the *Decretum*, in which he considered some of the practical difficulties arising out of the early theory of tithing, according to which a man had to pay tithes without distinction from his entire revenue as a personal religious obligation to the church where he received the sacraments, and particularly the problem of payment of tithes when men moved from one parish to another and yet still cultivated land in the previous parish. In one of the longest *dicta* in the entire *Decretum* Gratian examined the arguments of those who held that all tithes should be paid to the church where the payer received the sacraments, but realizing the havoc that the indefinite extension of this principle might play with the established revenues of the Church, he threw the weight of his own opinion on the side of fixity of receipts and decided that any baptismal church was entitled to the tithes from all the lands within its parish. 'For in so far as it affects the right to receive tithes,' he concluded, 'it is the same thing for the possessor [of the land] to move from one parish to another as for the possession to transfer from one parishioner to another.'[2] This view laid the basis, as Boyd pointed out, for the so-called predial doctrine which divorced tithes from the administration of the sacraments and treated them essentially as a charge on land rather than on persons,[3] and also for the compromise according to which

---

[1] *Decretum*, C. xxv; cf. A. J. Carlyle, *A History of Mediaeval Political Theory in the West*, II: *The Political Theory of the Roman Lawyers and the Canonists, from the Tenth Century to the Thirteenth Century* (Edinburgh, 1909), pp. 171-5.

[2] *Decretum*, C. XIII, q. I, *dictum post* c. I.

[3] Boyd, *Tithes*, pp. 139-40; cf. 247, who said that 'From at least as early as the time of Gratian to the close of the Middle Ages, it was essentially and primarily a charge upon the land'.

tithes from the produce of the soil were considered predial and
were owed to the priest in whose parish the land was located and
tithes from commercial, industrial, and professional revenues were
considered personal and owed to the church where the payer
received the sacraments.[1] Gratian thus foresaw and tried to avert
the kind of confusion that existed in England in the later Middle
Ages, when the tithe from a single field might be divided among
several churches and a prominent Franciscan was excommunicated for teaching that personal tithes might be used for the poor
rather than given to the parish priest.[2] By attaching tithes to the
land rather than to the person of the payer, however, he threatened
to undermine the entire policy of freeing monks from tithes.

    This inconsistency in the *Decretum* did not escape the sharp eyes
of the commentators, and Roland Bandinelli, the future Pope

    [1] Tithes from animals, which were raised on but not produced by the soil,
were later called 'mixed'. It is necessary to insist against those scholars who
claim that tithes were a purely agricultural due that these distinctions were new
in the twelfth century and that full payment of personal tithes from non-
agricultural revenues was always required in theory. The early Decretists
Roland Bandinelli, Rufinus, and Stephan of Tournai all recognized that the
distinction between predial and personal tithes was relatively new (see pp. 287–8
and 294–5 below). In a well-known letter to the bishop of Gran in Hungary,
Pope Lucius III (1181–5) held that people who move from one parish to another
should pay personal tithes from their agricultural produce, industry, and commerce within their new parish to the church where they received the sacraments and that the bishop might assign according to custom the tithes from goods
produced in the former or in another parish (Gregory IX, *Decretals*, III, 30, 20).
He thus insisted less rigidly than the Decretists on the fixity of receipts of tithes
from agriculture. Later canonists still disputed over 'whether tithes are a
predial or a personal prestation': see Stephan Kuttner, 'Some Unrecorded
Quaestiones', *Traditio*, XIII (1957), 507. See my article on 'Resistance to Tithes in
the Middle Ages' for some examples of papal insistence in the twelfth and
thirteenth centuries that tithes must be paid from all types of income, especially
in the diocese of Milan, where tithes seem to have been regulated by custom
and not paid from various products and revenues earlier than in other regions.
On personal tithes, which Viard believed were rarely paid in the later Middle
Ages (*Dîme*, II, 8), see Little, in *Eng. Hist. Rev.* LX, 67–88 (mostly on England);
Sylvia Thrupp, *The Merchant Class of Medieval London* (Chicago, 1948), p. 185;
and, for an example of tithes paid by a hard-headed Italian merchant, Iris
Origo, *The Merchant of Prato* (New York, 1957), p. 348.
    [2] F. W. Maitland, *Township and Borough*, Ford Lectures 1897 (Cambridge,
1898), p. 58, on divisions of tithes in England, and Little, in *Eng. Hist. Rev.*
LX, 67–8, on the case of William Russell.

Alexander III, in his *Summa* on the *Decretum*, written a few years after its publication, delayed his discussion of tithes from the thirteenth to the sixteenth case in order to take up together the problems of fixity of receipts and of monastic payment of tithes. 'That monks ought not to pay but to receive tithes', he said at first, 'is proved by authorities and reasons.' As authorities he cited the fact that the tribe of Levi paid no tithes and the canons of the council of Chalon and of Paschal II. As reasons he pointed out (which some theologians might not have accepted) that tithes were owed to the higher by the lower orders, that monks were of a higher order than priests, and that monks therefore need not pay tithes. He then refuted at length the two contrary arguments, both supported by texts in the *Decretum*, that established churches should not be deprived of their revenues, especially by monks and regular canons of whom a higher standard of conduct was expected than from other clerics, and that tithes should be paid only to baptismal churches. 'It should be noted at this point,' he said, 'that some monasteries are privileged and some are not. We therefore hold that monasteries privileged in this respect should not pay tithes to any other person; but the others, as some people hold, are bound to give tithes. It should also be noted that the opinion of many wise men differs on this point, for some claim that tithes are assigned by reason of the persons and others by reason of the lands.' The system of personal tithes, Roland explained, by which tithes were paid from every type of revenue to the church where the payer received the sacraments, prevailed in the Veneto and was in accord with the canons of Mainz (Chalon) and of Paschal II allowing monks and regular canons to keep the tithes from their demesne lands, but it might impoverish a church whose parishioners moved to another parish. Following Gratian, therefore, Roland personally supported the predial system which gave every church the tithes from all the lands within its parish. He admitted that monastic possession of tithes previously paid to parish churches was an exception to this rule. 'At this point we hold that nothing is held so generally that it cannot be modified in a particular. He who has the authority to modify canons also has the authority to interpret.' Just as under special circumstances, therefore, bishoprics and parishes might be divided or joined, so likewise monasteries might possess their demesne tithes. Like Gratian he based this right fundamentally on the control of the bishop over ecclesiastical property in his diocese and on the right of monks to perform pastoral functions. But even more than Gratian he recognized the inconsistency of this practice and of the predial system of tithes and sought to base the fact that many monks paid no tithes on concrete rights of possession of their own tithes rather than on an abstract freedom granted by the papacy.[1]

3. THE CRISIS OF MONASTIC FREEDOM FROM TITHES

The fears of the canonists were not without reason, and in practice the policy of freeing monks from tithes often had disastrous effects on the established revenues of the Church. Already long before the middle of the twelfth century complaints and disputes arose on all sides from previous owners of tithes who found themselves suddenly deprived of their property without just cause or compensation. At first the objections were comparatively few because the grants were rare, the recipients were usually poor, and their lands were often new lands from which no tithes had previously been paid. 'In judging Cistercian immunity', as Hirsch remarked, 'the financial factor must be given prominence';[2] and the payment of tithes would have imposed a severe economic burden on many new monasteries, while their freedom from tithes usually harmed no one. But these houses rapidly grew in wealth and soon not only accepted tithes from the labour of other men, which they had at first refused, but even sold the produce of lands from which they paid no tithes.[3] The foundation of new privileged monasteries and the spread of their holdings of land were a constant threat to all owners of tithes, and wealthy Cistercian abbeys sometimes refused to pay tithes which had for

---

[1] Summa mag. Rolandi, pp. 39–42.

[2] Hirsch, Klosterimmunität, pp. 144–5; cf. Muggenthaler, Zisterzienserkloster, pp. 33–4, who treated Cistercian immunity as an exclusively economic problem.

[3] Cf. pp. 190–2 above and Louis Lekai, Les moines blancs (Paris, 1957), p. 268.

centuries belonged to small and poor black Benedictine houses. The opposition thus grew in proportion to the number of tithe-privileges and the wealth of the recipient houses.[1]

One method of settling these difficulties was by arranging suitable compensation for the previous owners of the tithe. The Cistercians in particular, as Knowles and Mahn pointed out, often found that they could buy peace only by indemnifying the owner of the tithe with a lump sum in land or money or, more frequently, with an annual rent.[2] The hardship to the previous owner was thus reduced and the effect of the papal privilege was watered down if not annulled. As a rule these arrangements were made either voluntarily by the monks, who occasionally recognized the justice of the previous owners' complaints, or by the bishops and other local authorities who made it their business to protect the interests of the parish clergy and of other monasteries. As early as 1121/2 the archbishop of Sens required the Cistercians of Preuilly to make an allowance in kind to the priest of Egligny in return for the tithes from his parish;[3] the monks of Bonnevaux in about 1122 bought off for small sums the claims of several laymen to tithes from their produce,[4] and in 1123 the bishop of Orléans and an archdeacon secured the consent of the local lords and priests to an arrangement by which the Cistercian abbey of Cour-Dieu paid an annual rent of twelve pennies in return for the tithes from the 'priestly fief' of a parish.[5] Innocent II himself in his privilege for Ourscamp in 1131, which included no freedom from tithes, required the monks to pay seven shillings a year for

---

[1] A parallel problem existed in the Byzantine Empire, where the wealth and privileges of the monasteries were a constant source of concern to the emperors. In the twelfth century they tried to restrict the further acquisition of property by monks: see Peter Charanis, 'The Monastic Properties and the State in the Byzantine Empire', *Dumbarton Oaks Papers*, IV (1948), 51–118, esp. 82–7; A. A. Vasiliev, *History of the Byzantine Empire* (Madison, 1952), pp. 565–74; and George Ostrogorsky, *History of the Byzantine State*, tr. Joan Hussey (Oxford, 1956), pp. 291–2 and 329–31.

[2] Knowles, *Mon. Order*, p. 355, and Mahn, *Ordre*, p. 106.

[3] *Preuilly*, p. 6 (see p. 252 n. 2 above); cf. pp. 34–5 (1155) for an example of a rent to a monastery.

[4] *Bonnevaux*, pp. 86–7, no. 199; cf. Chevalier, *Regeste*, no. 3333 on the date.

[5] *GC*, VIII, instr. 502.

some land 'belonging both in tithes and in land tax (*terragium*) to the church of St Peter at Brétigny'.[1] The monks of Orval made many settlements of this sort, paying among others rents of twelve pennies to the *magister scholarum* Emelinus, ten shillings to the priory of Cons-la-Grandville, twelve pennies to two brothers in return for a fief of certain lands and tithes and a third of the tithes 'belonging to the altar', and twelve pennies to one priest and six to another in return for part of some tithes of which the other parts were given to them by laymen and clerics and confirmed by the archbishop of Trier.[2] Similar arrangements are found in the charters of the Cistercian abbeys of Écharlis, La Ferté, Igny, Rievaulx, Fontmorigny, Melsa (Meaux), Old Wardon, Grandselve, Longpont, and Cambron,[3] and it is probable that many of the private grants mentioned above were in fact made in return for a *quid pro quo*. They were thus sales of property, sometimes on an explicitly feudal or contractual basis,[4] and were often an essential complement to the papal privilege in order effectively to free a monastery from paying tithes.

More rarely the privileged monks agreed or were even forced to pay all or part of the tithes in question.[5] The monks of Tiron, for example, who were freed from paying tithes by Innocent II in 1132, were given some land from which the tithes belonged to the nuns of St Avit at Châteaudun and agreed in 1135 to pay to the nuns the entire tithe of goods produced by themselves and others

---

[1] *Ourscamp*, pp. 286–7; JL 7518; cf. pp. 275–6 (*c.* 1132) and 275 (1134) for other references to this transaction and 67–8 (*c.* 1140: rent to the monastery).

[2] *Orval*, pp. 11 (1138), 12 (1138), 15–16 (1141), 16–17 (1144), 17–18 (1145/56), 18–19 (1145/67), 20 (1149), 28–9 (1153/67), etc.

[3] *Yonne*, I, 310 (1136: Écharlis paid rent to parish priest); *La Ferté*, p. 66 (*c.* 1150, to two lay brothers); *St Martin des Champs*, II, 218–19 (1151: Igny paid rent in kind to monks); *Rievaulx*, pp. 27, 27–8, 28, and 29–30 (all 1153/67, to parish priests and monks); *Fontmorigny*, pp. 10–11 (1157/8, rent in kind to secular canons); *Old Wardon*, p. 15, no. 10 (*c.* 1160/70); *St Symphorien d'Autun*, pp. 73–5, no. 34 (1180: La Ferté paid rent in kind to monks); *Melsa*, I, 217–18 (*c.* 1182, rent in wax to parish church); and p. 264 n. 1, p. 192 and p. 273 for Grandselve, Longpont, and Cambron.

[4] In some of the grants to Orval and Rievaulx the tithes were called a fief or were recoverable if the rent was not paid.

[5] Cf. Viard, *Dîme*, II, 46, and the agreement between the Hospitallers and the canons of the church of the Holy Sepulchre, cited p. 276 n. 2 below.

on five arpents of the land, half of the tithes from the remainder of the land, and all the tithes of their animals and to the parish priest a third of their tithes 'except from the said vineyards and the monks' own animals and carts'.[1] In 1142/3 the abbot of St Peter at Chalon gave the woods of Grosne to La Ferté on condition that if they were to be inhabited the tithe should belong to the monks of St-Martin-de-Laives.[2] The dean of Noyon in 1145 gave the Cistercians of Longpont the demesne tithes from their grange at Héronval and the third which his church held out of the common tithe from all their agricultural produce in return for rents of twelve pennies and two sesters of grain respectively, and they were to pay 'the due tithe just like other labourers' from any land they cultivated outside the agreed boundaries.[3] In the foundation charter of Stoneleigh in 1155 Henry II gave the monks, among other property, 'the revenue of salt at Droitwich, that is, twenty-five loads saving the tithe of the canons of Kenilworth, that is, two and a half loads of salt, which they are accustomed to have'.[4] In 1154 the bishop of Cambrai gave the Cistercians of Cambron the church or altar 'in the precincts of which their church was founded' on condition that, as he said:

Since their order prevents their exercising the cure of secular souls, we keep in our hands the ecclesiastical benefice of the altar in order that the parish priest may receive the tithes from the produce and food of the peasants and the oblations and other parochial rights if there are any. The monks, however, should pay to the priest an annual rent of one measure of wheat and one sester of peas by the measure of the estate and should free him from the duties of *gîte* and from the synodals, and in return they may both freely possess the endowment of the altar and be free from all tithes of their own produce and food. If in the future they shall acquire any land in this territory which does not belong to them now, they should either pay tithes or make good to the priest by a suitable rent.[5]

---

[1] *Tiron*, I, 218–19.   [2] *La Ferté*, p. 101.
[3] *Héronval*, p. 3.   [4] *Stoneleigh*, p. 16; cf. introd. p. lix, on date.
[5] *Cambron*, p. 97. The *personatum* of this church, as distinct from the *dos* or landed property, apparently included the personal dues paid by the parishioners. On the synodals and other dues paid by the parish priests, see Cheney, *Becket*, pp. 150–1.

The spirit of equity which governed many of these compromises is here clearly expressed.

These arrangements were not always equitable and amicable, however, and many long and bitter conflicts were waged between the owners of tithes and monks who stood on the letter of the papal privilege and refused either to pay tithes or to give any compensation. These disputes were often taken into the courts, both secular and ecclesiastical, and occasionally broke out into open violence. The notorious controversy between the Cluniac priory of Gigny and the Cistercian abbey of Le Miroir, for instance, lasted almost twenty years and involved three popes as well as St Bernard and Peter the Venerable. It culminated in an attack on Le Miroir by the infuriated Cluniacs, who did damage estimated at the colossal sum of thirty thousand shillings.[1] More and more of these cases after about 1140 were taken to Rome, where they were either assigned to local judge-delegates or, if the dispute was sufficiently important, judged by the pope himself. Lucius II in 1144/5 instructed the archbishop of Milan to prevent his 'parishioners', both lay and ecclesiastical, from forcing the Augustinian canons of Crescenzago to pay tithes, and Eugene III repeated these instructions in 1145 in three letters of increasing severity.[2] In 1146 Eugene sent three cardinals to settle a dispute over the monastery of St Michael at Ventimiglia between the monks of Lérins and the canons of Ventimiglia. Among other things the monks complained that tithes had been exacted from their own produce by the canons, who replied that they had previously collected the tithes without opposition. The judges decided that in return for their demesne tithes and certain other rights the monks should grind the canons' grain without charge 'except for the usual benefice of the miller'.[3] Eugene also instructed the archbishop of Narbonne to prevent the bishop and canons of Maguelonne from forcing the new Cluniac house near Montpellier to pay tithes from the lands worked by its own monks.[4]

---

[1] See *Rev. bén.* LXX, 618.

[2] *APRI*, II, 341–3; JL 8695, 8774, 8775 and 8814. See *J. Ecc. Hist.* XIII, 178–9, on tithing in the diocese of Milan.

[3] *APRI*, I, 187; JL 8919.   [4] *Bull. Clun.* p. 58; JL 9628.

The long dispute between the Cluniac abbey of Seltz and the Cistercians of Neuburg was finally settled in 1151 in a secular court, and the Cluniacs gave up their claim to the disputed tithe in return for an annual rent of nine measures of grain for themselves and three for the local priest. The charter for Seltz said that 'We claimed the tithe from cultivated and uncultivated lands on the basis of our privilege, but they resisted on the basis of their privilege', which clearly shows how the new right of freedom from tithes often came into conflict with the old right of possession of tithes.[1]

Great difficulties arose in the Holy Land over the privileges of the Hospitallers, who according to William of Tyre both disregarded the excommunications and interdicts of the patriarch, appointed and dismissed priests without permission from the bishops, and 'completely refused to pay tithes from their estates and from all the revenues which have come to them by whatever right'. William went on to say that 'It seems to those who have carefully studied [the matter] that the church of Rome originally caused this great evil, although perhaps without knowing or weighing in the balance what was asked of it. For it unjustly freed the aforesaid house [of the Hospital] from the jurisdiction of the patriarch of Jerusalem, to which it had rightly been subject for a long time.' In a brief sketch of the history of the Hospitallers, William then repeated that they grew rich and were successively freed from the control of the abbot and the patriarch and 'henceforth showed absolutely no reverence for the prelates of the churches and completely refused [to pay] them tithes from any estates which have come to them by whatever right'. As a result, still according to William, the secular clergy were divided and split from many monasteries and hospitals which had grown rich from their generosity. In the spring of 1155, the patriarch of Jerusalem, the archbishop of Tyre, and six bishops from the Holy Land came to the new Pope Hadrian IV in Italy in order to protest against this situation. But William said that they were received with scant courtesy at the curia, which supported the Hospitallers, and the patriarch left after

[1] Würdtwein, *Nova subsidia*, VII, 151–2, no. 58, and IX, 351–3, no. 180.

several days of unprofitable discussion with 'his position injured rather than improved'.[1] William was clearly prejudiced on this matter, and a bull of Alexander III in 1168 proves that in fact the Hospitallers made important concessions with regard to tithes owed to the church of the Holy Sepulchre at Jerusalem.[2] But there is other evidence of trouble over tithes in the Holy Land,[3] and William's account shows above all the growing opposition to the new monastic privileges, and especially to freedom from tithes, in the second quarter of the twelfth century.

This attitude was found as much among monks as among bishops and priests, and it involved not only purely economic issues, important as these were, but also disputed questions concerning the independence of monks and their performance of pastoral work and manual labour. The disputes over tithes therefore heightened the hostility between the old and new monks. Peter the Venerable, in the letters written in 1135/7 to Innocent II and the papal chancellor Haimeric in connection with the controversy between Gigny and Le Miroir, complained bitterly at the threat to interdict the Cluniacs for claiming their tithes and at the Cistercian privileges, which contradicted both well-established precedents and 'many and ancient' papal privileges for Cluny. He warned 'that such a scandal is brewing from this [matter] that it may begin in our time but will not be finished in our age'. At the same time he wrote to the assembled Cistercian abbots in the chapter-general at Cîteaux saying that

---

[1] William of Tyre, *Historia rerum in partibus transmarinis gestarum*, XVIII, 3–8, in *Recueil des historiens des croisades: Historiens occidentaux*, I (Paris, 1844), 820–31 (quoted extracts on 820, 821–2, 826–7, and 830); tr. Emily Babcock and A. C. Krey, Columbia Records of Civilization, XXXV (New York, 1943), II, 234–50. On William's attitude towards the wealth and independence of the Templars, see Friedrich Lundgreen, *Wilhelm von Tyrus und der Templerorden*, Historische Studien, ed. Ebering, XCVII (Berlin, 1911), pp. 137–53.

[2] *PL*, CC, 473; JL 11382: the Hospitallers were to pay to the canons of the Holy Sepulchre 'tithes from all their possessions in the bishopric of Jerusalem which they grant to others to be cultivated and do not cultivate by their own hands or for their own use and tithes in accordance with the agreement made between you from their produce which is cultivated by their own hands or for their own use'.

[3] See Röhricht, *Regesta*, nos. 133 (1130), 239 (1145), etc., and Schnürer, *Templerregel*, p. 88 n. 1.

their freedom from tithes had harmed their good relations with
the rest of the Church and that they should pay tithes even from
goods produced by themselves 'lest you injure both yourselves
and us'.[1]

Further evidence of the growing protest is found in the
Liber de novitatibus huius temporis, which was addressed to the new
Pope Hadrian IV by Gerhoh of Reichersberg, who was generally
opposed to the possession by monks and regular canons of other
men's tithes but who defended their right to pay no tithes 'either
to soldiers or to secular clerics from the fields, vineyards, or food
of animals cultivated for their own use'. Gerhoh's opinion in
this matter was doubtless influenced by the experience of his own
canons, who had been forced to pay tithes by the bishop of
Regensburg before they were freed by Pope Eugene. He supported his view with the decrees of Urban I forbidding private
possession of church property,[2] of Innocent II, and of Eugene
III, and he urged the new pope to issue a similar statute, 'because
when Pope Eugene died it was thought by foolish men that his
statute concerning the non-payment of tithes by monks and
regular canons in places where they cultivate their lands by their
own hands and for their own use also died with him'. Gerhoh
maintained, as he had in his earlier works, that peasants must of
course pay tithes to the churches where they received the sacraments, but not spiritual men who needed no pastoral services
from priests. 'Oh marvellous desolation and detestable abomi-
nation of a desolation,' he cried, 'that those who should be supported by the tithes of the people are forced to give to secular
persons tithes from their labours, which by the dispensation of
the bishop they ought to receive from them for their own support.'
Under the guise of rigid, pharisaical justice, the bishops had
neglected the papal decrees and forced the monks and canons to
pay tithes.

I say that this little fox that destroys the vineyards lay concealed [wrote
Gerhoh, citing the Song of Solomon], but now it is aroused, as if the

---

[1] Peter the Venerable, epp. i, 33–5, in *Bibl. Clun.* 700–6.
[2] This decree was also used by Gerhoh in his *Opusculum de edificio Dei* (see
p. 163 above) and *Liber de laude fidei* (see p. 164 above and p. 278 below).

barking of the dogs of the Lord (that is, the apostolic teachings of Popes Innocent and Eugene) had already died down, and clearly thinks itself free to destroy the vines of the Lord Sabaoth with the tooth not now of the fox but of the wild boar. Let it therefore feel, father Hadrian, that the spirit of your predecessors still lives in you; let this most evil beast, I say, which has devoured Joseph, be severely chastised unless it stops its cherished evil-doing.[1]

In his *Liber de laude fidei*, written in 1158/9, Gerhoh again cited the decree of Urban I as evidence 'that tithes are owed to the poor of Christ' and the letter of Gregory the Great to show 'that they owe tithes to no man'. He also mentioned the decree of the council of Chalon-sur-Saône and praised the wisdom of the fathers there 'because they separate the demesne lands of the bishops, abbots, and monks from those which the peasants work for their own use, from which they rightly owe tithes to the priests who minister to them in spiritual matters'. He then described how Popes Innocent and Eugene freed monks from paying tithes from their own demesne. 'Some of the bishops at the council of Rheims [in 1148] tried to protest against this very beneficial and just practice, when Pope Eugene of holy memory was presiding, to whom he replied in this fashion: "You bishops nourish wolves on the pastures of the sheep, when you should be called shepherds of the sheep, and you do not grant the necessary sustenance to the poor of Christ from the tithes of the people, as you should, but rather you exact tithes from them."'[2]

Pope Hadrian IV was therefore faced at the beginning of his pontificate with a strong reaction against the policy of freeing monks from tithes. His immediate predecessor Anastasius IV, who was pope for only just eighteen months, had already reversed the policy of Innocent II and Eugene III in the case between Gigny and Le Miroir and had ordered the Cistercians to return to Cluny the seventeen thousand shillings paid as damages

---

[1] MGH, *Libelli*, III, 291-2. See pp. 162-5 above on Gerhoh's attitude towards monastic possession of tithes from the labour of other men. Cf. Pierre Mandonnet, *Saint Dominique* (Paris, 1937), II, 69-81, esp. 73-4, on the *canis dominici* and the concept of the foxes as the enemies of the Church.

[2] Gerhoh, *Opera inedita*, I, 208-9. This is the only source for the bishops' protest at the council of Rheims in 1148.

for the attack on their abbey,[1] and Gerhoh's work suggests that many local authorities were taking matters into their own hands. Hadrian had thus to decide whether to maintain the tithe-privilege unchanged or to modify, or even abolish it so as to protect the interests of the existing owners of tithes. During the first few weeks he issued several privileges containing the general freedom *Sane laborum*, including a confirmation for Aniane and new grants for the Benedictine abbey of St Martin at Tulle, the Premonstratensians of Braisne-sur-Vesle, and the abbey of Falera, which had become Cistercian in 1143.[2] But on 5 January 1155, exactly a month after his coronation as pope, Hadrian changed the formula in his confirmation for Prémontré from *Sane laborum* to *Sane novalium* and so restricted the application of the freedom from tithes to newly cultivated demesne lands and forced the monks to pay tithes from any lands from which tithes had previously been paid.[3] In his subsequent grants, both confirmations and new privileges, he made use almost exclusively of the formula *Sane novalium*.[4]

Hadrian was not in fact the first pope to restrict the freedom from tithes to produce from noval lands. Urban II in the late eleventh century specified noval tithes in his grants to St Jean-des-Vignes and Raitenbuch. Paschal II limited his grants for

---

[1] *PL*, CLXXXVIII, 1037–8 and 1067–8; JL 9866 and 9877. Early in 1155 the archbishop of Lyons and the bishop of Winchester arranged a final settlement by which the Cistercians agreed to return 11,000 shillings and to pay in the future an annual rent of seventy shillings in return for the tithes previously paid to Gigny (*Cluny*, v, 530–1, no. 4180). Cf. *Rev. bén.* LXX, 623.

[2] JL 9944, 9963, 9973 and 9978 (*IP*, II, 188). Schreiber, *Kurie*, I, 262, mistakenly said that Hadrian granted no privilege to a Cistercian house without 'the reactionary provision' limiting the freedom to noval tithes. Hoffmann, in *Hist. Jb.* XXXI, 717 n. 3, said that Hadrian gave any sort of tithe-privilege to only three Cistercian houses, which is also too few.

[3] *PL*, CLXXXVIII, 1377; JL 9972.

[4] See the examples cited by Schreiber, *Kurie*, I, 260–2, to which may be added *PU in Frankreich*, III, 30; JL 10076, 10157, 10170, 10180; *Fontmorigny*, p. 10; JL 10254, 10290 and (confirmations with the changed formula) JL 10003 a (St Mary at Josaphat), 10167 (St Stephen at Dijon), 10252 (Zwettl), *PU in England*, III, 267 (Crowland), *Preuilly*, p. 43, and *Old Wardon*, p. 19 (cf. the privilege of Eugene III on p. 17). On this restriction, cf. Pöschl, in *A. f. kath. KR*, XCVIII, 362.

Dietramszell, Lambach, and Baumburg to *decimas novalium vestrarum*. The episcopal grant of noval tithes to Ilsenburg in 1119 was confirmed by Popes Innocent II and Eugene III. Innocent also confined his privilege for Camp to tithes from uncultivated lands. And *novalium* were sometimes found in place of *laborum* in the privileges of Celestine II, Eugene III, and Anastasius IV.[1] Such limitations were presumably intended to protect the interests of those who already owned tithes from the monastery's lands, and they are evidence of a certain flexibility in the papal policy.[2] In practice, however, they were not always easy to apply. As Viard said, 'The question of knowing whether such and such a tithe was old or noval was a question of fact which was very difficult...to solve in many concrete cases'.[3] Eugene III in his bull for the abbey of St John at Parma vaguely defined *novalia* as lands 'which are newly cultivated and have not previously been cultivated for sixty, or fifty, or forty years or less'.[4]

Hadrian was the first pope to apply and justify this restriction generally, however. In a letter in 1155 to the monks of Pontida, who had refused to pay certain tithes, he wrote that 'We have decided that no other tithes than those which are known to come from newly cultivated lands should be granted to men of religion'.[5] The following year he wrote to the bishop of Halberstadt that 'The abbots of the Cistercian order have on account of the papal privileges taken from you without just cause the tithes from purchased lands of which you were previously accustomed justly to have the tithes. For we have decided that only the tithes of

---

[1] See p. 244 n. 4 above. Many monks with general privileges in fact principally or even exclusively cultivated new lands: cf. Dubled, in *Rev. d'hist. ecc.* LIV, 779–80. On noval tithes generally, see pp. 105–6 above, and Schreiber, *Kurie*, I, 279–81.

[2] Cf. Schreiber, *Kurie*, I, 253–5, and Mahn, *Ordre*, p. 106, who both said that these earlier restrictions to noval tithes were the result of regional and agricultural differences and were not exceptions to the general policy of granting full freedom from tithes.

[3] Viard, *Dîme*, II, 27.

[4] *PL*, CLXXX, 1061; JL 8790.

[5] *PL*, CLXXXVIII, 1586–7; Comp. I, III, 26, 15; JL 10444; *IP*, VI. 1, 159, no. 2 (under Pontirolo) and 394, no. 8 (under Pontida).

newly cultivated lands should be granted to religious men.'[1] He wrote in similar terms to the monks of the Vallombrosan abbey of Astino, requiring them to pay the tithes owed to a local priest.[2]

The most complete statement of this policy occurs in a newly discovered, undated decretal addressed to the English:

Certain bishops, abbots, and chaplains from both Italy and France have seriously complained to us that the abbots of the Cistercian order take tithes unjustly, saying that they have privileges from our predecessors and therefore need not pay tithes from their own cultivated lands; and thus it has occurred that, when they have acquired lands and property, the churches which have survived from the earliest cradles of the new-born Church have been destroyed. In view of such great damage and such serious destruction, we have therefore decreed at the prompting of wisdom and piety that the said Cistercian monks may keep the tithes from the noval lands which they cultivate by their own labour, [but] they should restore the others without any resistance to the churches in whose dioceses the lands and property are known to belong.[3]

The positive side of Hadrian's policy is shown by the privilege issued in April 1155 for the Augustinian canons of St Rufus near Avignon, in which he decreed 'that the authority of no privilege from either ourselves or our predecessors should prevent you from having in the future the tithes of all the lands from which you were at any time accustomed to have the tithes canonically and legitimately and of any church which is subject to you, to whomsoever these lands may belong'.[4] Since Hadrian himself had belonged to the community of St Rufus, and had been abbot for some years prior to his nomination as a cardinal (probably

---

[1] *Halberstadt*, I, 215; JL 10189 a.   [2] Comp. I, III, 26, 16; JL 10459.

[3] I am indebted for this text and for permission to use it here to Stephan Kuttner. It will be published by him and G. Fransen in their forthcoming edition of the *Summa* 'Elegantius in iure diuino' *sive Coloniensis*, Monumenta iuris canonici, I, I (Vatican City), ps. 9, c. 38; cf. J. F. von Schulte, 'Zur Geschichte der Literatur über das Dekret Gratians', *Sitzungsberichte der kaiserlichen Akademie der Wissenschaften* [*in Wien*], Phil.-hist. Kl. LXIV (1870), 130.

[4] *St Rufus*, p. 34; JL 10030.

late in 1149),¹ his grant to this house must have been inspired by his intimate knowledge of its affairs and probably especially by its losses of tithes. In the privilege he carefully separated the possession of land from the possession of tithes and decreed that a papal privilege for the owner of some land should not prejudice the right of the owner of the tithes from that land.

In the administration of his new policy, Hadrian occasionally tempered justice with mercy. His bulls for Aniane confirming its full freedom from tithes and instructing the bishop of Lodève to prevent the exaction of tithes from the produce and food of the monks were both issued late in 1154, before the change of policy.² But in a later bull, dated 16 February and previously attributed to Honorius II, he ordered the archbishops and bishops in whose dioceses the lands of Aniane lay to exact no tithes from the goods produced for the monks' own use and to prohibit 'the laymen in your parishes from complaining about these tithes'.³ William of Tyre remarked on the unfavourable reception given at the papal curia in the spring of 1155 to the patriarch of Jerusalem, who was seeking among other things a modification of the tithe-privileges of the Hospitallers,⁴ and although Hadrian never specifically confirmed the full freedom from tithes in his bulls for the Hospitallers, he is not known to have restricted their privilege to noval tithes.⁵ In his privilege for the abbey of St Cornelius at

---

¹ R. L. Poole, 'The Early Lives of Robert Pullen and Nicholas Breakspear' (1925), reprinted in *Studies in Chronology and History*, ed. A. L. Poole (Oxford, 1934), pp. 291-5.

² *Aniane*, p. 104; JL 9944, dated 12 December 1154 (confirming the privileges of Innocent II, Eugene III, and Anastasius IV, in *Aniane*, pp. 97, 99 and 102; JL 7432, 8953 and 9933), and *Aniane*, pp. 121-2 (not in JL), dated 12 December 1154/8 but probably issued at the same time as JL 9944. Hadrian also confirmed a bull of Anastasius IV protecting the rights of Aniane from lay and episcopal invasion: *Aniane*, pp. 118-19 (JL 9934) and 129 (not in JL).

³ *Aniane*, pp. 124-5; JL 7330, as by Honorius II and dated 16 February 1125/9 (see p. 234 n. 3 above), but Löwenfeld said that 'Hae litterae an recte Honorio II. ascribantur, non satis constat, quippe quae nonnullis Hadriani IV. epistolis intermixtae reperiantur'. The subject-matter and wording both support its attribution to Hadrian.   ⁴ Cf. pp. 275-6 above.

⁵ *Hospitaliers*, I, 176 (dated 19 December 1154, confirming the privilege of Anastasius IV [JL 9931], which protected the knights from molestation 'super decimis…et aliis que a sede apostolica indulta sunt'), 178, 179, 181, 183 and

Compiègne in 1157/9 he freed the monks from paying tithes of their own produce 'within the parish of your church'.[1]

As a rule, however, Hadrian adhered strictly to the principles of fixity of receipts and canonical distribution of tithes. On different occasions he insisted that the parish priests in the diocese of Worms pay the canonical quarter of all tithes to the bishop, that the parish priests on the lands of the Augustinian house of the Saviour at Venice must pay to the canons the tithes 'which have been canonically granted to their church by the privileges of the Roman church and the diocesan bishop', and that in the diocese of Milan the peasants must pay their tithes before subtracting the seed and other expenses and the lords must pay tithes from their portions of the crops.[2] In a bull for the monastery of SS Cosmas and Damian at Rome in 1157 he allowed that in certain churches 'the fourth part of the tithe, which is owed to the poor according to canon law' might be given to the monks 'as to the poor of Christ',[3] and he thus tacitly required the remaining three-quarters to be devoted to their canonical ends. In 1157/9 he confirmed a grant made by Count Alfonso of Toulouse to the cathedral of Arles of the noval tithes in the area of Argentières: 'By virtue of the office of supreme pontiff which has been imposed upon us by God, we are bound to do justice to our brother bishops and to maintain their rights unimpaired and complete.' He therefore ordered all his beloved sons, 'both clerics and laymen, monks, Hospitallers, Templars, and all men working the land at Argentières', to pay the tithes from all lands newly cultivated then and in the future to the archbishop of Arles.[4] In this case not even new lands worked by privileged monks were freed from tithes.

193, nos. 229, 233, 235–6, 239, 243 and 254 (all confirming earlier papal privileges without reference to tithes). In his bull for the cathedral of Arles cited below, Hadrian included the Hospitallers among those required to pay tithes.

[1] St Corneille de Compiègne, I, 155; JL 10510.

[2] APRI, II, 357 (1155), III, 189 (1157/8), and III, 198 (1154/9); JL 10080, 10488 and 10447. In a charter for Xanten in January 1155 he asserted the control of the archdeacon over all the noval tithes in the archdeaconry 'excepting those that may have been granted to other churches by papal privileges': Xanten, pp. 25–6; JL 9979.   [3] APRI, II, 360; JL 10299.

[4] EPRI, pp. 130–1, no. 236, and Hospitaliers, I, 194, no. 256; JL 10524. The charter of 1143 is printed in GC, I, instr. 97. Argentia is a common place-name

Hadrian also occasionally granted to churches the power to control the foundation of new churches on their lands. This right normally belonged to the diocesan bishop and was only rarely granted to monasteries.[1] A few examples are found, however, among the monastic privileges of Paschal II, Calixtus II, Innocent II and Eugene III,[2] and episcopal grants of this privilege were also known.[3] Peter the Venerable protested in his letter to Innocent II that some of the new houses of monks who were free from tithes had been established on lands belonging to Cluny 'without our consent [and] against canon law',[4] and Lucius II in two privileges for Cluny specifically authorized the abbot to control the building of churches and chapels in parishes belonging to Cluny and gave as his reason the duty of bishops to protect the rights and tithes of established churches.[5] Hadrian confirmed this in his general privilege for Cluny in 1155, specifying 'that in the future no order or religious house other than Cluniac may be placed in your parishes, in order that the goods and rights which have been granted to your church by the kindness of the Roman pontiffs may not be reduced or taken away by the spread of some new or intruding religion'.[6] He made similar grants in 1156 to the

---

in France: cf. Auguste Longnon, *Les noms de lieu de la France* (Paris, 1920–9), p. 152; it was translated as 'Argens' in *Hospitaliers*, I, 194, but it probably refers to Argentières in Bouches-du-Rhône.

[1] Cf. Gregor Ender, *Die Stellung des Papstes Calixt II. zu den Klöstern* (Greifswald Diss., 1913), p. 55.

[2] JL 6082 (1106, for the abbey of the Saviour at Brescia); 6201 (1108, for St Bertin); *PU in Frankreich*, NF III, 48 (1109, for La Capelle); Calixte II, *Bullaire*, II, 165 (JL 7049, confirming JL 6082 in 1123) and 338 (JL 7167, confirming JL 6201 in 1124); *APRI*, I, 139 (JL 7408, for Gorze in 1130); *PU in den Niederlanden*, p. 116 (1135, for Lobbes); JL 8016 (1139, confirming for St Bertin); JL 8801 (1145, for St Peter at Ghent; dropped by Hadrian IV in JL 10228). The bulls of Alexander III in *PU in England*, I, 372–4 (cf. p. 302 n. 4 below), show that the abbey of St Florence at Saumur also had this privilege.

[3] Cf. Round, *Calendar*, p. 443, no. 1228 (1119/38: archbishop of York for Holy Trinity at York).

[4] Peter the Venerable, ep. I, 33, in *Bibl. Clun.* p. 701.

[5] *Bull. Clun.* pp. 53–4; JL 8621–2 (1144); cf. Gaston Letonnelier, *L'Abbaye exempte de Cluny et le Saint-Siège*, Archives de la France monastique, XXII (Ligugé–Paris, 1923), p. 51.

[6] *Bull. Clun.* p. 68; JL 10069.

abbey of Bagno in Romagna and in 1159 to his own old house of St Rufus near Avignon, forbidding anyone to sell or usurp its tithes and to build a church on its lands without the permission of the abbot.[1]

Hadrian's policy towards monastic tithes has commonly been described by historians as harsh and reactionary. Schreiber, for instance, wrote that Hadrian was 'not friendly to monasteries' in this matter and desired principally to protect episcopal finances; and his reaction was called 'brutal' and harmful to monastic finances by Viard and too early and too vigorous by Mahn, who attributed it to 'the traditionalist and authoritarian spirit of the English pope'.[2] This view fails to take into account, however, the circumstances in which the policy was formulated and the clear statements of its purpose in Hadrian's own documents. It was designed to correct a situation which would only have been aggravated by continuing his predecessors' policy, such as Gerhoh advocated, and there is no evidence that in general it did more harm than good to monastic finances, since it protected the revenues of many established houses while still freeing from tithes any monks who were willing to cultivate new lands. By restricting but not abolishing the privilege, Hadrian tried to establish the freedom from tithes on a realistic basis and to remove the need for private arrangements modifying the effect of the full privilege. It is true that Hadrian had a strong will and applied his new rule vigorously,[3] and had he lived longer he might have enlarged the number of exceptions in order to deal with individual cases. 'He is one of those figures of medieval history,' said Stubbs, 'of which what little we know is suggestive of a great deal more that we should desire to know. He was unquestionably

---

[1] JL 10203 (IP, v, 125–6, no. 7) and St Rufus, p. 48 (JL 10571); for a similar grant to a non-monastic church, see JL 10050.

[2] Schreiber, Kurie, I, 263–5 and 276–7; Viard, Dîme, II, 43–4; Mahn, Ordre, p. 107; cf. Hoffmann, in SMGBOZ, XXXIII, 437–9; Pöschl, in A. f. kath. KR, XCVIII, 361; and Dubled, in Rev. d'hist. ecc. LIV, 781 n. 1.

[3] On Hadrian's character, see John of Salisbury, Policraticus, VI, 24, and VIII, 23, ed. C. C. J. Webb (Oxford, 1909), II, 67 ff. and 410–11, and Metalogicon, IV, 42, ed. C. C. J. Webb (Oxford, 1929), pp. 217–18; cf. Raymonde Foreville, in Histoire de l'Église, ed. Fliche and Martin, IX. 2, 27–8.

a great pope; that is, a great constructive pope, not a controversial one, like those who preceded and followed; a man of organizing power and missionary zeal; a reformer, and, although he did not take a wise way of showing it, a true Englishman.'[1] Disregarding the final remark, recent research has tended to confirm that he was an active and skilled administrator, although a conservative theorist, and that his policy towards monastic tithes should be seen in a framework not of reactionary authoritarianism but of constructive reform.[2]

The most complete contemporary statement, and still perhaps the best short estimate, of Hadrian's policy towards tithes was given by his friend and admirer John of Salisbury in the *Policraticus*, which was finished late in 1159, soon after Hadrian's death.

At first, while religion rejoiced in poverty and poured out the very bowels of its own neediness for the necessities and use of others, the monastic professions became vested with privileges which, after the necessity for them had passed away and their charity grew cold, are now regarded rather as instruments of avarice than of religion. For, lo, all these privileged persons seek their own advantage and Jesus, who is preached in public, is either altogether absent or else kept hidden in the background. Hence it is that the blessed Hadrian when he saw these privileges being thus turned into a means of avarice, not wishing to revoke them altogether, yet restricted their scope by the limitation that what such men may withhold from the fruits of their labour should be interpreted solely with reference to lands newly brought under

---

[1] William Stubbs, 'Learning and Literature at the Court of Henry II', *Seventeen Lectures on the Study of Medieval and Modern History* (Oxford, 1887), p. 151.

[2] On his work in the organization of papal finances, expectative privileges, and confirmations of lay and urban privileges, see Guillaume Mollat, 'Les graces expectatives du XIIe au XIVe siècle', *Rev. d'hist. ecc.* XLII (1947), 81; Cheney, *Becket*, pp. 78 and 85–6; and D. P. Waley, 'Pope Boniface VIII and the Commune of Orvieto', *Transactions of the Royal Historical Society*, 4th ser., XXXII (1950), 121. With regard to monastic exemption, as with freedom from tithes, his policy was more cautious than that of his immediate predecessors: cf. Knowles, in *Downside Review*, L, 426, and Foreville, in *Histoire de l'Église*, IX. 2, 38. Walter Ullmann, 'The Pontificate of Adrian IV', *Cambridge Historical Journal*, XI (1955), 233–52, stressed that in his controversies with Frederick Barbarossa and the Byzantine Emperor Manuel, Hadrian made no substantial additions to papal theory (p. 236).

cultivation. For thus they will be able to enjoy their privileges without serious infringement of the rights of others.[1]

The change in papal policy also had important repercussions in the area outside direct papal influence. To the canonists it showed the way to a reasonable reconciliation of the conflicting principles of monastic freedom from tithes and of fixity of receipts, since Hadrian firmly based his policy on the predial doctrine that tithes were essentially a charge upon land and must continue to be paid to their owner even if the cultivator moved or possession of the land changed hands. The Bolognese Decretist Rufinus, for instance, whose *Summa decretorum* was written about 1157/9, admitted the contradiction between the thirteenth and sixteenth cases in Gratian's *Decretum*. He explained the transformation of tithes from a personal into a predial due as a result of the development of parishes from indefinite regions into areas with fixed boundaries; and he maintained that all tithes from agricultural produce were predial and belonged to the church of the parish in which they were raised and that tithes from other revenues, as from trade and handicrafts, were personal, 'which each man should pay to that church in the place he lives and hears the daily offices or, to use the old terminology, to that church where he receives the food of his redemption'. Following Pope Hadrian, however, Rufinus made an exception for tithes from newly cultivated lands, which he allowed monks to keep; and in his commentary on Gratian's *dictum ante* C. XVI, q. I, c. 42, on the payment of tithes by monks, he said that when Gratian wrote that monks need not pay tithes from fields cultivated for their own use, 'This should be understood strictly as only from new lands, for from other lands they ought to pay tithes to those churches in whose parishes the lands lie, as we assigned [them] above in C. XIII, q. I, on the basis of Hadrian's canon, unless some monasteries happen to have a special privilege from the pope

[1] John of Salisbury, *Policraticus*, VII, 21, *ed. cit.* II, 197–8, tr. John Dickinson, *The Statesman's Book of John of Salisbury*, Political Science Classics (New York, 1927), pp. 318–19. John was in some respects prejudiced against the new orders of monks, but his intimacy with Hadrian IV gives high authority to this passage, which has been overlooked by all historians of tithes.

concerning the non-payment of tithes in any way'. Again in his commentary on the decree of the council of Chalon in 813 allowing bishops and abbots to receive the tithes from their own fields, he specified those 'which they make fruitful by new cultivation, as is said in Hadrian's decree' and stressed that members of the *familia* must pay their tithes to the churches 'in whose territory are the fields from which the tithes are taken'.[1]

The author of the *Summa* 'Elegantius in iure diuino', compiled at Cologne about 1169, especially used Hadrian's decretal addressed to the English in his discussion of payment of tithes by monks.

Pope Hadrian settled this question in the decretal letter addressed to the English [he wrote], so that they ought to [pay tithes] from old fields, [but] they ought not to from noval lands which they cultivate themselves. And since their serfs and hired workers acquire all that they acquire in cultivating previously uncultivated fields not for themselves but for their lords, the produce should therefore be taxed in accordance not with the law of the serfs but with the privilege of the lords. This does not apply to tenants or share-croppers or *ascripticii*.[2]

Stephen of Tournai based his commentary on C. XVI, q. 1, of the *Decretum* almost entirely on the works of Roland Bandinelli and Rufinus. Like them he distinguished personal from predial tithes, and he cited Hadrian in support of the predial doctrine.

These [tithes] are given by reason of the lands [he wrote], for by whomsoever they are cultivated, whether by its parishioners or by other men, [a church] should not be deprived of the tithes from the lands within its [parish] boundaries. And this can be seen from the new decree of Pope Hadrian. For although some say that monks wherever they cultivate lands should pay no tithes except to their own monastery, Pope Hadrian said that they should pay to those churches in whose boundaries the lands lie, except for the tithes coming from their new lands, which the pope allows them to keep by a special privilege.[3]

---

[1] *Die Summa Decretorum des Magister Rufinus*, ed. Heinrich Singer (Paderborn, 1902), pp. 332–5; cf. Kuttner, *Repertorium*, pp. 131–2.

[2] See p. 281 n. 3 above.

[3] *Die Summa des Stephanus Tornacensis über das Decretum Gratiani*, ed. Friedrich von Schulte (Gniessen, 1891), pp. 217–18 and 222–3 on C. XVI, q. 1; cf. Kuttner, *Repertorium*, pp. 133–6.

The change in papal policy also increased the pressure from the local authorities on the privileged monks either to pay tithes or to give adequate compensation for the tithes from which they were technically free. The mere rumour of Eugene's death, according to Gerhoh, encouraged the bishops to neglect the papal privileges; the little foxes of reaction were aroused and tried to destroy the vines of monastic freedom from tithes not only under Hadrian but also during the long pontificate of his successor Alexander III. In a case between the canons of Kenilworth and the Cistercians of Combe and Stoneleigh, for instance, Archbishop Theobald of Canterbury wrote to the bishop of Coventry in 1155/9 'that the Cistercian monks living in their parishes of Stoneleigh and Smite should pay full tithe to them [the canons] from both the food of animals, from agricultural produce, and from everything from which tithes were customarily paid to the canons and to the said churches before the entrance of those men [the Cistercians]'.[1] Even under Popes Innocent II and Eugene III the Cistercians might have had to pay a rent in lieu of the tithe, but this decision in such direct violation of their privileges clearly reflects the change in papal policy. Many priests and monks who had lost their tithes on account of the earlier policy now laid claim to their previous property. John of Salisbury described in two letters written about 1154/61 for Theobald of Canterbury how the dispute between the Cistercians of Coggeshall and the Cluniacs of Rumilly was brought successively before the archbishop of Canterbury, the bishop of Thérouanne, the archbishop of Canterbury again, and finally the pope at Rome.[2] Decisions in both the ecclesiastical and secular courts, which tended to be controlled by conservative interests, increasingly favoured the former owners of the tithes.[3]

[1] Saltman, *Theobald*, p. 364 (cf. the grant to Stoneleigh cited p. 273 above).

[2] John of Salisbury, epp. 3–4, *ed. cit.* I, 5–6. The prior of Rumilly in this case accused the Cistercians of 'depriving him of the church and the tithes of the parishioners, whom they had driven from their lands and homes', in order, presumably, to work the land themselves. The abbot of Coggeshall replied that he held the church in return for an annual rent, but he was unable to prove his claim before Theobald (cf. *Rev. bén.* LXX, 607). The outcome of the appeal to Rome is not known.

[3] Cf. the cases involving Fontmorigny (1170/1) and Les Écharlis (1177) in *Fontmorigny*, p. 24, and *La Charité-sur-Loire*, pp. 166–7 (see *Rev. bén.* LXX, 608,

The refusal of a privileged house to pay tithes might be met with violence and even excommunication. Abbot Henry of Cîteaux, who later became cardinal-bishop of Albano, wrote to Alexander III that the monks of Déols, 'trusting in arms rather than laws', had attacked the Cistercian abbey of Nerlac in the hope of recovering tithes for which they had already received a 'suitable commutation'.[1] Archbishop Roger of York in 1164/81 excommunicated the Cistercians of Rievaulx and laid an interdict on their abbey because they refused to pay tithes from their own produce.[2] And during the reign of King John in England, a priest revived a claim to some tithes which had not been paid for over thirty years and seized a quantity of grain from the monks of Melsa (Meaux). He and his men were excommunicated by the papal legate, but the abbot agreed to pay an annual rent of twenty shillings and finally bought out his claim altogether for the lump sum of a hundred marks.[3]

Sometimes the monks were required to pay tithes even from newly cultivated lands from which no tithes had previously been paid. The bishop of Strasbourg in 1156 gave a chapel to the Cistercians of Neuburg on condition that 'they pay tithes to the parish priest of Still from all lands which have been newly opened both now and in the future, except for the glebe (mansus dotalis) of the chapel'.[4] The chronicler of Lorsch listed under the year 1165 many grants made to the Cistercians by Abbot Henry, 'who kept on both sides a measure of equity by which they received the use of the property and he and his successors derived no little profit from the annual rents'. Among these grants was one of some uncultivated woods to 'the poor of Christ' at Schönau, on condition that they would pay a rent to Lorsch and the local

for accounts of these cases and the full text of the former), which were both tried in secular courts, and the decision of the bishop of Angoulême in the case between St-Amant-de-Boixe and the Templars in 1171: Roger Grand, *Saint-Amant-de-Boixe*, offprint from *Bulletins et Mémoires de la Société archéologique de la Charente* (Angoulême, 1940), pp. 61–2.

[1] *PL*, CCIV, 222; cf. Mahn, *Ordre*, p. 110.
[2] *PU in England*, I, 458–9, no. 188.
[3] *Melsa*, I, 311–13.
[4] Würdtwein, *Nova subsidia*, IX, 355–6, no. 182; Wentzcke, *Regesten*, no. 557.

priest in order, as the charter said, 'that the produce of their labour should also be of profit to my church'.[1]

In one way or another the effect of the papal privileges was thus limited and sometimes almost annulled. As Wilkes pointed out for the Cistercian abbey of Himmerod, 'Although it was technically freed by the *exemptio totalis* from an obligation to pay tithes, in fact Himmerod had to pay them at least indirectly. It was confronted by secular lords as well as by parish priests. The document cited above of Hillen in 1157 already shows that on the basis of special agreements the abbey had to pay a rent in money and in produce to laymen in place of tithes.'[2] In 1167 the abbey of Cîteaux itself agreed that its 'amicable composition' of several disputes with the cathedral of Autun should supersede any previous charter or privilege from the pope or other authority.[3] The archbishop of Besançon maintained in his settlement of the dispute between the dean of St Stephen and the abbey of Belle-vaux in 1174 that 'Concerning the tithes which the monks say have been assigned to them by apostolic privilege, we say what the Roman curia itself is accustomed to explain, that is, that they should keep for themselves the tithes of noval lands'.[4]

This pressure on the privileged monks to, in effect, pay tithes now came not only from the disgruntled previous owners of the tithes but also from ecclesiastics who felt that the new orders were now too rich and strong to warrant privileges freeing them from tithes.[5] Even Gerhoh conceded that there was a sort of pharisaical justice in forcing the monks to pay tithes, and John of

[1] *Chronicon Laureshamense*, s.a. 1165, in MGH, SS, XXI, 446–8; cf. Mahn, *Ordre*, p. 106.

[2] Karl Wilkes, *Die Zisterzienserabtei Himmerode im 12. und 13. Jahrhundert*, Beiträge zur Geschichte des alten Mönchtums und des Benediktinerordens, XII (Münster, 1924), p. 125.

[3] *Autun*, I, 101.

[4] *GC*, xv, instr. 42; cf. Mahn, *Ordre*, p. 108.

[5] Most scholars are agreed that at least by the end of the twelfth century the privilege was increasingly unnecessary, and even abused, and that by arousing dispute and hatred it tended to do more harm than good: cf. Angelo Manrique, *Annales cistercienses* (Lyons, 1642–9), I, 239, s.a. 1132, cap. 5.4; Vacandard, *St Bernard*, II, 488 ('ce privilège exorbitant'); Pöschl, in *A. f. kath. KR*, XCVIII, 372 ff.; Knowles, *Mon. Order*, p. 355; Mahn, *Ordre*, pp. 109–11; Donnelly, *Laybrotherhood*, pp. 38–9; Cheney, *Becket*, p. 13; etc.

Salisbury, who was less sympathetic than Gerhoh to the new orders, frankly considered that the privileges had been turned to the ends of avarice. It has already been seen that Alexander III shared a general concern in the second half of the twelfth century over the growing wealth and worldliness of the Cistercians, and in 1169 he even threatened to revoke their privileges. 'For if you have deserted the original institutions of your order', he wrote, 'and wish to change to the common laws of other monasteries, you will also have to be judged by the common law, since it is fitting that those who submit to the same life as others should feel the same legal discipline.'[1] He did not specifically mention freedom from tithes in this letter, but it was certainly among the privileges which he had in mind.

Peter of Blois explained the situation clearly and strongly in two letters written on behalf of Archbishop Richard of Canterbury in about 1180. In the first he wrote to Alexander III that:

We indeed know that many popes granted these exemptions for the sake of the peace of the monasteries and on account of the tyranny of the bishops, but the matter has now been reversed. For the monasteries which have obtained this benefit of most damnable freedom either by apostolic authority or (which is more common) by interpolated bulls have become involved in more strife, disobedience, and neediness, so that many houses which are well known for sanctity and religion either never wanted to have these immunities or rejected them as soon as they obtained them.[2]

In the other letter, addressed to the abbot of Cîteaux and the Cistercian chapter-general, Peter said that:

The prayers and tongues of all men would have risen to praise your sanctity had you not stolen what is not yours, had you not taken the tithes from monks and clerics.... According to the Bible tithes are the tribute of needy souls. And what is this unjust immunity, that you should be exempt from paying the tithes with which the lands were burdened before they became yours and which were previously paid to churches on account not of persons but of lands? And why should

[1] Cf. p. 194 and n. 4 above.
[2] Peter of Blois, ep. 68, in *Opera omnia*, ed. J. A. Giles (Oxford, 1847), I, 204-5; cf. Cheney, *Becket*, p. 99.

the right of another person be endangered if the lands have come into your possession? For according to the common view the lands came to you with their burden.... The soldiers in France claim for themselves the right of tithing, disregard your privileges, and extort tithes from you by force. Rise against them, not against clerics and the churches of clerics; remember that at one time you were clerics and received the sacraments in their churches.... We have not set our mouth against heaven (*Non ponimus os nostrum in coelum*), nor do we dispute the act of the pope. But if the lord pope as a special indulgence gave you a privilege at a time when your order rejoiced in poverty, when the bowels of its poverty were freely poured out for the uses of the poor, it could be tolerated at that time because it was introduced on account of necessity, although it contributed to the common injury. But now, when your possessions have multiplied even into immensity, these privileges are regarded as instruments of ambition rather than of religion.

He went on to say that no papal privilege allowed the Cistercians to steal, and urged them to return their ill-gotten gains. He even threatened to excommunicate anyone who gave or sold to the Cistercians land from which tithes were owed and said that the king would confiscate any property given to the Cistercians against his wishes. He then again urged them to give back the tithes to their rightful owners. 'For if you keep the tithes only from newly cultivated lands, as Pope Hadrian of blessed memory decreed, the damage done to us will be more tolerable, [because] we have not felt its advantages. But as the philosopher said, what is possessed with pleasure and profit is not lost without grief.'[1]

Here were gathered a formidable array of arguments against the Cistercian freedom from tithes: arguments drawn from the Bible and canon law, from the nature of the monastic order, from the original purpose of the privilege, and from the hardship to the previous owners of the tithes. Peter relied especially on the principle of fixity of receipts and the predial doctrine of tithes and, while paying lip service to the papacy, he in effect questioned the

---

[1] Peter of Blois, ep. 72, *ed. cit.* I, 248–50. The close textual similarity between parts of this letter and the passage from the *Policraticus* cited pp. 286–7 above, suggests either that Peter used the work of John of Salisbury or that they drew on a common source.

authority even of the papacy to transfer arbitrarily possession of ecclesiastical revenues. He made no effort to conceal his opinion that the Cistercians had abused their privileges, taken unfair advantage of their benefactors, and grown rich at the expense of others. Walter Map attacked the Cistercians on the same point in his *De nugis curialium*, which was written about 1182: 'They say with the Pharisee that "We are not as other men are", but they do not say "We give tithes of all we possess".'[1]

Pope Alexander III was consequently faced with many inherited difficulties, and when deciding how to act on the question of monastic tithes he found himself in a dilemma created by his predecessors. On the one hand was the continued need of some monks for full freedom from tithes and the open flouting of the papal privilege by the local authorities; on the other was the growing opposition to the privilege in influential circles and the realization, which Alexander himself shared, that many of the privileged monks had outgrown the need for freedom from tithes. He had to steer a course between the extremes of rigid enforcement and complete abolition of the privilege, both of which would have caused confusion and hardship, and he had to decide in the case of every monastic privilege to include either a full freedom from tithes, a freedom from noval tithes only, or no freedom at all.

Alexander's practice in fact varied widely, and his policy was in some ways to follow no policy.[2] Although as papal chancellor he had had a hand in making earlier policy, he differed from Hadrian in being a lawyer by training, and already in his *Summa* on the *Decretum*, written in the 1140's, he laid down the principle with respect to tithes that every general rule had its exceptions and that every canon could be interpreted by the proper authority. He realized that the predial doctrine (to which, following

---

[1] Walter Map, *De nugis curialium*, xxv, ed. M. R. James, Anecdota Oxoniensia, IV, 14 (Oxford, 1914), p. 42, and tr. Frederick Tupper and Marbury Ogle (London, 1924), p. 53 (and introd. p. xxi, on the date).

[2] On Alexander's tithe-policy, see Schreiber, *Kurie*, I, 265–9; Hoffmann, in *SMGBOZ*, XXXIII, 439–45 (largely based on Schreiber); Viard, *Dîme*, II, 42–4; Foreville, *Église et la royauté*, p. 419; Mahn, *Ordre*, pp. 107–11; Boyd, *Tithes*, pp. 142–4.

Gratian, he adhered personally) did not entirely prevail in practice or in canon law and that the rights of a privileged monastery must be respected.[1] Also unlike Hadrian, Alexander lived long enough to change and modify his own policy. Indeed, the greatest difficulty in discerning any clear pattern in his policy towards tithes is that many of his most important decisions are not dated. 'As a maker of case law,' said Maitland, 'Alexander is second to no pope, unless it be to Innocent III.'[2] His decretals concerning monastic payment of tithes are found in all subsequent canonical collections and in spite of their *ad hoc* nature and inconsistency, laid the basis for the final solution of the problem.[3]

Clearly Alexander's most pressing task was to bring order into anarchy, to stem the tide of reaction, and to prevent the local authorities from taking the law into their own hands and interpreting the papal privileges as they saw fit. This he did in three ways: by specifically dissociating himself from Hadrian's policy, by restoring full freedom from tithes in some privileges changed by Hadrian, and by enforcing obedience to the papacy and respect for its privileges. He apparently had a sort of standard letter which he sent on different occasions to the bishop of Thérouanne and to the archbishop of York.

Although we wish greatly to love and encourage you and all our brothers and co-bishops in everything proper [he wrote to the bishop of Thérouanne], we are unable without manifestly and wilfully obstructing justice and opposing our predecessors' decrees to hear or heed in any way either you or anyone else concerning the matter about which we have often been asked of compelling black and white monks and regular and secular canons to pay tithes from the hired lands which they hold either for a definite period of time (*ad terminum*) or for a fixed rent (*ad firmam*), so that we may not seem to persecute the religious spirit which we are bound to love and encourage in others even if we do not have it in ourselves. Since, indeed, our predecessors allowed religious men not to be forced to pay tithes to any man from

---

[1] See pp. 268–70 above.

[2] F. W. Maitland, *Roman Canon Law in the Church of England* (London, 1898), p. 124.

[3] The following discussion is based largely upon Alexander's decretals and could be greatly expanded by an examination of all his monastic privileges.

the produce which they raised by their own hands or for their own use or from the food of their animals, we do not see how we can force them to pay these tithes. Our predecessor Pope Hadrian of blessed memory then interpreted 'tithes of produce' according to his own desire (*pro sua voluntate*). But it is proper for us to remove it from an attack of this sort, since we do not remember ever having read in the Old Testament that the Levites paid tithes to the Levites. We also know that in the New Testament, as you are aware, it was established that the people should pay tithes to those churches in which they hear the holy office and receive the other ecclesiastical sacraments throughout the year.[1]

The letter to Roger of York, which may have been occasioned by the excommunication of the monks of Rievaulx for refusing to pay tithes, was substantially the same, except that it said that monks were immune from tithes rather than not bound to pay tithes and specified that Hadrian changed *labores* into *novalia*. It was included in several canonical collections.[2] In a letter to the archbishop of Rheims and the bishop of Thérouanne in 1174, Alexander wrote that 'We believe that you are aware that our fathers and predecessors the Roman pontiffs permitted, and we have now renewed, that all the monks of the Cistercian order should not be forced to pay to anyone tithes from their own produce which they raise by their own hands and for their own use or from the food of their animals'.[3] The use of the term *innovatum* here shows that Alexander consciously revived the policy of full freedom for the Cistercians after the restriction by Hadrian.

To mark his return to the earlier policy Alexander restored the

---

[1] *PU in Frankreich*, NF IV, 394–5. Desiderius was bishop of Thérouanne from 1169 to 1181, and this letter was probably written after JL 12358 (1174) cited below.

[2] JL 13873, most recently edited by Jean Leclercq, *Études sur saint Bernard et le texte de ses écrits*, Analecta sacri ordinis Cisterciensis, IX. 1–2 (Rome, 1953), p. 199, who dated it 'avant 1160'. This seems to be too early. In the *Thesaurus*, I, 600, it is embedded in a letter from Gerard of Clairvaux to Desiderius of Thérouanne written about 1180. In Gilbert Foliot, *Epistolae*, ed. J. A. Giles (Oxford, 1846), II, 72–3, it is included in a letter attributed to Alexander together with a series of other canons concerning monastic freedom from tithes, most of them also in the First Compilation, which was drawn up about 1188/92. The text histories and dates of these two letters need further study.

[3] *PL*, CC, 979; JL 12358.

term *labores* in many privileges for Cistercian houses which had been granted freedom only from noval tithes by Hadrian.[1] Above all he sought to enforce the full freedom by his bulls *Audivimus et audientes*, of which he sent at least three dozen to bishops all over Europe and of which the earliest known example was issued in 1174.[2] The operative section, which expressly forbade the substitution of *novalia* for *labores* in Cistercian privileges, was included in the *Decretals* of Gregory IX:

You should know that it has come to our attention that some of you have tried to exact and extort from our beloved son the abbot and monks of the Cistercian order tithes of the produce which they raise by their own hands or for their own use and have perverted by a wicked and malicious interpretation that section of the papal privilege in which the Cistercians are allowed that no one should exact from them tithes of the produce which they raise by their own hands or for their own use. For they claim that 'new lands' should be understood in place of 'produce'. Since therefore we desire to foster the monks of this order by apostolic kindness and to take greater care that no one will have an opportunity to spite them or unjustly to molest them, we order you by this apostolic charter not to allow this to be done. For if we had meant only 'from new lands' in the places where we put 'from produce', we should have put 'from new lands', as we have put in the privileges of some other [monks].[3]

The exact wording of this letter varied considerably. In the privilege for Cambron in 1178, for instance, Alexander referred to the 'wicked and sinister' interpretation of those who claimed that 'de *novalibus* should be understood where it is known that de *laboribus* is written'.[4] But the intention was always to insist upon full freedom from tithes.

---

[1] See the examples given by Schreiber, *Kurie*, I, 261–2, to which may be added *Preuilly*, pp. 44 and 50–2. Mahn, *Ordre*, p. 108 n. 1, suggested that the privilege for Pontigny in February 1160, in which the *novalia* was retained (PL, CC, 85; JL 10624), was the result either of the conservative habits of the papal chancery or of the fact that Alexander had not yet decided to restore *labores* in all Cistercian privileges.

[2] See the lists in Schreiber, *Kurie*, I, 268 n. 1, and Mahn, *Ordre*, p. 108 n. 3.

[3] *Decretals*, III, 30, 12; JL 13859.

[4] *Cambron*, p. 12; JL 13038.

He also issued a rarer standard letter, *Per ordinem Cisterciensem*, which survives in copies for Bellevaux and Old Wardon and in several canonical collections in versions addressed to Rievaulx, Cumhir, and the Cistercians generally.[1] In it Alexander said that many privileges had been sought from the papacy to support the claims of monks and secular clerics in their disputes over tithes with the Cistercians. To prevent the infringement of their privileges, therefore, he decreed that the Cistercians need not reply to a claim 'if there is no reference to the Cistercian order in the letters which have been obtained from the apostolic see against you in matters of tithes and other things which the apostolic see has granted to your order'.

From these sources alone it might appear, and some historians have concluded, that Alexander completely abandoned the restriction to noval tithes introduced by Hadrian and returned to the policy of Innocent II and Eugene III.[2] These documents applied principally to the Cistercians, however, and were mostly issued towards the end of his pontificate, though the dates are not all certain. Towards other orders and during the early years of his pontificate he seems to have been less indulgent and sometimes explicitly adhered to Hadrian's restriction. The famous canon *Ex parte*, for example, is found in different manuscripts addressed to the bishops of Tarragona, Troyes, and other dioceses and is cited here from the *Decretals* of Gregory IX:

It has come to our attention on your behalf, as you know, that the white, black, and certain other monks have on account of the privileges given them by the church of Rome presumed to take from the churches under your jurisdiction their revenues of tithes. We certainly do not want you to be unaware that our predecessors of holy memory granted to almost all religious men the tithes of their own produce. But our predecessor Hadrian of good memory granted only to the Cistercians, Templars, and Hospitallers the tithes from the produce which they raised by their own hands or for their own use; he allowed

---

[1] *EPRI*, p. 203 (1171/81); *Old Wardon*, p. 20, no. 15 (1159/81); *Decretals*, I, 3, 6; JL 13846.

[2] Cf. Canivez, in *Dict. d'hist.* XII, 903, and Donnelly, *Laybrotherhood*, pp. 45 ff.

other [monks], however, to pay no tithes from their new lands which they cultivated by their own hands and for their own use, from the food of their animals, and from their gardens; and in these matters we have imitated him.[1]

Alexander cannot have believed that Hadrian, under whom he had served as chancellor, had really granted full freedom from tithes to the Cistercians, Templars, and Hospitallers; and it is probable, as his final words imply, that his intention in making this distinction was to create a precedent for his own policy, or at least to justify some of his own privileges. For although he occasionally granted full freedom from tithes to black monks and canons, in some cases he introduced the limitation to new lands even into privileges where Hadrian had granted full freedom. He put *novalia* in place of *labores*, for instance, in his privilege for the monks of Aniane, whose full freedom had been particularly asserted by Hadrian.[2] The grant to Gellone was restricted to noval tithes in 1162, and those for Tiron and Ramsey, which had been first granted in 1132 and 1141, were restricted in 1175/6 and 1178.[3] A complete examination of Alexander's monastic charters would probably reveal other examples in which he restricted the freedom for black monks and canons. Only two of Alexander's decretals in the First Compilation and the *Decretals* of Gregory IX asserted full freedom for the Cistercians and military orders; the remainder either required the monks to pay tithes or arranged a compromise.

In several bulls Alexander insisted that the full freedom applied only to goods produced by the monks themselves or for their use. There was nothing new in this limitation, of course, but it was occasionally neglected by the privileged monks. 'Although by the kindness of the apostolic see', he wrote to an anonymous abbey, 'it has been granted that you need not pay tithes to anyone from your produce which you raise by your own hands or for your own use, you are not, however, allowed on this account to

---

[1] *Decretals*, III, 30, 10; JL 14117.
[2] *Aniane*, p. 130 (5 August 1160/81, perhaps 1165).
[3] Tisset, *Gellone*, p. 222 (JL 10769); *Tiron*, II, 101; *Ramsey*, II, 137 (JL 13079a).

withhold from anyone the tithes of your lands which you grant to other men for cultivation.'[1] In 1175 he wrote to the Hospitallers in the province of Toledo that:

Since we have heard that you presume without the permission or grant of the diocesan bishops to keep the tithes of the workers on the estates which you acquire, we consider this to be improper and contrary to the arrangement of the holy fathers, and by the authority of this letter we order you not to presume without a grant from the diocesan archbishop or bishop to keep in any way the tithes of the workers on the estates which you have acquired or may in the future acquire and from which the bishops used to have the tithes, but you should allow and require the tithes to be paid in full to the said archbishop or bishop.[2]

In a letter to the monks of *Neubothe* (perhaps the Cistercian abbey of Newbottle in Scotland) he further maintained, apparently in direct opposition to his statement in the letters to Desiderius of Thérouanne and Roger of York, that the full freedom applied only to lands owned by the monks and not to rented lands. The monks of Holy Cross had complained to the pope that Newbottle had 'rented and received at farm from many laymen the fields from which they used to have the tithes and a great part of their support'. The pope therefore decided that:

Since these monks are heavily and excessively burdened by this, and it was not the intention either of ourselves or our predecessors that you should pay no tithes from possessions which you rented, we order you to pay in full to those monks the tithes from the fields which you have rented in their parishes and from which they used to receive the tithes or to reach an agreement with them so peacefully and friendlily that no cause for scandal should arise between you and that you appear to reach out for more than was granted to you.[3]

Both this and the letter to Roger of York, in which rented lands were explicitly freed from tithes, were included in the First

---

[1] Comp. I, III, 26, 11; *Decretals*, III, 30, 11; JL 14068.
[2] *Hospitaliers*, I, 334–5, no. 485; JL 12519.
[3] Comp. I, III, 26, 6; *Decretals*, III, 30, 8; JL 14023.

Compilation, but only the letter to Newbottle appeared in the *Decretals* of Gregory IX, and the weight of Alexander's authority was therefore ultimately opposed to including rented lands within the scope of the privilege.

On several occasions Alexander even required fully privileged monks to pay tithes from their demesne lands. He wrote to Archbishop Thomas of Canterbury in 1162/70 that 'The duty of dispensation imposed upon us by God advises and urges us in many ways to care for all the churches of Christ, and we should preserve their rights intact and unimpaired'. He then ordered the Cistercians of Boxley to pay tithes in full, 'including from cultivated lands in which houses were previously built', to the local parish church, 'and in the same way that tithes were previously paid even from pastures, we wish that tithes should now be paid in full from these lands which have been changed to growing crops'.[1] Here as in the case between Rumilly and Coggeshall the Cistercians had presumably turned out the former inhabitants and destroyed their houses in order to cultivate the lands themselves. Alexander discussed this point in greater detail in a letter to the bishops of Worcester and Hereford, which was attributed to Hadrian IV in the *Decretals* of Gregory IX, concerning an arrangement between an abbey and a priest 'that the monks would pay in full to the priest and his church during his lifetime all the tithes of grain and all vegetables except for the small tithes which the priest declared quit for the sake of the elevation (*exaltatio*: presumably the construction) of the monks' church'. Subsequently the abbot obtained full freedom from tithes from the pope and a grant of the entire estate on which the priest's church was built from the king; and 'when he had expelled all the workers of this estate, he cultivated all the land of the said parish for his own use and withdrew the revenues owed to the church'. Alexander insisted, however, 'that they inviolably maintain and preserve the previous agreement and composition, in spite of the said privilege, unless (which we do not believe) it contains a reference to the transaction'.[2] He thus required the monks to

---

[1] Comp. I, III, 26, 18; *Decretals*, III, 30, 4; JL 11660.
[2] Comp. I, III, 26, 17; *Decretals*, III, 30, 3; JL 14144.

continue paying tithes from the grain and vegetables raised on their demesne.[1]

The essence of Alexander's policy with regard to monastic tithes was in fact to preserve the rights of all churches, including of course the privileged monasteries, and to maintain as far as possible all existing agreements. He fully realized that many of the conflicts could not be solved at law and was always ready to promote and confirm an equitable compromise. In one surviving canon taken from an unknown letter he simply decreed 'that if a composition concerning tithes shall be made between you and any ecclesiastical person, with the assent of the bishop or archbishop, let it remain fixed and unshaken for all time'.[2] On many occasions he tried to avert controversies by arranging amicable settlements. In a charter of 1162, for instance, the bishop of Rodez confirmed some tithes which had been given to the nuns of Nonenque by the abbey of Villemagne at the request of the pope.[3] In two letters to the archbishop of York and the bishop of Durham in 1171/81, following the excommunication of the monks of Rievaulx for not paying tithes, Alexander ordered them to preserve the compositions made by the monks, who, as he pointed out, were technically free from tithes and therefore not required to make any composition at all.[4]

These interventions were frequently in favour of the former owners of the tithes. In response to a complaint from the monks of Tournus in 1165, he wrote to the Templars in the dioceses of

[1] Cf. Comp. 1, III, 26, 19 and 22; JL 13978 and 14000, requiring privileged monks and Hospitallers to pay tithes in full from their own lands and animals. Neither was included in the *Decretals* of Gregory IX, doubtless because they were redundant.

[2] Comp. 1, 1, 27, 2; *Decretals*, 1, 36, 2; JL 14191.

[3] *Nonenque*, p. 5.

[4] *PU in England*, 1, 462–4, nos. 193–4; cf. 372–3, nos. 109*a* and 109*b*, where Alexander settled a dispute between the Templars, who claimed the right to build a church anywhere on their lands, and the monks of St Florence at Saumur, who cited their right to control the building of churches in their parishes. The pope decided that the Templars might hold the church they had built but that the monks' church should keep all parochial rights, especially tithes. He thus protected established revenues without hindering the construction of a new church, as in cases over freedom from tithes.

Lyons and Chalon urging and advising them 'like peaceful men to reach an agreement with the monks in the interests of peace in order that they may receive some consolation for the tithes which they have lost', even though they were not legally bound to pay tithes.[1] In 1168 he confirmed the agreement between the Hospitallers and the church of the Holy Sepulchre in Jerusalem over the demesne tithes of the knights.[2] When some Cistercians who had been asked to pay tithes complained to him, he replied:

Since it is improper for monastic honour and religion to engage in disputes and controversies, we require, advise, and urge you by apostolic charter to make a composition peacefully with the said abbot and monks concerning those tithes and other tithes in order that the reputation of your religion may not be tarnished by controversies of this sort. For when the Roman church gave to your order the privileges concerning tithes, the abbeys of your order were so rare and poor that it could not rightly scandalize anyone; but now by the grace of God they have multiplied and grown rich in possessions so greatly that many ecclesiastics often complain to us about you.[3]

Towards the end of Alexander's pontificate there is evidence that the Cistercians themselves began to realize that their privileges often defeated the ends for which they were designed and were seriously concerned over the wealth and consequent criticism of their order. The abbots in the chapter-general at Cîteaux in 1180 (stimulated perhaps by Alexander himself or the letter from Archbishop Richard of Canterbury) decreed that:

because of the serious scandal which increases daily in all places on account of [our] keeping of tithes, we ordain and firmly order that whoever among you from now on acquires fields or vineyards from which churches, monasteries, or other ecclesiastical persons have customarily received the tithes up to this time, you should pay [them] without opposition, unless by chance you have already received them as a gift or have made a composition or are able to acquire [them] peacefully in the future.[4]

---

[1] *PL*, CC, 364; JL 11190.   [2] See p. 276 n. 2 above.
[3] Comp. I, III, 26, 9; *Decretals*, III, 30, 9; JL 14004.
[4] *Statuta*, ed. Canivez, I, 86–7.

The chapter-general ten years later went even further and in order to refute the charges of avarice decreed that Cistercian abbeys in the future should acquire land only by gift and not by purchase.[1]

At the end of the twelfth century, after Alexander's death, it was more or less established that in principle the Cistercians and the military orders were entitled to full freedom from tithes, and other monks and canons to freedom from noval tithes only and that in practice all monks were expected to take into consideration the interests of the owners of the tithes, to be willing when necessary to make a composition and even to pay tithes, and generally to treat their privilege as a basis for negotiation rather than as a rigid right. Bernard of Pavia, looking back over papal policy in his *Summa decretalium*, written in 1191/8, said of tithes that 'They are given by laymen...but should also be by clerics and monks, except for their own produce and food...Pope Hadrian interpreted this as from new lands...but this interpretation at first displeased Alexander III...but later he approved of it, as I learned in his curia, except for privileged monasteries and religious houses'.[2]

Bernard included many of Alexander's decisions concerning tithes in the so-called First Compilation or *Breviarum extravagantium*, which was composed between 1188 and 1192 and which, according to Kuttner, 'drove all previous collections of decretals from the field'.[3] He also included three interesting canons which are found for the first time in several canonical collections of the late twelfth century and which were probably forged during the pontificates of Hadrian IV or Alexander III in order to defend the claim of monks to receive but not to pay tithes.[4] In the first,

---

[1] *Statuta*, ed. Canivez, I, 117–18; cf. Hoffmann, in *Hist. Jb.* XXXI, 714, and the secondary works mentioned p. 195 n. 5 above.

[2] Bernard of Pavia, *Summa decretalium*, III, 26, 3, ed. E. A. T. Laspeyres (Regensburg, 1860), p. 105 (the omissions in the passage quoted are the relevant decretals); cf. Gabriel Le Bras, in *Dict. de droit can.* II, 785, on the date.

[3] Kuttner, *Repertorium*, p. 322.

[4] The correspondences between the Comp. I and eight other canonical collections are listed in Emil Friedberg, *Die Canones-Sammlungen zwischen Gratian und Bernhard von Pavia* (Leipzig, 1897), p. 182 (on III, 26). According to

which was attributed variously to Augustine and Popes Boniface, Gregory, and Eugene, it was decreed:

that monasteries should in no way be forced to pay tithes from their own fields, since if they [tithes] should properly be given to orphans and pilgrims, it is improper to exact them from those who are made poor men for the sake of him to whom the tithes belong. For if the poor of the Lord are his inheritance, the inheritance of the poor should be paid to the poor, that is, to those who for fear of him have given up what they could possess and have followed him naked and subjected themselves to the power of another.[1]

According to a second canon, which was attributed to Pope Gregory (or to the council of Tribur in one collection), 'We establish by apostolic authority that no abbot should keep tithes or first-fruits or other rights which belong canonically to the bishops without authorization from the pope or from the bishop in whose diocese he lives'.[2] The third canon, attributed to Pope John, established 'that tithes and oblations of the living and the dead are appropriate for those who possess nothing in the world, have chosen voluntary poverty, and wish to remain in their monastery under a rule, in whom Christ is fed and clothed'.[3] In the Frankfort collection this canon is followed by the remark, prefacing Alexander's advice to the Cistercians to give compensa-

information kindly sent by Stephan Kuttner, they also appear in the *Coll. Londiniensis IV* (Kuttner, *Repertorium*, pp. 283–5); Gilbert Foliot, ep. 350, *ed. cit.* II, 73–4; *Coll. Oenispontana*, ed. Friedrich Maasen, in *Sitzungsberichte der kaiserlichen Akademie der Wissenschaften [in Wien]*, Phil.-hist. Kl. XXIV (1857), 65 (at the end of the long note); *Coll. Francofortana*, ed. Stephan Kuttner, in *Sav. Zs.* LIII, Kan. Abt. XXII (1933), 374; and *Coll. Tanner*, ed. Walther Holtzmann, in *Festschrift zur Feier des Zweihundertjährigen Bestehens der Akademie der Wissenschaften in Göttingen*, II: *Philologisch-Historische Klasse* (Berlin–Göttingen–Heidelberg, 1951), p. 119. The first and third were also cited in the treatise on whether monks should preach, in Clm 27129, fo. 116r. The origins of these collections suggest that the canons were forged in France or England, but they are not always found together and may have originated separately in spite of their similarity. They were not included in the *Decretals* of Gregory IX. Cf. the forgeries made a century earlier to justify the performance of pastoral work by monks (cited p. 166 n. 3 above).
[1] Comp. I, III, 26, 14.   [2] Comp. I, III, 26, 20.
[3] Comp. I, III, 26, 21. In the *Coll. Casselana*, 'of another' is added after 'rule'.

tion for tithes, that 'privileges concerning tithes have been given to religious men because of poverty and love and now the old churches are oppressed on account of their multitude'.[1] These collections thus included a thorough mixture of canons, and in them could be found a precedent and a reason for almost any specific action regarding monastic payment of tithes.[2]

This policy was finally codified in the thirteenth century by the Fourth Lateran Council and in the *Decretals* of Gregory IX. The council decreed that the Cistercians must in future pay tithes from all newly acquired lands from which tithes had previously been paid.[3] The formulas used by the papal chancery in the later Middle Ages freed the Cistercian, Carthusian, and military orders from paying tithes of produce raised by themselves or for their use, and of their orchards, fishponds, and the food of their animals, on all lands which they had acquired before the General Council in 1215 and on new lands only, from which no tithes had previously been paid, which they had acquired since 1215. The black Benedictines and Augustinian and Premonstratensian canons were freed from tithes only of the produce from newly cultivated lands.[4] The principle of a limited right of monks to pay no tithes was thus definitely accepted, and the compromise proposed by Alexander III in *Ex parte*, ostensibly based on the policy of Hadrian IV, became both the law and the practice of the Church.

---

[1] Kuttner, in *Sav. Zs.* LIII, Kan. Abt. XXII, 374.

[2] Friedberg, *Canones-Sammlungen*, pp. 181–2, lists the collections in which all these canons are found.

[3] *Decretals*, III, 30, 34; cf. Viard, *Dîme*, II, 45; Mahn, *Ordre*, p. 112; and C. R. Cheney, 'A Letter of Pope Innocent III and the Lateran Decree on Cistercian Tithe-Paying', *Cîteaux*, XIII (1962), 146–51.

[4] Michael Tangl, *Die päpstlichen Kanzleiordnungen von 1200–1500* (Innsbruck, 1894), pp. 229–49.

CONCLUSION

A FTER the twelfth century the problem of monastic tithes moved into a new phase and lost its distinctive character. The issues of possession and payment of tithes by monks were settled in principle and were merged into the legal complexities of late medieval property rights. Everyone recognized that tithes were owned by some monks and were not paid by others. Tithes became in effect a form of real property, a due owed from the land; and their payment depended solely upon the productivity of the soil, unless they had been commuted to a fixed amount, and not upon the personal position of the owner or worker of the land. The customary owner could not be deprived of his rights either by the transfer of the land into the possession of a monastery or by the movements of the tithe-payers from one parish to another.

From a broad point of view, however, monastic tithes were only one of a long series of problems arising from the acquisition of property by ecclesiastical institutions, which in theory had no right to certain types of property and were not bound by the same responsibilities as other owners. Parallel issues continued to arise throughout the later Middle Ages, and successive efforts were made to protect established rights by such measures as the statutes of mortmain, limiting the right of churches to acquire property, and the inquests *ad quod damnum* held before the foundation of new monasteries. Even today no entirely satisfactory solution has been found to the steady accumulation by tax-free institutions of property from which taxes were previously paid. Indeed, the theory and origins of the modern practice of freeing religious, educational, and charitable institutions from taxes are far from clear. The decision of the House of Lords in 1949 that contemplative communities are not legally charitable set aside the earliest precedent for such freedom and may be one of a series of decisions protecting established rights more carefully and defining more strictly the types of institutions and property from which no taxes are required.[1] In the Middle Ages the pressure for such decisions was more effective than it is now largely because the losers were not the governments, which lose the taxes, but private institutions and individuals who complained loudly when they lost their tithes and other rights. Hadrian IV and Alexander III worked out in comparatively few years the distinctions and limitations which solved the problem of monastic tithes. But Peter the Venerable was more of a prophet than he knew when he said in the 1130's that in principle the freeing of any institution from a common burden like tithes would create difficulties which might begin in his time but would not be finished in his age.

The entire history of monastic tithes as they have been studied here was influenced by this overriding concern with property interests, which contributed largely to the overthrow of the early principles of tithing. Custom made law, and once a monastery had by any means established its customary right to receive tithes, the theory that monks should not own tithes was disregarded, and both ecclesiastical and secular authorities accepted the new theory of monastic possession of tithes. In the twelfth century the issue was still debated by theorists, but even the monastic reformers were unable to reverse a practice consecrated by five centuries of abuse. The process of 'realization'—the increasing emphasis on the 'real' or proprietary elements rather than the personal relations—affected all society after the ninth century,[2] and in the sphere of ecclesiastical revenues it can be seen in the canonical principle of fixity of receipts and the predial doctrine of tithes, which proved the greatest barrier to any theory of general monastic freedom from tithes. At every turn the history of monastic tithes was marked by the fervent respect of men in the Middle Ages for precedent and established rights and by their hard-headed realism in dealing with disputes over property.

A second factor running throughout the history of monastic tithes, and showing that they cannot be studied apart from the broad developments of medieval history, was the change in the

---

[1] *Report of the Committee on the Law and Practice of Charitable Trusts*, British Command Papers, 8710 (London, 1952), p. 33, cap. 129.

[2] Cf. Ganshof, *Feudalism*, p. 135.

structure of the Church. Above all, monks came to be regarded as the regular branch of the clerical order, and in spite of the efforts of the monastic reformers to reassert the independence and special character of their order, monks increasingly resembled the secular clergy in status and even in functions. Thus they were equated with the one group of Christians who were traditionally expected to receive and not to pay tithes, and this change justified at the same time possession of tithes by monks and the practice of granting monks their own tithes and freeing them from tithes.

Another aspect of this change in the structure of the Church was the rise of the papacy in the eleventh and twelfth centuries to a position of supremacy in the affairs of the Church. Even when allowance has been made for the importance of custom and the initiative of the recipients and local authorities, it was above all the papacy that legalized monastic possession of tithes and freedom from tithes. The popes of the Reformed Papacy repeatedly asserted, within limits, the right of monks to own tithes; and the personal policies of Paschal II and Innocent II, as shown in their bulls, established the principle that not all monks need pay tithes, although the opposing canonists, monastic theorists, and conservative interests were supported by early precedent, canon law, and practicality. But even Gratian, who otherwise adhered to the predial doctrine of tithes, gave way to *Decimas a populo*; and Thomas Aquinas, who said that 'according to ordinary law' clerics who performed no pastoral duties must pay tithes, cited *Novum genus* to show that the papacy might grant a certain freedom from tithes. Hadrian IV and Alexander III then resolved the practical conflict between the two ancient illegalities. It was the papacy above all that sanctioned these modifications in the theory and practice of monastic tithes, and in this matter as in others it stands out as the great normative force in the workings of the Church in the Middle Ages.

APPENDIX

MAITLAND once remarked that 'People can't understand old law unless you give a few concrete illustrations; at least I can't'.[1] Here, therefore, are descriptions of nine characteristic cases concerning tithes, which were too long to be included in the text and which have been chosen out of many similar cases in order to illustrate special points and generally to give an idea of the complexity of litigation over tithes in the twelfth century.

I. The famous case between the bishopric of Treviso and the abbey of St Hilary at Venice lasted almost two centuries and involved a notable series of forgeries on both sides.[2] It seems to have begun in the middle of the tenth century, when the bishop laid claim to the tithes from two prosperous estates named Pladano and Ceresaria, now swallowed up in the lagoons, which belonged to the abbey of St Hilary, though they may at some earlier time have belonged to the see of Treviso. The abbot therefore forged a charter, attributed to Charles the Fat in 883, confirming his possession of these two estates and their tithes,[3] and this forgery

[1] Quoted by R. L. Schuyler, 'The Historical Spirit Incarnate: Frederic William Maitland', *American Historical Review*, LVII (1952), 309.

[2] The relevant documents are printed in *Padova* and, better edited, in the MGH, *Dipl.*

[3] *Padova*, I, 32–3, no. 16, and MGH, *Dipl.* Charles III, no. 183. This charter is an alleged confirmation of a grant by Charlemagne, saying that he had received Pladano and Ceresaria from the bishop of Treviso and given them to St Hilary. It was definitely condemned as a forgery by Kehr in the MGH edition in 1937, but previously its authenticity was doubted by Giuseppe Marzemin, 'Le abbazie veneziane dei SS. Ilario e Benedetto e di S. Gregorio', *Nuovo Archivio Veneto*, NS XXIII (1912), 100, and defended by Roberto Cessi, 'Un falso diploma di Lotario (839) ed il delta di S. Ilario', *Atti e memorie della R. Accademia di scienze, lettere ed arti in Padova*, NS XXXVII (1921), 134 n. 1. Cessi was principally concerned with *Padova*, I, 17, no. 8, a grant to St Hilary of Pladano and its tithes forged probably in the fourteenth century, but he incidentally defended the authenticity of the alleged charter of Charles III and the grant by Charlemagne which it confirmed, and he thus accepted that the two estates had once belonged to the see of Treviso.

was confirmed by genuine charters from Otto II in 981, Henry II in 1008, and Conrad II in 1025.[1] Two can play the game of forgery, however, and in the middle of the eleventh century Bishop Rother of Treviso interpolated a reference to the abbey of St Hilary and to the tithes of Pladano and Ceresaria into the list of possessions in the privilege granted to Treviso by Henry II in 1014,[2] and in 1047 Henry III confirmed both this expanded version of the 1014 privilege[3] and a privilege granted to Treviso by Conrad II in 1026, which contained no allusion to the disputed tithes.[4] Rother then established his claim to the tithes before a synod at Treviso in 1048/51, presided over by the patriarch of Aquileia. But the abbey appealed to the emperor, at whose order both sides met with the bishop of Torcello and other men who swore that the tithes belonged to the abbey, and in a document dated 1052 Rother formally renounced his claim to the tithes.[5] Bishop Aclinus of Treviso repeated this renunciation before a synod at Altino in 1070/7.[6] Meanwhile, however, the bishops secured two confirmations of their claim to St Hilary and the disputed tithes from Henry IV, in 1065 and 1070;[7] and Henry's privilege for St Hilary in 1091 included no reference to the tithes, though it forbade any payments by the men of the abbey to the

---

[1] *Padova*, I, 94–5, 118–19, and 145–6, nos. 65, 87 and 110, and MGH, *Dipl.* Otto II, no. 240, Henry II, no. 185, and Conrad II, no. 46. The diploma of Henry II referred to charters of Otto I, II and III, of which the first and third are lost; and Bresslau, the MGH editor, suggested that the forged grant of Charles III may therefore have been first authenticated by Otto I. The authenticity of Otto II, no. 240 and Henry II, no. 185 seems indisputable (see the remarks by Kehr on Charles III, no. 183); Conrad II, no. 46 was based on Henry II, no. 185, but it seems to have been tampered with in the middle of the twelfth century.

[2] MGH, *Dipl.* Henry II, nos. 313 a (without the interpolation) and 313 b (with the interpolation), based on Otto III, no. 225.

[3] MGH, *Dipl.* Henry III, no. 201 b, with excellent notes by Bresslau giving an account of the forgeries before this date.

[4] MGH, *Dipl.* Conrad II, no. 66, confirmed by Henry III, no. 201 a.

[5] *Padova*, I, 195–6, no. 159.

[6] See the charter of Henry V cited p. 312 n. 2 below. The date is determined by the pontificates of Bishop Aclinus (1070–86) and the Patriarch Sigehard (d. 1077): Gams, *Series*, pp. 774 and 803.

[7] MGH, *Dipl.* Henry IV, nos. 174 and 231.

duke or to the bishop.[1] Henry V, on the other hand, supported the abbey against his father and the bishop, and in a charter of 1110 he said that he had forced Bishop Gotpul to renounce all claims to St Hilary and he confirmed the tithes of Pladano and Ceresaria among other possessions of the abbey.[2] The privilege for Treviso from Henry V in 1114 contained no reference to the abbey,[3] whereas the privilege for St Hilary from Lothar III in 1136 was based on the charter of 1110 and confirmed the abbey's possession of the tithes.[4] These were severe blows to the episcopal claims, but in 1142 the bishop made a final effort and secured from Conrad III a confirmation of the old privileges including possession of St Hilary and the disputed tithes.[5] This grant seems to have precipitated the final solution, since in August 1143 the abbot lodged a complaint before the papal legate Cardinal Goizo of St Cecilia, the patriarch of Aquileia, and the bishop of Ferrara, sitting at St Mark's in Venice, and they forced the bishop once and for all to restore the tithes to the abbey.[6]

II. A less exalted and shorter, but no less persistent, controversy was waged in the late eleventh century between the nuns of Ronceray and the monks of St Nicholas at Angers over the tithes of Montreuil-sur-Maine.[7] The nuns had bought the land from Rainald of Châteaugontier and his wife Burgundia, who owned it as her dowry, but the monks claimed the tithes and advanced three successive arguments to support their claim in the court ot Bishop Geoffrey of Angers. First, they said that they had owned the tithe before the nuns bought the land. 'This claim accomplished nothing,' according to the charter, 'since in a judgement witnessed by (coram) Count Fulco, in the sight and hearing of the monks, the seller explained what he was not selling: that is, the

---

[1] MGH, Dipl. Henry IV, no. 417, which was probably composed by the recipient and may not be entirely authentic.

[2] Padova, II, 40-1, no. 49; Stumpf 3044.

[3] Giambatista Verci, Storia della Marca trivigiana e veronese (Venice, 1786-91), I, Documenti, pp. 12-13, no. 10; Stumpf 3104.

[4] MGH, Dipl. Lothar III, no. 100.

[5] Ughelli, Italia sacra, v, 519; Stumpf 3435.

[6] Padova, II, 313, no. 419; IP, VII. 2, 173, no. 1. The later forgery, cited p. 310 n. 3 above, suggests that the abbey was still unable to hold the tithes in peace.

[7] Ronceray, pp. 145-6 (1095/1100).

knightly fief, and Ralph the son of Brefrid, and the custom in wine from three-quarters of the vines for the monks' work of charity. There was no mention of the tithe in that judgement, however, and since they were silent then they lost now.' Second, the monks said that the tithe was not part of Burgundia's dowry, but this was disproved by two witnesses. Lastly, the abbot said that his monk Herbert could testify that Burgundia had given the tithe to St Nicholas before selling it to Ronceray, but since Herbert was then away in Normandy, the court decided against the monks. After Herbert's return, the abbess and the monks gathered before Rainald and Burgundia to hear the oath, and 'the abbess was ready to deliver a man who would deny this for her by oath, but the monks would not receive him'. They were apparently unwilling to put their claim to the test of oath or ordeal and thus were forced to accept the justice of the nuns' case.

III. In a letter written in 1112/18, the bishop of Turin told the archbishop of Milan about the tithes of Scarnafigi,[1] which had been held from the bishop of Turin by the Countess Adelaide of Turin (1035–91)[2] and given by her, with the permission of the bishop, to the nuns of St Peter in Turin on condition that they never be given away. The nuns, however, granted a quarter of the tithe, without investiture by the abbess, to a son of the Viscount Bruno, named Marchisius, who in turn gave it as a benefice to a knight named Seniorinus. When after some years Adelaide heard of this, she took the tithe away from Marchisius and Seniorinus and gave it back to the nuns, who held it during the abbacies of Bertha, Romana, and Emilia.[3] Meanwhile both

---

[1] *Scarnafigi*, pp. 241–3 and, in an abbreviated form, Fedele Savio, *Gli antichi vescovi d'Italia: il Piemonte* (Turin, 1898), pp. 354–5. On the dates of Bishop Mainard (1100–1117/18) and Archbishop Jordan (1112–18), which determine the dates of the letter, see Ughelli, *Italia sacra*, IV, 132–5 and 1045; and Savio, *Piemonte*, pp. 353–5 and *La Lombardia*, I: *Milano* (Florence, 1913), pp. 472–5.

[2] C. W. Previté-Orton, *The Early History of the House of Savoy (1000–1233)* (Cambridge, 1912), pp. 187–250.

[3] Cf. the documents from St Peter at Turin published by F. Gabotto, in the *Cartari minori*, Biblioteca della Società storica subalpina, LXIX (Turin, 1912–23), III, 144.

Marchisius and Seniorinus died without children, and the death of the Countess Adelaide in 1091 was followed by a succession dispute between Henry IV's son Conrad and Adelaide's nephew Boniface of Vasto, who established his control over the southern part of the county.[1] Otto, the brother of Marchisius, then claimed the tithe 'as a paternal benefice' from Boniface and gave it to Seniorinus' brothers, who took a third rather than a quarter, as before, of the tithe. After three years, however, the nuns complained to Boniface that they had been deprived of tithes which they had held in peace for over thirty years. Boniface sent them to the bishop, who returned the tithe to the nuns after Otto had been summoned and had refused to appear before either the bishop or Boniface. The brothers of Seniorinus, however, said that Otto's refusal to appear should not prejudice their right to hold the tithe and refused to accept the judgements in favour of the nuns given, first, in the court of the bishop and, second, by a group of judges chosen by both sides. The bishop therefore sent the case to the archbishop of Milan, whose decision is unfortunately not known.

IV. Different issues were involved in the case between the abbey of St Andrew near Bruges and the bishops of Tournai over the church of Ghistelles, which had been given to the abbey early in the twelfth century by Bishop Lambert of Arras (1093–1115) in return for a rent of eighteen shillings a year. Pope Calixtus II confirmed this grant in 1118. 'After our fathers had ruled the church of Ghistelles with dignity and praise for over forty years,' wrote the chronicler of St Andrew, 'and after its tithes and revenues had greatly increased owing to the industry and care of the venerable Drogo and his successors our monks', Anselm, the first bishop (1146–9) of the new see of Tournai, within which the abbey lay, raised the rent to twenty-seven marks, which the monks agreed to pay. When Bishop Everard (1173–91) claimed that the monks had no right to hold the church, however, 'a very great controversy' broke out. The papal legate Cardinal Peter of St Crisogono finally arranged that the monks should divide the revenues of the church with the bishop and pay no rent in

---

[1] Previté-Orton, *Savoy*, pp. 255–8.

the future, and Pope Celestine III approved this settlement in 1195.[1]

V. The abbey of Ste Croix at Bordeaux became involved in a dispute over the tithes of Lignan,[2] which it had acquired from Gaucelinus of Génissac and his family, first for a mortgage of eight hundred shillings of four pennies each during the abbacy of Peter of Beyssac (1132–8) and then six years later by purchase for a horse worth five hundred shillings.[3] The abbey then granted the tithe to Robert of Malagent in return for an annual rent of four quarts of grain and a relief of five shillings when the lord changed. During the abbacy of Arnold of Vayrines (1182–1210), however, Robert's son Gerald, who had inherited the tithe from his father, mortgaged it to Robert of Lignan for seven hundred shillings and thus deprived the abbey, according to the charter, of both the tithe and the rent. The abbot therefore appealed to Peter Gaubert, 'who was at that time guardian of the peace (*dominus pacis*)' and who supported the abbey; but all parties concerned gathered 'in the cloister before the door of the abbot's chamber', and the abbot agreed to redeem the tithe from Robert for seven hundred shillings on condition that Gerald would not take the tithe from the church and would continue to pay the rent. This settlement was then ratified by the archbishop.

VI. The tithes of the estate of Mose in the diocese of Halberstadt were the subject of a three-sided dispute between the monastery of Our Lady at Magdeburg, the canons of St Paul at Halberstadt, and Albert the Bear of Saxony.[4] In a composite document, drawn

---

[1] *Chronica monasterii sancti Andreae iuxta Brugas*, ed. A. Goethals, Recueil des chroniques, chartes et autres documents concernant l'histoire et les antiquités de la Flandre occidentale (Ghent, 1844), pp. 20–1. The dates of the bishops concerned may be found in Gams, *Series*, pp. 251 and 495. The relevant papal bulls are lost.

[2] *Ste Croix de Bordeaux*, pp. 111–13; on the dates of the abbots, see A. Chauliac, *Histoire de l'abbaye Sainte-Croix de Bordeaux*, Archives de la France monastique, IX (Ligugé–Paris, 1910), pp. 76–93.

[3] The contract specified that if there was any change in the money before the pledge was redeemed, it would be paid at the choice of the abbey in money of four pennies or sixteen silver marks.

[4] The three relevant charters are in the chartulary of *Unser Lieben Frauen zu Magdeburg*, pp. 16, 17 and 27–9.

up in 1160, Albert recorded that he had held this estate from the archbishop of Magdeburg, that he had granted it as a benefice to Count Otto of Hillersleben, that Otto had returned it to him, and that he had returned it to Archbishop Conrad (d. 1142), who gave it to the abbey of Our Lady. Albert and his men still claimed the tithe of Mose as a benefice from the bishop of Halberstadt, however, and in a charter of 1145 Archbishop Frederick and Bishop Rudolf explained that:

Although this tithe is [now] worth twelve shillings a year as a benefice, the estate of Mose was partly uncultivated and partly cultivated by Slavs who paid no tithe at the time we gave the use of the tithe to the church of Our Lady, so that the tithe was worth either nothing or only what was exacted not by the justice of the Church but by the armed violence of the Margrave Albert's men, since his vassals (*illa ab eo inbeneficiati*) seriously oppressed the monks of Our Lady on the other property of the estate. The monks could not bear this and spent over twelve talents to redeem the tithe, which was resigned to the marquis by his men and to us by the marquis and was granted by us to the monks to be held for ever.

At the same time, however, the canons of St Paul at Halberstadt also claimed the tithe, and Bishop Rudolf recorded in a charter also dated 1145 that 'A controversy was waged over this tithe between the Margrave Albert and the brothers of St Paul, who said, "The tithe is ours", and showed the privileges given them by bishops; but he said, "No, it is my possession", and counted it among the benefices held from us. They [held] only a charter; he held the tithe, but not without protest.' Both sides finally resigned their claim on condition that the tithe be given to the monks of Our Lady, who in return gave the canons an estate worth ten shillings a year and gave to the margrave, in addition to the twelve talents spent to redeem the tithe from him and his men, 'the more powerful compensation of many prayers'.

VII. Pope Lucius II in 1144 wrote to the four abbots of Arlanza, San Millán de la Cogolla, Oña, and Silos that 'If justice and order should be kept in secular affairs, how much the more should confusion be excluded from ecclesiastical matters. Therefore we order by this letter that you should not take from the estates of your monasteries any tithes which belong according to the canons to our venerable brother Bishop Peter of Burgos, but you should send them to him intact and in peace.'[1] In 1150 Eugene III wrote again to the same abbots and to the abbot of Cardeña saying that he had instructed the bishops of Coria and Segovia to settle their dispute over the episcopal third.[2] In June 1152 he asked the bishops of Salamanca and Segovia to judge the tithe-case between the archbishop of Burgos and the abbey of Oña and wrote to the archbishop in September of the same year that he had ordered the abbot to pay 'to you without the subterfuge of an appeal that part of those tithes which is owed to the bishops according to the canons'.[3] Following this victory, the archbishop accepted an estate named Rebilla from the abbey in return for the disputed episcopal third of the tithes and the parochial rights in all its churches, in addition to various other tithes.[4] This settlement was confirmed in 1155 by the papal legate Cardinal Jacintus of St Maria in Cosmedin,[5] and later by Alexander III, Innocent III, and Honorius III.[6] Meanwhile, in 1153, the clerical and lay vassals of Oña promised to pay their tithes to the abbey,[7] which henceforth therefore received all the tithes from its lands and churches.

VIII. The record of the evidence taken in the dispute between the bishop of Brescia and the abbey of Leno in 1194–5 over the tithes of thirteen estates gives a detailed picture of the division of parochial rights in northern Italy in the second half of the twelfth century.[8] The witnesses were not entirely consistent and clear, but

---

[1] *Oña*, I, 223–4. This and the subsequent papal documents associated with this case are not in JL.

[2] *Ibid.*, I, 250–1.

[3] *Ibid.*, I, 252–3 and 254.   [4] *Ibid.*, I, 256–7.

[5] *Ibid.*, I, 261–2 (for Burgos) and 263–4 (for Oña); on this legation see Säbekow, *Legationen*, pp. 48–51.

[6] *Oña*, I, 269 (1159), 274–5 (1163), 471–2, and II, 497–9, 505–6, 510–11, and 515–16.

[7] *Ibid.*, I, 257–9.

[8] *Leno*, pp. 136–87. This little-known account was kept by the Brescian notary Ambrosio Vitti at the request of the arbitrators in the case and contains the testimony, often verbatim, of thirty-seven witnesses, most of them citizens of standing in their communities and some with memories reaching back over fifty years.

they more or less agreed that the tithes from six of the estates belonged to the bishop and were held from him as fiefs by various laymen, often with a quarter reserved for the parish priest, and that the tithes from the other seven estates were divided, usually by quarters but once by thirds, between the bishop and the abbot. Sometimes the divisions were very elaborate. At Leno itself the abbot owned between four-fifths and nine-tenths (the evidence varied) of the tithe, of which part was held as a fief by a layman, and the remainder belonged to the bishop and was held from him by the lords of Rodigo, who had granted it to the lords of Corzaghetto. At Gottolengo, the tithes were classified into those from free tenures, from the abbey's own land, and from newly cultivated lands. Of the tithes from free tenures, the bishop owned three-quarters, which were held from him by the lords of Concésio and from them jointly by the three sons of Otto of Milan, and the abbot held one-quarter, which he had granted to the parish church. These tithes were collected together and then divided between the priest and Otto's three sons. All the noval tithes, however, and all the tithes from the abbey's own lands, which were held by the lords of Lavallo, belonged to the abbot, who therefore altogether owned more tithes at Gottolengo than the bishop, although he was not, as one witness put it, lord of the tithes but only of the abbey.[1]

IX. Finally, a very detailed account (placed last on account of its length) of a trial which was marked by a great deal of chicanery is found in one of the treatises on the controversy between the abbeys of St Remy and St Nicasius at Rheims.[2] The entire dispute was extremely long and complicated and involved a variety

---

[1] *Leno*, p. 187. Likewise at Pavone the abbot owned all the tithes from land held by peasants and belonging to the abbey and a quarter of the tithes from free tenures, which was held by the priest; all of these together made up more than half the total tithe; the remaining three-quarters of the tithes from free tenures belonged to the bishop and were divided as fiefs between the lord of Rodigo and James of Martinengo, who had granted their three-eighths respectively to Dalfinus of Carthegnano and the sons of Albricus of Capriano.

[2] Hermann Meinert, 'Libelli de discordia inter monachos S. Remigii et S. Nicasii Remenses agitata tempore Paschalis II papae', *Festschrift Albert Brackmann* (Weimar, 1931), pp. 259–92 (quoted passage on pp. 274–7).

of issues,[1] and the passage translated here concerns the tithes of Vrilly, which were claimed both by the monks of St Nicasius and by the canons of St Timothy, a dependency of St Remy. As will quickly be apparent, this treatise was written by a monk of St Remy, whose prejudice should be taken into account. Following the death of Abbot John of St Nicasius, he wrote in chapter eleven, the new Abbot Jorannus, in about 1103,

decided to persecute the church of St Remy and St Timothy with all his body and soul; and after he had come to an agreement with the Archbishop Manasses and his advisers the Provost Ralph and the *scholasticus* Odelricus and other canons of Notre Dame, he pestered them for a certain tithe of St Timothy until at last he had the tithe adjudged away from them by a very false judgement.

12. In the presence of the archbishop the lord Provost Ralph brought this claim for the church of St Nicasius against the canons of St Timothy concerning a certain tithe which belonged to St Nicasius from the church of St Sixtus, and he said that Dudo the dean of St Timothy and other brothers had claimed the tithe from some land of Peter the chamberlain from master Godfrey, who held part of this tithe, and Abbot John of St Nicasius, who [according to Dudo's claim] had unjustly taken it from St Timothy and its canons and usurped it for themselves. The abbot of St Nicasius and master Godfrey had replied to this claim that they and their predecessors had held that tithe from that land belonging to Peter for thirty-one years in peace and unchallenged. A judgement on this claim and the reply had been sought, and the judgement had been that if the abbot and master Godfrey could prove their claim by oath through two men, they should henceforth hold the tithe in peace. Witnesses to this fact were ordered to come forward; they came forward; it was put to the oath. The Lord Archbishop Rainald ordered that they should take the oath outside Notre Dame, near the apse of the church, [but] the canons of St Timothy refused to hear this [oath] and went away. After the time of the harvest, however, the canons of St Timothy came with their armed men (*auxilio*) to that land and took the tithe from St Nicasius and the lord Provost Ralph, who held the part of the tithe after the death of master Godfrey. The canons were informed of this injury by

---

[1] The dispute was finally settled by Paschal II in April, 1113; *Reims*, I, 264–9 (JL 6352), where there is a long note on the controversy.

the abbot of St Nicasius and the lord Ralph in a friendly and neigh-
bourly fashion, and they recognized that they had taken this tithe from
them unjustly and returned it from their storehouse to the man of the
lord Ralph. Later, however, this land remained uncultivated for a
long time until Peter's son Hugo, who owned the land, had it planted
with vines. The vines were planted, the harvest came, but the canons
with renewed injury took the entire tithe from the church of St Nicasius and the Provost Ralph.

13. The lord Abbot Azenarius of St Remy rose up at this claim,
and because it attacked him, since all that place was his and he had to
care for the canons as for his monks, he sought a delay in order to
consult with the Archbishop Manasses, obtained it, took counsel, [and]
came back. When permission had been received from the archbishop,
he instructed a certain cleric to reply for himself and his canons.

14. The cleric therefore arose and replied that the lord abbot and
the clerics clearly remembered the claim brought by the Dean Dudo
and other canons against the Abbot John and master Godfrey, that
witnesses had sworn, the tithe had been returned, [and] they had
subsequently done them no injury. They were ready to show which
land had been in question and to prove by proper and synodal judgement what had been adjudged and examined. They were ready to prove
by canonical judgement that the church of St Timothy and its canons
had held the tithe from the land belonging to Peter for sixty years and
more in peace and unchallenged and that there had been no interruption
of this possession.

15. In addition (*Ex habundantia*) the lord abbot of St Remy and his
canons offered as a witness of this fact the tithe-collector who had
received the tithe from this land in the time of Archbishop Wido
[1033–55] and had given it to the brethren in peace and unopposed. To
confirm this they also had the tithe-collector in the time of the lord
Archbishop Gervase, the tithe-collector in the time of Archbishop
Manasses of Gornay, the tithe-collector in the time of Archbishop
Rainald, and the tithe-collector in the time of the living lord Archbishop Manasses. Furthermore, Peter's serfs who during his lifetime
ploughed and sowed that land, reaped the harvest, [and] gave the
tithes, were present and were ready and willing to assert that for
twenty years they had given the tithe from that land to the tithe-
collector of the canons and that no one else had asked [for the tithe].
After Peter's death, furthermore, his son Hugo received the land by
hereditary right, tilled the land with his plough and sowed it with his

seed for twenty years and more, paid the tithe to St Timothy, [and] was asked by no one else. Hugo affirmed this fact and was ready to maintain this truth either by divine judgement or by secular duel. The abbot of St Remy and his canons were furthermore ready to confirm this same truth through seven, ten, even twenty or more suitable and elder townsmen, by whatever law it might be judged.

16. The lord Archbishop Manasses ordered a judgement to be made on this claim and reply. The judges arose, went into council, returned from consulting, and asked, since a synod was very near, for a delay until that synod [1103 or 1105].

17. On the first day of the synod the abbot of St Nicasius and his spokesman the lord Ralph arose [and] asked to be given a judgement. At this the lord Lambert, who was prior and dean of the church of St Remy at that time, arose [and] said that the lord abbot of St Remy was absent because by the order and permission of the archbishop he had gone to a dependency (*obedientia*) of St Remy in order to treat with the tyrants who had on that same day burned a farm of St Remy in his presence; and since the claim had been made principally against him [the abbot] and he had replied through his spokesman for himself and his monks, the dean, as was just, asked the archbishop on behalf of the abbot for a delay until the following day, when he would come and hear the judgement in person. In short, he could not have a delay. The lord archbishop ordered judgement to be made and advised them to judge justly under pain of anathema and on their obedience.

18. At this order from the archbishop the suitable and elder laymen arose and said that they had previously held the land which was under discussion. But it was useless. The archbishop threatened to imprison them unless they were silent. The dean of the priests, in accordance with his orders, arose, went into council, summoned whom he wished, came back, [and] gave judgement that if the abbot of St Nicasius, who had made the claim, could produce those persons of the synod who had been present at the synod on that day, had heard the claim concerning Peter's land, and had seen the tithe from this land of Peter and his son Hugo adjudged to the lord abbot and confirmed by the legal oath of witnesses, then they [the monks of St Nicasius] should hold it henceforth. This judgement was followed by no one, and no one was found who would follow it. On the contrary, Richer the cantor of Notre Dame arose and said that the judgement concerning the claim of many men would be delayed until the following day, and the same abbot

who according to this judgement should have had the witnesses then sought and obtained a delay until the following day.

19. On the following day the lord abbot of St Remy came to the synod [and] asked to be given a judgement, or at least for a repetition of what had been done for him in his absence. To this the archbishop replied that no claim had been brought against him and he had made no reply; but the lord abbot wished to prove by legal evidence both that a claim had been brought against him and that through his spokes-man he had replied for himself and his canons. In short, this was not allowed him by the archbishop; indeed, he was forbidden by a threat to speak any more. The abbot of St Nicasius arose [and] produced three priests who had witnessed this matter. Then the dean [Lambert] arose [and] said that one of these priests had been summoned that day into the synod by the archbishop concerning an anathema and had not been cleared by any excuse in the presence of everyone; it was established that the second lived in concubinage, [and] the sacrament was presented to the third. The canons, however, saw that they were oppressed by the judgement and were about to lose unjustly by false witness the tithe which they had owned for so long a time in peace, and they appealed to the justice of Rome. The abbot of St Remy also wanted to leave so as not to hear this oath, but the archbishop forbade him to leave on his obedience. But it was useless. The judgement was then more strongly confirmed, the sacraments were sworn, [and] the tithe was adjudged away from the canons.

INDEX

The following abbreviations are used: abb. = abbess, abbey; abp. = archbishop; abt. = abbot; bp. = bishop; card. = cardinal; emp. = emperor; k. = king; pr. = prior, priory; and, for the affiliations of religious houses, Aug. = Augustinian; Ben. = Benedictine; Camal. = Camaldolese; Carth. = Carthusian; Cist. = Cistercian; Cl. = Cluniac; Prem. = Premonstratensian; Sav. = Savigniac; Vall. = Vallombrosan. These indications are mostly taken from Cottineau, *Répertoire*. Changes in affiliation are indicated by a hyphen.

Page references alone are given for entries appearing in both the text and the notes on the same page. Note references apply to the entire note, even when continued on the following page.

Aachen, 33, 77; councils in 816 and 817, 40 n. 5; council in 818/19, 40; St Adalbert (Ben.), 79
Aaronites, 10, 16, 43
Abbo, abt. of Fleury, 54 n. 4, 56, 80–1, 84, 147, 165, 181 n. 1
Abelard, 15 n. 2, 144, 151, 158
Abingdon (Ben.), 105, 116, 118–19, 224 n. 8, 225; abts., *see* Ingulph, Rainald
Abraham, patriarch, 10, 14, 15, 16, 17, 109
Achardus, bp. of Langres, 67 n. 5
Aclinus, bp. of Treviso, 311
Acquanegra (Ben.), 238, 261
Acy (Cl.), 248 n. 3, 250 n. 1
Adalbert, abp. of Mainz, 119 n. 2, 154 n. 4, 263
Adalbert, provost of Speyer, 167
Adalhard, abt. of Corbie, 60, 202
Adam of Dryburg, 30 n. 3
Adam of Ely, clerk of Earl Robert of Leicester, 110
Adelaide, countess of Turin, 313–14
Admont (Ben.), 101, 117, 120 n. 3, 136
Adraldus, abt. of Breme, 88
Aelfric, 50
Afflighem (Ben.), 137, 226–7
Agapitus II, pope, 75, 211
Agaune (St Maurice-en-Valais; Ben.-Aug.), 95 n. 3
Agobard, abp. of Lyons, 32, 201 n. 1
Aiglibertus, bp. of Le Mans, 58
Aimoin of Fleury, 80
Airard, bp. of Chiusi, 209
Airard, bp. of Nantes, 85–7, 114 n. 4
Alba, bp., *see* Benzo
Albano, card.-bps., *see* Boniface, Henry, Matthew

Albert the Bear, duke of Saxony, 123, 222, 315–16
Alcuin, 16 n. 2, 33–4
Alexander II, pope, 54 n. 4, 84, 89, 95, 209 n. 4, 215, 216, 244 n. 3
Alexander III, pope, 3, 93, 110, 120 n. 6, 123, 128 n. 2, 148, 161, 184, 194, 200 n. 1, 220, 221, 260 n. 2, 268–70, 276, 284 n. 2, 288, 289, 290, 292, 294–303, 304–5, 305–6, 308, 309, 317
Alfonso, count of Toulouse, 283
Altenberg (Cist.), 238, 262
Altino, synod in 1070/7, 311
Amatus, bp. of Oléron, abp. of Bordeaux, 89 n. 4
Amberloux, 78
Ambra, 78
Ambrose, St, abp. of Milan, 17, 18 n. 4
Amiens, bp., 109, 122
Amiterno, 59
Amulo, abp. of Lyons, 36
Anacletus II, anti-pope, 238, 247–8, 260 n. 1
Anastasius IV, pope, 209 nn. 2, 3, 244, 278, 280, 282 nn. 2, 5
Anchin (Ben.), 226 n. 2; abt., *see* Gelduin
Andrew of Strumi, 137
Angers, bp., 122 n. 2, 203, *see also* Geoffrey; le Ronceray (Ben.), 119 n. 3, 122 n. 3, 125, 135, 312–13; St Aignan (canons), 203; St Aubin (Ben.), 87, 119 n. 3, 122 n. 2; St Nicholas (Ben.), 122 n. 1, 124 n. 5, 125, 312–13
Angles (Ben.), 124 n. 5
Angoulême, bp., 289 n. 3; St Cybard (Aug.-Ben.), 113 n. 3

INDEX OF SECONDARY AUTHORS